# BEING HUMAN DURING COVID

# Being Human during COVID

### Kristin Ann Hass, Editor

University of Michigan Press
*Ann Arbor*

For questions or permissions, please contact um.press.perms@umich.edu

Published in the United States of America by the
University of Michigan Press
Manufactured in the United States of America
Printed on acid-free paper
First published November 2021

A CIP catalog record for this book is available from the British Library.

*Library of Congress Cataloging-in-Publication data has been applied for.*
ISBN 978-0-472-03878-7 (paper : alk. paper)
ISBN 978-0-472-90250-7 (OA)

https://doi.org/10.3998/mpub.12136619

We would like to recognize the generous support of the College of Literature, Science, and
the Arts and the Michigan Humanities Collaboratory at the University of Michigan for the
Fulcrum edition of this volume.

Credit for cover art: Laura Koroncey

# Contents

*Acknowledgments*                                                                    ix

Introduction:
  Living with the Virus That Knows How We See Each Other                              1
    *Kristin Ann Hass*

**PART I: NAMING**

Chapter 1. This Virus Has No Eyes: Telling Stories in the Land of Monsters  23
    *Christopher Matthews*

Chapter 2. Facing Our Pandemic                                                      43
    *Sara Blair*

Chapter 3. Living on Loss of Privileges: What We Learned in Prison         64
    *Patrick Bates, Alexandra Friedman, Adam Kouraimi,*
    *Ashley Lucas, Sriram Papolu, and Cozine Welch*

Chapter 4. Not Even Past: Archiving 2020 in Real Time                        72
    *Michelle McClellan and Aprille McKay*

**PART II: WAITING**

Chapter 5. Waiting = Death: COVID-19, the Struggle for Racial Justice,
    and the AIDS Pandemic                                                           93
    *David Caron*

Chapter 6. Buddhism, the Pandemic, and the Demise of the
    Future Tense                                                                    117
    *Donald Lopez*

Chapter 7. COVID Diary: Hands, Nets, and Other Devices                       122
    *James Cogswell*

Chapter 8. Social Distances in Between: Excerpts from
    My COVID-19 Diaries                                                             132
    *Amal Hassan Fadlalla*

**PART III: GRIEVING**

Chapter 9. Grief and the Importance of Real Things during COVID-19     153
  *Suzanne L. Davis*

Chapter 10. Looking Backward in Order to Look Forward:
  Lessons about Humanity and the Humanities from the
  Plague at Athens     176
  *Sara Forsdyke*

Chapter 11. Protests, Prayers, and Protections: Three Visitations
  during COVID-19     181
  *William A. Calvo-Quirós*

Chapter 12. Soliloquous Solipsism     199
  *Melanie Tanielian*

**PART IV: MORE WAITING/SHELTERING**

Chapter 13. Finding Home between the Vincent Chin Case and
  COVID-19     219
  *Frances Kai-Hwa Wang*

Chapter 14. Caged with the Tiger King: The Media Business and
  the Pandemic     221
  *Daniel Herbert*

Chapter 15. Prosthetics for Right Now     233
  *Nick Tobier*

**PART V: RESISTING**

Chapter 16. COVID-19's Attack on Women and Feminists' Response:
  The Pandemic, Inequality, and Activism     243
  *Abigail J. Stewart*

Chapter 17. The Virus That Kills Twice: COVID-19 and Domestic
  Violence under Governmental Impunity in Nicaragua     250
  *Eimeel Castillo*

Chapter 18. "Our Steps Come from Long Ago": Living Histories of
  Feminisms and the Fight against COVID in Brazil     256
  *Sueann Caulfield*

Chapter 19. Making Sense of Sex and Gender Differences in
  Biomedical Research on COVID-19     266
  *Abigail A. Dumes*

Chapter 20. Digital Encounters from an Intersectional Perspective:
   Black Women in Argentina                                        271
      *Marisol Fila*

Chapter 21. The Media Discourse on Women-Led Countries in the
   COVID-19 Pandemic: Using Germany as an Example                  281
      *Verena Klein*

Chapter 22. Coronavirus Capitalism and the Patriarchal Pandemic
   in India: Why We Need a "Feminism for the 99%" That Focuses
   on Social Reproduction                                          287
      *Jayati Lal*

Chapter 23. Whose Challenge Is #ChallengeAccepted?
   Performative Online Activism during the COVID-19
   Pandemic and Its Erasures                                       312
      *Özge Savaş*

Chapter 24. COVID-19: Nigerian Women and the Fight for
   Holistic Policy                                                 318
      *Abiola Akiyode-Afolabi and Ronke Olawale*

PART VI: NOT WAITING

Chapter 25. COVID-19 through an Asian American Lens:
   Scapegoating, Harassment, and the Limits of the
   Asian American Response                                         329
      *Roland Hwang*

Chapter 26. The High Stakes of Blame: Medieval Parallels to a
   Modern Crisis                                                   336
      *David Patterson*

Chapter 27. Unmuting Voices in a Pandemic: Linguistic Profiling
   in a Moment of Crisis                                           344
      *Nicholas Henriksen and Matthew Neubacher*

Chapter 28. Quarantine Rebellions: Performance Innovation in
   the Pandemic                                                    357
      *Anita Gonzalez*
*Contributors*                                                     389
*Index*                                                            397

Digital materials related to this title can be found on the Fulcrum platform via the following citable URL: https://doi.org/10.3998/mpub.12136619

# Acknowledgments

Sometime in the spring of 2020, Alex Stern, my colleague in the Department of American Culture and Associate Dean for the Humanities at the University of Michigan, suggested that the Humanities Collaboratory should do something to give humanists a voice in this moment. *Being Human during COVID* is a result of that suggestion. So, first, thank you Alex. The Humanities Collaboratory team has turned our attention to this project and moved it from an idea batted around in a Zoom meeting to both a print and digital volume in record time. Thanks to Sheri Sytsema-Geiger for her considerable energy and for keeping us on track, as always. Thanks also to the Humanities Collaboratory steering committee—Kerstin Barndt, Sara Blair, Tabby Chavous, Anne Cong-Huyen, Angela Dillard, Christiane Gruber, Khaled Mattawa, Peggy McCracken, and Arthur Verhoogt—for their support of this project.

The editorial board we assembled for *Being Human during COVID* is made up of game, smart, and hardworking folks. Samer Ali, Anne Cong-Huyen, Sandra Gunning, Tiya Miles, and Johannes von Moltke read and reread these essays and guided me in making hard decisions while the world seemed to be spinning off its axis. Darcy Brandel joined as an ad hoc editorial board member when an additional reader was needed. I am grateful for their collective dedication to this project.

Audrey Becker has worked with me at every step of the way, and she stepped up when it all seemed a little overwhelming. This project would not have happened without her heroic efforts. I am especially grateful for her skills as a reader and her eye as a grammarian. Thank you, Audrey!

Charles Watkinson at the University of Michigan Press welcomed and encouraged this idea. Thank you, Charles. Thanks are also due to our production editor Mary Hashman and to copyeditor Richard Isomaki. Thanks also to Anna Pohlod for helping to keep us organized and moving forward. Thanks to Lena Lee and Kseniya Dzhala for their research. Finally, throughout the process, Sara Cohen has been a smart and inspiring partner—even as she has been sharing space with Carlo, a kindergartener and drawer of rainbow pictures, in school on Zoom.

# Introduction

## Living with the Virus That Knows
## How We See Each Other

*Kristin Ann Hass*

In August 2020, at the Democratic National Convention, now-vice president Kamala Harris made this observation: "This virus, it has no eyes, and yet it knows exactly how we see each other and how we treat each other."[1] She captured something essential about being human during COVID: it has challenged us, and it has revealed us to ourselves in very specific terms. Living with this wicked-smart virus has been a dramatic and multivalent experience. We have struggled to name it; we have waited for it to come to our doors and we have waited for a cure and then we have waited some more; we have grieved more than 350,000 deaths in the United States (and counting) and nearly two million deaths worldwide; we have waited for tests and vaccines and leadership and then we have waited some more; some have violently resisted public health measures and some have resisted the personal and political chaos and violence that the virus has stirred;[2] some have not had the luxury to wait and some have determined not to wait anymore; and then we have all waited some more. Each of these responses have been revealing and have been shot through with fear and dread and frustration and prejudice, and, on a few occasions, with a thrilling sense of hope.

In the United States, half the country has watched aghast as President Donald Trump has shockingly, cruelly, and recklessly sought to deny the reality of the virus and to use the pain it has wrought to his personal advantage.[3] (Jane Mayer's September 2020 story in the *New Yorker*, "A Young Kennedy, in Kushnerland, Turned Whistle-Blower" could be the most chilling reporting on the virus.)[4] The other half of the country, however, has cheered him on with full-throated support for his denial and jocular joy in the mocking of science and medicine and compassion and knowing things.[5] (I was stuck at a light in January behind a car with two brand-new bumper stickers. One read, "The Coronavirus is a Hoax" and other read, "Uber.")

Vice President Harris's observation that the virus reveals us to ourselves referred, in part, to these divisions that existed and have been cracked further open by the virus. (Wearing a mask has become a political marker as much as a public health imperative.) But she is also getting at something deeper and more specific: the disproportionate deaths among Black, Latino, and Indigenous people. The virus found, burrowed into, and has given heightened visibility to our deepest cultural fault lines. I don't think it came as a surprise to anyone who pays attention that the poor, the old, and the socially vulnerable are more susceptible to the fallout of the disease. It would be hard to be surprised that women who are working and raising children, especially economically marginalized women—in the United States and around the world—would suffer most and in the most violent terms. This, despite the fact that more men are dying from the disease than women. But as it became increasingly clear that race—not just age or economic status or geographic location—is a marker for increased vulnerability to the virus, a deep, insistent inequality took on a profound new visibility. In late March into April and May 2020 it slowly became clear that people of color of all social-economic classes are more likely to get sick and more likely to die from COVID.[6] The virus actually does know how we see each other.

COVID has shaken the globe, and in the United States it has laid bare both the worst in us and, on occasion, the best in us. I have had a recurring thought over the last eleven months that might usefully convey a sense of what it has been like to live while the virus has raged. It may seem overwrought or melodramatic, but I can assure you that it is the real meditation of an optimist knocked off her feet. I have come to feel, for the first time, that I can understand how the Second World War followed so quickly on the heels of the First World War. As a historian, I have spent two decades feeling that no matter what I read or how I broke it down, I couldn't understand, couldn't feel in my bones how it could happen. (I know what happened, I just could not get to *how*. How could people have sought more violence and chaos so quickly?) Then one day in the spring when the virus and the denial and the political vitriol and the cruel inequity and the unemployment and the hunger and the murder of Black Americans by police and the protests in the streets were all spiking together, I felt like I could understand. When we watched George Floyd get murdered and the president of the United States defend a young man who used his stimulus check to buy a weapon he used to murder BLM protesters, I felt like I could understand.[7]

This volume is dedicated to trying to name what it feels like to be human as the virus rages. It asks its authors to draw on scholarly expertise and lived experience to try to make sense of an unfamiliar present in which days can seem like months and a year like a day. This is no mean feat.

We have invited scholars across a range of specializations—Buddhist studies and classical archaeology and musicology and the history of art, and many more—to share their thinking to help us to see, to name the experience of COVID through their perspectives as scholars and as humans. As we waited and worked through the pandemic, we watched as many of the questions that occupy us, rather quietly, as scholars of the humanities were dramatically transformed by COVID-19. Our inquiries have taken on dramatic new lives before our eyes, becoming shared life-or-death questions about how human societies work and how culture determines our collective fate. Every question we ask—about grieving and publics, about the social contract and individual rights, about race making and xenophobia, about ideas of home and conceptions of gender, about narrative and representations and power—has taken on a new urgency for all of us. So we invited scholars at the University of Michigan to contribute to this volume, and they gamely jumped in. Our remarkable editorial board includes Samer Ali, Anne Cong-Huyen, Sandra Gunning, Tiya Miles, and Johannes von Moltke. They have selected and edited this work and reminded me of both the broad range of our collective expertise and the relative homogeneity of our class experience. (Darcy Brandel also generously read the poetry for us.) And Audrey Becker has shepherded and gone deep into the weeds in all elements of this project.

We have divided this work into six thematic sections that reflect, themselves, a bit of the experience. They are "Naming," "Waiting," "Grieving," "More Waiting/Sheltering," "Resisting," and "Not Waiting."

## PART I: NAMING

The first, and maybe the last, business of facing the unknown seems to be the naming. I remember listening to the TV anchors in the morning of September 11, 2001, struggling to name what was happening before their eyes. Is this Pearl Harbor, they asked. Antietam? Or Hurricane Andrew? Naming gives us a hook, a context, a place to start the process of comprehension. The literal naming of the virus that has killed 1.92 million people to date was first a matter for scientists—it is a coronavirus of some kind. Then naming was a matter of politics in the United States, where President Trump was determined to give it a name that encouraged racist and xenophobic blame for the virus. Finally, there was modest victory for science as the name that took hold is one that identifies a particular, new coronavirus and links it to the year in which it emerged—hence COVID-19. It is a serviceable name—it is a specific reference to what the virus is and when it came to be, but it doesn't begin to name what it feels like, how it has changed us, what it has taken from us. It is a name that abbreviates the virus family, but it will explode with meanings across time. It has already become exponentially bigger than the virus itself, and that is saying a lot. In fact, a big part of being human during COVID has been about trying to name, to understand, to contain, to get our arms around something that is at once quite singular—a particular mutation of a common microorganism and spectacularly multifaceted—reaching into nearly every corner of the planet and changing things there.

But even before the naming could take the form of anything like a noun, there was a more inchoate experience of trying to grasp the unknown, trying to feel or sense perimeters of the amorphous. My first fumbling attempts at this led me to the vivid memory of being on an airplane that was on fire. Maybe the most shocking part of that experience was the heavy, dense silence that fell over us after the captain made his succinct, clipped announcement that we were aflame and were going to make an emergency landing. It wasn't at all like it is in the movies—there was no screaming or running up and down the aisles. There was no activity whatsoever except for clutching. I sat, like the lot of us, in stone silence clutching my children, hardly daring to breathe.

In March 2020 the plane on fire seemed like a decent beginning to try to understand the experience of the pandemic. It captured the facing of a terrifying unknown, the sense of being suspended in time, the experience of waiting for some ghastly, deadly thing to happen, and the fascinating business of witnessing collective (early) acquiescence. As much as anything, I was struck by the relative quietness of the whole thing. There was suffering and fear, and plenty of people had to go out into the unknown every day, but the streets in most places were quiet. I kept asking people—on the phone—if someone had told you that the whole world was going to be shut down over the course of a few weeks in response to a deadly plague, would you have ever imagined it to be so orderly? Or so still, at least at first? Where I live, and where most but not all people live, those who could just went home and hunkered down. I was fearful in Whole Foods and unable to sleep in my soft, familiar bed, but the experience of the empty streets did not match the commotion of the cinematic figures waving their arms and howling their fears that I guess I had imagined a deadly virus sweeping the globe might inspire. I was aware, of course, that my experience was not universal and that it was going to be important to track and to try to understand experiences beyond my own.

In the first section, literary scholar Christopher Matthews reflects on monsters and how the stories we tell create them and help us to manage their presence amongst us. In "This Virus Has No Eyes: Telling Stories in the Land of Monsters," Matthews tries to capture the experience of grabbing hold of meaning, of a name and of a narrative in the early days of the virus with the help of monster stories. He reminds us that "monster stories are quite often less about the monster itself—the goblins and their backstory—than the human response, good or bad, blinkered or enlightened, to crisis, to transformation, to catastrophe." He brings us to a sharp call for a conscious knowing—for rejecting a hazy unconsciousness of an unknown beast—to know and to name what it is costing all of us. Literary and visual culture scholar Sara Blair grapples with how we have tried to name the virus by capturing it in images, by *visualizing* life with COVID. In "Facing Our Pandemic," she asks, "How do we make sense of the mounting intimate and collective losses, the untold injuries to personhood and human being? . . . How do we give a face to the experience of the pandemic's violence, or begin cultivating new forms of response to the systemic realities it exposes?" She walks us through a series of powerful images, made mostly by amateur photographers, that work to capture, to show, what it is like to be human during COVID. Blair deftly reveals a kind of complicated renaissance of the portrait as a vivid response to a new, pointed need to see each other and to be seen in the context of both the pandemic and the social justice movement. We need to see the faces hidden behind PPE and the faces scarred by masks, and we need to see the faces of a movement that calls us to acknowledge what has long been in plain sight. In "Living on Loss of Privileges: What We Learned in Prison," Patrick Bates, Alexandra Friedman, Adam Kouraimi, Ashley Lucas, Sriram Papolu, and Cozine Welch have created (and transcribed) a web series in which formerly incarcerated people respond to the near constant refrain that the COVID lockdowns are like being in prison. This series responds to what could be a galling comparison with compassionate lessons taught by former prisoners on how to manage the experience of losing basic privileges. Artaysia Mallisham talks about the importance of self-care, Romando Valeroso shares his experience of the importance of structure, and Juan Juan Willis describes how important venting was for him—venting through writing poetry and songs. Individually and taken together, these personal accounts offer powerful instruction, and they contribute to the work of naming of this experience. Finally, Michelle McClellan and Aprille McKay share their practice of trying to name the experience of the virus for the future—of collecting artifacts for the Bentley Historical Archive that will tell the story of living through the virus for future historians. In "Not Even Past: Archiving 2020 in Real Time" they share a sampling of the items they've collected so far: a photograph of a forty-eight-year-old, beloved campus bus driver named Troy Dixon who was killed by the virus in April 2020; a comedic film made by an undergraduate about the monotony of the lockdown; and the handwritten diary of a professor of music. They also share the challenge of collecting, of naming what we don't yet fully understand.

PART II: WAITING

Part of the quiet of the first months of the pandemic, for those of us outside of hospitals and clinics, was an unfamiliar kind of waiting—waiting in March and April and May and then June and July and August and then waiting in months that blur together and lose their shape. Waiting that flattened time. Waiting for news, waiting for research, waiting for sick people to get better, waiting for leadership, waiting for an explanation of the deadly social distinctions made by the virus, waiting for grocery deliveries, waiting for a vaccine, waiting for a cure, waiting for test results, waiting for better tests, waiting for no more waiting, waiting for less unrest in the streets, waiting for more unrest in the streets, waiting for a return to normalcy, waiting for a new, better normal.

To be sure, waiting has not been uniform or equitable or even about a clear, familiar passage of time. The essays in this part work to capture pieces of this wild waiting. David Caron leads off this section with "Waiting = Death: COVID-19, the Struggle for Racial Justice, and the AIDS Pandemic," in which he asks us to think about waiting but also about patience and impatience. He considers waiting in the context of the AIDS crisis and the long civil rights movement against the waiting we are doing now. He beautifully pulls us through multiple kinds of waiting, and then he offers some hope. He writes, "I remember what it felt like to wait with other people—and then to have enough" and reminds us that George Floyd's murder came, in the midst of so much waiting, as a potent call not to wait for justice for Black Americans. Donald Lopez's "Buddhism, the Pandemic, and the Demise of the Future Tense," walks us through a different approach to thinking about biding time—about stopping time. He starts with Buddhist concepts of suffering, explaining that the most pernicious is the suffering of conditioning—the almost unseen habit of always waiting for suffering in the next moment, "over which we have no control." Certainly this felt resonant in the early months of the pandemic. For those of us who remained healthy and outside of hospitals, the state of waiting for the other shoe to drop, for the virus to darken your own door, was an active, if abstract, kind of suffering. As Lopez describes it, "the fact that we have no control over the future, no matter what models we construct, no matter what scenarios we project, no matter what plans we make" can, once it becomes the focus of our attention, be consuming. It can rob us of our confidence, he writes, of speaking in the future tense. (When I read this in June 2020, I thought I understood what he meant, and then in November and January, as the deaths continued to mount and chaos intensified, I felt this in my bones.) For Buddhists, in Lopez's formulation, letting go of the future tense is not so much about "living in the moment" as it is about surrendering the self to survive the present. He explains, "As soon as we recognize that we do not exist in the way that we have always imagined, that we do not exist in the way that we imagine ourselves in this year of politics and plague, then the future, and all the horror that it holds, will end." Waiting, then, is made survivable by reframing our most basic understanding of existence. Visual artist Jim Cogswell's "COVID Diary: Hands, Nets, and Other Devices" takes another approach to waiting. His first set of images, of hands, was made in the first week of March as the storm approached. He frames them with an homage to their narrative potential. In these images, his hands are not wringing; they are floating among bits of color that look, presciently, like a hybrid of the COVID virus and bullet holes in glass. There is a sense of free fall in these images that is heightened when, inspired by a palimpsest of tragedy, he stretches back to ancient Greece and introduces free-floating fragments of nets into the images in "Nets and Other Devices," work made in May and June 2020. The conversation he evokes across time, with bits of tragic iconography and neon orange traffic cones, captures palpable sensations of suspended time. This part ends with Amal Fadlalla's moving "Social Distances in Between: Excerpts from My COVID-19 Diaries." She reflects on the ways in which waiting out the virus in a home that is not fully a home for a transnational woman of color casts shades of meaning on the now ubiquitous term—social distancing. Comparing her experience of the lockdown in a Midwestern college town to that of her sister, who is a doctor in Saudi Arabia, and her sister in Sudan, who is negotiating the virus and dramatic political transformation, she asks us to think about multiple forms of distance. She explains, "I use 'enhanced social distancing' here to highlight myriad other social boundaries and divisions that we have normalized, embodied, and taken for granted over the years." She shows us the hardening of some of these distinctions as she waits for the crisis to pass, but she also takes us with her as she walks her neighborhood. She shows us, with small interventions and daily familiarity, the process through which some—but not all—of these distinctions loosen as she finds herself walking past "Black Lives Matter" and "We Support That Woman from Michigan" yard signs and connecting to a gardening neighbor aptly named Angel. For her, waiting creates the space for something else to bloom.

PART III: GRIEVING

In all of the waiting it would seem like there would be time for grieving. In March, 4,331 Americans were killed by the virus. In April, the total rose to 59,646 souls. May saw the death toll reach 100,783. June: 120,258. July: 145,507. August: 175,751. September: 199,080. October: 222,625. November: 259,690. December: 336,802.[8] People seem to have struggled to know how to grieve at this scale. On May 24, 2020 the *New York Times* ran a front page with the headline "U.S. Deaths Near 100,000, an Incalculable Loss" and a list of the names, ages and hometowns of those who had died.[9] On August 30, 2020 the City of Detroit organized fifteen long group funeral processions in Belle Isle Park to remember Detroiters lost to the virus. At the Queens Museum in New York City, a parking lot was transformed into a loving memorial with a twenty-thousand-square-foot mural portrait of a masked doctor.[10] Another, bigger project—the COVID Memorial Project—offers both a site on which to post a memory of someone killed by the virus and a large-scale projection project, to enable people to project memorial slideshows on buildings. They also placed thousands of small American flags on the National Mall in September to try to commemorate the dead and to convey a sense of the scale of the loss.[11] This is something, but it is not commensurate with the scale of loss. It is not as if grief has been banished, but one of the most remarkable aspects of being human, in the United States, during COVID has been the relative absence of public grief. This is not to suggest that there has not been intense, sustained, wrenching private grief—there have been more than 350,000 occasions for it. But despite the list above, which could be expanded to include many, many more local efforts, we have not—despite the time some have had on their hands—seen the kind of mass outpourings of public grief that have been so central to American civic life in the last forty years.

Where is the grief? And when do we grieve? You might speculate that, because the virus has hit some communities, especially communities of color, harder than others, grief has been segregated, and to some extent this is probably true. But this doesn't align with the story of public grief in the contemporary United States. A very short version of that story is that after the social disruptions of the Vietnam War, public commemoration experienced a dramatic revival, and shared practices emerged around public memorials that involve the leaving of things at sites of bombings and shootings and car accidents and natural disasters. This has been a remarkably robust, participatory culture of commemoration. (Think flowers and teddy bears and flags at Ground Zero or Parkland or at the site of Michael Brown's murder.) This practice emerged from the grief of communities of color who lost a disproportionate number of young men to the Vietnam War and has become common practice. It has also been a kind of centrifugal force in a tense and divided nation. We have gotten good at grieving together. We haven't been able to agree on a lot, but we have shared grief and we have valued collective grieving. The stories behind the fight to build the 9/11 memorials and the fights to build new war memorials on the National Mall reveal a deep investment in shared grief. All of this makes the relative absence of public grief for the nearly four hundred thousand Americans lost to the virus all the more remarkable. If you were told, in 2019, that we would lose the same number of people that we lost on 9/11 every day for months and that the streets would not be flooded with grievers, that the media would not be saturated with stories of loss, that Facebook would not have been turned into a solemn stream of tears, that, in fact, a large part of the population would be denying the fact of these deaths, I am not sure you would have believed it.

Certainly, the scale of the losses is part of the problem. President Trump's cruel denial of the reality of these losses is also part of the problem. The fact that people are dying in isolation in hospitals also contributes to the muted response. Published photographs of mass graves look like they are from another time and place; it is hard to believe that they were taken here and now. The images of mobile morgues set up in hospital parking lots and on city streets look like they're trucks lined up at loading docks at Target, not makeshift storage for the dead, not the simple reality of mass death.

I wonder if the enormous energy and passion that millions of Americans gave to the Black Lives Matter movement in 2020 is linked to all of the free-floating, bottled-up collective grief. The murder of George Floyd before our eyes in an unspeakable nine minutes and twenty-nine seconds unleashed some of this grief, along, of course, with rage that turned out to be impossible to contain. I know that for many the most intense pain of the virus came as the news reports about the racial bias of the virus started to come in. (No, no, no, oh God, please no.) George Floyd is not the first Black man or woman we have witnessed being murdered by the police. These murders have been an open fact of life in the United States since its inception. They have been the subject of periodic public outrage and they have continued. Trayvon Martin, Eric Garner, Michael Brown, Tamir Rice. We knew their names before George Floyd was killed. Was there a connection between the quiet grief Americans were holding in May 2020, the sense of helpless disbelief that the virus really does know how we see each other, and the intense national and global response to Floyd's murder? The work of movement activists is likely the key driver, but the need for millions to take to the streets, even in the pandemic, could well be linked to the problem of COVID grief. It certainly was a powerful expression of collective grief. When Harris told us that the virus knows how we see each other, she made an argument for the ways in which these griefs are connected. The divisions among us that the virus has required us to see, to feel, to carry inextricably, bind the loud, outraged grief for Floyd and the quiet, camouflaged grief of the souls stored in refrigerator trucks in parking lots across the country.

The essays in this section take up COVID and grief. Suzanne Davis helps us to think about the quotidian nature of mourning in her essay "Grief and the Importance of Real Things during COVID-19." Davis, a curator at the Kelsey Museum of Archaeology, takes up three distinct objects to do this because, as she writes, "Historical artifacts—and sometimes an awareness of their absence—can help us make sense of this brutality, acknowledge grief, and find hope in the world." She walks us through the story of "a painted limestone grave marker in the collection of the Kelsey Museum; a cardboard box taped shut for shipping in 1948 and never reopened, now in my father's office; and a fork with a wood handle and three spindly steel tines that I use on a daily basis." She argues that "each artifact encodes trauma and loss, but is also a mechanism for remembrance—becoming a vessel for specific stories of the collective brutality and beauty of life." Sara Forsdyke turns to ancient history in her essay, "Looking Backward in Order to Look Forward: Lessons about Humanity and the Humanities from the Plague at Athens." She takes up a plague that killed more than a third of the population of Athens in 430 BCE. Describing the social breakdowns that were more terrifying than the disease, she writes, "One clear lesson is that societies must reinforce institutions of social cohesion that build bonds of familiarity and trust between citizens in order to survive the disruptions caused by pandemics." William A. Calvo-Quirós's essay, "Protests, Prayers, and Protections: Three Visitations during COVID-19," invites us into an intimate community of grievers and thinks about the relationship between grief and grievance. He tracks a resurgence of religious practices related to deities and saints, and tries to capture something of the "innumerable private and public acts of piety, such as virtual masses, rosaries, and Zoom religious events, [that] have populated the news." He finds saints, in a broad Latinx diaspora, evoked on COVID masks and for the Black Lives Matter movement. He shares his experience of joining a Zoom rosary group—which devotes most of its meetings to requests for prayers for people they know who are suffering from the disease or its brutal social impacts. The final essay in this section is Melanie Tanielian's powerful "Soliloquous Solipsism: An Attempt to Put Words to a Loss of Words." She draws us in, with text but mostly with images, to her experience of loss as a loss for words. She writes, "My humanness, like a smartphone losing its battery power one tiny percentage point at a time and diminishing its screen's pixels, turned pitch black. Grief immobilized years of training in narrating historical deaths with the sole political goal of historical justice, historical accuracy, and meaning making of the historical." So she turned to making images, images of her body—muted, in pain, and very much alive—to express a private grief that raged within her that the lockdown had unlocked and that could not be abstracted. This work is, in part, about what grief opened up in her, and in that way it puts the question on the table for all of us. What has grief given us? What has it enabled? And what has it taken away? The image that I keep coming back to for grief during COVID is of a free radical slamming around in a body—both loose and trapped, dormant and radioactive, very much alive and heavy with the potential.

## PART IV: MORE WAITING/SHELTERING

Of course, as all of this raged around us there has been a whole lot more waiting. Tense waiting. Quiet waiting. Noisy waiting. Homeschooling while working from home waiting. Waiting for work. Waiting for help. Waiting to get a good night's sleep. Waiting to get out of the house. Waiting for grocery deliveries. Waiting for bleached groceries to dry. Waiting for a vaccine. Waiting for a cure. Waiting for better tests. Waiting for test results. Waiting to see what happens next. And, of course, waiting for the presidential election to come and then waiting for it to be over. And then waiting for it to be over some more. Waiting and sheltering. Hunkering down.

Movement within the waiting inspires Frances Kai-Hwa Wang's poem, "Finding Home between the Vincent Chin Case and COVID-19." She opens with the line, "First I heard from the high schoolers at Chinese School that all their parents were stocking up on rice and bottled water." Her next line is "Then I heard about the fights breaking out in the California Costcos. Don't mess with Asian Aunties." She jokes about how "America went crazy for toilet paper" and shares her struggle to feel at home in the state where Vincent Chin was murdered in 1982 by men who were punished with a $3,000 fine. But across the arc of the poem she comes to embrace Michigan as her home, after holding it at arm's length for twenty years, not because of the rise in anti-Asian violence but because of the pushback against it in old and new media. She writes, "As the hashtags surge #StopAAPIHate #washthehate #IamNotA-Virus #hateisavirus #StandAgainstHatred, / And Big Gretch starts trending. / I feel, for the first time in all these years, like I belong here. Like I am not alone here. Like this can be home here." Daniel Herbert takes up a very different set of questions about waiting at home. He writes about the watching we are doing while we are waiting and the impact the virus has had on the industry and the culture of watching in "Caged with the Tiger King: The Media Business and the Pandemic." Herbert tracks the impact of the shutdown on all aspects of the media business—production, distribution, and consumption. He writes, "As we imagined how we might conduct ourselves and find relief and even pleasure in a world where public and group interactions appeared threatening, our use of home entertainment—and the business that enables it—seemed more important than ever." And he asks, "Did *Tiger King* really offer a picture of Hollywood's 'new normal?'" Bringing us through this, he wants to show "how the streaming media practices encouraged and enabled by industrial changes are bound up in other processes of social division." Certainly there is forbidding resonance in the image of millions of people, myself included, disappearing into the awful world of the Tiger King, which felt like parody, real-time political reporting, salacious gossip, and actual participation in the abuse of vulnerable young people. *Tiger King* left you wanting more and needing to take a shower and heartbroken, if also temporarily distracted from actual political insanity and abuse and death.

Nick Tobier's contribution, "Prosthetics for Right Now," offers a sense of play that is quite distinct from the passive ugliness of the *Tiger King*. He writes briefly about the ways in which people waiting all over the world tried to connect: "Think about what we saw—either directly or via news. Italians serenading one another from their balconies. New Yorkers nightly at 7:00 p.m. cheering from windows for frontline health care workers." He asks us to "think about where we were in March 2020. Largely home (if you had the luxury of working from home); hoarding or searching for toilet paper, yeast, flour; thrust into school closures with improvised learning plans; and watching from near and far as COVID cases surged in Detroit, Milan, New York City while Donald Trump insisted that the virus posed no more danger than the seasonal flu." He recommends Rebecca Solnit's *A Paradise Built in Hell* on communities forged by disaster, and then he offers a series of practical and impossible designs intended to facilitate community in this crisis. He introduces Solnit to remind us that disaster "shocks us out of slumber—but only skillful effort keeps us awake."

## PART V: RESISTING

What we have lost in our public spaces and how we might hope (or work) to reimagine them as more equitable and more just is a central theme in the experience of being human during this pandemic. What we have lost in our domestic spaces is a more intimate and, often, much more pressing question. This part of this volume is written by nine individual authors who are part of a collective project to capture the stories and experience of feminist activists across the globe. The Expanding Global Feminisms Project, supported by the University of Michigan's Humanities Collaboratory, is building an archive whose purpose is to provide raw material for scholars of women's movement activism to use in teaching and research. The essays they contribute here draw on these sources and lay out the deadly sharp edges of the gender divide of the COVID experience. They make plain, in indelible terms, another level at which the virus shows us how we see each other.

In her introduction to this section, "COVID-19's Attack on Women and Feminists' Response: The Pandemic, Inequality, and Activism," Abigail Stewart tells us, "The essays . . . consider what the scholars associated with the Global Feminisms Project, regardless of their own national origins and different disciplines, have learned during this period about the situation of women generally, and feminist activists in particular, during this very difficult time." She promises that the essays in this part demonstrate "the creative, courageous, and forthright way feminist scholars and activists have met the new challenges to women's lives posed by this global pandemic," and they make good on this promise. They offer some of the most vivid concentrations of suffering in the pandemic in this volume.

Eimeel Castillo's essay, "The Virus That Kills Twice: COVID-19 and Domestic Violence under Governmental Impunity in Nicaragua," tells the story of the violence against women that has been such a crushing part of being human during COVID. She writes, "The impunity and lawlessness that reign in Nicaragua are key to understanding how the pandemic has worsened the already existing epidemic of domestic violence and femicide," and she demonstrates the invaluable work of women's organizations as the state takes a repressive turn. Sueann Caulfield, in "Our Steps Come from Long Ago: Living Histories of Feminisms and the Fight against COVID in Brazil," walks us through "the emergence of a diverse array of women activists at the forefront of efforts to defend vulnerable populations through direct action and political lobbying" in the context of multiple failures of leadership. She shows us how Black feminist, LGBTQ+, and pan-Indigenous organizations have been crucial for vulnerable communities. In "Making Sense of Sex and Gender Differences in Biomedical Research on COVID-19" Abigail Dumes notes the history of inattention to sex and gender in medical research and the relative uptick in interest in gender in COVID-19 research in an effort to understand why the virus is killing more men than women. She advocates for an opportunity to push for more intersectionality in medical research. Marisol Fila also writes about how Black, LBGTQ+, and feminist activism has been crucial in the face of repressive policies that intensify the inequity of the impact of the virus. In "Digital Encounters from an Intersectional Perspective: Black Women in Argentina," Fila describes the agility with which activists have turned to digital platforms to continue their work. Verena Klein takes up different leadership styles and outcomes along gender lines during COVID in "The Media Discourse on Women-Led Countries in the COVID-19 Pandemic: Using Germany as an Example." Jayati Lal shows in vivid detail that "the disparate effect of the coronavirus on women workers has also deepened gender inequalities globally." Her essay, "Coronavirus Capitalism and the Patriarchal Pandemic in India: Why We Need a 'Feminism for the 99%' That Focuses on Social Reproduction," focuses on India but offers global implications for the impact of patriarchy and capitalism on the unjust distribution of the pain of the pandemic. Özge Savaş's essay, "Whose Challenge Is #ChallengeAccepted? Performative Online Activism During the COVID-19 Pandemic and Its Erasures," finds similar themes in Turkey. She describes both the particular vulnerability of women and LGBTQ+ activists and the limitations of online activism, arguing that "we need feminist global solidarity without the erasure of our differences, centering the voices of those whose struggles are compounded by sexist, racist, ableist, capitalist, and xenophobic institutions." In the last of these compelling essays, legal scholar and activist Abiola Akiyode-Afolabi and anthropologist Ronke Olawale argue that women in Nigeria are experiencing disproportionate vulnerability to the disease and increased domestic violence. They argue that despite "the lockdown, nonprofit women's organizations in Nigeria supported vulnerable women in the country." Across these essays there is moving and inspiring evidence of all kinds of existing feminist organizations stepping up to resist the forces that sharpen the gendered edges of the inequities wrought by the virus. All of these women and organizations across the globe are making powerful arguments for not waiting while we are all supposed to be waiting.

PART VI: NOT WAITING

Since the beginning of the pandemic, "not waiting" has taken all kinds of forms. French scientists mapped the genome of the virus between January 24 and January 29, 2020.[12] Michigan governor Gretchen Whitmer set emergency operations into motion on February 28, 2020, and schools were closed on March 13.[13] Teachers were back at work, online, within a few days. Unemployed people, 15% of Americans by April, volunteered and advocated for each other in record numbers.[14] In June a stunning number of individuals and organizations made impassioned, public antiracist statements. A massive, inflamed political battle was waged—and that too involved waiting. A vaccine was developed in record time; doctors started getting vaccinated in December. Not waiting has been, in other words, intense and tumultuous. The essays in this final part reflect this. They call for mobilizing against racism, for using caution when laying blame, for noticing less obvious forms of prejudice that have been heightened by the conditions of the pandemic, and for acting out.

Lawyer and activist Roland Hwang's essay "COVID-19 through an Asian American Lens: Scapegoating, Harassment, and the Limits of the Asian American Response," describes "a second pandemic that Asian Americans face—an epidemic of anti-Asian hate," and he calls on his readers to push back. He writes, "I am struck by how a portion of the US population is quick to blame Asian Americans for the spread of COVID-19, perpetuating the 'perpetual foreigner' stereotype, a persistent view of Asian Americans as not quite 'real' Americans." He reminds us of the history of anti-Asian racism and makes it clear that while the current violence and hate is linked to that history, what is happening during COVID is "being choreographed and stoked by President Trump and members of his administration who call the pandemic 'Chinese flu' or 'Kung Flu,' to pointedly stir up anti-Asian hate to activate a long history of racism." Hwang calls on us to see this mobilization of racist tropes for what it is and to respond accordingly. Historian David Patterson turns to Rome in 589 CE to think about a history of plagues and our efforts to understand them and to assign blame for them in his essay, "The High Stakes of Blame: Medieval Parallels to a Modern Crisis." He rejects the impulse of individuals to blame themselves—for getting sick or for getting someone else sick—and reminds us that blaming the other in pandemics has a long history. Christians blamed Jews for a plague in France in 1348, just as Americans have blamed Asians, and Italians have blamed Muslim migrants in 2020. He tells us leaders have long sought to blame God or to duck blame by denying pandemics and writing them out of histories. He concludes that from Rome in 589 CE into the present, "the behavior of a virus is made a proxy of governmental competence: nature is supposed to reflect the excellence of ruling authorities." Linguists Nicholas Henriksen and Matthew Neubacher call our attention to a less sweeping but still active form of prejudice that has been intensified by the virus. In "Unmuting Voices in a Pandemic: Linguistic Profiling in a Moment of Crisis," Henriksen and Neubacher note the increased importance of virtual communication in 2020 and explore the structures of linguistic profiling and its relevance amid the pandemic and the social inequality that has come to the forefront. Drawing on their research on Andalusian speakers, they contend that "examining the automatic, split-second judgments we make about a speaker may seem like an inconsequential act of protest, but as we further depend on audio-reliant communication platforms, this represents a crucial step toward continuing our evolution into a less-prejudiced society."

The final essay in this section and this volume is a dynamic, explosive, inspiring catalog of the work of artists who have decided quite emphatically not to wait, despite closed theaters and galleries and performance spaces, but instead to make and to share and to push for change with their pressing and vivid work. Anita Gonzalez's "Quarantine Rebellions: Performance Innovation in the Pandemic" is a series of brief essays that "break down how isolation of individuals from their artistic communities has led to creative reflection and eventually direct, embodied political action." She writes, "Like a blinding light of merciless whiteness, the health crisis and its accompanying economic breakdown revealed cracks and crannies of deeply imbedded inequities, making them clearly visible," and she tracks how artist after artist has "created powerful movements of change within performance communities and beyond at a time when it is difficult not to be engulfed in isolation and despair." Gonzalez and these artists leave us not only invigorated but with a new set of intellectual and creative tools for responding to the virus that knows how we see each other.

This volume doesn't seek to offer a totalizing vision of being human during COVID-19. And it certainly misses big important elements of the experience. Its contributors are all gainfully employed by a big university, and most are riding out the virus in the upper Midwest. These are pretty significant limiting factors to start off with. We don't include the perspectives of Uber drivers and small business owners and the cleaning staff at nursing homes and people of all faiths or political positions. What we do is seek to give readers a hit of the painful, complicated, fascinating experiences—of the naming and waiting and grieving and resisting and the not waiting—as we are making sense of them from our positions as scholars and eyewitnesses. In this spirit there is one more element of the experience that Gonzalez evokes and that is alive in a number of these essays—Fadlalla, Blair, Davis, Calvo-Quirós, Wang, Caulfield, Savaş—that seems worth including. For all of the bad and the ugly, people across the globe have responded to the pandemic with good. We have cheered hospital workers at shift changes and taped handmade "Thank you, nurses" signs to our windows. Neighborhoods put on stuffed animal scavenger hunts for locked-down kids. Experts and novices figured out how to sew masks and have been cranking them out month after month. In my county, people donated in record numbers to local food banks, and the University of Michigan and the National Guard worked together to distribute the food.[15] The owner of a small local tea shop started making 250 lunches a week for public school kids who were missing their school lunch.[16] More than five hundred University of Michigan medical students volunteered to provide childcare to frontline medical workers, deliver groceries to vulnerable populations, and sit (virtually and in person) with COVID patients so they would not die alone.[17] The list could go on and on and on. Teachers doing drive-bys to wave at their students from their cars; neighbors getting groceries for each other; tidy streets suddenly dotted with "Black Lives Matter" and "Thank You Health Care Workers" signs. The desire of so many to help, to reach out, has been palpable since early March 2020.

As this volume goes to press, it is hard to say where we are. We have vaccines that are reaching a few but are mostly bottled up in bureaucracy. We are seeing the greatest numbers of both cases and deaths at any time during the pandemic. We are seeing the greatest political catastrophes of generations. (My revisions of this introduction were interrupted by a phone call from a friend—"Turn on your TV, armed Trump protesters have taken the Capitol.") To return to the sketch of a metaphor I began with, I am not sure if we are still on the burning plane waiting for it to land or if we have landed and are just waiting for the ground crew to put out the secondary fire caused by the rough landing. Either way, as the work here makes clear in many different ways, we, collectively, are the ground crew—and we have a clear sense of the work to be done.

January 2021

*Notes*

1. https://www.washingtonpost.com/politics/2020/08/20/kamala-harriss-conv ention-speech-annotated/
2. There are too many examples of violence—including murdered security guards and, in Michigan, a plot to kidnap and harm the governor. https://www.washingtonp ost.com/nation/2020/05/04/security-guards-death-might-have-been-because-he-wo uldnt-let-woman-store-without-mask;https://abcnews.go.com/Politics/fbi-michigan -gov-kidnapping-plot-texts-small-gatherings/story?id=73698990
3. https://www.theatlantic.com/health/archive/2020/10/trump-covid-denial /616946/
4. https://www.newyorker.com/magazine/2020/09/28/a-young-kennedy-in-kus hnerland-turned-whistle-blower
5. The violence of Trump supporters on January 6, 2021, coincided with a record number of daily COVID deaths in the United States. https://www.chicagotribune.com /coronavirus/ct-nw-covid-19-deaths-january-6-20210107-a3d3nn4tvfdwhnpyb2tqjyq quq-story.html
6. https://www.hopkinsmedicine.org/health/conditions-and-diseases/coronavi rus/covid19-racial-disparities
7. https://www.washingtonpost.com/investigations/2020/11/19/kenosha-shoo ting-kyle-rittenhouse-interview/?arc404=true and https://www.nbcnews.com/polit ics/national-security/internal-document-shows-trump-officials-were-told-make-co mments-sympathetic-n1241581
8. https://covidtracking.com/data/national/deaths
9. https://en.wikipedia.org/wiki/U.S._Deaths_Near_100,000,_An_Incalculable _Loss
10. https://www.npr.org/2020/12/08/940802688/hardly-any-1918-flu-memorials -exist-will-we-remember-covid-19-differently
11. https://www.npr.org/2020/12/08/940802688/hardly-any-1918-flu-memorials -exist-will-we-remember-covid-19-differently Other mural projects have been taken up in California and other states as well. https://www.nbclosangeles.com/news/loc al/boyle-heights-rose-river-memorial-project-honors-victims-of-covid-19-pandemic /2491791/
12. https://www.pasteur.fr/en/press-area/press-documents/institut-pasteur-seq uences-whole-genome-coronavirus-2019-ncov

13. https://www.clickondetroit.com/health/2020/03/24/michigan-coronavirus-ti meline-key-dates-covid-19-case-tracking-state-orders/

14. https://www.cnbc.com/2020/11/06/unemployed-americans-are-turning-to -advocacy-work-amid-covid.htm

15. https://www.clickondetroit.com/all-about-ann-arbor/2020/10/07/ann-arbo rs-food-gatherers-addresses-record-breaking-food-insecurity-during-pandemic/

16. https://www.secondwavemedia.com/concentrate/features/businesscovid190 541.aspx

17. https://mmheadlines.org/2020/05/during-pandemic-medical-students-volun teering-to-ensure-that-no-one-dies-alone/

# PART I

# Naming

# CHAPTER 1

# This Virus Has No Eyes

## Telling Stories in the Land of Monsters

*Christopher Matthews*

> This virus has no eyes, and yet it knows exactly how we see each other.
> —Senator Kamala Harris, accepting the nomination for vice president at the 2020 Democratic National Convention

## TINY INVISIBLE BEASTS

A story might keep you safe. A story might protect you.

In Terry Pratchett's *A Hat Full of Sky*, his 2004 novel about a young witch learning her craft—which turns out to be more midwifery than magic, less casting of spells than tending to the sometimes-icky bodily needs of folk with few resources—our hero, Tiffany Aching, begins to adapt to the tasks demanded of her. Trimming the toenails of the elderly and bathing the dead, she philosophizes: "You did the doctoring work as neatly as you could, and if it was on something oozy, then you just thought about how nice things would be when you'd stopped doing it."

Tiffany's assessment seems to be that such work is unpleasant but honest, and yet the bare facts of human health and sickness only get her so far. For example, although the Raddles, one of the hardscrabble village families on Tiffany's rounds, had been told (repeatedly) about the problem with their privy—that "it was far too close to the well, and so the drinking water was full of tiny, tiny creatures that were making their children sick"—this knowledge has made no difference in their behavior: "They'd listened very carefully, every time . . . and still they never moved the privy." Then Tiffany's powerful new mentor swoops in with a radically different approach:

Mistress Weatherwax told them it was caused by goblins who were attracted to the smell, and by the time [she and Tiffany] left that cottage, Mr. Raddle and three of his friends were already digging a new well the other end of the garden.

Honest Tiffany objects. "It really *is* caused by tiny creatures, you know," she bravely reminds her imposing elder. But Mistress Weatherwax, the Jedi master of witches, schools her:

> You have to tell people a story they can understand. Right now I reckon you'd have to change quite a lot of the world, and maybe bang Mr. Raddle's stupid fat head against the wall a few times, before he'd believe that you can be sickened by drinking tiny invisible beasts. And while you're doing that, those kids of theirs will get sicker. But goblins, now, they make sense *today*. A story gets things done.

Mistress Weatherwax operates somewhere between folklorist and public health communications director. She is no antiscience magician, but a translator of science into image, into fable.

A story gets things done. Especially a story about goblins. We might say Weatherwax has done nothing more or less than mobilize a handy fear, a fear so obvious and cliché—goblins are scary, they'll eat you, your children, up—that its readiness-to-hand is its virtue.

Is this what monster stories are, ideally, good for? While fear—or stories that mobilize "fear," meaning anxiety about the unknown implications of something perceived as an emergent threat—can precipitate horrors (bigotry, racist violence, anti-immigrant attacks), could such stories, looked at from the right angle, also prompt virtuous action? Can fear be not just a technique of ignorance but a system of knowing? Or even of virtuous not-knowing? A means of nudging those who are frustratingly, blithely certain toward uncertainty—which, in some contexts, might be the same as goosing the complacent into virtuous action? Can fear teach us to care, or can it redirect our caring toward more beneficial ends?

Monster stories are quite often less about the monster itself—the goblins and their backstory—than the human response, good or bad, blinkered or enlightened, to crisis, to transformation, to catastrophe. Such stories of fictional human responses to fictional, imaginary threats might, therefore, give us conceptual tools for reading and critiquing—and imagining—human responses to actual threats.

CATASTROPHE

March 2020, the pandemic hovering in the wings, shifting shape, seeming vague and far away, then crisp and near. I remember, sort of, my imperfect understanding of what was coming. We were all turning into amateur epidemiologists, deputized by the latest article to wonder and worry about contagiousness, the longevity of the virus on different surfaces, whether cats could get it, whether dogs could spread it, how a ventilator works, and how many the nation needed, right now, to avoid catastrophe.

It seems quaint, now, to imagine a catastrophe so localized, pinned to a particular moment, still coming—rather than already here, so thoroughly here, continuously unfolding, unrolling luxuriously, over miles, over months.

My students and I were reading *Dracula*. It was a whole course about monster stories, primarily grounded in the British nineteenth century. In some sense, you might say, it was a whole course about catastrophe—about the invisible, about what's coming, what's encroaching, about circling the wagons, about contested cultural definitions of "threat," its proximity or distance, its alienness, its uncanny intimacy, as it waits at the gates, or hides among us.

"I long to go through the crowded streets," Count Dracula taunts Jonathan Harker, his clueless guest, "to be in the midst of the whirl and rush of humanity, to share its life, its change, its death." This is Dracula getting excited about moving to the great human buffet that is London. Harker has come east, to bring Dracula the paperwork that will help him go west. It is a novel that asks us to fear the foreign and to value proper documentation.

Until March, I hadn't quite realized the whole course was about catastrophe. Yes, we had been working all along to take monstrosity seriously as a trope, as a literary mechanism of real social critique and political import. Connecting Mary Shelley's novel *Frankenstein*, for instance, with Samuel Taylor Coleridge's poem "The Dungeon," a critique of the cruelties of solitary confinement and its ability to transform human beings into criminals—proposing that Shelley's novel is also about the manufacturing of a criminal, more than the making of a human—we saw the relevance to contemporary debates about the carceral state and the demonization of the incarcerated. Then, the pandemic was suddenly upon us, and the virus seemed nothing so much as an external disruption, a blockage getting in the way of our evolving hypotheses.

Pretty soon, though, it started to seem that the pandemic was, in some sense, what our class had always been about. I went a little mad with literary parallels. *Dracula*, I declared one day, was a pandemic novel. *Influence* had become one of our theoretical watchwords—for the kinds of dangerous relationships traced out in Stevenson's *Jekyll and Hyde* and Wilde's *The Picture of Dorian Gray*, which elevates the term to a kind of code for wonderful, intoxicating, unnerving transgressions—and now everyone was talking about the historical parallels between this virus and influenza, and did my students know the word came from the Italian for *influence*? I had never set out to teach some kind of "Everything I Need to Know I Learned from a Monster Story" class, but I couldn't resist the imagistic and conceptual connections these tropes seemed to be throwing before us with every twist in the story of the pandemic itself—with every lurch and stumble of our flinching, blinkered national response to it.

Two days later, our campus was on lockdown.

I kept thinking about monsters. Their readiness to hand. The unlikely wisdom of fear.

While there are certainly ways to see the virus as a sort of monster—and such an analogy is one of my essential premises here (virus as goblin, as tiny beasts, as vampiric infection)—I really want to focus on something else: not virus as monster, but pandemic as monster story; not the "beast" in isolation but the drama of the human response *to* the beast. I want to think specifically about the ways in which competing monster tropes become methods of imagining different kinds of communal responses *to* pandemic, and by extension different definitions of the communal, the national, the human. Monster stories are on some level always about defining the community, imagining what threat or incursion or mutation will inspire the community to either reinforce its defenses or reconsider and revise its boundaries. And about doing the head-scratching work of figuring out how just, how fair, how good, such a response really is.

I admit, we could mean almost anything by "monster story," since they are slippery and ubiquitous. The concept of "monstrosity" has for millennia been associated with hybridity, transition, and amalgamation, and the stories too, which of course span continents and centuries, can be told and deployed to serve all kinds of agendas. A monster story might, for instance, demand its listeners admit their ignorance and expand their sympathies. Or it might invite its readers to get riled up about some perceived threat. It might help us align our efforts with something I find myself calling "Virtue," a primarily service-oriented impulse: we move the privy, we benefit (even if blindly so) from the expertise of those who know, we protect the vulnerable from illness, we reassert some bond of mutual care. Or a monster story might help us align our efforts with what we might generally call "power," a primarily self-, comfort-, and "security"-oriented impulse: we realize the goblin isn't really one of us, we decide it's easier to chase it out of town than bother with the privy, we assert our in-group boundaries, we feel more human for having cast out what we refuse to call human, we feel righteous in the casting out of the grotesque enemy.

Summer came, and the pandemic was still here, although its form had shifted. The end of summer came, and it was still here, its presence vast and familiar, shadowy, heavy, empty, and stretching. As the seasons passed, all kinds of stories were battling it out, not all of them on the side of Virtue with a capital *V*. But they were all ready-to-hand.

### INVASION

So many jokes about time's elasticity—*Today is March 243rd*—and memory a kind of empty box. It does take some work to remember: March, the pandemic hovering in the wings, and we were reading *Dracula*. We talked about the vampire's use of blood as a form of invasion, as a misogynistic and homosocial technique for building his power within England, the empire he planned to colonize from within. *I long to go through the crowded streets* . . .

In one of the most remarkable, grotesque schemas of the novel, Dracula sets his sights on the arguably polyamorous Lucy (who has already wondered aloud why she can't simply marry all three of the men who have pledged their love for her). Embodying a perverse kind of wish fulfillment, Dracula drains Lucy's blood night after night, and, to keep her alive, her chivalrous lovers repeatedly volunteer for transfusions, pumping their blood into her.

Only to have Dracula suck it right back out again.

I drew a kind of hourglass on the board: three men, all putting their blood into Lucy, and Dracula drinking the men's blood through her. Lucy as a vessel for men's blood, for an exchange between men. "Your girls that you all love are mine already," the Count will later declare, "and through them you and others shall yet be mine." The narrative makes it clear, but somehow drawing it on the board reveals the gruesomeness. I think I hear actual gasps behind me as I finish the chart.

Around this same time, the closing of campus feeling imminent, and necessary, a rather horrifying image of the virus's "deadly tentacles" was making the rounds: a world map filled with blood-red arcs, representing a ghastly global infiltration.

This, too, is a monster story. The world has been scribbled over, all movement and no stability; boundaries erased, painted over with red venom. A bloody spread, liquid, sprouting and spurting, infiltrating. Quite scary.

Figure 1.1. The BBC debunks a viral image from Ireland's *The Sun*. BBC News source: "Coronavirus: How a Misleading Map Went Global," February 19, 2020.

But the image is a false one. It's actually a map of airline flight paths, misrepresented as infection. According to the BBC, the University of Southampton's World Population Project included the image—as "a map illustrating global air travel"—in a series of posts about their research into likely movement out of Wuhan, China, in the weeks before the city went into lockdown. The researchers received messages asking if the graphic "represented the findings of the study," leading the team to clarify that it was only "intended to show the extent of the global air network." Still, according to the university, "somehow, from this, an incorrect story has spiraled."

The map was, the BBC reports, "picked up by several Australian news outlets" and "appeared in the online editions of [UK media outlets] the Sun, Daily Mail and Metro." One Australian TV station used the graphic in an online video that claims the map "predicts the spread of the global outbreak" and that the red lines "represent five million Wuhan residents who fled the city." (In the BBC's tally from February 2020, that video had been viewed more than seven million times.) American conspiracy theorist Glenn Beck claimed that "UK researchers had tracked the mobile phones of 60,000 people that had left China and then produced a travel map." The image in figure 1.1, from a site connected to the *Irish Sun*, still readily came up in a Google search in late August.

"The chart is frightening," Beck said.

In class, we talked it over: Dracula's reverse transfusions, Lucy as conduit. We worked to see what might lie behind this horror, what the novel was asking us, expecting us, to feel and to fear. Dracula is scary because, like any good monster, he has been well engineered to scare. Like any literary monster, he is an artifact, a thing made to fulfill a function. To understand the artifact is to understand the function for which it was made, which is to understand the social conditions in which such a thing could be put to use, literally or conceptually. This probably means Stoker's audience was well positioned to fear the mingling of blood, the infiltrated bedroom, the machinations of foreigners, the depleting of masculine goodness through the fickleness of female desire, and the general corruption of a set of cultural logics that had, for a very long time, comfortably equated blood with heritage, sex, race, and nation.

"To know her is to love her," Dracula says, meaning England, and so much more. Dracula's great threat, you could say, the thing Stoker expects his audience to fear, is how the Count's access to the *women* of England gives him access to the bloodlines of England, to the genetics of England, and thus to England as a nation—if we mean nation as ethno-state, where racial identity and citizenship are conceptually intertwined. Stoker asks us to fear Dracula as a threat to racial purity and thus national sovereignty, as though the two were the same thing.

A monster is a made thing, and the fear it cites and invokes is a made thing. But the fear most likely comes first.

*An incorrect story has spiraled.* The misreading of the map reveals a lot, asking us as it does to see circulation *as* infection, boundary crossing *as* diseased invasion. An airline's map of triumphal global reach, the thick arcs of interconnectivity, not unlike a cell phone company's boastful graphics of its tremendous "coverage," represented, or imagined, as essentially identical to, interchangeable with, a nightmare of viral infiltration. This is what Stoker invites his readers to worry about too. Invasion, of body, nation, and bedroom, of each through the other. Bloody tentacles of some foreign beast.

Our own president asked us to fear something similar: not the virus itself—he asked us to disregard the virus, to disbelieve the scientific fact of the virus—but the infiltration of a foreign adversary. A monster story: "Chinese virus," "Kung Flu." A story designed to get something done. Specifically, to retread an easy, clichéd fear and solidify domestic power by invoking international danger. This was not a story designed to get anyone to move the privy, but to distract us with a little feel-good xenophobia: cast out, discursively at least, the goblins, and all will be well.

GOOD FEAR

It's summer, and I have begun to take my mother on long drives in the country whenever I visit. We are both happy hermits, but I am the kind of son who thinks she needs to get out sometimes. I am the kind of hermit who loves a good wander, and although I dislike driving for the sake of driving, a pandemic requires flexibility. We have discovered old farm roads snaking their way through bright-green swampland, old dime stores where my mother tells me she would, as child, order hot dogs sliced down the middle and served on a hamburger bun—a kind of Midwestern delicacy. She tells me her father, whom I never knew, used to take her and her brothers on long Sunday drives like this, flipping a coin at intersections to see which way to go, letting the coin decide, to add a little chaos and increase their chances of getting lost. A good kind of lost.

My mother admires the towns we drive through, but they are mostly shells, the ruins of places that probably functioned pretty well fifty or a hundred years ago but are now only half-inhabited. Sometimes I think we could be almost anywhere. We see a lot of Trump signs. We drift down little Main Streets, stop for gas, haunt the curbside outside an ice cream joint we found online, wondering if we dare, but almost no one is wearing a mask.

We are listening to Philip Glass's Violin Concerto No. 2, *The American Four Seasons*, second movement, and the violins sear, slice high, wobble and descend, and repeat. I suppose it feels "American" because there is a wide-openness to the sound, a gesturing toward vastness, a speaking into canyons. Also heartbreak, deep wells of need, almost everything feeling lost. It is music for isolation, for looking out of windows, for a sense that, just outside of the window, the world that seems beautiful is not exactly not-beautiful, but, while being beautiful, tainted. Hiding something.

On our drives I sometimes think of the Raddles. Maybe these folks, the ones without the masks, are under the sway of the wrong story. One about bravura or might or the value of fearlessness. Maybe they need a story that will make them properly afraid.

Percy Shelley, in his preface to Mary Shelley's *Frankenstein*, argues that the story is not merely "a series of supernatural terrors" but a tale that uses such materials to achieve "a point of view . . . for the delineating of human passions more comprehensive and commanding than any which the ordinary relations of existing events can yield." We don't necessarily go to monster stories because they get things "right," but because—if we trust Percy on this one—they can be a vantage point from which we see how cruelly humans can behave when afraid, and how stupidly they can behave when they fail to be afraid.

Look at that flight path map: Even when real fear is called for, and real action, it can mutate into something ugly. Its audience is a roomful of pitchforks. One thing that especially bothers me about that map: how could anyone who has ever flown, who has ever looked in the back of the in-flight magazine, not immediately recognize it for what it is?

My mother and I drive deeper into the country. Empty villages, farms with equipment here and there that seems abandoned in the middle of the day, vast arching machines shooting water on crops without a person in sight. Still, when we find little pockets of people, on a main street, outside a bar, a group of men looking at each other trying to figure out how to get something heavy out of the back of a pickup truck, there seems to be no fear. They don't seem to care how close they stand. They watch us as we drive by.

I think about *Dracula*'s opening chapters: an upstanding young middle-class man, a lawyer from the metropole, about to be both married and promoted—such are the signs of his goodness, his deep abiding *normalcy*, of his function as a representative of the homeland—takes a train further and further east, until the landscape becomes wilder, and the people dress funny, and eat strange food, and make weird signs when he tells them he's on his way to visit the Count in the old castle up there. After more than a century of reading such tales, we can see it a million miles away: Jonathan Harker, on top of the world, scoffing a little at the picturesque natives making the sign of the cross over him, will soon come to realize that the superstitions of the locals are pretty much spot-on. They are the knowledgeable ones, and he'd better listen.

Am I Harker, meandering out of my element, far from the city and shocked that the locals don't share my sensibilities? Should I listen to the wisdom of the villagers? Ice cream awaits.

But we don't get out. Almost no one is masked. We keep driving.

## BAD CERTAINTY

In moments when it seems a little tingle of horror might do my brain and body good—might wake me up on a soporific afternoon back-country drive—I often think of all the terrible horror movies I managed to watch during my poorly monitored after-school TV-time as a child. Santa Cruz had a channel that served them up in cheesy, heaping cauldronfuls. I think about *Night*

Figure 1.2. Still from the *Night of the Living Dead*. "They're coming to get you, Barbara." Directed by George A. Romero (1968; Image Ten).

*of the Living Dead*, George Romero's weirdly rough and strangely compelling zombie flick from 1968—on basic cable within ten years—and of the line that launches its fleshy terrors: *They're coming to get you, Barbara.* It's said mockingly, in a vaguely Karloffian voice, in a cemetery, by a brother to a sister. She has spotted a stranger stumbling in the distance and finds him unsettling. Her brother is unsympathetic, and teases, with this distillation of all things horror—*They're coming to get you.*

It's a mantra that perfectly encapsulates one of the recurring moral epistemologies of such tales: the fearful aren't wrong (that guy really is, we quickly learn, a zombie), and the cocksure are going to pay (the brother will be attacked and zombified in due course, thank you very much).

We tend to think fear makes people do bad things—and perhaps it does, and the danger of *white* fear especially has a long, and increasingly well-documented, history as a motor for repeated, consequence-free violence against Black and brown bodies. Still, I want to make some room for this other possibility, that fear can be . . . just. That fear might, sometimes, be aligned with a virtuous uncertainty, and lack of fear with the arrogance and violence of blinkered dogma. (Are those police—in Minneapolis, in Louisville, in Ferguson—really "afraid," or isn't it some deep abiding *certainty* that enables the violence?) In the cemetery, the sister's fear doesn't mobilize any ugly bigotry; it's her brother's *lack* of fear, the obnoxious fraternal knowingness of his taunt, that is both repellant and deadly.

His sister's fear is a metric for her alertness to what she doesn't know. She will survive, if not the film, at least its first half hour. Her fear is, very broadly speaking, good.

Back in my mother's own little town, surrounded, we fear, by the overly certain, we live large and order pizza. When I go to pick it up, I pause on the empty sidewalk outside the restaurant and put my mask on—not out of fear, I want to say, because I don't want to be accused of simply acting from fear, but out of knowledge, and smart uncertainty, and care for others. But this is increasingly, on our drives, what I'm using "fear" to name: a system of unknowing that might nudge us toward broader, and better, caring. I open the swinging door with a pinky. (Are surfaces still vectors of transmission? I don't know.) Inside, the tables are full, people are hunched over beers and slices, laughing, leaning, gesturing. I feel like a foreigner, there in my mask, painfully obvious, unsure where to stand, but it takes whole minutes before anyone even notices me.

The end of Romero's film famously doubles back to a new, more systematic, and deadlier version of the brother's arrogance. Here, the morning after the apocalypse, the only survivor, our Black hero, Ben (Duane Jones), the one person who managed to keep his head on straight and barricade the farmhouse quickly enough to save himself—and, for a while, a handful of white folks, including poor Barbara—from the waves of the undead. He wakes up to the police, alongside what appears to be a gaggle of deputized white farmers, and a helicopter in the air, patrolling the fields and shooting the last few zombies.

The men close in on the farmhouse. Our hero looks out the window. The white men see him. And, sure of what they see, one of them raises a rifle. He shoots, with a horrible casualness.

Why do the superstitious locals in your average monster story seem to hold the secret—if only the fancy city-slickers would listen—but here we are, my mother and I, surrounded by whole villages of the incautious, the unafraid, the overly sure? Partly, maybe, it's that the wrong stories are getting told. And partly it's about proximity: the Londoner naively hiring a coach up to the castle *benefits*, a little, from the wise fear of those who have lived *in the shadow of the castle*.

But a virus thrives in cities (which is why Dracula can't wait to get to London, *to be in the midst of the whirl and rush*). This virus thrives in cities. These folks on our drive, they don't live in the shadow of the castle. I do.

The men congratulate themselves on one more zombie down.

Figure 1.3. Still from the *Night of the Living Dead*. Ben, surviving. Directed by George A. Romero (1968; Image Ten).

## OUT ON THE EDGES

Sometimes a story, especially one with goblins in it, represents a kind of epistemological shortcut, a chance to shift behavior, an intervention. There is a long tradition of using monster stories as *warnings*, mnemonic devices for insufficiently risk-averse children or somewhat dull-witted adults: Don't go into the forest alone, beware the edge of the lake. Don't drink the water.

I'm thinking about the people at the edges. And about the difference between one story, in which people who feel themselves constantly under threat resent being asked to take care, versus another story, in which those who are exposed at the margins fall, repeatedly, to disease and rifles, because not enough people have taken care. But, even these days, it can be hard to know where the edges really are.

Monsters usually attack, in some sense, the cultural center: standard notions of family, of rank, all the emblems of "normalcy." Frankenstein's creature, in the quintessential example, kills off his creator's family, culminating in the murder of Victor's new bride, Elizabeth—another wisely fearful sister (she and Victor were raised together), armed with nothing but healthy uncertainty and small clues, doomed by another brother insufficiently afraid (despite being in possession of rather more substantial clues, including having heard his own creature tell him, "I will be with you on your wedding night").

*They're coming to get you, Barbara.*

Sometimes the monster attacks the centers of power—literally or figuratively—because the story itself wants us to reconsider the nature of that power. Sometimes the monster attacks the center because the story asks us to be afraid of whatever's not in the center.

The thing is, by the end of either kind of story, the cultural center is usually just fine. The white men, in the fields, circle the farmhouse. Someone like Ben may have temporarily, almost accidentally, inhabited the role of hero, defended his own human holdout; but, at the end, the normal structures rush back in, the "center" recovers its power. Ben could defend the house at night from the encircling undead tottering to his doorstep; he cannot defend it in the daylight, from the encircling white men, who stomp across the fields but whose power is not zombie-like, whose power is their ability to see Ben as just another body that needs to be put down.

Sometimes the center is right there in an old wheatfield, an old farmhouse, a forgotten village. Ben has sweated through the night to stay alive, to survive an incomprehensible infection; but the real survivors are the men who didn't even have to try, and for whom a monster story is not so much a drama of survival as a ready mechanism for domination.

The monster is the response to the monster: as though the pasty-white zombies stumbling through the fields at night were really just a kind of nightmare foretelling the real aggressors, the daylight men, the sheriff, all those deputized locals, so handy with a rifle, the helicopter buzzing happily overhead.

*This virus has no eyes, and yet it knows exactly how we see each other.* The virus has of course laid bare (what was already all too clear) this cruel double-attack within American inequity, this nightmare/daymare onslaught. The virus-monster finds its way most readily to the exposed, the vulnerable, the marginalized—and fresh on its heels, as though the virus were mere symbol, even more violence against Black and brown people in our streets and on our borders; the militarized suppression of protest; the sacrifice of whole factories and prisons full of human beings, where the virus has spread gleefully, because those factories and prisons have been designed to operate on the margins of power, to be powered by the despair of brown and Black people. A real-world monster-story, a reassertion of entrenched power, over the vulnerable, the literally marginal.

In Angela Carter's "The Werewolf," from her 1979 collection *The Bloody Chamber*, a harrowing retelling of what we've come to think of as "Little Red Riding Hood" (in the Grimm telling; originally from the traditional French tale "Conte de la Mère-Grand," or "The Story of Grandmother"), even a little village can represent the center of power. It begins with scarcity, like so many witch-worrying tales (cf. "Hansel and Gretel"), but this is the kind of need and anxiety that ends up projecting and protecting normal power, not challenging it: "Cold; tempest; wild beasts in the forest. It is a hard life. Their houses are built of logs, dark and smoky within."

Such scarcity seems to require superstition, as an additional reinforcement, a spiritual fencing round in the absence of physical security. In the shadow of the castle, you make the sign of the cross. They know the value of a good goblin story here:

At midnight, especially on Walpurgisnacht, the Devil holds picnics in the graveyards and invites the witches; then they dig up fresh corpses, and eat them. Anyone will tell you that. Wreaths of garlic on the doors keep out the vampires.

*Anyone will tell you.* Such certainty. The village is the center, from which the monsters are projected, to mark the outlands on the map, from which the stories are deployed to purify the boundaries.

Of course a child is sent through the woods to grandmother's house, but she is never really in danger: she is armed with stories, and a knife, and the certainty her village has armored her with, weaponized. Yes, a wolf attacks, but it doesn't go so badly for the child:

It was a huge one, with red eyes and running, grizzled chops; any but a mountaineer's child would have died of fright at the sight of it. It went for her throat, as wolves do, but she made a great swipe at it with her father's knife and slashed off its right forepaw.

The child wraps up the severed wolf's paw in a cloth. At her grandmother's, the child finds the old woman in bed, sick, feverish. Out falls the wolf's paw, onto the floor—except now it's an old woman's hand, "toughened with work and freckled with old age." Her grandmother's hand.

The child pulls back the sheets and confirms her suspicions: a bloody stump. Her grandmother writes "like a thing possessed," but this is not a story in which grandmothers, or witches, or wolves, have much of a chance. "The child was strong, and armed with her father's hunting knife."

What else does the child require, besides a dangerous certainty and the weapon of the father? The certainty of her tribe—"The child crossed herself and cried out so loud the neighbours heard her and come [*sic*] rushing in." And the neighbours "know the wart on the hand at once for a witch's nipple," so, in this certain knowledge, "They drove the old woman, in her shift as she was, out into the snow with sticks, beating her old carcass as far as the edge of the forest, and pelted her with stones until she fell dead."

Carter has us in a terrible quandary: we know these stories, we must root for the girl who beats back the wolf. But Carter is determined to show us how readily this heroism curdles.

It's only a happy ending if you're rooting for the center, the hub of power. "Now the child lived in her grandmother's house; she prospered." The center is unscathed—a transfer of ownership, a slight dynastic shift, and the winner takes her rightful place.

Was there ever a werewolf? Is this simply a case of manufacturing an excuse to claim the grandmother's property? And it's all so much cleaner when the whole community does the killing for you. The knife can sever a paw, a hand, but it's the social power that kills, by saying, *You know what this is. The signs tell you what you think they will tell you. These names for the threats were on your lips already and here they are before us—proof that we were right. Your violence is virtue.*

I have had this line in mind lately: "When a nation broadcasts its heroism, no citizen is safe" (from Andres Neuman's novel *Fracture*).

Don't know where the edges are? Find out where the grandmothers are being "sacrificed on the altar"[1] of the . . . what to call it? The economy, the myth of national heroism, the wrong stories. *Anyone will tell you.*

Stories make things happen. Carter's reminds us to root for the grandmothers, and the wolves, and the grandmothers who might be wolves, and the wolves who might be grandmothers.

Sometimes the monster is our response to the monster.

## TRANSFORMATION

Early fall. We are adapting. Events—lockdown, loss of connection, an entirely screen-based social world, the sense, at times, that "flattening the curve" was an impossible ask for our particular nation—are no longer conducive to ordinary relations. My daughter has started to cringe when characters in movies get too close to each other.

Back from one of those drives with my mom, bringing her into the house, there is a text from home: for the second time this week, my daughter has a bad headache and a fever. Do we need to get her tested? My partner and I know the answer, but we have to ask each other anyway. I do not tell my mother.

A local hospital, a drive-through test. The results will take three to five days. To get the results you have to sign up for access to the online medical-record portal, which requires an application, which should be approved, we are told, in six to nine days. It is a bad system.

And the pandemic is a moving target. Our understanding of the disease has shifted and modulated over weeks and months—as it should, of course, as we collectively develop our knowledge of how the virus lives among us and spreads between us. After a grocery trip, I no longer wash the cheese, I no longer Lysol the milk. But I'm not entirely sure that I shouldn't.

My daughter will not be positive. I assume? I have been arguing for the virtues of uncertainty, but now I crave absolute, concrete, black-and-white knowledge. Of course I do. Where else would comfort come from? Could I find comfort, if I squinted, if my nervous system were better aligned with my principles, in some ongoing unknowability?

"We take it as a given that uncertainty is always bad," *The Atlantic*'s Eric Weiner writes, "and, conversely, that certitude is always good." In his "Preparing Your Mind for Uncertain Times," Weiner aims to shield readers from some of the pandemic's psychological torment by training us to become more comfortable with uncertainty. While we might actively seek out the occasional bit of "benign uncertainty" offered by a mystery, our natural aversion to uncertainty makes us miserable, Weiner argues, in the kind of "darker . . . malign uncertainty" we face now: "Not only the immediate suffering of illness and job loss caused by the pandemic, but its open-ended nature. We don't know when it will end." Weiner's solution is to follow the Stoics, among others, and to increase "our tolerance for uncertainty," so that it "never metastasize[s] into panic."

But I'm not so sure I want to simply *tolerate* such malignity. I don't want *calm* uncertainty; fear might be wise—and maybe panic appropriate—when the instabilities are no mere uncomfortable by-product (of novelty, of disease) but a central, systemic feature of our crisis, a pandemic goosed and amplified into a catastrophe by a mendacious, antiscience, authoritarian-curious executive branch.

But if Weiner's uncertainty seems too placid, is there such a thing as radical uncertainty? Maybe one version can be gleaned in Jeff VanderMeer's "This World Is Full of Monsters" (2017) and its portrayal of a protagonist transformed, deeply remade, by the arrival of a story-creature:

> A tiny story, covered in green fur or lichen, shaky on its legs. It fit in the palm of my hand. I stared at the story for a long time, trying to understand. The story had large eyes that could see in the dark, and sharp teeth.

Does a story-creature *crave* stories, or is it *made* of stories? To be a monster is to be on this edge, between identity and appetite. To be the edge. Either way, VanderMeer makes the story the monster, and the monster the story. As our narrator sleeps, with the cute little beast in his hands, the story "gnawed its way into my belly and . . . crawled up through my body into my head. When I woke, gasping my resistance, the story made me stumble out the door of my house and lurch through the dark down my street, giddy and disoriented, muttering, 'Do not stop me. Do not stop me. Story made me this way. Story made me this way.'"

*A story makes things happen.* If a monster hijacks your (likely mistaken) sense of possessing a real self that makes authentic choices, maybe it is indeed Mistress Weatherwax's kind of story, the kind that "makes things happen," that is the real monster. In the sense that monsters change things by revealing the errors of our comfort. Which is another reason why, I think, my students and I so often root for the monster.

I think of Mary Shelley's affection for her creature, and her creature-story, as though they were the same thing—*It fit in the palm of my hand*—her sweet parental command to her novel in a later edition: "I bid my hideous progeny go forth and prosper."

Indeed, in VanderMeer, the story bids the human go forth. And what starts as horror—the domestic invasion, the transformation at home that gets, inevitably, loosed upon the streets—shifts into an irresistible, undefinable, and radical transformation, away from the old human self, inching its ways toward something that looks less like terror and more like liberation. We go from the distressing weirdness of "the story-creature" sprouting "out of the top of my skull in a riot of wildflowers," to "somehow it felt right"—to, eventually, a wide-eyed surrender to non-, or trans-, or extra-humanness, not even an "I" anymore but a "we" in the final sentences. In this new "we" form the narrator is "flung up into the stratosphere" with "a holy roar," and "we were joyous. We were ecstatic as the stars came at us, no longer veiled, and we saw them in all of the glory that was both ours and theirs." This is an apocalyptic unveiling of the cosmos achieved through loss of self—thanks to a monster story: "We could tumble forever and never die, and every sighting of a star filled us like a tiny bliss, a flower opening up and opening up and never fading."

This weightless vision of an exploded self makes me a little sick to my stomach, but VanderMeer asks us to loosen our grip on the question of "being human." Being human is complicated. Maybe overrated. Is it a shape, a particular body, a behavior, a mind, a pronoun, a citizenship? Monster stories are places where we can ask these questions. Where we can toy with radical uncertainty, let it bloom from our skulls.

Monsters teach us something. Not that we should literally, blindly, invite the virus itself to infect us, transform us. But maybe that we *should* let the *pandemic* change us. It already has. Maybe we should take the uncertainty that has metastasized and use it to expand our sense of who counts within our tribes. Maybe we will learn to fear the right things.

September, when I was a kid, and the seasonal turn meant the grass had a crunch to it and the trees began to rattle, I liked to stomp around, to imagine myself stomping around, in the woods, or more accurately the desiccated gullies behind our California ranch house, beautifully alone. If any villagers saw me, they would be sore afraid. These days, I wouldn't trust any white boy who fantasizes too much about making people fear him, but this is a tender memory, and I don't think I relished any power, just some whiff of poetic openness, some aloneness, some hint of shape-shifting. A hint of empathy with outcast things.

*Story made me this way.*

A couple of years ago, my daughter decided to dress up as Mary Shelley for Halloween. We cobbled together something to approximate the fashion of a modest young woman of Shelley's time. She carried around a basket with her novel in it, waited to see if anyone would notice and figure it out. I was her creature, in boots, and a too-small suit jacket that made my arms look weirdly long. I lumbered, but not too close. She wanted to go to each door by herself. I watched from the street.

*I bid my hideous progeny go forth*, she did not say.


## FINALLY, KNOWING

In January of the Before-Times, I asked my students a silly question, from a cheeky entrance exam given to 2018 applicants to Oxford's All Souls College:

Would you rather be a vampire or a zombie? I had no particular pedagogical goal besides breaking the ice.

My students turned it into a meaningful debate. At first, they overwhelmingly chose vampire, because they felt that that condition offered, despite its horrors, some level of self-awareness, some humanness left intact, even a lushly cinematic suffering that held some appeal. Besides, with all that immortality, not to mention a short list of pretty decent superpowers, you could probably manage a few workarounds and have some fun.

Then a small group, only a couple at first, spoke up for the zombie life.

Yes, being a zombie would probably stink. You would be mindless, animalistic, falling apart, and all appetite. But really, these brave students floated, wouldn't you, as a vampire, be just as dead inside and rotten and driven by appetite? And wouldn't it be *better* to be mindless amid such torment? Wouldn't you *want* unconsciousness? Maybe it would be the best way to survive your corrupted state. A kind of mindfulness, a kind of monster zen.

More hands shot up. Several vampires converted.

*Affording a point of view,* Percy asserted, *for the delineating of human passions.*

The longer the pandemic has lasted, the more I think many of us have newly felt our condition to be zombie- or vampire-like—locked away, longing for touch, our bodies seeming weirder, more fragile, less outfitted for the social world, the longer we stay inside. We are all slightly grotesque, and very alone, the twin attributes of any classic monster.

And, not incidentally, hemmed in by sickness and death, by literal death and stories of death, by death outside our doors, death and sickness in our own houses, and abstract communal death and sickness told through numbers too large to comprehend.

How does one survive in such a time? Each method of survival implies an ethics.

The vampire generally understands that the lives of others are the cost of his own survival. A perverse trolley problem, one the vampire traditionally answers rather too easily. Because appetite overrides. The zombie, being hollowed out, comes to the same conclusion but without awareness, without calculation.

In the Before-Times, I rather adored my students' sudden counterintuitive embrace of zen zombie-hood, as the less painful of two kinds of existential pain. But now, six months in, nine months in, staring into the new year, I think I'd go back to vampire. Because unconsciousness doesn't seem like a virtue now. We should know the pain we cause. We should know how much the sacrifices others are making enable us—people like me, at home, watching the empty sidewalks out my window, snow suddenly falling—to stay safe in our castles.

### Note

1. See Milbank, "America's Seniors, Sacrificed on the Altar of Reopening," for context.

### References

Belam, Martin. "Would You Rather Be a Zombie or a Vampire? An Answer to Oxford Uni's Hardest Question." *The Guardian*, October 8, 2018. https://www.theguardian.com/culture/shortcuts/2018/oct/08/would-you-rather-be-a-zombie-or-a-vampire-an-answer-to-oxford-unis-hardest-question.

Carter, Angela. "The Werewolf." In *The Bloody Chamber*. New York: Penguin Classics, 2015.

Milbank, Dana. "Opinion: America's Seniors, Sacrificed on the Altar of Reopening." *Washington Post*, May 27, 2020. https://www.washingtonpost.com/opinions/2020/05/22/americas-seniors-sacrificed-altar-reopening/

Pratchett, Terry. *A Hat Full of Sky*. New York: Harper, 2004.

Reality Check team. "Coronavirus: How a Misleading Map Went Global." BBC News, February 19, 2020. https://www.bbc.com/news/world-51504512

Shelley, Mary. *Frankenstein*. Edited by J. Paul Hunter. New York: Norton, 1996.

Stoker, Bram. *Dracula*. Edited by Glennis Byron. Peterborough, Ontario: Broadview Press, 1998.

VanderMeer, Jeff. "This World Is Full of Monsters." Tor.com, January 23, 2018. https://www.tor.com/2017/11/08/this-world-is-full-of-monsters/

Weiner, Eric. "Preparing Your Mind for Uncertain Times." *The Atlantic*, August 25, 2020. https://www.theatlantic.com/family/archive/2020/08/how-embrace-uncertainty-pandemic-times/615634/

# CHAPTER 2

# Facing Our Pandemic

*Sara Blair*

What would it mean to picture the invisible forces threatening our health and well-being, even the possibility of a meaningful civic life, in the time of pandemic? How do we make sense of the mounting intimate and collective losses, the untold injuries to personhood and human being? As the moment of COVID-19 in the United States has intersected with #GeorgeFloyd, #Minneapolis, and Black Lives Matter, the questions are only more urgent. We all know the CDC image of the coronavirus, a fungal white tennis ball studded with blood-red triangular spikes (https://phil.cdc.gov/Details.aspx?pid=2 3311). Johns Hopkins's state-of-the-art dashboard (https://coronavirus.jhu .edu/map.html), with its interactive tracking maps, gets over a billion hits a day. From the atomic scale to the global, we look to see what we're up against. How do we give a face to the experience of the pandemic's violence, or begin cultivating new forms of response to the systemic realities it exposes?

Much of my work happens in the interdisciplinary space of visual culture studies, which often raises questions about how to make abstract systems of power visible. From that perspective, I've found myself increasingly attuned to portraiture as a project in the time of COVID. In the United States, portrait images of fellow citizens have long been a resource for exploring the meaning of our Union: celebrating and critiquing it, imagining it in more perfect form. (Frederick Douglass was a master of this project. The most-photographed nineteenth-century American, he used the portrait as a critical form of democratic art, an unprecedented resource for combatting anti-Black racism under slavery and beyond.) In the United States, photography's historical adjacency to the Civil War, still the most fatal war in US history, made it inevitable that the portrait would have a critical social function: bringing ordinary Americans face to face with loss, documenting the lived life of the dead. But photography has also aligned itself in its unfolding practice with the exercise of state power, producing mug shots and surveillance images, supporting the pseudoscience of physiognomy, racial typology, and eugenics.

With its wide range of effects, from memorial to surveillance, social tax-onomy to self-declaration, photographic portraiture continues to lend itself to experiments with making inequities visible. Can it also help us think about how readers, viewers, and citizens who are hailed very differently by the "we" of "we the people" might go on to face them? In what follows, I want to consider some of the ways portraits are being made and used during the pandemic, and how they offer us opportunities to account for the histories it exposes—and to question our habits for encountering the human being of strangers and fellow citizens.

Early in the pandemic, as coronavirus was creating the first hot spots in the United States, frontline health care workers sought to make themselves visible (my students would say "relatable") to the highly vulnerable patients they were triaging, intubating, and providing with urgent and end-of-life care. The use of portrait images as an extension of standard medical IDs and a fea-ture of PPE, which had become essentially DIY, made sense. Robertino Rodri-guez, a respiratory therapist at Scripps Mercy Hospital San Diego, whose ER gear leaves almost none of his face uncovered, decided to make a gigantic, laminated badge, a Photomat-style torso shot he taped to his coverall. He posted a selfie on Instagram featuring his badge: a portrait of his portrait. That image inspired other emergency care providers, like Pasadena-based nurse Derek DeVault and coworkers, to follow suit. We could say the project went viral, as it was picked up by CNN, Fox, the *New York Post*, and other old-media news outlets coast to coast.

To find this image please go to:
<https://doi.org/10.3998/mpub.12136619.cmp.4>

This was the kind of human-interest story coronavirus begged. Here were heroic first responders (comparisons to 9/11 were already standard) whose competence and empathy were alike reassuring, and not just for terrified COVID patients. The recirculation of their self-portraits as soft news, how-ever, elided the face at least some care providers meant to put on the crisis. In particular, it ignored their messaging about civic responsibility. DeVault's accompanying Instagram post reads: "Thank you to all the healthcare work-ers out there for battling on the frontlines. To all those who are staying home, huge shout out to you! I know that is also not easy."[1] His portrait was made and shared not just to humanize caregivers for their patients, and so to improve the experience of illness, perhaps even medical outcomes. It also asked viewers to imagine and make contract with a distribution of risk and diminished agency—support for those who work the front lines from those who stay home, as well as the reverse. Shared responsibility for the well-being of all was still, at this stage of COVID, presumed to be a shared value. And, it was further presumed, we would be more determined to achieve it because we had looked into the eyes of our digital neighbors and fellow Americans, had faced and taken heart from their experience. This is the durable, misleading promise of the photograph: the arrested yet moving image that changes hearts and minds, if not the chronic conditions of social experience.

The presumption that photographs of our fellow humans can "bestow" humanity, or make it real to us in a distinctive way, is as durable and indispensable as it is misleading. What has happened to this presumption in the time of pandemic? Adopted as a mode of humanizing health care workers for their most vulnerable patients, the portrait quickly became a strategy for humanizing health care workers for the rest of us, an America increasingly divided and divisible. During the month of March, citizens in New York and other cities were gathering at 7:00 p.m. each night on balconies and front stoops to clap and bang pots in celebration of health care workers (https:// www.businessinsider.com/videos-people-cities-cheering-healthcare-work ers-windows-rooftops-same-time-2020-4). By April, however, others were entering public spaces in order to declare their independence (https://www .vox.com/policy-and-politics/2020/4/30/21243462/armed-protesters-mic higan-capitol-rally-stay-at-home-order) from public health appeals, social distancing, state and local edicts—and democratic governance itself. With sharply rising death rates and increasingly painful awareness of the policy failures leaving care facilities scrambling to provide PPE and health guidelines, ER and ICU workers began posting very different kinds of face-offs.

St. Petersburg, Florida, neurology nurse Megan Patterson was one of many hospital personnel posting selfies with visible evidence of the toll exacted by protective gear itself, worn continuously during punishing thirteen-hour shifts (and, during a critical period of the initial wave, redeployed, against guidelines for its use).

To find this image please go to:
<https://doi.org/10.3998/mpub.12136619.cmp.5>

She noted in a March 21, 2020 Instagram post:

I'm not afraid when I'm at work. I'm doing what I was trained to do. I'm afraid when we run out of resources—supplies and staff. COVID19 is real and it's here. Stay home, wash your hands and stop buying all the things that healthcare workers need to do their job. When we don't have what we need to take care of you, we too will become ill . . . then who's left to take care of you and your loved ones?[2]

Likewise, @Genithecrankynurse, a self-described "angry, punk nurse" from Indiana "who won't shut up until the US is a good place to live," tweeted a selfie with this caption: "This is what you look like [note the second person] after wearing an N95 mask all day. We don't have enough of anything. We need @SenSanders more than ever now. Help us help you."[3]

To find this image please go to:
<https://doi.org/10.3998/mpub.12136619.cmp.6>

Bernie Sanders, champion of Medicare for all, would drop out of the presidential race three weeks later, but the circulation of such images continued. Their focal point is their subjects' stigmata: the reddened skin <link to: https://www.instagram.com/p/CDhfPzcg51_/>, chafing, and bruises <link to: https://www.instagram.com/p/CCkFyFXj3pA/>, trace evidence of their unrelieved and dangerous labor. Offered up on social media threads, such marks index the insufficiency not just of health care provisions or national leadership. These portraits of unmasking register an even more pervasive disease than COVID: the sense that the political bands that have connected us with one another have been rapidly dissolving.

How such images might have informed political sentiment is hard to gauge, given the speed with which they were repurposed. Almost simultaneously with such robust threads as #COVIDnurse, #maskmarkings, #frontlinehealthheroes, and #nurselife, portraits of the unmasked featured in an ad campaign dropped by global marketing agency Ogilvy for Unilever Corporation's Dove brand.[4] Titled "Courage is Beautiful" (https://www.youtube.com/watch?v=sQOq0-ODBbc), it went "right for the heart" of viewers "with a message of gratitude for health care workers tirelessly working on the front lines."[5] The video flashes a succession of portraits of doctors and nurses, many shot by award-winning Italian photojournalist Alberto Giuliani (no relation to Rudy), their faces scored, bruised, and otherwise damaged by their protective gear.

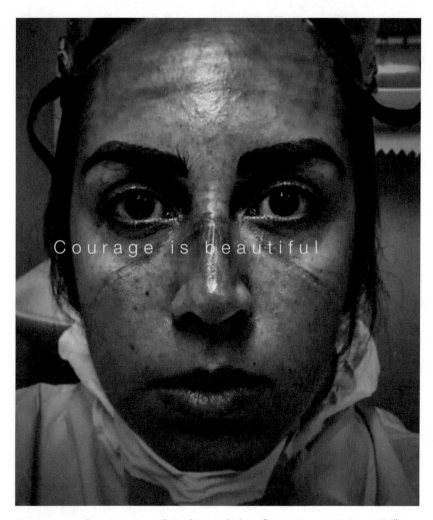

Figure 2.1. April 8, 2020 screenshot of Amanda from "Dove: Courage is Beautiful" video, Ogilvy London UK.

Marketing professionals and many consumers responded enthusiastically. The campaign certainly suggested, as a self-identified creative on Twitter noted, "how marketing and advertising communications have influence in media during challenging times."[6] "Influence," here, might be a euphemism for the power to redirect attention. To what degree does humanizing the labor of health care workers—which has been nothing but extraordinary—draw focus away from systemic political failures or the hard facts of disparity in the

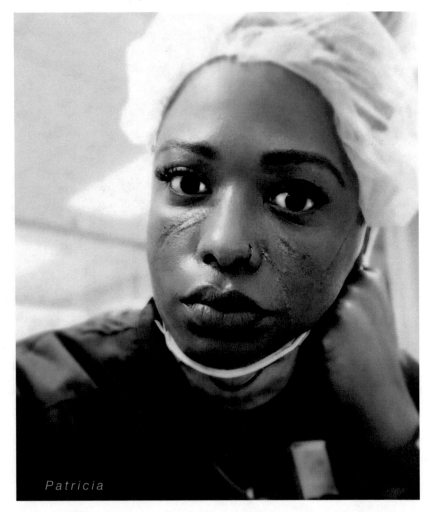

Figure 2.2. April 8, 2002 screenshot of Patricia from "Dove: Courage is Beautiful" video, Ogilvy London UK.

pandemic's impact and outcomes (even among those workers themselves)? How long does recognition of the ethical power and courage, the "beauty," of frontline workers, medical or otherwise, obstruct a view of the structural conditions that underlie their efforts? Can the humanism of the portrait be separable from neoliberal and corporate contexts of its invocation?[7]

These are the kinds of questions that arise when the professionals show up—professional photographers, that is, whose work in the portrait form is always an intricate play of interactions and effects. Like other citizens of the pandemic republic, photographers have struggled with work under the regime of social distancing, masking, and stay-at-home orders. In response, many have experimented with what remains when the studio and even the street are off-limits as spaces of social and photographic encounter. For some image-makers, pandemic restrictions have become a context for meditating on the push-and-pull, the intimacy and distance, of photography itself, and on the promises it makes in the current moment about what kind of knowledge it offers of authentic human being(s).

One of the durable notions of the photograph, a self-authenticating humanism, is that the mutual gaze of portrait subject and viewer is a meaningful form of community. When we are barred from moving beyond certain physical thresholds—the window, the doorway, the stoop—the camera can powerfully dramatize both the urge to connect with fellow Americans and impediments to connection. Many photographers, consequently, began shooting "doortraits," images of everyday subjects occupying such thresholds. Stephen Lovekin, primarily a celebrity and events photographer currently providing content for the Shutterstock agency, began turning his camera on fellow residents of his Brooklyn neighborhood, Ditmas Park, in late March 2020. Consistent with its demographics, many were creative professionals—filmmakers, advertising or media consultants, fellow travelers in the production of images. Titling the project *Words at the Window: Self Isolation and the Coronavirus*, Lovekin asked his subjects to display personal messages as part of their self-presentation (https://www.instagram.com/p/B-v6g70jbfK/).[8]

Among these images is the window portrait of the family of John and Stephanie Stislow, co-principals of their eponymous visual branding firm. The subjects enact the aspiration to be a part of their community as they dwell apart from it. The physical architecture of their double window, and the photographic space it creates, separate the child's face from the hand that holds aloft their sign; the visible integrity of the body is broken. The core message here is a riff on the concluding promise of Walt Whitman's "Song of Myself": "Missing me one place, search another, / I stop somewhere waiting for you." Shadowing the portrait's hopefulness about communal and democratic experience, though, is the question of what we are waiting out, and what that waiting exposes. Across thresholds and gulfs of experience and access, how inclusive can the second-person address be? Who can feel hailed across time and social distance by such messages; how quickly do they become evidence of a form of civic feeling that no longer seems possible?

To find this image please go to:
<https://doi.org/10.3998/mpub.12136619.cmp.9>

Even as their subjects offer us a compellingly open gaze, Lovekin's portraits point us to the question of what it means to look "through" the doorway, the window, or the aperture. Speaking broadly, all photographic images obscure the fact of their own mediation. The conventions of portraiture—the frontal view, the returned gaze, the exclusion of everything beyond the moment and the frame—become a screen through which we gaze on others, with the conviction that their photographs lay bare some truth of their experience or social being, and perhaps consequently of our own. But the photograph always masks as much as it unmasks, and the context of the pandemic has been an opportunity to reconsider that fact for our times.

Confined to home quarters, without access to subjects, managing their own experiences of pandemic, many photographers have made images that explore the relationship of the camera to the screen or mask. Minneapolis-based Alec Soth, celebrated for his large-scale projects in the lineage of such chroniclers of American banality as Walker Evans, Diane Arbus, and William Eggleston, altered his practice with such questions in mind. "Nowadays," he noted in a recent *New York Times* interview, "it feels like everything is seen through panes of glass."[9] Shooting on his iPhone through binoculars and the windows of his car—that is, through multiple screens—he has been making images that convey the limits not just of intimacy but of any social knowledge we achieve through the camera. They reflect the grim reality of our moment: "distance, distance, distance."[10]

That distance is by no means merely aesthetic, and its matter is deeply shaped by experiences of racism and inequity, as recent work by rising young artists like Chad Browne-Springer (https://www.courant.com/ctnow/arts-th eater/hc-ctnow-black-photographers-covering-protests-20200708-gsdxy4ok 2nhuna6mv77tfvxqve-story.html) and Eric Hart Jr. (https://www.instagram .com/p/CC6e3NeJPAa/), and other photographers of color, brings home.[11] In the aftermath of the murder of George Floyd, with ongoing protests against police violence and anti-Black racism, sustained unemployment, and staggeringly high infection rates and coronavirus deaths in the United States (over 178,000 total as of this writing), "pandemic" signifies a whole array of systemic, interlocking threats. How might the singular image, captured in a singular moment, explore the dynamic force of their intersection?

New York–based photographer Peter DeVito, a 2019 graduate of the Fashion Institute of Technology who began his professional career by focusing on gender inclusivity, racial diversity, and body image, has been making images on FaceTime and disseminated on Facebook and Instagram. In one series, he makes portraits of models wearing face masks on which they display messages linking the experience of coronavirus to realities of anti-Black racism and other social threats. Although the models remain unnamed, DeVito posts their personal narratives in lieu of his own commentary. That work clearly fed his follow-on project, *Black Voices Matter*, in which DeVito has invited Black models to choose a message that he digitally overlays onto their faces: the medium is the mask.

The resulting portraits are accompanied by separate images, posted as swipe-throughs, of narratives written in the models' handwriting[12]—another kind of index to the use of the portrait as a space of agency, which non-Black image-makers might hold for subjects of color. Nikolas Ray's face/mask reads: "It doesn't matter if you voted for Obama."

To find this image please go to:
<https://doi.org/10.3998/mpub.12136619.cmp.11>

Cozy, @cozboylenz, chose a partial list of Black Americans killed by police. Like fitted PPE, it extends across the full width and height of the subject's face, contoured to its angles and planes; "Say Their Names" is printed in red—the only color in all these grayscale portraits—across the subject's lips. Thus embodied, the models' chosen texts are at once life narratives, political declarations, pleas, and manifestoes. A partial lens onto the experiences of Black Americans, they turn discomfort back onto presumptively white viewers, for whom various questions arise. Do the texts have a protective function for their subjects or readers—or for their subjects with respect to their readers? Indexed to black skin, do they become white masks? Is the effect of such portraits to compel non-Black viewers to confront what they project onto Black bodies?

To find this image please go to:
<https://doi.org/10.3998/mpub.12136619.cmp.12>

Beyond the mask as a fraught object and metaphor, our current pandemics share a singularly grim challenge: the problem of making death—violent, unnecessary death—available for apprehension, and part of a collective understanding of our democracy. Bystander and viral digital images, usually handmade, fueled antiracism activism and protest across the United States during the summer of 2020, and images of the victims of police and white vigilante violence have been central to the impact of Black Lives Matter almost since its inception (https://www.latimes.com/entertainment-arts/story/2020-06-02/george-floyd-instagram-art-tributes-portraits). But even the gruesome, gone-viral footage of murders in real time hasn't fully faced the dead, as it flickers between the urgent logics of crime scene evidence and memorial.

In fact, some of the most telling of these images have been made or critically shaped by perpetrators.[13] Although the horrific cell phone video of Eric Garner's death on July 17, 2014, was shot by a friend, police officers whose actions it captures quickly move to block visual access to Garner. The video made and released by Gregory McMichael, among the three white men eventually charged with the murder of Ahmaud Arbery, records the gunshots that killed him and his body falling to the ground, also with a partial and distanced view. The excruciating raw footage of George Floyd's death captured by rote on the bodycam of then-officer Tou Thao offers a view of Derek Chauvin's knee on Floyd's neck but no access to Floyd's face, or even his body, as he calls out "Mama" and "I can't breathe." Much of its searing power derives from the steady mechanical gaze it trains on bystanders as they grow in number and intensity of opposition: we see the gruesome progress of Floyd's killing reflected in their faces. Only after his body has been removed does the camera shift focus back to the site where he was felled. Another officer stoops to pick up a shoe, the only material evidence remaining.

By other logic, bodies are also made to disappear as the last resort of pandemic. Journalistic conventions, deathways, HIPAA regulations, and legal injunctions against photography in particular spaces have kept our COVID dead almost entirely out of sight—except as unfaced corpses in coroners' offices (https://www.toledoblade.com/local/Coronavirus/2020/04/17/lucas-county-coroner-coronavirus-presents-challenges/stories/20200414075), makeshift and mobile morgues (https://www.nytimes.com/2020/04/02/nyregion/coronavirus-new-york-bodies.html), or piles of body bags (https://talentrecap.com/ny-nurse-shares-devastating-photo-of-piling-dead-bodies-in-trash-bags-amid-coronavirus/). The gravely ill have likewise been screened—sometimes literally—from view.

In a *New York Times* op-ed of May 1, 2020, art historian and African American studies scholar Sarah Lewis points to the loss beyond loss that accrues when we lack "images that represent the full impact of the coronavirus crisis"—

Figure 2.3. Nursing facility, Kirland, Washington, February 29, 2020. Courtesy of Elaine Thompson/AP.

when, as CNN Business correspondent Brian Stelter noted back in March 2020, "We're not able to see inside the emergency rooms and intensive care units where this invisible demon is being fought."[14] In other words, we lack portraits, in the fullest sense of the term, of those whose lives have been lost, needlessly or even criminally. The portrait series shot by in-house photographer Jeff Rhode at Teaneck, New Jersey's Holy Name Medical Center of a critically ill patient named Louie, with his consent, is the exception that proves this rule (To find this image please go to: <https://www.wbur.org/hereandnow/2020/05/12/photogra pher-hospital-coronavirus-pandemic>). (Rhode has noted that he put down the camera as this subject was dying, without family present, to hold his hand during his final moments.)[15]

In spite of photography's limits and the problematic assumptions it may condition, the visual register of personhood remains a critical resource for the collective work of response, both memorial and potentially reparative. This is presumably why the display of portrait photos has been a shared practice of protest across pandemic contexts, in demonstrations against police killings of Black Americans like Breonna Taylor (https://www.cnbc.com/2020/06/18/bre onna-taylor-kentucky-ag-cameron-updates-police-killing-probe.html) as well

Figure 2.4. Nurses and healthcare workers mourn and remember their colleagues who died during the outbreak of the novel coronavirus during a demonstration outside Mount Sinai Hospital in Manhattan on April 10, 2020 in New York City. Photo by Johannes Eisele/AFP via Getty Images.

as actions by health care workers, like the Good Friday demonstration outside New York City's Mt. Sinai Hospital focused on colleagues lost to coronavirus and its failed policy context (https://ktla.com/news/coronavirus/u-s-averages-over-1000-coronavirus-deaths-daily-for-16-straight-days/). One indicator of the still powerful necessity of portrait images to the broader work of reckoning with social injuries has been the strategies that chroniclers of our American life have adopted to address—and even showcase—the unavailability of auratic photographs, vestigial traces of the singular human face.

The front page of the *New York Times* on May 24, 2020, was designed to mark the now-distant milestone of one hundred thousand COVID deaths in the United States (https://www.nytimes.com/2020/05/26/learning/the-front-page.html). The paper's staff created its grayest-ever front page—that is, absent any graphics or photographs, in color or black and white: "a first in modern times."[16] Editors considered and then chose against an array of photo portraits of the dead in favor of a "hugely dramatic" listing of the names of one thousand victims, each followed by a brief account of the subject's unique personhood excerpted from obituaries published in media outlets across the nation. They added this self-referential subtitle: "They Were Not Simply Names on a List. They Were Us."[17] The absence of images becomes a meditation on the problem of reckoning, at scale, with the uniqueness, the nonreproducibility, that images can preserve.

While the editors of the *Times* went retro, reaching back to nineteenth-century visual conventions to face the toll of COVID death, some photojournalists turned to digital technology. Working with drones at the height of New York's first wave, they captured still images (https://news.artnet

Figure 2.5. Burials take place on Hart Island on April 9, 2020 in the Bronx borough of New York. Photo by Andrew Theodorakis/Getty Images.

.com/art-world/nypd-confiscates-drone-hart-island-1838187) and videos (https://www.washingtonpost.com/history/2020/04/27/hart-island-mass -grave-coronavirus-burials/) of mass COVID interments on Hart Island, the city's burial ground for its unclaimed dead and the largest mass grave in the United States.[18] The function of that site as a potter's field of more than a million bodies, including scores of AIDS victims still unidentified, drove home both the dehumanization and the structural inequalities underlying COVID illness, treatment, and death. No COVID victims can be seen, only the bulldozed earth waiting to enclose them. The invisibility of the dead as persons is the point: what we register as missing, confronting the stark image of their absence.

Both kinds of strategies remind us that we have not seen their faces. Facing that fact is a critical part of reckoning not only with the scope of loss but with the practices of response to it for which we are differently yet collectively responsible. Photographs of our fellow Americans, citizens, workers, and social agents remain indispensable to this reckoning, even as we may struggle to recognize the limits of the knowledge they offer. The unfolding work of BLM activists and allies helps suggests the way portraits can make such work possible. It's worth recalling that George Floyd had lost his employment at a restaurant under Minnesota's stay-at-home orders and was posthumously identified as positive for the coronavirus.[19] The confluence of threats, risks, and forms of violence he has come to embody—public health, economic, and social pandemics—may help explain why his image has remained so powerful as a point of departure for imagining responsive forms of justice and democratic feeling alike.

Take, for example, the context of public statuary and activism during summer 2020 against the iconography of anti-Black racism. Across the nation and the globe, monuments were being toppled, icons destroyed. Judicial action in Richmond, Virginia, prevented the removal ordered by Governor Ralph Northam of a statue of Robert E. Lee on the city's former Monument Avenue. Undaunted, activists responded by transforming the object: painting it with slogans, using it as a setting for continuous community gathering and justice-oriented memorial. Their repurposing has been shaped by a pointed use of portrait imagery. In mid-June, BLM activists began projecting the gone-viral portrait image of Floyd onto the site, from its graffitied plinth to its equestrian sculpture. (https://www.dailystandard.com/world_pictures/index.php ?pict_id=25908). Wrapping around the image of Lee and white supremacist history like a mask, a cloak of empowerment and protection, the portrait here also serves as a kind of unveiling and an invitation to another way of seeing. Illuminating the monument, it exemplifies the practice of seeing through received history, holding all citizens accountable for the latter's reproduction and afterlives, suturing it to the human face of what it has refused and suppressed.

This reparative call to justice by way of the portrait was taken up by members of Floyd's family, who would shortly afterward partner with Change.org, the crowdsourcing citizen change agent, to sponsor the George Floyd Hologram Memorial Project (To find this image please go to: <https://www.wusa9.com/article/news/local/virginia/george-floyds-family-gathers-in-richmond-to-unveil-hologram/291-97090ce6-9db3-4a88-813d-eaceb3912fff>). Launched on July 28, 2020, it featured a hologram of Floyd's image projected against the backdrop of various Confederate monuments, intact and removed, beginning with the statue of Lee.[20] Both installations, notably, require nightfall and the cloak of darkness to be visible. Dramatizing illumination, they transpose the signification of blackness and of light. In a similar vein, Floyd's portrait speaks volumes to very different kinds of self-portraits staged at the same site in daylight. Everyday citizens and activists have made the palimpsestic plinth a backdrop for their own remarkably powerful portraits—like that of teenagers Kennedy George and Ava Holloway, shot

Figure 2.6. An image of George Floyd is projected on the base of the statue of Confederate General Robert E. Lee on Monument Avenue, Monday, June 8, 2020, in Richmond, Va. Courtesy of AP Photo/Steve Helber.

by photojournalist Julia Rendleman in tutus and en pointe, fists raised in a Black Power salute (https://www.instagram.com/P/CBD40VC18ju/?hl=en).[21]

That declaration of love and power was made to be seen by community members, but also by viewers outside the community—by Black Richmonders and white others, for whom the photographer is a stand-in. Portraits are intensely complex rhetorical acts, and the logic of this one has something to suggest for the COVID moment. To account for those who have been injured, harmed, or lost to our pandemics requires fellow citizens to dwell in their looks back, to reckon with the full weight, affective and social, of the desire to be seen, to count rather than merely to be counted.

Images that compel this work are even now being made, testing the empathy that photographs have historically sought to condition and often presumed as an end in itself. *The Human Faces of COVID-19 New York City*, a recent project of award-winning photojournalist Peter Turnley, features many subjects who retract their gazes or offer them as a challenge and an invitation: how to imagine the pandemic as a shared experience, across material differences, as we acknowledge the various limits to that imagining?

Figure 2.7. In this June 5, 2020 photo, fourteen-year-old Black ballerinas Ava Holloway and Kennedy George pose in protest at the Robert E. Lee monument in Richmond, VA. Photo by Julia Rendleman/Reuters.

Figure 2.8. Roxie, 90, the Upper West Side, New York, March 30, from "The Human Face of Covid: New York 2020." Photo: Peter Turnley.

A shot by photo-documentarian Michael Christopher Brown on Los Angeles's Skid Row, in a series tracking the effects of coronavirus on homeless individuals, raises similar questions about the project of facing social costs and losses, as the larger-than-life portrait image compelling the viewer's gaze and the living subject shrouding his own from view contend. In a different register, rising photographer Vanessa Leroy has also insisted on what we are unable to bring into view, de-facing the portrait as a mode of knowledge and encounter to give intensely material form to the question of how we see America and Americans, who is protected and who is marked by its symbols.

As we continue to face devastating, still-unfolding uncertainties, conjuring the life that has been lost, and how so and why, remains a critical need. Across unyielding social distances as well as social distancing, the portrait can create encounters that are productively unresolved, compelling us to look, urging us to ask how we might earn the right. This is the powerful, speculative work that the gaze of the portrait, steady, returned, challenging, unavailable, can offer us in the time of pandemic. It would be up to us—viewers, Americans, whoever we are—to respond by reimagining what just looking requires and what it means.

Figure 2.9. Man outside Midnight Mission, Skid Row, LA, 2020. Photo courtesy of Michael Christopher Brown.

Figure 2.10. Altar of Stars Part 2. Photo courtesy of Vanessa Leroy.

## Notes

1. Derek DeVault (@derekdevault), "Saw this idea on IG," Instagram post, April 20, 2020, https://www.instagram.com/p/B-pkFlBDb-i/?utm_source=ig_embed

2. Megan Patterson (megansm16), "I'm not afraid when I'm at work," Instagram post, March 16, 2020, https://www.instagram.com/p/B-BEJ-dj5AW/

3. (Genithecrankynurse), "This is what you look like after wearing an N95 mask all day," Tweet, March 18, 2020, https://twitter.com/genithecrankyn1/status/124043 8695326560256. See also "In Harm's Way," *New York Times*, May 4, 2020, an invitation to doctors, nurses, and health care workers to "share your story and photos from the coronavirus frontlines." https://www.nytimes.com/article/doctors-treating-coronavi rus.html

4. Unilever Corporation, "Courage Is Beautiful," YouTube video, 0.30, April 8, 2020, https://www.youtube.com/watch?v=sQOq0-ODBbc

5. Abby Gardner, "Dove's New 'Courage Is Beautiful' Campaign Shines the Spotlight on Health Care Workers," *Glamour*, April 10, 2020, https://www.glamour.com/sto ry/dove-courage-is-beautiful-campaign-healthcare-workers

6. Ashley Grace (@ohashlilies), "As Dove is well recognized for their authentic Real Beauty ads," Tweet, April 10, 2020, https://twitter.com/ohashlilies/status/12484 74366746095618?ref_src=twsrc%5Etfw%7Ctwcamp%5Etweetembed%7Ctwterm%5E 1248474366746095618%7Ctwgr%5E&ref_url=https%3A%2F%2Fwww.scarymommy .com%2Fdove-courage-video-healthcare-workers%2F

7. For an account that puts this project in the context of photographic practice, see Hannah Abel-Hirsch, "Exhaustion and Emptiness: Faces of Those on the Frontline," *British Journal of Photography*, April 15, 2020, https://www.bjp-online.com/2020 /04/exhaustion-and-emptiness-faces-of-those-on-the-frontline/

8. Steven Lovekin, "Words at the Window," New York, March 2020, Shutterstock, https://www.shutterstock.com/editorial/news/exclusive-%E2%80%90-words-at-the -window%2C-new-york-2020-03-27

9. Alec Soth, cited in Meara Sharma, "Eight Photographers' Pictures from Isolation," *New York Times*, April 29, 2020, https://www.nytimes.com/2020/04/29/t-magazi ne/photographers-coronavirus-isolation.html

10. Soth, cited in Sharma, "Eight Photographers' Pictures."

11. A powerful recent photo essay on the responses of Black photographers to conditions of self-isolation and social distancing, written and curated by Deborah Willis, is "Sources of Self Regard: Self-Portraits from Black Photographers Reflecting on America," *New York Times*, June 19, 2020, https://www.nytimes.com/interactive/2020 /06/19/arts/black-photographers-self-portraits.html. See also "We Can't Go Back to Normal: Twelve Young Photographers Share Their Stories about How the Events of 2020 Have Shaped Them," *Washington Post*, July 20, 2020, from which my own curation has been in part drawn. https://www.washingtonpost.com/graphics/2020/national /photography/young-photographers-COVID-protests/

12. Access to these handwritten narratives, or even manifestoes, is available on the linked Instagram posts as right-click pages, at https://www.instagram.com/p/CC rQ1J9B_Cv/ and https://www.instagram.com/p/CBv7FdSBK-o/, respectively.

13. The relevant citizen and police videos are widely available on social media and the web. I refrain from reproducing screenshots or linking to footage here.

14. Sarah Lewis, "Where Are the Photos of People Dying of COVID?," *New York Times*, May 1, 2020, https://www.nytimes.com/2020/05/01/opinion/coronavirus-pho tography.html. Brian Stelter, cited in Lewis, "The Scariest Aspects of the Coronavirus Are What We Can't See on TV," *CNN Business*, March 26, 2020, https://www.cnn.com /2020/03/25/media/coronavirus-television-reliable-sources/index.html. The force of this absence globally was made clear in news reporting on the decision of Carlos Castillo, archbishop of Lima, to have his church filled with more than five thousand photographic portraits of those who had died in Peru to that point in the COVID pandemic, thereby staging a critique of a national health system "based on egotism and on business" and linking failures of public health leadership with looming economic contraction and its inequitable costs. "Peru Archbishop Fills Cathedral with Portraits of COVID-19 Victims," *The Guardian*, June 14, 2020, https://www.theguardian.com/wo rld/2020/jun/15/peru-archbishop-fills-church-with-portraits-of-COVID-19-victims #:~:text=At%20mass%20on%20Sunday%20the,faces%20%E2%80%94%20none%20of %20them%20alive

15. Rhode discusses the project, and his portraits of front-line medical workers and of Louie are included in a video posted to the hospital's YouTube channel, "N.J. Photographer Is Documenting the Inside of a Hospital during COVID-19 Pandemic," YouTube video, 3:37, May 26, 2020, https://www.youtube.com/watch?feature=youtu .be&v=-MJ9pe4T-z8&fbclid=IwAR33EGKCE8lVJyhCv7vKUmS6e3jd3k4qFHRrFc9T QjCU6KFF44PytpKj07Y&app=desktop. See also Jeremy Hobson and Allison Hagen, "Hospital Photographer Says Documenting the Pandemic Poses a 'Unique' Safety Challenge," WBUR *Here & Now*, May 12, 2020, https://www.wbur.org/hereandnow/20 20/05/12/photographer-hospital-coronavirus-pandemic

16. Tom Bodkin, chief creative officer of the *New York Times*, cited in John Grippe, "The Project behind a Front Page Full of Names," May 23, 2020, https://www.nytim es.com/2020/05/23/reader-center/coronavirus-new-york-times-front-page.html. By comparison, see the *Washington Post*'s image-based "Faces of the Dead" project, last updated July 31, 2020, https://www.washingtonpost.com/health/2020/04/24/coronav irus-dead-victims-stories/?arc404=true

17. Bodkin, cited in Grippe, "Project."

18. As Lewis notes, at least one such photographer had his drone and footage impounded. See Christopher Robbins, "NYPD Seizes Drone Of Photojournalist Documenting Mass Burials on Hart Island," *Gothamist*, April 17, 2020, https://gothamist .com/news/nypd-seizes-drone-photojournalist-documenting-mass-burials-hart-is land

19. Scott Neuman, "Medical Examiner's Autopsy Report Reveals George Floyd Had

Positive Test for Coronavirus," NPR, June 4, 2020, https://www.npr.org/sections/live
-updates-protests-for-racial-justice/2020/06/04/869278494/medical-examiners-auto
psy-reveals-george-floyd-had-positive-test-for-coronavirus

20. Joseph Guzman, "George Floyd Hologram Will Be Projected over Confederate
Monument," Changing America, July 28, 2020, https://thehill.com/changing-america
/respect/equality/509474-george-floyd-hologram-will-be-projected-over-confederate

21. Julia Rendleman, *Ballerinas Kennedy George, 14, and Ava Holloway, 14, Pose in
Front of a Monument of Confederate General Robert E. Lee in Richmond after Virginia Governor Ralph Northam Ordered Its Removal*, Keep Fronting, n.d., https://keepfr
onting.tumblr.com/post/627037480583102464/grupaok-ballerinas-kennedy-george
-14-and-ava. See also Sarah McCammon, "In Richmond, Va., Protestors Transform a
Confederate Statue," NPR, June 12, 2020, https://www.npr.org/2020/06/12/876124924
/in-richmond-va-protestors-transform-a-confederate-statue

# CHAPTER 3

# Living on Loss of Privileges

## What We Learned in Prison

*Patrick Bates, Alexandra Friedman, Adam Kouraimi,*
*Ashley Lucas, Sriram Papolu, and Cozine Welch*

### PROJECT DESCRIPTION

In many posts on social media, comparisons have been drawn between the experience of coronavirus lockdowns and being in prison. *Living on LOP: What We Learned in Prison* is a video series initiated by formerly incarcerated artists Patrick Bates and Cozine Welch that reflects on this comparison. *Living on LOP*, a production of the Documenting Prison Education and Arts team of the Carceral State Project, features the stories of formerly incarcerated people who teach us what they learned in prison that can now help us all adjust to life during the pandemic.

In Michigan prisons, "loss of privileges," or LOP, is a broad designation for a range of punishments that incarcerated people can suffer as a result of a disciplinary action. Depending on the severity of the offense of which a person is accused, LOP can mean anything from restrictions of one's time in the prison yard to a stay in solitary confinement. As producer and host Bates explains, the name contains three different meanings.

> [The first is] in reaction to misconduct in prison. What happens as a punishment for any misconduct is that you can be put in the hole for isolation or you can be put on LOP. [The second is the] bigger meaning, the loss of privileges as far as the loss of privileges from society in prison. The third meaning would be the loss of privileges from what people [in the free world] are dealing with right now. Loss of privileges such as not being able to go get your haircut or go to the movies. Those are privileges, not rights.[1]

The literal and metaphorical meanings of LOP offer a bridge between those who have experienced isolation in prison and those in the free world who may be struggling to cope with the limitations of the pandemic. LOP enables the narrators of each episode to showcase their thoughtfulness, compassion, wisdom, and expertise as people who have survived incarceration.

Awareness of the carceral state and mass incarceration is now increasingly present in the conscience of the public as the worth and "justice" of the criminal justice system is being sharply called into question during the pandemic. There is an undeniable link between the social and racial inequities that have been exposed during the pandemic and the revolutionary response to the murder of George Floyd. As calls to defund and abolish the police continue to gain force throughout the nation and the world, now is a critical moment to honor and listen to those who have been most impacted by the criminal justice system and to advocate for dismantling the systems of racism and oppression that have led to the incarceration of nearly 2.3 million people in the United States. We hope this series offers a sense of grounding, wisdom, and hope as we all look forward to the construction of a truly just world.

## ARTAYSIA MALLISHAM: SELF-CARE

PB: I'm Pat Bates, and this is *Living on LOP*. "LOP" stands for "loss of privileges," for misconduct inside of a prison. The lessons former prisoners learned during isolation can be used today and moving forward in our lives. This week we're with the amazing Artaysia Mallisham. She's going to show us about self-care.

AM: Hi. My name is Artaysia Mallisham, and I served nine years and six months at Women's Huron Valley. So during my experience being locked up, I learned how to do my own hair, how to do my own makeup, and to take care of myself to make me feel confident. When I first went to prison, I had to go to level 4, because I had to do nine months to the day before I was cleared to go to level 2, with general population. So during that time I was under twenty-three-hour lockdown. I was only able to come out one hour a day, and within an hour I had to shower, use the phone, try to do my hair, iron, cook, all those things. So within an hour I didn't have time to do all those things. So after I did everything that was important to me, like using a phone and cooking and all of those things, when I would go to my room, I would teach myself how to do my hair—from braiding, twists, or anything—and I would also do my bunkie's hair. So once I

Figure. 3.1. Artaysia Mallisham talks about the importance of self-care during isolation and how her experience learning to do her own hair and makeup helped her build confidence during her period of incarceration. Photo courtesy of Sriram Papolu.

went to general population, by the prison still being overpopulated, I still felt the need to do all those things myself in my room. We had access to hair tools and other critical tools, but by the prison being overcrowded, it was just easier for me to still do my own hair.

I eventually learned how to do my own makeup by playing with it. Doing my eyebrows, getting ready, I wanted to feel good and look cute for visits when my family came: my son, my grandmother, my father. So that's what I did. When you go to prison, so much is stripped from you, down to everything you feel about yourself— feeling good, feeling confident—all those things are taken. So I used those tools I learned to make myself feel confident, and I also did other people's hair and makeup for visits when their family came, to make them feel better. So now through the isolation, I feel like all those things—like the beauty supply stores, closed-down hair salons and nail salons—I definitely feel like this is a time where people can learn to do their own hair. You can go watch YouTube tutorials on doing hair, nails, anything, and you definitely can do it if you apply yourself.

## ROMANDO VALEROSO: STRUCTURE

PB: I'm Pat Bates, and this is *Living on LOP*. "LOP" is "loss of privileges," for misconduct inside of a prison. The lessons former prisoners learn during isolation can be applied today as well as moving forward in our lives. This week we're with the great Romando Valeroso, and he's here to show us how to have structure.

RV: My name is Romando Valeroso. I was released from prison on April 10, 2018, after having served forty-five years of a life sentence. During my period of incarceration, I was on a lockdown in the late 1970s due to a TB epidemic. During that period of time, everyone in the prison thought that they were gonna be the next person to die from this epidemic. Everybody became frustrated not knowing exactly what was going to happen, me included.

I had just started studying Islam, and so I took that period of time during that lockdown to learn Arabic. I learned prayers one line at a time until I was able to recite the whole prayer, and I did that with a number of prayers. And it became my way of dealing with that lockdown. It gave me purpose, clarity, and gave me peace of mind to do that, because in doing so, it gave me like a regimen, a structure in my life, something that I could do every day—something that I had to look forward to every day, to deal with the lockdown. That same regimen, that same structure, followed me throughout the rest of my period of incarceration, as well as when I returned to society. When the governor issued a stay-at-home order, I naturally became a little frustrated, thinking, "What am I gonna do?" But then that situation that happened in the early seventies came back into play, and the same structure I had found in prison with my prayers—I used that same thing here. I pray every day. I make my five obligatory prayers every day. I make them on time. . . . I make them on time because I know that if I miss one prayer, it's not guaranteed that I'm gonna be here to make the next prayer. Because we're not guaranteed anything in this life.

And so that's my regimen in life. That's my structure, and it gives

Figure 3.2. Romando Valeroso shares how he implemented structure into his life while in prison through prayer. This allowed him to cope with incarceration by giving him peace, calm, and clarity. He explains how we can all implement a little more structure in our own lives during the pandemic to reap similar benefits. Photo courtesy of Sriram Papolu.

me clarity. You, too, can find that same peace of mind, believe me. It's just finding something that will help you find clarity in your life, something that will give you peace of mind. And by finding structure in your life, by putting something regimental in your life, every day it will help you through that period of time. And that's what I wish for each and every one of you during these difficult times.

## JUAN JUAN WILLIS: VENTING

PB: I'm Pat Bates, and this is *Living on LOP*. "LOP" is "loss of privileges," for misconduct inside of a prison. The lessons former prisoners learned during isolation can be used today, as well as moving for-

Figure 3.3. Juan Juan Willis shares how he used music while in prison to vent, allowing him to relieve stress and frustration. He discusses the importance of venting and transmuting negative energy into something productive and offers advice on how we can all do this today. Photo courtesy of Sriram Papolu.

ward in our lives. This episode features Juan Juan Willis, aka Zaza Juan, and he's here to tell us how to vent in a stressful situation. Juanito!

JJW: What's up? What's up? ¡Oye! ¡Oye! ¿Qué pasó? (*to the camera*) And you gotta be bilingual, too, a little bit.

We're going to start off with Juan Willis, aka Juan Juan, aka Zaza Juan, bka Juanitos. But, you know, that's another segment though, you know. But I served twelve years in the Department of Corrections, man. But I used music to help me vent and cope with my twelve years because that was a vessel for me. I always messed with music, just messed with music, as when I was young. So when I got locked up, that was something I never experienced before—like going, *Now you're going to do some real time.* Like, it's a couple days in the precinct, thirty days or something like that. No, you're going to do some real time. About to be away from your family. So I ordered a bunch of pads from the store, and they—and if you've been to the county, they taxing you like $2.50, $3.00 a pad. And I just got the writing and venting and writing down my life events, what was going on, what I always did.

So when you hear my music and hear me venting, I'm venting. For real. No cap. And it helped me deal with all type of stuff. Man, you isolated. You by yourself. You feel like you're alone. You and that bitch—just, your freedom got snatched. Most important, your freedom got snatched. You got all types of emotions and stuff running through you just building up, escalating, and to de-escalate, I took to the pen and pad. And like I said, that code for me, solitary confinement—really, I really honed in and tried to craft my skills. Because you really in there. You in that—you in that—you in that small—you in something—you in something smaller than this, and they cut—you in something smaller than this. You in something smaller than this. And they bring that slot up. They bring that slot up to—you ain't coming out that bitch all day. And they bring your trays through. They bring your trays to the slot, and your last meal coming at three-thirty, four o'clock. You ain't getting nothing else, man, for real.

So I used—I used that in there and just—and just wrote. Whether it be poetry—I put whole songs together. Just spoken word. Anything, I just write. What you gain from venting is a stress reducer and a stress reliever. And if you know—and if you know about stress, it's stress. It's a deadly and a silent killer, man, and it's for real. And stress—and stress will kill you. And a lot of people will be stressing and don't even know you're stressing. And you'll have—and it's just—it's heavy, and it's a heavy toll on the body physically, emotionally. So expressing yourself in a positive way is critical. Because if you don't, and it leads—and it leads to negativity. That's what they said. Idle time is the devil's playground, and that's true. And you find yourself getting off in the stuff you know you got no business getting off into. But you can do positive stuff. You can vent. It's ways you can vent and express yourself in positive ways.

A lot of people don't know that they're unconscious. I'm conscious now, but don't get it twisted. I'm still a savage. This is people's first time being incarcerated, so to speak. They never went through this. We went incarcerated on a smaller scale. They got the world incarcerated right now. So they—a lot of people don't know how to cope. We ain't never been through this before. They can find that they home. They can't come outside. They gotta watch TV. We've been doing this. I've been locked up. This ain't nothing to me. I'm like this! (*Mimes lying down with a remote control, changing channels on the television.*) You seen the meme they have of Kermit the Frog? I got the remote like this. This ain't nothing. I ain't stressing. I'm good! And I'm still venting. Now I'm going to the studio though, so, you know, we still gettin' it. You know, we still get it on, but just this is not— people not—and you got to understand that people's way of life has been flipped upside down. When I went to the—when they first put them—put them handcuffs on me—when SWAT came and got me, my life was flipped upside down the same way. Everybody—people going through the same thing. They straight. Kids not in school, so now you got—you got extra activities that's going on in households where people was out and about moving. They had their schedules going on. Now all that's came to a halt, so now we're spending more time with each other than we would normally do. And they don't know how to vent. People don't know how to cope and vent. But the ones that do, they exercise and find other ways to vent. So I urge everybody, just find your find your peace and your serenity and vent, please. Please.

### Note

1. Patrick Bates, and Cozine Welch, interview by Ashley Lucas, June 18, 2020, https://www.youtube.com/watch?v=-uEZqKs7keU

# CHAPTER 4

# Not Even Past

## Archiving 2020 in Real Time

*Michelle McClellan and Aprille McKay*


### INTRODUCTION: ARCHIVAL PRACTICE AND THE CHALLENGE OF COLLECTING THE NOW

In the early days of the coronavirus pandemic, many commentators looked to the past for a frame of reference. Some called the events of 2020 "unprecedented," while others drew parallels with the influenza pandemic of 1918–20. The frequency of comparisons like these is one clue that many people already see current events as "historical." Predicting that historians and community members of the future will want to know and remember what this time was like, archives and museums across the United States and around the world launched "contemporaneous collecting" initiatives, sometimes called "rapid-response collecting," to document COVID-19. Archivists at the Bentley Historical Library at the University of Michigan seized this opportunity to experiment with this new technique, quickly spinning up a crowdsourced COVID collecting program while the world around us was adapting to the demands and strictures the virus has placed on our lives and communities. The technique exposed questions for archivists in this special context: What is "archival?" Who decides? What perspective do we lose if we try to make that determination while an event is still happening? How do we cope with the randomness and heterogeneity of items submitted by the public and make them findable and comprehensible by our constituencies? This essay explores some of the challenges of documenting the events of the current moment and examines examples of material gathered through the initiative to offer some preliminary reflections on the experience.

Collecting the present brings opportunities, but also challenges conventional archival practices, raising questions about the nature of archives and the role of archivists. Individuals have long documented their own lives, of course, and anyone who saves photos, files away her correspondence, or maintains a group of treasured objects may be said to "curate" her own collections. Such self-documentation has been made even easier with the rise of digital cameras, smartphones, and other technologies that facilitate recording and disseminating everyday experiences. Indeed, almost two decades ago the historian Roy Rosenzweig, a pioneer in the use of digital technologies in historical documentation and interpretation, observed that the internet meant that everyone could become an archivist.[1]

But formal archives, like the Bentley Historical Library, do more than chronicle individual lives. They serve as stewards of collective memory, with a dual mission to preserve historical materials and to make them accessible for research, education, personal interest, and other purposes. Archives provide the foundation for many humanities disciplines, as the acknowledgments sections of scholarly monographs and journal articles often make clear. They also can underpin a sense of community and cultural identity.[2] Archives are not simply warehouses or aggregations of unrelated items; rather, archivists select materials to be included, then provide context and structure that add value and even meaning. Archivists create and manage metadata, write finding aids, staff reading rooms, transfer fragile digital files to avoid obsolescence, and more—all to ensure that archival records are "discoverable" and will remain useful to successive generations of researchers.

Each archive has its own unique mission, different goals for collecting, and different constituencies to serve. The Bentley Historical Library's mission is to collect materials that document the history of the University of Michigan and the state of Michigan beyond state government, and its collections are about evenly divided between these two priorities. The collections of Michigan congressman John Dingell, architect Albert Kahn, the Detroit Urban League, and the University of Michigan Athletic Department are a few examples. In all, the Bentley holds more than eleven thousand individual collections, comprising more than seventy thousand linear feet of physical records, as well as digital records and websites that comprise more than 120 terabytes. As field archivists for each of the two collecting domains (the university and the state), the two of us are charged with adding new materials to the collections. Significantly, the Bentley does not purchase material; all of the materials held at the Bentley have been donated by individuals or organizations, or transferred to the Bentley as part of the university's stewardship of its own records.

Our efforts to collect archival materials to represent the university and the state of Michigan are necessarily incomplete and selective.[3] Aside from the obvious constraints imposed by limited resources, our decisions about what is important and interesting are influenced by the culture, institutions, anxieties, and political moods of our times, as well as by our personal histories and relationships. Power is replicated through the archives: political leaders and university presidents transfer well-tended and extensive collections of records to the Bentley, while the experiences of students or essential workers are more elusive. But although the records of the elite may serve to allow the perspectives and messages of the powerful to speak over time, archives also serve as an important resource for accountability for our public institutions, supporting critique and memory.

Researchers at the Bentley have asked time and time again to see one student scrapbook that contains a facemask from the 1918 influenza epidemic. Nestled on the page with report cards and a newspaper clipping is a plain cloth rectangle with ties, along with a card explaining how to wear the mask "to prevent influenza." Even before COVID-19, the artifactual quality of this mask drew viewers' attention, with at least one observer wondering whether any virus could possibly have survived on it. Now the mask seems all the more poignant and powerful as a window onto an earlier public health crisis. Casual observers, students, historians, and archivists all appreciate, whether consciously or not, that that student kept the mask and card and affixed it in his scrapbook, and then donated the scrapbook to the Bentley.

This mask is one of the few pieces of evidence the Bentley can provide to illustrate how students at the University of Michigan experienced this earlier epidemic. There was no formal "university archives" at that time (the Bentley's "Michigan Historical Collections" was not founded until 1935)—but today, as field archivists, we have the opportunity and obligation to collect strategically. We are very aware that this is our moment to ensure that meaningful experiences are not neglected. Are there actions we can take now to catch the stories of those in our community who are impacted by COVID? How can we connect with people whose voices matter, but whose accounts might not come to the archives in the routine way? Exhausted health care workers, students who were abruptly sent home in the midst of their senior year, labor activists arguing for safer working conditions, international students and workers worried about their visas, and COVID patients in the hospital all have important perspectives that belong in the archives.

Our sense of urgency is redoubled because today information is almost exclusively created digitally. No longer can we be sure that photographic prints or letters to loved ones will survive in a shoebox or a file cabinet. Images, recordings, correspondence, journals, newsletters, and essays are

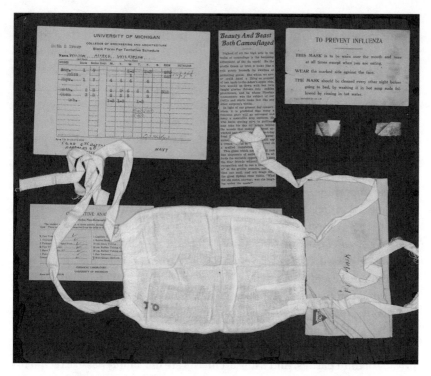

Figure 4.1. Alfred Wilkinson Wilson scrapbook, 1916–21. University of Michigan, Bentley Historical Library.

all "born digital" and most often are never printed to paper. And unlike the offices of the powerful—the governors, the senators, the university presidents of this world—everyday actors do not have administrative aides to help them organize and preserve the records of their lives. Information about the pandemic is largely digital, and our very experience of it has been transformed into something virtual. So we needed a way to capture websites, public notices, photographs, petitions of faculty and community members, Zoom town meeting recordings, virtual commencement celebrations and more—before that information was overwritten, files were lost, and people moved on to new concerns.

The impetus to collect the present is not unique to this moment. Archivists, historians, artists, and social scientists have long sought other ways to document their own times. One example is the "Mass Observation Project," an initiative that began in the United Kingdom in the 1930s.[4] A small group of scholars and artists sought to create an "anthropology of ourselves" by documenting everyday life in Britain. Volunteer participants were invited to keep diaries and respond to periodic surveys, while a small number of paid investigators observed and made notes about the behavior of others. These efforts continued for several decades and have been since collected into an archive at the University of Sussex. The impetus behind many oral history projects is similar: to self-consciously create a record that will preserve a story for posterity. Events such as 9/11, Occupy Wall Street, and the Pulse Nightclub shooting have also inspired institutional contemporaneous collecting efforts.[5]

But collecting the present runs counter to conventional archival practice in some important ways. Archivists usually acquire groups of documents at one time, all sourced from one creator, with a substantial lag-time between the date they were created and the date they were acquired. Indeed, it is usually a sense of closure or transition—when the significant event has ended or at least passed through a recognizable turning point—that transforms material into something "archival." It is a central tenet of archivists that not everything can be saved; the passage of time affords an important sense of perspective, making it easier to determine long-term significance ("enduring value" in archival parlance). In addition, time often serves to mute the sensitivity of certain information and to meliorate ethical concerns about the privacy of third parties. And while archivists are not simply passive recipients of records, collecting the present can require a more active role in shaping the historical record than many archivists were trained to expect.

There are risks, therefore, in collecting when time pressures mean that the archivist's role in appraisal is substantially transformed, in some ways diminished or altered beyond recognition. But there are also risks in waiting too long, as demonstrated by the lone facemask that remains in the student scrapbook.

Our challenge in documenting COVID-19, then, is to ethically capture a diverse range of voices across different record formats, and to do so while the events in question are still unfolding. How could we be as inclusive as possible, conform to archival best practices regarding ethics and privacy, and respond to current events in a timely fashion?

## DOCUMENTING COVID-19 AT THE UNIVERSITY OF MICHIGAN

One tactic was to create "Documenting COVID-19 at the University of Michigan," targeting students, staff, and faculty of the University of Michigan and inviting them to submit items that would document their experience of the pandemic.[6] In the call for contributions, we listed examples of the kinds of documents that would be welcomed, including COVID-themed class assignments, syllabi for redesigned classes, photographs of essential workers performing their tasks, and journal or diary entries of what it is like to recover from the virus.[7]

The Bentley is not alone in undertaking contemporaneous collecting.[8] Indeed, many archives followed the lead of Katie Howell of the University of North Carolina–Charlotte,[9] who created the collecting form we used, and the University of Virginia, which created a Digital Collecting Toolkit after the Charlottesville "Unite the Right" rally.[10] Archivists serving on the Society of American Archivists' Tragedy Response Initiative Task Force have collaborated to create "Documenting in Times of Crisis: A Resource Kit," where colleagues share tools, techniques, and "lessons learned."[11] Here in Michigan, other institutions have undertaken COVID collecting, including the state archives,[12] Michigan State University,[13] the Ann Arbor District Library,[14] the Detroit Historical Society,[15] and the Reuther Library at Wayne State University,[16] to name just a few.

Archivists' collective experience will emerge in our professional literature over the next few years. Here we discuss some examples of material that donors transferred to the Bentley this way and offer a few preliminary thoughts. In many ways, the experience so far has highlighted more questions than answers.

In defining our scope, we elected to restrict our collecting project to members of the University of Michigan community for a few reasons. First, we had no way of knowing how big the takeup would be. Would we receive thousands of submissions? Would this overwhelm our limited staff? How could we articulate for a statewide public what kinds of contributions would be of potential historical value? Since we had never undertaken a general solicitation for contemporaneous materials before, we decided to limit the scope to a more concrete set of potential donors, those who were affiliated with the University of Michigan.

We were aware that other Michigan archival institutions were also engaging in contemporaneous collecting. Limiting the project to the U-M allowed us to exploit our local expertise and personal connections and prevented duplication of effort and redundancy with other organizations. The U-M is a large public university with a federated operation and a major medical center, located in southeast lower Michigan, which was a hotspot early in the pandemic. As a result, members of the U-M community could potentially offer a variety of perspectives on the ways in which the pandemic affected signifi-cant sectors of American society, including health care and higher education.

Focusing on the U-M community would give the resulting collection a coherence that would ultimately make it more comprehensible for research-ers. It would sharpen the quality that archivists sometimes call "aboutness," helping to answer the questions "What is this collection about? What is it good for?"

We knew that the method we were going to use to collect the materials would use a Google submission form. Because everyone in the University of Michigan community is familiar with Google collaboration tools and has a Google account, we knew we would not have to provide work-arounds and tech support for individuals without these skills. In addition to serving as the portal through which submissions were made, this form asked the person submitting each item to provide a description of the item and identifying information (although not all donors responded in detail) and addressed other mechanics of the transfer of materials. Contributions began on April 20, 2020, and collecting is ongoing, though most submissions occurred in the April—June timeframe. The project has been quite successful attracting sub-missions. At this writing, we have acquired contributions from 137 donors.

After classes moved online in mid-March and before the end of the semes-ter on April 30, some instructors at the University of Michigan reconfigured class assignments to include reflection on the present moment. We called on deans' offices and instructors already familiar with the Bentley to spread the word that the archives would like to preserve students' COVID-themed coursework. Several enthusiastic instructors quickly incorporated a contri-bution to the archives into their curriculum. For example, David Sweetman gave the following assignment to his Organizational Studies class:

> The UM Bentley Historical Library is collecting stories of our experiences during this unprecedented time so that future generations can learn from our experiences. For this extra credit assignment, submit at least one long para-graph or at least a one-minute video recording about your lived experiences during this time via Canvas discussions.

Twenty-two students made contributions. Twenty-three members of Adam Eickmeyer's class, Perspectives on Healthcare, responded with short essays to this prompt:

Answer the following questions 1) How has the pandemic affected you, and how have you adjusted? This could be academically, professionally, etc. 2) What are some positive things that have come from this situation? If not for you, for someone else? 3) What things from this course or other courses have helped you understand the problems posed by the virus? 4) What do you hope for after the pandemic subsides?

Submissions have been made by students from twelve different courses. By acting quickly, we were able to add student-made videos and journal entries that reflected their experiences during the upheaval caused by the epidemic. In all, 70% of the contributions have come from students, and the large majority related to a class assignment.

Publicity for the initiative (beyond the outreach to instructional faculty during the semester) was launched on May 11, 2020, and several news outlets promoted the project as a positive story in the midst of a frightening part of the pandemic.[17] Our team also reached out to specific communities within the university, informing them of our project and asking leaders to encourage their constituencies to add their stories or documents. We contacted labor unions and organizations of instructors, graduate students and healthcare professionals, units responsible for student housing, dining, transportation, custodial services, information technology, construction, and student athletics. These messages, individually targeted to more than forty different university constituencies, were sent in June and July. This outreach effort was less successful than we had hoped. While we did not ask contributors how they had learned of the project, only fifteen contributors submitted items after these messages were sent.

Overall, the submitted materials tend to speak to the earlier days of the pandemic, as we suspect our community's sense of novelty may have been replaced by COVID fatigue. We received fifty-two submissions during the last ten days of April, sixty-three in May, twenty in June, nine in July, one in August, six in September, one in October, two in November, and one in December. Toward the end of the fall 2020 semester, Bentley archivists once again reached out to professors to ask them to encourage their students to submit items to the project. As of this writing, we have not yet learned if those solicitations will yield contributions.

Our goals were to gather individual perspectives from people whose experiences are not as routinely documented in the archives. The submission form did ask contributors to categorize their relationship with the university, and it is clear that students and staff predominated. As of January 12, 2021, the distribution of contributors was as follows:

| Student | 96 |
| Staff | 32 (15 of whom collaborated on one submission) |
| Faculty | 7 |
| Community member | 2 |
| Patient | 0 |

We had hoped that a crowdsourcing model in which people contribute their own material directly would yield a wide range of voices. Yet these results remind us that individuals must have a reason to donate materials; if they do not already have a relationship with the collecting institution or a direct incentive to make a contribution, they may not feel moved to do so. The structure of class assignments brought in substantially more items, for example, than community members contributed. That said, the materials submitted are diverse in format, topic, and theme, reflecting the ways in which the pandemic affected people associated with the University of Michigan.

GLIMPSES FROM THE COVID PROJECT

What follows are examples of items contributed by a selection of project donors. Though only a relatively short period of time has passed since the items were donated, already our perspectives have changed in ways that allow us to see new significances and meanings. For example, our call for contributions specifically solicited photographs of essential workers. Staff member Larry Skrdla submitted a photograph of Troy Dixon, who worked at the U-M for thirty years, the last ten as a bus driver. At the University of Michigan, as on many large campuses, students and staff rely on the bus system to move between dormitories and classroom buildings, and from satellite parking areas to central campus offices. The framing of the photo—through the open doors toward the driver as if the viewer were stepping onto the bus—is thus quite familiar to many people affiliated with the U-M. Dixon, the driver, is shown smiling broadly and giving a thumbs-up sign. This cheerful, everyday image poses a jarring contrast to the information that Skrdla provided with his submission: that Dixon had passed away at the beginning of the pandemic. Skrdla did not say when the photo was taken (although the green trees and grass in the background suggest that it had been taken some time prior to the start of the pandemic, which hit Michigan in March 2020). Neither does he mention whether Dixon's death resulted from COVID-19, though it is certainly implied.

Figure 4.2. Troy Dixon, University of Michigan bus driver by Larry Skrdla. University of Michigan, Bentley Historical Library.

Since Dixon's death, many more Michiganders have died from the virus, while social distancing measures have prevented survivors from gathering to grieve and remember their loved ones. Skrlda's contribution creates a memorial in the university's archives, ensuring memory of Dixon will persist in a context that emphasizes his service.

Other submissions presented a very different tone. Undergraduate Tiger Russell Yeh submitted his video *Heavy Headed*, created for Terri Sarris's Film, Television, and Media class. It's a lighthearted look at accessing pharmaceutical help to get through an isolated and virtual semester.

The four-minute film opens to a first-person perspective of a waking student. We see his desk as he tries to do homework: multiple screens, tea, stacks of books, a cell phone with distracting dog photos. Then suddenly we shift perspectives to see a representation of the subject's brain, populated by a man with an aluminum foil hat wearing a "dopamine" name label. We see him struggle to lift a dumbbell labeled "focus." Returning to the first-person view of the student, we see him open a pill bottle labeled "D-booster." After the student swallows the pill, Dopamine is suddenly able to lift the dumbbell in fast motion. The student accomplishes hours of work, until there is a sudden crash and the student falls asleep again. He wakes and starts again, but today rejects the pills in favor of escaping his apartment for a bike ride. Dopamine begins dancing. The student throws his books in the garbage, and we see a screen showing that all his class assignments are late. At the end there are legends: "Lazy," "slacker," "just.try," "we all have it," "listen for once," "idiot," "stop moving," and "it's my worst enemy."

Looking at this video several months after it was first contributed evokes

Figure 4.3. Screen capture from "Heavy Headed" by Tiger Russell Yeh. University of Michigan, Bentley Historical Library.

new comparisons with the explosion of TikTok videos during the pandemic. Legions of Americans were moved to create short videos about their coronavirus experiences and to share them via this social media platform. Though TikTok videos are less than a minute, the ubiquitous availability of cell phone video cameras has encouraged individuals to engage their own creativity in ways that resonate with Yeh's. We suspect that the passage of more time will allow us to further reflect on the student experience of the pandemic and the adequacy of the pedagogical support they received from the university during this unprecedented time.

Several donors let us know they are keeping journals that were still in progress, since the pandemic is ongoing. For example, Tiffany Ng, the university's professor of carillon, submitted a photograph of handwritten pages from her journal documenting the change in the natural and urban soundscapes of Ann Arbor during the lockdown, and anxieties of being an Asian American during a significant rise in anti-Asian racism. On her submission form, dated April 30, 2020, she notes, "I am a musicologist and sound studies scholar, so I have been keeping this journal for future historians of sound." The photographed journal page describes a hike in a park and hearing the sound of river water flowing over a dam. We will follow up with her and with others who have signaled their interest in the project whose commemoration efforts are ongoing. We will learn then whether they persisted with their journals over the many months of the pandemic or whether journaling fulfilled an expressive need during a shorter period of time. As archivists, we are intrigued, and can easily imagine that these items will be interesting and unique, but we need to be patient and wait until an appropriate period of time has passed to ask to see the completed work.

As we wait, it is worth noting how the photograph of Ng's diary pages functions as a kind of placeholder, a digital surrogate of the handwritten diary. At the time that Ng offered her diary, we could not accept physical donations. In an effort to slow the spread of the virus and to "flatten the curve" of the rate of infection, the Bentley Library adopted significant restrictions on face-to-face interactions and on the transfer of materials. In keeping with a series of executive orders by the Michigan governor and following general public health principles, the library has been closed to the general public for months. The library began to open for research for individuals directly affiliated with the University of Michigan two afternoons a week beginning in September, and began to accept the transfer of physical materials in a garage setting on a very limited basis beginning in November. Between March and August the Bentley Library was not even able to accept mail. That means that donors have not been able to get physical materials to us. For the same reasons, the field archivists have not been able to go to people's homes and offices to collect items. Because of concern about the extent to which the virus might live on materials such as papers and books, the Bentley—like other archives and libraries across the country—has had to adapt new practices even for so-called contactless transfer.

In the case of Ng's diary, the digital stand-in for a document that is still being written evokes the suspended animation that many people feel in the midst of the pandemic and the degree of isolation it has imposed. It also reminds us that we do not know how long the pandemic will go on, a narrative uncertainty that stands in stark contrast to the usual transition of before and after that marks historical materials as archival.

Working on this project has caused us to reflect on the similarities and differences between journalists and archivists. Like journalists, we too are trying to document society. Like a journalist, an archivist is not usually a protagonist in the action to be documented, but neither is she a passive (read: neutral) observer, simply accepting whatever material comes her way. The following example illustrates how journalistic content creation and archival fieldwork overlap during the pandemic while also highlighting the distinct role of the university archives in ensuring institutional accountability. The U-M College of Engineering's communications department published a

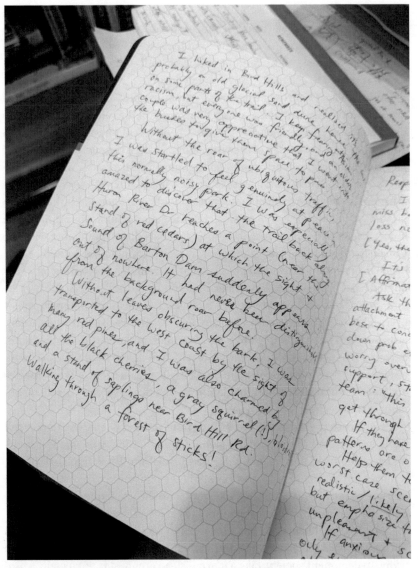

I hiked in Bird Hills and realized it's probably an old glacial sand dune because on some parts of the trail. I kept fearing racism, but everyone was friendly, and a couple was very appreciative that I went into the bushes to give them space to pass.

Without the roar of ubiquitous traffic, I was startled to feel genuinely at Peace in this normally noisy park. I was especially amazed to discover that the trail back along Huron River Dr reaches a point (near the stand of red cedars) at which the sight + sound of Barton Dam suddenly appears out of nowhere. It had never been distinguishable from the background roar before.

Without leaves obscuring the bark, I was transported to the West Coast by the sight of many red pines, and I was also charmed by all the black cherries, a gray squirrel (?, blondish) and a stand of saplings near Bird Hill Rd. Walking through a forest of sticks!

Resp
I
miss b
loss n
[yes, the

It's
[Affirma
Ask th
attachment
base + conc
down prob e
worry over
support, st
team: this
get through
If they have
patterns are o
Help them t
worst case sce
realistic/likely
but emphasize t
unpleasant + sc
If anxiou
only s

Figure 4.4. Journal of Tiffany Ng, professor of carillon. University of Michigan, Bentley Historical Library.

Jeff Lockhart <jwlock@umich.edu>                                    Sun, Jul 19, 2020 at 12:17 PM
To: "Cunningham, Rebecca" <stroh@med.umich.edu>

Dear Rebecca,

Thank you for your quick and thoroughly considered reply! I really appreciate it.

I'm worried that if there is not capacity for surveillance testing with 4 thousand people now, there will not be capacity for testing even
symptomatic people in the Fall, when over 71 thousand students, faculty, and staff return to campus. Most of them will not be
following such strict distancing and PPE protocols as current lab staff are. Does the university have any estimates of testing capacity,
outbreak size, infection rates, or similar for this Fall? These ought to be public record, but I cannot find them among the provost
reports, EHS guidance, or Maize and Blueprint plan.

Thank you,
Jeff
[Quoted text hidden]

Figure 4.5. Email message, Jeff Lockhart to University of Michigan vice president of research Rebecca Cunningham. University of Michigan, Bentley Historical Library.

video blog ("vlog") of graduate students' experiences during the pandemic.[18] Each video features an engineering graduate student talking frankly about coping during the pandemic. Presumably the vlogs posted by the College of Engineering fulfill rhetorical goals of the institution: they serve to support students and help them feel less alone, they help alumni understand the plight of graduate students and potentially donate funds, and they provide an opportunity for the students to give real feedback about their experiences, among others. The Bentley will collect these videos, independently from the crowdsourced COVID collecting project, as part of our standard mission to document the university.

While not very many of the contributions submitted to the project are critical of the university, certainly a few are. For example, one student donated an email exchange with the administration questioning the U-M's COVID-19 testing strategy.

Jeff Lockhart, a PhD candidate in sociology, made five contributions to the project in July and an additional one in September. Lockhart is one of the leaders in the Graduate Employees Organization (GEO), which was strongly critical of the administration's response to the pandemic, and called a strike of all graduate student instructors on September 8, 2020. Lockhart took advantage of our call to ensure that the archives preserved noninstitutional accounts of the pandemic response. In addition to correspondence with university administrators, Lockhart contributed a summary of the provost's reopening plans created to focus graduate student advocacy, a scatterplot of the effect of the pandemic on the job market for sociology PhDs, and a collection of his own pandemic-related tweets. Lockhart's submissions show the potential of the Bentley, as an institutional archive, to preserve perspectives that hold the institution accountable, both as the events are unfolding and for purposes of later analysis.

## ARCHIVES, DIVERSITY, AND POWER

The Bentley's collecting initiative has unfolded against the backdrop of wider debates about user-generated content and inclusivity in the archival record. For many archives engaged in contemporaneous collecting, including the Bentley, building a more diverse historical record has been an important goal (diverse in format, perspective, and underrepresented voices). While it is too early to draw definitive conclusions about what has been contributed through this project, it is clear that a crowdsourced approach does not erase constraints and challenges that have been there all along. The material that has come in so far skews toward students and class projects. None of the student contributions were compelled since participation was always voluntary, but sometimes contributors received extra credit for submitting an assignment to the archives. The power dynamic between student and instructor is implicit in the texts and films the students contributed. Also, despite reaching out to specific campus constituencies with calls for contributions, we have not succeeded in documenting important perspectives and experiences, such as the voices of custodians and patients at the hospital, for example. Our experience shows that a crowdsourced approach may be the next step in creating inclusive archives, but we must ensure that it does not exacerbate existing biases and gaps in archival holdings.

In this as in any other crisis, those most affected may have the least time and energy to document what they are going through. Indeed, there is a debate in the archival field about the extent to which it is appropriate to try to gather documentation from individuals and communities who are living through traumatic events.[19] So for example, the racial disparities in health outcomes from COVID-19 emerged quickly as an important aspect of the pandemic, including in Detroit and southeast Michigan. Yet families going through such trauma and loss are not likely to want to, or to have the capacity to, document their pain for posterity right now, and for archivists to reach out to them at such moments is exploitative and cruel.

In this context, the advantages of a collecting initiative like this can also be disadvantages. The Google submission form allows people who are relatively tech-savvy to submit material and complete the transaction, including release forms related to privacy and use, easily. But it also means that the donation process is less collaborative than usual, when a field archivist often confers with a prospective donor at some length about the materials to be documented, gaining important information and insight that helps contextualize the collection for future users. From the limited information he provided via the Google form, we do not know, for example, whether staff member Larry Skrdla, who submitted the photograph of bus driver Troy Dixon, knew Dixon personally. Was there a particular reason that image was taken or preserved, or was it a routine staff photo? Did Dixon participate actively in making this photo of himself, or is it a representation that only reflects Skrdla's perspective? Knowing such additional details would not change the reality of Dixon's death, but it might deepen the meaning ascribed to the photo and how it wound up in the archive.

More generally, an important part of building representative archives is developing and maintaining relationships with donors. Such relationships are especially significant in the case of individuals and groups whose voices are not as well represented in institutional archives such as the Bentley. We hope that this kind of collecting initiative will add materials that would not have been captured otherwise, but we knew from the start that it would not be the only tool we used to collect material related to the pandemic. It does not substitute for targeted outreach and relationship building by field archivists who try to see the big picture, and so we hope that it will yield leads and new connections as well as content.

CONCLUSION

Archivists always straddle the past, present, and future, collecting materials in the present that document the past and securing them for future use. And archivists are never simply passive recipients of records created by others; we always make judgments about value and meaning in selecting records to preserve. Today, however, the intensity of the COVID-19 pandemic, professional activism, and the ephemeral nature of materials generated in response to crises create a sense of urgency to collect in new ways in order to document the present as we are living through it. This crowdsourcing initiative to collect COVID-19 materials represents a nimble response and, in theory at least, should ensure the preservation of materials that might otherwise be lost. But it asks us as archivists to adjust our role, raising questions both philosophical and practical. We are taking a more active step in shaping the historical record by asking for materials to be produced, while also compressing our typically deliberative process of appraisal. Rather than accessioning collections with a clear provenance, we are soliciting a wide variety of heterogenous materials whose processing requires new, potentially much more time-consuming, methods. In a sense, this is a hybrid approach, as we attempt to harness the energy of crowdsourced digital content while fitting it into the procedures of an established institutional archive to guarantee preservation and access.

Given that the pandemic and the collecting initiative are still ongoing, we cannot yet assess whether the quality and amount of records gathered will be worth the effort. We are taking inventory of the materials that community members are donating and thinking about how to reach out to those whose experiences are not yet represented. We are devising new workflows for making these materials available for research and considering how to evaluate the success of our efforts. While our conclusions can only be partial at this point, we have learned that this type of outreach and crowdsourcing, including the invitation to prospective donors to create materials for the archive, can be one tool in building inclusive archives. It is not a substitute for cultivating ongoing relationships with individuals and communities, an important part of building diverse archival collections. Furthermore, the meaning and significance of the records we collected through this initiative will be determined in part by future users of the archive, and not by us at all. One thing we know for sure, then, is that time will tell.

### Notes

The authors would like to thank Nancy Bartlett, Bentley Historical Library, for her encouragement, suggestions, and incisive feedback as we worked on this essay.

1. Roy Rosenzweig, "The Road to Xanadu: Public and Private Pathways on the History Web," *Journal of American History* 88.2 (September 2001): 546. Here Rosenzweig was riffing on Carl Becker's famous presidential address to the American Historical Association in 1931, "Everyman His Own Historian."

2. Terry Cook, "Evidence, Memory, Identity, and Community: Four Shifting Archival Paradigms," *Archival Science* 13 (2013): 95–120.

3. These is extensive scholarship on this point. See, for example, Michel-Rolph Trouillot, *Silencing the Past: Power and the Production of History* (Boston: Beacon Press, 1995).

4. http://www.massobs.org.uk/

5. Diane Nester Kresh, "Courting Disaster: Building a Collection to Chronicle 9/11 and Its Aftermath," Library of Congress Information Bulletin, September 2002, https://www.loc.gov/loc/lcib/0209/sept11.html; Megan O'Shea, "Guide to the Occupy Wall Street Archives Working Group Records," Tamiment Library & Robert F. Wagner Labor Archives, March 20, 2019, http://dlib.nyu.edu/findingaids/html/tamwag/tam_630/; Historical Society of Central Florida, Pulse Nightclub Shooting collection, Sep-

tember 2018, https://archive-it.org/collections/11001

6. https://docs.google.com/forms/d/e/1FAIpQLScUiCdxNjCS2HUf41XEJnjLhYh Vp-_i3SAkjgKeIbdvoD_zsA/viewform. The Bentley team that worked on the project was led by Caitlin Moriarity and includes Steven Gentry, Emily Mathay, Aprille McKay, Sarah McLusky, and Brian Williams.

7. https://bentley.umich.edu/news-events/news/help-the-bentley-archive-u-ms -pandemic-experiences/

8. Katherine J. Wu, "As COVID-19 Reshapes the World, Cultural Institutions Collect Oral Histories," *Smithsonian Magazine*, April 7, 2020, https://www.smithsonian mag.com/smart-news/COVID-19-reshapes-world-cultural-institutions-collect-oral -histories-180974613/; Pam Schwartz, Whitney Broadaway, Emilie S. Arnold, Adam M. Ware, and Jessica Domingo, "Rapid-Response Collecting after the Pulse Nightclub Massacre," *Public Historian* 40.1 (2018): 105–114, https://doi.org/10.1525/tph.2018.40 .1.105; A. L. Neatrour, J. Myntti, and R. J. Wittmann, R.J. (2020), "Documenting Contemporary Regional History: The Utah COVID-19 Digital Collection," Digital Library Perspectives, July 20, 2020, https://doi.org/10.1108/DLP-04-2020-0025

9. https://library.uncc.edu/contribute-your-stories-COVID-19-outbreak

10. http://digitalcollecting.lib.virginia.edu/toolkit/

11. https://www2.archivists.org/advocacy/documenting-in-times-of-crisis-a-reso urce-kit

12. https://www.michigan.gov/mhc/0,9075,7-361-99041_99042---,00.html

13. https://lib.msu.edu/branches/ua/COVID19/

14. https://aadl.org/pandemiclog

15. https://detroit1967.detroithistorical.org/detroit-quarantine

16. https://reuther.wayne.edu/COVID-19

17. "Bentley Historical Library Seeks to Archive Pandemic Experiences of U-M Community," May 11, 2020, https://arts.umich.edu/news-features/bentley-historical -library-seeks-to-archive-pandemic-experiences-of-u-m-community/; "University of Michigan Bentley Historical Library Seeking Submissions to Document COVID-19 Pandemic," https://www.mlive.com/news/ann-arbor/2020/05/university-of-michi gan-bentley-historical-library-seeking-submissions-to-document-COVID-19-pand emic.html; Meredith Bruckner, "University of Michigan's Bentley Historical Library Wants Your Help Documenting COVID-19 Pandemic," All about Ann Arbor, May 13, 2020, https://www.clickondetroit.com/all-about-ann-arbor/2020/05/13/university -of-michigans-bentley-historical-library-wants-your-help-documenting-covid-19-pa ndemic/

18. Joseph Xu, "Grad Students Coping under COVID-19," March 30, 2020 https://ne ws.engin.umich.edu/2020/03/grad-students-coping-under-covid-19/

19. Eira Tansey, "No One Owes Their Trauma to Archivists, or, the Commodification of Contemporaneous Collecting," June 5, 2020, http://eiratansey.com/2020/06/05 /no-one-owes-their-trauma-to-archivists-or-the-commodification-of-contemporane ous-collecting/

# PART II

# Waiting

# CHAPTER 5

# Waiting = Death: COVID-19, the Struggle for Racial Justice, and the AIDS Pandemic

*David Caron*

> Hoping for a life more sweeter
> Instead I'm just a story repeating
> —Leon Bridges, "Sweeter"

Since the COVID-19 pandemic began to spread across the planet, a great deal of human activity has involved waiting. We're waiting to know how the situation will unfold and when the crisis will end. We're waiting for a cure and a vaccine. We're waiting to hear whether we'll have our job back, or for a government check to come. We're waiting for our lives to return to normal, yet we expect that the world won't be the same after such thorough disruption. In places where entire populations were urged to stay at home and venture out only when strictly necessary, people found themselves suddenly deprived of access to spaces defined, in one form or another, by interactions with fellow human beings—and thus deprived of these very interactions. Waiting, then, may appear like the epitome of temporal nothingness or, at best, strangeness. We're living "in these unusual times," "in these weird times," "in these crazy times," or whatever similar phrase we started to reflexively attach to "I hope this email finds you well." In the face of so much uncertainty, waiting can also turn into a demanding emotional task, leading some to introspection when sociality as we knew it has all but vanished. Furthermore, we are urged to wait, even ordered to, because the resolution of the crisis is supposed to depend in part on our patience with restrictions in our lives. Some are reacting angrily at such disciplining, worried about government overreach and lost freedom. Some, too, are waiting to see what the world will look like on the other side of a catastrophe that has upended our economies and shed a new light on deep social inequalities in the face of illness and death. But as the pandemic shows no sign of ending and with the knowledge that more pandemics are to come, as predictable as this one, one must ask: What if there is no "other side of this"? What exactly are we waiting for? For many, time suspended has provided an opportunity to imagine a different future, regardless of the pandemic's outcome, and to facilitate the advent of social justice now rather than simply wait for it to happen. The year 2020 is an election year in the United States, after all, and as I write, people are marching in the streets of many American cities and towns to demand that our future world not be one where Black people keep getting murdered by the police or lynched by self-appointed neighborhood vigilantes. Some people are tired of waiting. As Martin Luther King Jr. wrote in 1963: "For years now I have heard the word 'Wait!' It rings in the ear of every Negro with piercing familiarity. This 'Wait' has almost always meant 'Never.'"[1]

I remember another time when I, too, was sick and tired of waiting. These were the years between 1981 and 1996, when AIDS was ravaging vulnerable communities in this country and worldwide in the face of shocking indifference; years when our hopes for a cure kept rising every few months only to be betrayed soon after, sometimes for no other reason that some publicity-seeker had garnered attention from the media; years when we understood that waiting for other people to care made little point because they wouldn't—ever. Waiting with others, albeit not with everyone, soon led to a mix, at once toxic and salutary, of despair, rage, grief, and fatigue that spurred a new kind of activism, a kind that arose from the absolute certainty that if we kept waiting, we were all going to die. As I witness the current uprising for racial justice in the midst of another deadly pandemic, I think back with some degree of hope of AIDS activism, of how a new disease helped us rethink the categories of race, gender, sexuality, and sociality off which death fed. And I remember what it felt like to wait with other people—and then to have enough.

But what is waiting?

In *Passing Time: An Essay on Waiting*, a slim, smart and often aggravating volume at once analytical and poetic, cultural critic Andrea Köhler peers into Western philosophical and literary traditions in order to reclaim waiting as the very stuff of life and a human and humane counterforce to the increasingly frantic pace of modern existence. The essay closes with these lines: "And every time our wishes are granted too easily or quickly, a vengeful God exacts his due: we forfeit the rewards of patience. Caerus, the lucky moment, presupposes waiting—the gift of time—excruciatingly long sometimes, and sometimes blissfully wasted, but always a gift" (135–36). We know this story; it feels good indeed, but the nostalgia reeks of privilege. I look into Köhler's essay less to refute it than to mine its consensual sentiments for insights into the problematic ways in which a historically gendered rhetoric of waiting has been deployed during the COVID-19 pandemic and has unexpectedly (or not) dovetailed with the struggle for racial justice.

Köhler pays close attention to three defining dimensions of waiting that also characterize our current experience and that I just briefly sketched: introspection, wisdom, and creativity. As we wait, we turn our focus inward and examine our emotions in search of truth and authenticity; the willingness to delay satisfaction is supposed to lead to maturity in the individual and, says Freud, culture in the group; and waiting ( for the future) constitutes something akin to a gestation period as we look into ourselves for continuity through renewal. In Western cultures—and, I would argue, specifically *modern* Western cultures—the ability to wait has come to signify individual and social virtue. Still, I prefer to see waiting (and the refusal to wait) as a political act rather than a virtue. Here's why.

From Jews waiting for the Messiah to Christians waiting for his second coming, from Penelope to the protagonists of *Waiting for Godot*, from damsels in castles longing for their knight to return to the wives of fishermen scanning the horizon, waiting occupies such a central place in Western religious, literary, and artistic imagination that some find it an apt metaphor for the human condition and for our investigations into the sublime nature of love, God, death, and the like. This very Western approach to universality may well contain a kernel of existential truth, but with a deadly pandemic raging around me I feel much more inclined to look at our current moment in a more down-to-earth fashion. Liminal in nature, waiting works as a hinge all at once in time, space, and society, and thus serves as an organizer of social relations.

Waiting uncomfortably dilates the present moment and makes us aware of our situation between past and future events, whence perhaps the urge to reflect on it in vast existential terms we would prefer to avoid. As Harold Schweizer remarks in his essay *On Waiting*, "The waiter—the impatient waiter—is an unwilling student of philosophy. When we wait, we who have no time to philosophize are made philosophers against our will" (25). But we don't wait only in time; we wait in space, too, which involves specific material conditions. Waiting rooms, queues, antechambers, and all sorts of halls started to dot Europe's built environment with the advent of modernity in the Old World. As new economic activities and modes of transportation emerged, so did new configurations of time and subjective relations to it. Transportation schedules, time zones, and pocket watches began to appear in the nineteenth century and reflected the larger concerns of the age and how they made their way into the daily lives of individuals.[2] Where and how we wait exposes who, but more importantly *what*, we are in relation to a set of social interactions and institutions in a given culture and at a given time in history. Put differently, waiting produces identities in situation. I can in turn be a patient at the doctor's, a client at the bank, a traveler at the airport, a friend or relative at the hospital, a concertgoer on a sidewalk, and so on. I am where I wait and what I wait for. And I change accordingly as the transient nature of my situations reminds me of the unevenness that defines human beings.

Since the spaces where we wait are public or semipublic, chances are we're not there alone. Shared waiting spaces don't just house us or locate us; they organize bodies and lay out the parameters of their interactions. Chairs or ropes may tell us how we should position ourselves in a given space and in relation to other people's bodies. When Walt Disney created his amusement parks, for instance, he also invented the snaking line. The clever trick allowed customers eager to have fun to look at each other and enjoy some kind of collective entertainment before the actual ride, thus filling time with something other and more pleasurable than waiting. Disney essentially took our minds away from the dread of existential mulling simply by rearranging bodies in space. They don't call Disneyland the happiest place on earth for nothing.

Today, we have sidewalk and floor markings six feet apart and yellow tape over seats we mustn't use, and as they direct our bodies, these spaces also regulate sets of cultural norms regarding civility, obedience, privacy, and a variety of taboos. See, for example, how French people wait for the bus, all bunched up together, while the English will form orderly lines. In some places, crossing the street when it isn't your turn may be frowned upon, even with no car in sight. If you go see a therapist in France, chances are you will be the only patient in the waiting room and you will leave, unseen, from a back door after your session. An American counterpart, however, may not take such precautions, and that, of course, tells us something about the social perception of mental health issues in different countries. And while we may share our excitement with strangers standing next to us in line before a game or a show, we are more likely to keep to ourselves at the doctor's or at the bank because health and money remain private matters even in a public place. Waiting, in other words, reveals much about a given culture.

Waiting doesn't only map out various social relations horizontally, though. Not everyone waits in the same way even though we may be, or seem to be, waiting for the same thing. Think of business-class airport lounges and lines for "elite members." Think of the people who walked right into that club because they're famous or very beautiful and you're just some nobody behind the velvet rope. Waiting distributes power. One of my students recently wrote in a paper that the planet had become "a pandemic waiting room." Indeed, what have our governments and public health officials done if not police our bodies by mandating how, where, and with whom we are to wait? And when another student remarked that "not having to wait is the definition of privilege," she may have been referring to coronavirus testing but expanded her remark to apply broadly to waiting in general. To be sure, the modalities of waiting don't just delineate social roles, they distribute authority unevenly. The doctor has power over you; so do the banker and the airline representatives, and oftentimes they signal that power first by exercising their authority to make you wait. As Helmut Puff shows in "Waiting in the Antechamber," antechambers developed in European palaces in the early modern period in order to distribute power in relation to the sovereign and among people of different ranks. Waiting, in that sense, played an active part in the consolidation of monarchical power. At the court, "knowing the art of how to wait" and not to speak out of turn could make all the difference in your social and political success (29). To wait often entails obeying a set of rules and submitting to limitations on our dominion over ourselves. How we deal with these limitations, then, inevitably implicates our sense of self in relation to modalities of power. This holds true for African Americans urged to wait quietly for their civil rights; for queer people and other minorities told to calm down and wait for the cure that will surely come; and today to, say, women made to hunker down at home with an abusive spouse.

In *A Lover's Discourse*, Roland Barthes notes, "*To make someone wait*: the constant prerogative of all power" (40). Barthes is discussing love in this essay, which necessarily brings up the question of gender. To be sure, waiting, in Western cultures but not only, has long been a gendered activity. Women are often made to wait for men and depicted that way in countless artistic representations and cultural production. They wait for men to return from work or from war, from prison perhaps, or just to call back. Here too, waiting organizes social roles and interactions. In premodern Europe, it divided domestic and military tasks, for example, while in the modern era it played a crucial part in producing gendered concepts of the private and the public as different and unequal spheres of human activity.

In particularly brutal circumstances, waiting can become a ruthless mode of exercising power over other human beings. As Köhler observes, largely following Siegfried Kracauer, "There's a reason that the arbitrary authority of bureaucracies has come to epitomize the torture of waiting as well as the brutality of dictatorships at large. The government agency is the quintessential modern waiting room. There, the meaninglessness of waiting penetrates every fiber of those waiting" (49). Many of us will never forget the photos of acts of torture committed against Iraqi war prisoners by American soldiers in Baghdad's Abu Ghraib prison. Most iconic of all was the picture of a prisoner standing on a box, hooded, his naked body only covered with some sort of poncho, with electrodes attached to his fingers and penis, waiting for the pain of electricity running through his body to come at any time, or not at all. Perhaps more than the pain, waiting itself constituted the act of torture.[3] And in Charlotte Delbo's concentration camp memoir, *Auschwitz and After*, repeated scenes of endless roll calls endured every day by prisoners standing in the bitter cold of Polish winters convey the full extent of their dehumanization, as she expresses in this poem:

> SS in black capes have walked past. They made a count. We are waiting still.
>
> We are waiting.
>
> For days, the next day.
>
> Since the day before, the following day.
>
> Since the middle of the night, today.
>
> We wait.
>
> Day is breaking.
>
> We await the day because one must wait for something.
>
> We do not await death. We expect it.
>
> We await nothing.
>
> We await only what happens. Night because it follows day. Day because it follows night.
>
> We await the end of the roll call. (22; translation modified)[4]

Waiting without a future or a past; waiting extended into an endless present of suffering; waiting for the sake of waiting: realizing the anguish at play in making people wait as a means of dehumanizing them makes us look less than kindly upon universalizing musings on the whole thing as a trope for the human condition. Would Samuel Beckett have written *Waiting for Godot* before Auschwitz? I doubt it, but if he had, we wouldn't have read it the same way. Waiting is always situated, including in history.

With the advent of Western modernity and the Anthropocene, ancient notions of time shifted from a cyclical to a linear model as an organizer of human lives. What Barbara Adam terms "timescapes of modernity" describe the demands that global industrialization has placed on our experience of time at the expense of the environment. Building on Adam's ideas, Rosemary Robins points out, in "Waiting for Rain in the Goulburn Valley," that the cyclical time of the eternal return of the seasons and of the human activities they supported provided people with a set of expectations rooted in nature and inevitability. The linear concept of time that accompanied the shift from agrarian economies to increasingly industrial ones transformed the human experience into one defined by uncertainty—an uncertainty only magnified today by global warming. While nature can always play tricks on us and force us to revise our expectations, the advent of the Anthropocene gradually removed these expectations (and will possibly remove nature itself at some point) from our experience of time and replaced them with the never-ending narrative of progress and the anxiety that comes with it.

One important thing to remember is that even the word "waiting" didn't always mean what it means now. In various forms, and different languages, it originally referred to social rather than subjective life, as attested by etymology. The same Germanic root gave us the English "wait," "watch," and "wake"; Latin origins connect the French *attendre* (to wait), the Spanish *attender* (to attend, to heed, to care, to nurse), and the English "attend," "attention," "attendance," and so on. "Waiting," which once meant to serve and to attend to the needs of others (a meaning still extant in "waiter" and "lady in waiting," for example), took on its full current subjective dimension in the modern era. Köhler goes as far as to make the following assertion: "*Waiting* in the common modern sense was apparently first recorded as far back as the thirteenth century. Not until the eighteenth century, however, did it accrue those adverbial facets and specifications that testify to its more painful side. Since the age of Romanticism, one waits *with longing, impatience,* or *in agony*" (25). These emotions do figure prominently in premodern literature, often in relation to a lover's absence. In most cases, however, they have no direct association with the specific words we now use to signify the act of waiting; waiting in English, *wachten* in German, *attendre* in French, for example.[5] Just as "taste" expanded from the gustatory to aesthetic judgment and "tact" from touch to a form of thoughtfulness, so does the modern sense of "waiting" reflect Western modernity's new focus on the subjective characteristics of the self and Cartesian body-mind dualism. Qualities once ascribed to bodies and their interactions with other bodies or with the material world came to define the subject of the new humanism. And just like taste and tact, waiting, thanks to its new meaning, was tasked not just with attesting to culture and conveying it but with inscribing norms within the deeper recesses of subjectivity, making each individual the carrier and enforcer of a social order without which he or she would not exist.

This subjective, affective dimension of waiting seems to have developed alongside new ideas on the value of time concurrently with the Industrial Revolution and the shift to the linear model of time. Glossing a letter in which Mozart expressed his exasperation at having to wait for his aristocratic hosts in a cold room with only a lousy piano, Puff notes, "From the vantage point of an industrious society, waiting was time spent unproductively—time that could and should have been put to better uses. The lack of measurable results therefore was one of several sources of frustration for those kept in this state" (29). And at this level too, the shift entailed more than the establishment of a culture centered on the principle of an autonomous self; it created hierarchy and inequality among individuals. In the modern age, mastering good taste, tactfulness, and what Puff called "the art of how to wait" served to separate the grain from the chaff.

What, then, does this all play out in a pandemic?

Think of how some of us have started to examine our affective reactions to the current crisis. As more and more people started to suffer from illness, loss, economic hardship, hunger, or domestic violence, those lucky or privileged enough not to be too adversely affected by the situation have marveled, anguished, or both at the peculiar stillness that characterizes lives lived under lockdown. Both emotions are perfectly understandable. The new, unfamiliar texture of the present, once too evanescent to be noticed but now thickened with all sorts of affect, has led many to turn their attention inward. We may first experience our retreat from the world and its multiple entanglements as absence and lack, but to focus on ourselves may allow us to see such withdrawal as excess, too—an excess of time that suddenly reveals all that was presumably lacking in our regular lives, starting with self-awareness. What are we supposed to do with all this unused time, some wondered, if not take it as a gift and a unique opportunity to scrutinize ourselves and our reason for being in a world whose interconnectedness became impossible to deny almost overnight?

Counterintuitive as it may sound at first blush, global crises often lead people to introspection. This may be due to the fact that global solutions to global problems seem so far beyond the grasp of individual agency that, rather than give in to the despair of helplessness, we turn to what we do have access to—ourselves. This is especially true when access to others beyond our household has become impossible or, at best, mediated with technologies that seem to alienate us as (much as) they connect us. When we shine a light on our feelings in the hope of making sense of them, we ultimately seek self-empowerment in the face of the powerlessness that defines our waiting, but we do so by ignoring the social forces that are shaping our present.

Indeed, what can feel so confusing with the waiting that accompanies a crisis so overwhelming that many of us as individuals may feel that we have no control over it is that it affects us differently and on different scales at once. That would be the case with any world event with observable effects on people's daily lives, of course. Consider, for example, the repercussions of World War II, reaching into the inner workings of Western domesticity and the psyches of newly decolonized people. But it is especially true in the case of a global health crisis, which engages the entire planet and people's bodies simultaneously. This ain't my first rodeo, you see. I remember all too well how the AIDS pandemic made me feel as a sexually active gay man having to negotiate the terms of intimacy under the clouds of mass deaths, widespread panic, and the especially vile forms of exclusions and discrimination faced by the most vulnerable among us. We were not "all in this together" back then, as the feel-good slogans of so many COVID-era commercials would now have us believe; it felt rather as if "all this was in us" instead. I will come back to the HIV/AIDS pandemic in a bit. For now I want to stress how the scalar derangement one may experience in such a context—when contracting a microscopic virus feels as though you've also absorbed something planetary in size—prompting questions as ecological as they are ontological about the nature of the self and its relation with everything else. Am I in the world, or is the world in me? Or both at the same time?[6]

Introspection, however, has also been shared quite publicly as of late. Authors, artists, and social media personalities are documenting their experiences in real time. Psychologists and advice columnists are encouraging us to express our emotions in the name of self-care. And OMG those COVID dreams! Even social events on Zoom can feel, and look, like sharing our aloneness, each of us boxed in like *Hollywood Squares*, the walls of our prison in the background. In the very Western collective turn to the self that characterized the COVID moment, at least up to the police murder of George Floyd and its aftermath, I see no yearning for community, no transformation of modernity's norms and values but, rather, their intensification. As I suggested earlier, waiting defines and disciplines the self in relation to other selves and to the culture at large. Waiting during COVID is no exception.

As Köhler would have it, "Even when we are waiting in the company of others, each of us is actually waiting alone. Like sleep, waiting cannot be shared—by playing games or telling stories, for instance; it can only be outsmarted individually" (43). In the foreword to the English translation of the essay, Mark Lilla remarks in the same vein that, as we wait, "we then experience our very selves. Just as no one can take a bath for you, no one can wait for you" (14). I disagree. In reality, cultural forces—and thus collective dynamics—suffuse the act of waiting from the start. The emotions we feel, be they pleasant or unpleasant, derive from these very forces and what place they have assigned us in the social food chain. One doesn't wait alone but always with the cultural forces that predetermine what waiting is, means, and does in the first place. And if it involves "our very selves," it is only in the ways these selves get policed.

When one doesn't know how to wait, destructive forces can run rampant and make society unsafe for all of us. The ability to wait—that is, to make oneself wait—presumably becomes the vector of self-discipline, without which no sociality can exist at all. In modern, democratic societies, power is no longer exercised by the sovereign over the people but by the people over themselves. The antechamber is now located in ourselves. For the most part, when our (democratic) governments urge us to wait patiently at home until we can safely start to return to our normal lives, they are of course acting reasonably given the circumstances, and one would be wise to abide by their recommendations. But beyond and above our current situation, what governments ask us is to defer the satisfaction of our desires and to present that deferral as the mature, responsible, and civilized thing to do. The ability to wait isn't a self-redemptive virtue like any other; it is a sign of personal development and an engine of civilization. The genius of modernity consists in having merged these two dimensions—the individual and the societal—into one. As Michel Foucault asserts in his later work on what he terms "governmentality," modern Western subjects learn how to self-discipline, exonerating governments from their duties toward the people as a result. Calling some people irresponsible, as we have repeatedly observed during this pandemic, allows governments, local or not, to shift the burden of responsibility entirely, presenting themselves not as responsible leaders in charge of the situation but rather, as not responsible for any bad outcome.

To underscore that point, we demonize a college student on spring break who tells a TV reporter that he won't let the pandemic get in the way of his fun. From the safe and hyper-othering and objectifying perspective of a drone camera shot, we look down horrified at a crowd of young revelers on the streets of Daytona Beach or masses of bodies packing a swimming pool in the Ozarks. And each time, a local official comes on television to stress that these people, who are endangering the welfare of the community, are in fact outsiders, visitors from out of town—not "from here," not "us." In the early years of the AIDS pandemic, the "culprits," the modern poisoners of wells, were similarly designated as geographical, social, or sexual others who, having disrespected national, cultural, or behavioral boundaries, were now putting the rest of us at risk; as unrestrained pleasure seekers who turned away from mature forms of sexuality predicated on reproduction and the family; as compulsive travelers without roots or commitment to home and country whose very mobility suspiciously resembled that of the virus itself. And of course, we are constantly reminded that the whole COVID crisis was triggered by someone in a distant, nonwhite country that didn't respect the foundational separation between civilized human and wild animal.[7] As for the instances of so-called looting and the destruction of property that have occurred during a few of the protests following George Floyd's murder, many observers are prompt to dismiss these acts of uncontrolled violence as politically illegitimate.

And so as soon as countries and localities went into lockdown to slow the spread of the virus, officials deployed a rhetoric that appealed to our collective maturity and insisted on how trivial, how *inessential* the things we had to give up for a while actually were, if we took the time to think about it. Many a tweet, meme, or Facebook post, in the early days, reminded us that our elders had to put up with much worse during world wars and the like, and that having to sit on our couches watching Netflix looks like a small sacrifice in comparison. If we are to survive this as a city/country/planet, we are told, we must all behave like responsible adults and think in the long term for the benefit of all. When our own president speaks or behaves irresponsibly in the face of grave risks, critics emphasize his impulsiveness and childishness, contrasting him with someone like National Institute of Allergy and Infectious Diseases director Anthony Fauci—the voice of reason and knowledge that vouches not only for Fauci's own maturity but for that of the culture that was built on these very principles. As a modern Western nation, we want to recognize ourselves in the wise scientist, not in a president with no consideration for factual truths and who is famously unable to restrain his impulses and contain his words.

To the extent, then, that the injunction to wait appeals to the very foundations of what makes us a functioning community, and not simply to our mettle in the face of exceptional circumstances, it inevitably spills beyond its stated limits. Why not wait forever? In "Waiting Out the Crisis," anthropologist Ghassan Hage has observed how some cultures exalt the ability to wait out a crisis together as a form of heroism that signals one's belonging to the community. Conversely, those unable or unwilling to endure unfortunate but temporary circumstances "like the rest of us" (102) are thought to set themselves apart from the group. Hage reminds us of Jean-Paul Sartre's example of a queue at a bus stop forming a "series" of people who remain indifferent to and isolated from each other and thus do not form the sort of collectives whose agency would make them difficult to govern.[8] And Hage concludes:

> Crisis today is no longer felt as an unusual state [but] is a kind of permanent state of exception. In this sense, enduring the crisis becomes the normal mode of being a good citizen and the more one is capable of enduring a crisis the more of a good citizen one is. As usual, this takes on a racial, civilizational and class dimension: the ones who do not know how to wait are the "lower classes," the uncivilized and racialized others. (104)

For Sartre, the moment a series of mutually alienated people begins to fuse, the newly formed group radically threatens the order of things. And this, comments Alain Badiou in his reading of Sartre, can only happen when prompted by external factors:

> It is worth noting that Sartre, borrowing an expression from Malraux, calls this event an apocalypse. The apocalypse means that the series dissolves into a fused group. The mediation this requires is itself partly external: it is the awareness of its intolerable nature that dissolves the series and creates a new reciprocity. If, for example, the bus we are waiting for in passive indifference does not come along, there will be protests and mutterings. People will start to talk to each other about the inhumanity of their external conditioning. (22–23)

As I wrote earlier, and as we've all heard many times, we're waiting to see what life will be like "on the other side of this." But this begs the question, which I posed at the outset: What if "this" has no other side?

Consider, for example, the two very different waves of protests that the refusal to wait any longer has spurred since the lockdown started. First, far-right activists and other Trump supporters, almost all of them white and some armed, staged relatively small rallies in state capitals, starting with Lansing, Michigan, and targeting primarily states run by Democratic governors who had imposed some degree of restrictions on the population. Advocating for individual freedom, most participants in these rallies defiantly refused to wear the protective face masks that, for them, have come to symbolize government overreach. Some went as far as planning to kidnap and kill a governor and other elected officials. Their slogan: "Liberate Michigan!" (or some other blue state). The second wave of protests, as we know, followed the murder of a Black man, George Floyd, by the Minneapolis police and called for a radical rethinking of law enforcement. The event eventually triggered a deep reconsideration of racism in America's past, present, and future. With a focus on community and unity, nearly all participants wore face masks, which in this case became markers of care and consideration for others. Their slogan: "Black Lives Matter!"

For the white nationalist pro-Trump protesters, the wait itself induced suffering, and they demanded that it end so that they might pick up their lives where they left them off. They were not exactly waiting *for* anything other than a return to the past as it was. I imagine that, to them, the present had become an experiment in lack, and they possibly experienced stay-at-home injunctions as emasculating. Women are the ones who are supposed to wait at home, not men. The anxiety that this feeling of feminization triggered manifested itself as masculinist self-destructiveness, a quasi-fascist mode of negative heroics perhaps best embodied by Trump's own nihilistic defiance in the face of reason and science. The second protesters, on the other hand, are asking for certain old practices to stop and for new ones to be invented in their stead. For a long time now they have been expecting something to arrive—namely, racial justice—and they are tired of waiting for it. Interestingly, the specific and especially horrific violence long suffered by trans people of color became the theme of a June 14 rally in Brooklyn that was attended by thousands. To them, the present is filled with possibility and promise, including in matters of gender and sexuality.

As we have seen, the refusal to wait, even when it takes the form of a collective rebellion, does not in itself bespeak progressive politics—or politics at all, for that matter. Yet both kinds of protests have been disruptive in their own way in that they threw a monkey wrench into the modes of governmentality embodied in waiting. The first protesters were criticized by some as low-class and irresponsible far-right activists; the second, by others, as far-left race rioters and anarchists hell-bent on sowing chaos. Both have been dismissed to some extent as politically immature, either because they brought military-style assault rifles into government buildings, for example, or for demanding that the police be completely abolished.

But as implied by the modern notion of developmental maturation—be it personal, cultural, or political—the suspension of time that waiting embodies isn't just about the present moment; it is also about the future, of course. I wrote earlier that waiting can feel like a gestation period. I don't want to make too much of the fact that the historical period I have been invoking also produced our current apparatus of sexual norms, reproductive ideology and mandatory heterosexuality, as Michel Foucault tells us,[9] but I didn't choose the gestation metaphor at random either. With patience and our souls at rest, Köhler notes, "The great idea lies in wait" (73), and "Something is brewing within us" (74). Even if one does not subscribe to such nineteenth-century Romantic notions of creativity (after all, stupid or simply small ideas lie in wait far more often than great ones), the truth is that when we are waiting, even for the bus, the present moment finds itself defined by the future, filled with something that hasn't happened yet, may still never happen, but that we envision with varying degrees of intensity and affect depending on what it is exactly that we are waiting for. Clearly, unless we are running late to something truly urgent, waiting for the bus will not feel as emotionally charged as waiting for news of a loved one with COVID. Either way, as we are in the process of waiting, the present—that is, the only temporality we can ever be said to actually experience—is brimming with something that doesn't exist, something like fiction. Barthes, again, beautifully renders the sort of world-making that we engage in as we wait for the one we love and invent all kinds of scenarios to explain why they haven't arrived yet. Waiting can indeed spur invention. Köhler sees the daydreaming of children made to wait as "our first exercise in utopian thinking" (40).

In the first phase of what we could call the COVID moment (I see the ensuing uprising for racial justice as the second and concurrent phase of that moment rather than a separate occurrence), a large portion of our time has been filled with questions about what the future will hold after the pandemic.

We know that professional activities will start again, but under what conditions? How many will never get their job or their business back? I'm an academic living in a college town. As of this writing, I do not have any idea what the next semester will look like in terms of teaching. And will this crisis hasten the demise of my favorite used bookshops and record stores? The owners of the one and only gay bar in Ann Arbor have already announced that they will not be reopening the place. Will giant corporations take over the entire town? We expect that our lives will be different *after*, but we don't yet know how; we try to imagine, with trepidations sometimes and at other times with hope. But we can also create.

More explicitly perhaps than introspection and maturation, envisioning the future—the third aspect of waiting under COVID—is fraught with politics. And in that respect, the aftermath of George Floyd's murder has worked as an astonishing accelerant that all of a sudden has radically upended expectations. Given the mistakes and even gross incompetence that characterized government responses to the pandemic around the world, so many of them caught unprepared by an event numerous epidemiologists and others had long forecasted, much of the conversation about the future has turned around how to be ready next time. We expect, or hope, that some leaders will eventually pay the price for their failures, probably at the ballot box. But until the sudden irruption of demands for racial justice, the talk remained focused on improving our current systems, not on radically changing them. In this context, too, the rhetoric of perfectibility falls in line with the framework of modernity and its political expression in the form of liberal democracy—a project whose existence depends precisely on its perpetual incompletion. Individuals and societies must thrive for betterment, aspire to perfection. But because a society predicated on perfectibility can never achieve perfection without destroying itself at the same time, our goals must never be attained. We must wait forever. Nothing is more politically dangerous than the refusal to wait.

We may still lack the necessary historical distance to explain what exactly made the murder of George Floyd at the hands of a white police officer ignite into nationwide, and then worldwide, protests. In the context of the pandemic, however, the prospect of having to wait quietly for yet another dismissal of charges or a non-guilty verdict may have felt unbearable. But the irruption of the protests undoubtedly owes to the fact that African Americans and Latinxs have been disproportionately affected by the pandemic, contracting the virus, becoming sicker, and dying from it at far higher rates than whites. Not to mention that poorer Black and brown people often perform what we have started to call essential tasks, which put them at greater risk of infection, while they do not possess the economic clout or union representation that would allow them to demand safer working conditions and remuneration commensurate with the value of their labor. The odious murder of an unarmed Black man, one in a long and disgusting series, happened on top of that reality. Whereas the COVID-19 pandemic may have initially appeared to place everyone at equal risk with its plague-like randomness, the reality of course is that, like almost all epidemics before it, this one has preyed more ruthlessly on some of the most socially vulnerable. In that sense, COVID-19 has a lot in common with HIV/AIDS, and I'd like to turn now to that not-so-ancient history for useful insights into the current moment.

The first thing to keep in mind about the HIV/AIDS pandemic is that it hasn't ended yet. We are still waiting for a cure and a vaccine almost forty years into the known epidemic. Ask Dr. Fauci; he was there. For some of us, watching him on TV again feels a bit like reconnecting with an old acquaintance. I remember the sobering announcements, back then, about the unique difficulties that a retrovirus such as HIV presents, and that we should be very patient because it might take as long as five years to develop a vaccine. Five years . . . I remember the miracle treatments and the "This is it!" moments and all the other false hopes, and today I feel like telling my younger or straighter friends not to pay too much attention to up-to-the-minute developments on the COVID research front. Those of us who were formed politically by the AIDS crisis understand the fragility and transience of knowledge in the midst of a frightening pandemic. And we know that, if they're going to ask for our patience, demand it even, scientists must appear to know something we don't about the future. Even if they don't.

The second thing to remember about the HIV/AIDS pandemic is that, today, African American and Latino gay men as well as men who have sex with men (MSM)[10] are still at far greater risk of contracting the virus and dying from its complications than anyone else, with white gay men and MSM coming third and African American women fourth. Transgender people have also seen an increase in infection. With the opioid crisis of the past several years, HIV incidence has risen in poor, rural, white populations, which prompted a rapid national reaction and a surge in policy decisions from the very politicians, such as then-governor of Indiana Mike Pence, who had done their utmost to impede the fight against HIV. But African Americans have remained uniquely vulnerable to a disease that hardly anyone wants to talk about anymore but that still killed 15,820 people in this country in 2018—a quarter of a century after the arrival of very effective life-prolonging treatments.[11] Anyone thinking that COVID-19 has *revealed* the racial inequalities embedded in American health care clearly hasn't been paying attention. When it comes to HIV/AIDS, we're definitely not in this together and never have been. There were no history-making banner headlines on the front pages of the *New York Times* and the rest of the country's newspapers when the number of AIDS-related deaths reached one hundred thousand sometime in 1990. In 1983, Larry Kramer, the playwright and AIDS activist who died recently, wrote a now-famous column in a gay publication, the *New York Native*, entitled "1,112 and Counting." This is 2020 now, more than seven hundred thousand people have died of AIDS in the United States, and we're still counting.

Larry Kramer's exhortation conveyed one central message: we cannot wait. As a cofounder of the AIDS activist group ACT UP–New York in 1987, he once gave a speech before which he asked two-thirds of the people in attendance to stand up, telling them they would all be dead within five years. And then he said, "If my speech tonight doesn't scare the shit out of you, we're in real trouble. If what you're hearing doesn't rouse you to anger, fury, rage, and action, gay men will have no future here on earth. How long does it take before you get angry and fight back?"[12] With its slogan "Silence = Death," ACT UP called on us to turn into raging queens and embarked not only on a series of spectacular public actions but also on a radical critique of the systemic causes of the AIDS pandemic, such as homophobia, racism, mass incarceration, the policing of drug use, immigration policies, the criminalization of sex work, and so on. Predictably, the activists were criticized from the right for being too impatient and violent, and from the left for being naive and politically immature. The impact of AIDS on vulnerable minority communities and their very association with the disease may have been initially clearer than that of COVID, which in fact explains government inaction and public indifference, but Black Lives Matter today, like ACT UP back then, reminds us that, in an exclusionary system, anything harmful that occurs will always harm the excluded most. And now we hear that COVID will exacerbate HIV-related problems. One pandemic feeding off another. "The virus doesn't discriminate," they said then and they say now. Like hell it doesn't. Anyone affected by AIDS knows that. Waiting = Death.

Köhler's and Lilla's conception of waiting as essentially subjective and unshareable rests on the affective dimension of the experience, which they understand as somehow universal in nature and, save for its material conditions, outside the reach of history. As Lilla writes, "The child who cries when his mother leaves the room gets his first lesson in life: we wait alone" (14). But who is this "we" exactly? As I suggested earlier, the autonomous self that is invoked in such dehistoricizing statements is nothing more than a specifically modern Western construct claiming universality. And mainstream discourses often present stay-at-home isolation during the pandemic as an individual or private experience, endlessly mirrored and visually rendered on computer screens during Zoom sessions, so as to appear to confirm its universality. We recognize that differences exist, of course. Unequal gender roles, risks of domestic violence, hunger, and mental health issues may affect some people and not others during the pandemic, but separation seems to remain a uniting factor no matter what your circumstances. Yet any member of a group that has been socially marginalized precisely by being denied access to this dominant model of selfhood possesses the ability to experience something like waiting as relational rather than isolating.

Waiting specifically as a member of a group differs both from what we may call existential waiting (such as waiting for God, death, and the like) and from strictly situational waiting ( for the bus, for the doors to open, etc.). For a marginalized group, instances such as waiting for a cure for AIDS or for a rise in the minimum wage, while neither universal nor individual, are inherently political. As John Rundell remarks in "Temporal Horizons of Modernity and Modalities of Waiting": "In modernity, because there are multiple worlds, there are also multiple boundary positions, multiple forms of waiting, and hence multiple forms of unease" (45). In other words, within the disjointed experience that is this modernity, different kinds of people experience time and relate to the future in different ways. Think, for example, of queers without children; of young African Americans with narrower social expectations and a shorter life expectancy than their white peers; of girls who keep hearing that they can achieve anything they put their mind to when in reality most cannot; of migrants and refugees in search of a better future (or simply a future); of trans people whose transitioning ushers in the person they have in fact always been; of low-income people living from paycheck to paycheck; of old people who, well, you know . . . Even medical ethics mandates that, if limited, care be given by priority to those who can reasonably expect to have a longer future, as if a young Hitler might be worthier of saving than a mature Nina Simone. And who remembers the complete indifference that met the so-called junkie pneumonia that decimated IV-drug users in New York City in the late 1970s and turned out to have been AIDS? What future did these people have anyway, right?

It bears repeating that, just like anti-Black racism in the United States, AIDS was and remains genocidal in nature. This belief, which I have expounded on in my work over the years, finds an early and near perfect expression in the passage from Leo Bersani's famous essay, "Is the Rectum a Grave?," in which Bersani encapsulates the principle that even though the Reagan administration—or any other government—did not engineer the AIDS pandemic the way the Nazis organized and perpetrated the extermination of the Jews, its systematic indifference amounted nonetheless to the sort of genocide always contained in the thought that if some segment or other of the population did not exist, the rest of us would be better off. As Bersani puts it:

> At the very least, such things as the Justice Department's near recommendation that people with AIDS be thrown out of their jobs suggest that if Edwin Meese would not hold a gun to the head of a man with AIDS, he might not find the murder of a gay man with AIDS (or without AIDS?) intolerable or unbearable. And this is precisely what can be said of millions of fine Germans who never participated in the murder of Jews (and of homosexuals), but who *failed to find the idea of the holocaust unbearable.* (201)

I don't think I ever felt more connected to a collective sense of gayness than I did during the worst years of the AIDS crisis. I never felt less alone than when we, as a group, had been marked as expendable; when we, as a group, feared not just death but extinction; and when we, as a group, waited for a cure. This communitarian form of waiting produced an awareness of how situated—that is, neither individual nor universal—the experience of AIDS actually was at the time. My fears, my sadness, my rage never felt like mine alone back then the way it does now. When ACT UP demanded that we turn our grief into anger, they didn't deny affect; they turned it inside out, as it were, and made it collective and thus political. On January 22 and 23, 1991, for instance, ACT UP–New York coordinated a number of spectacular public actions in a "Day of Desperation"—a name ACT UP–Paris kept for their yearly World AIDS Day march—overturning what we normally understand by desperation, one of the most isolating of emotions. As etymology reminds us, desperation entails no hoping but also no waiting. The activists even moved the work of mourning from the realm of the psyche and into the streets in what they termed political funerals, during which a coffin could be walked down a city street and a lover's ashes scattered over the White House lawn.[13] And the literature of AIDS often consisted of first-person memoirs by gay men who were themselves about to die, but who first told the stories of those no longer able to, making each book a collective autobiography that not only spoke to its gay readers but also included them in the collective experience.[14] Similarly, many African American men likely hear the stories of Trayvon Martin, Eric Garner, Michael Brown,

Tamir Rice, Philando Castile, Ahmaud Arbery, George Floyd, and Rayshard Brooks, whose name I had to add to the list as I revised this essay, and know that it is theirs too and that only by telling these stories repeatedly can they have a chance to postpone and perhaps avoid meeting the same fate. "Say his name," goes the injunction in Black Lives Matter events, an injunction now complemented by the African American Policy Forum's #SayHerName campaign after the police killing of Breonna Taylor and other Black women. When contemplating the possibility of extinction, telling stories means more than recording the past; it conveys the possibility of the future.

The tale of Scheherazade comes to mind. Predictably, Köhler and Lilla read her story as a parable for the human condition and the singularity of the waiting experience.[15] Canadian queer filmmaker John Greyson, however, makes a very different use of the old tale in his 1993 musical *Zero Patience*. For him, and for his characters, the Arabian princess becomes an inspiration and a symbol of resistance in the face of AIDS. Early in the movie, we meet a character named Zero. Inspired by Patient Zero, a much-demonized gay flight attendant whose sexual promiscuity was said to have hastened the spread of HIV in North America, Zero has already died when the story begins. But his ghost sings a song that urges us to clear his name and to keep repeating his story—a story that, when watching the movie in 1993, the audience understands to be that of all the people with AIDS, already dead or likely to be soon: "Tell the tale / Save my life / A life I could have had / Just like Scheherazade / Tell the story / Tell the story." While in the title song, these words in the first person are sung by a group of AIDS "terrorists" who vandalize a natural history museum with an HIV exhibit: "If patience is a virtue, then I'm a sinner from hell / 'cause I only want one thing, I just want to be well / Well now / If patience is a virtue, then I've got none."[16] Scheherazade turns storytelling into a tactic of postponing death. For communities facing the genocidal threat of AIDS, it becomes a way to reaffirm the collective dimension of waiting or refusing to wait and, with that, envision the possibility of a future for, if not all individual members perhaps, the collectivity that makes gay lives possible in the first place.

Like waiting itself, storytelling is as much about the future as it is about the past. Anticipation, hope, dread, and similar emotions that imply causality anchor waiting to a logic of continuity connecting past and future. Fiction, on the other hand, may be untethered from linear logic and envision something that doesn't exist but perhaps could. Unlike monuments, such as the statues of slave traders and Confederate generals that have been coming down this summer and are but markers of institutional oblivion and rewriting, stories of past and present injustices, in particular, aim to go beyond mere memorialization. As the singing ghost in *Zero Patience* suggests, the kind of memory these stories intend to produce may feel like haunting and entail a disordering of time. The dead entrust us with a mission not just to seek justice for past misdeeds but to establish it for the future. And given that justice must not be incomplete if it is to be at all, such a quest cannot be incremental. Justice either is or isn't, which makes it different from our modern notions of rights. African Americans have rights, but they do not have justice. Activist storytelling may thus become the vector of political imagination and a form of world-making.

Indeed, one of the most striking outcomes of the story of George Floyd spreading around the world has been the conversation about abolishing the police—an example of and a call for radical political imagination as the only way forward after decades of useless reforms and incremental progress. The history of policing in the United States shows that African Americans have always been defined as "those who must be policed and not helped." The French government's policies during the COVID crisis pointed to a very similar and equally perverse logic. When the authorities mandated that people stay confined at home unless they had a compelling reason not to—such as buying food or medication and performing an essential task—anyone leaving home had to carry a self-written note justifying why they were outside. One may be tempted to laugh at this ridiculous manifestation of France's love of paperwork, but in reality the move served to make everyone subject to policing. And the usual profiling practices made police controls far worse for minorities in poorer, less white, and already disproportionately policed neighborhoods. The message was clear and revealing. The fact that the people must serve the police and not the other way round doesn't result from some malfunction of the system; it inheres in the system and guarantees its perpetuation. To demand, then, that the police force be defunded, or even abolished as we know it, signals a departure from the modern idea of perfectibility at the core of all reforms. The story of George Floyd, and with it those of all the other victims of police brutality, doesn't call for progress but for discontinuity, for disruption.

I wrote earlier that to wait had a different meaning before the modern era and that etymology reminds us of the old bond between waiting and caring. As I hope I have managed to convey in these pages, the modern shift in meaning betrays a profound and pernicious cultural shift in focus toward an inner sense of self and away from understandings—and practices—of being as relational. If I am drawing attention to a word's history, I am not implying that we should restore its obsolete senses, let alone return somehow to modes of social relations that organized premodern cultures. Rather, by reminding ourselves of the lives that words could have had, we can allow the ghosts of meanings past to haunt and destabilize the present and envision a future in which the injunction to wait would remain attached to the duty to care—that is, to watch out for injustice and to attend to the needs of others. Many of us live in societies that work to amplify vulnerability, not alleviate it. This isn't anything new, of course, especially in times of plagues and mass migrations, but one of the most noxious teachings that the AIDS crisis has entrenched in our cultures is the unquestioned principle that we must protect ourselves from those weaker than we are. In that respect, that pandemic was emblematic of the reactionary turn that also started forty years ago. With this pandemic and the murder of George Floyd resonating in cities around the world, are we now witnessing the beginning of something else at long last? Haven't we waited long enough?

### Notes

1. King, "Letter from Birmingham Jail."

2. For a fascinating overview of these developments in the nineteenth century, see Doane, *Emergence of Cinematic Time.*

3. We now know the identity of the man in the picture—and for that matter the fact that he is indeed a man—thanks to the investigation that followed the leaks of the photographs and videos taken at Abu Ghraib. Understandably, many who have written on the story think that using the man's name helps restore the humanity that his torturers sought to erase. I respect that view and would never claim that it is somehow erroneous. As precisely a view, it can neither be proven nor disproven. That said, I choose not to name the man for two reasons. First, he did not himself come out as the man on the photo and never sought public attention. He was outed. Personally, if the image of my torment had been displayed all over the world as his was, I know I wouldn't want my identity revealed. Second, I think that, in certain discourses, the idea that a name humanizes a person ultimately stems from the modern Western valorization of the individual subject and/as its self-realizing autonomy. As a scholar who understands personhood in other than humanist terms, I find this notion ontologically problematic. In my view—and again I make no truth claim here—a person doesn't require a name, or a gender, or a face, to be (considered) fully human.

4. "Les SS en pèlerines noires sont passées. Elles ont compté. On attend encore. / On attend. / Depuis des jours, le jour suivant. / Depuis la veille, le lendemain. / Depuis le milieu de la nuit, aujourd'hui. / On attend. / Le jour s'annonce au ciel. / On attend le jour parce qu'il faut attendre quelque chose. / On n'attend pas la mort. On s'y attend.

/ On n'attend rien. / On attend ce qui arrive. La nuit parce qu'elle succède au jour. Le jour parce qu'il succède à la nuit. / On attend la fin de l'appel" (Delbo, *Auschwitz et après*, 1:37).

5. I thank Blake Gutt for his help with this particular point.

6. The unfolding climate catastrophe raises similar questions, as it starts to affect everyday lives in measurable ways.

7. Just as the novel coronavirus is believed to have crossed the animal-human boundary in a Chinese wet market selling and butchering wild animals, such as bats, for human consumption, so too did HIV first infect humans who were killing chimpanzees for food in Cameroon.

8. In *Critique of Dialectical Reason*, I am using Sartre's example because it concerns waiting, obviously, but his analysis reaches beyond this and takes aim at various forms of social activities that bring people together only on the surface and actually enforce isolation and political impotence.

9. See Foucault, *The History of Sexuality*, vol. 1: *An Introduction*.

10. The distinction between "gay men" and "men who have sex with men" in HIV/AIDS prevention work became crucial with the realization that many men who seek same-sex sexual encounters do not tend to identify as gay and are therefore not receiving or processing information designed with gay men in mind.

11. For more detailed information, see https://www.hiv.gov/hiv-basics/overview/data-and-trends/statistics and https://www.cdc.gov/hiv/basics/statistics.html

12. See https://en.wikipedia.org/wiki/Larry_Kramer

13. For more on the central role affect played in ACT UP, see Gould, *Moving Politics*. On ACT UP–Paris specifically, see Broqua, *Action = Vie*.

14. On what he calls "dual autobiography in AIDS memoirs," see Chambers, *Untimely Interventions*.

15. How Köhler can describe the eventual wedding of Scheherazade with a serial killer of women as a happy ending is rather disturbing (*Passing Time*, 44, 47).

16. All music and lyrics by Glenn Schellenberg.

## References

Adam, Barbara. *Timescapes of Modernity: The Environment and Invisible Hazards*. London: Routledge, 1998.

Badiou, Alain. *Pocket Pantheon: Figures of Postwar Philosophy*. Translated by David Macey. New York: Verso, 2009. Translation of *Petit panthéon portatif*. Paris: La Fabrique, 2008.

Barthes, Roland. *A Lover's Discourse: Fragments*. New York: Hill and Wang, 1978. Translated by Richard Howard. Translation of *Fragments d'un discours amoureux*. Paris: Seuil, 1977.

Bersani, Leo. "Is the Rectum a Grave?" *October* 43 (Winter 1987): 197–222.

Broqua, Christophe. *Action = Vie: A History of AIDS Activism and Gay Politics in France*. Philadelphia: Temple University Press, 2020.

Chambers, Ross. *Untimely Interventions: AIDS Writing, Testimonial, and the Rhetoric of Haunting*. Ann Arbor: University of Michigan Press, 2004.

Delbo, Charlotte. *Auschwitz and After*. New Haven: Yale University Press, 1995. Translated by Rosette C. Lamont. Translation of *Auschwitz et après*. 3 vols. Paris: Minuit, 1970–71.

Doane, Mary Ann. *The Emergence of Cinematic Time: Modernity, Contingency, the Archive*. Cambridge, MA: Harvard University Press, 2002.

Foucault, Michel. *The History of Sexuality*. Vol. 1: *An Introduction*. Translated by Robert Hurley. New York: Vintage Books, 1980. Translation of *La volonté de savoir*. Paris: Gallimard, 1976.

Gould, Deborah B. *Moving Politics: Emotion and ACT Up's Fight against AIDS*. Chicago: University of Chicago Press, 2009.

Greyson, John, dir. *Zero Patience*. 1993.

Hage, Ghassan, ed. *Waiting*. Melbourne: Melbourne University Press, 2009.

Hage, Ghassan. "Waiting Out the Crisis: On Stuckedness and Governmentality." In *Waiting*, edited by Ghassan Hage, 97–106. Melbourne: Melbourne University Press, 2009.

King, Martin Luther, Jr. "Letter from Birmingham Jail." https://www.africa.upenn.edu /Articles_Gen/Letter_Birmingham.html. Accessed June 4, 2020.

Köhler, Andrea. *Passing Time: An Essay on Waiting*. Translated by Michael Eskin. New York: Upper West Side Philosophers, 2011. Translation of *Lange Weile: Über das Warten*. Leipzig: Intel Verlag, 2007.

Puff, Helmut. "Waiting in the Antechamber." In *Timescapes of Waiting: Spaces of Stasis, Delay and Deferral*, edited by Christoph Singer, Robert Wirth, and Olaf Berwald, 17–34. Boston: Brill / Rodopi, 2019.

Robins, Rosemary. "Waiting for Rain in the Goulburn Valley." In *Waiting*, edited by Ghassan Hage, 76–85. Melbourne: Melbourne University Press, 2009.

Rundell, John. "Temporal Horizons of Modernity and Modalities of Waiting." In *Waiting*, edited by Ghassan Hage, 39–53. Melbourne: Melbourne University Press, 2009.

Sartre, Jean-Paul. *Critique of Dialectical Reason*. Translated by Alan Sheridan-Smith. London: NLB, 1976. Translation of *Critique de la raison dialectique*. Paris: Gallimard, 1960.

Schweizer, Harold. *On Waiting*. New York: Routledge, 2008.

# CHAPTER 6

# Buddhism, the Pandemic, and the Demise of the Future Tense

*Donald Lopez*

What does it mean when the things that we teach in the classroom come true? I have asked myself this question over the past year as our world has been stricken with an unfamiliar form of suffering, a suffering that somehow seems new. Yet Buddhists have analyzed the nature of suffering for more than two millennia. Although we have learned, with good reason, to be skeptical about eternal truths, Buddhism may have something to offer as we ponder our particular pain.

Almost every fall for the past thirty years, I have taught a course called Introduction to Buddhism. Early in the semester, I spend a week on what is probably the most famous Buddhist doctrine: the Four Noble Truths. According to tradition, this was the Buddha's first sermon after his enlightenment under the Bodhi Tree, delivered to a group of five ascetics in a place called the Deer Park outside the city of Varanasi in northern India. One prominent Buddhist school places this epochal event in 531 BCE.

Each of the four truths is typically rendered by a single abstract noun: suffering, origin, cessation, and path. As the Buddha's first teaching, these four words are the subject of considerable commentary, but one might gloss them to say that (1) life is qualified by suffering, (2) there is a cause of that suffering, (3) there is a state in which suffering has ceased, and (4) there is a path to that state. Of the three or four hours I spend talking about the four noble truths each fall, about half ends up being devoted to the first: suffering. There I explain that the Buddha enumerated eight types of suffering that humans must undergo: birth, aging, sickness, death, losing friends, making enemies, not getting what you want, and getting what you don't want.

There is another description of suffering that one finds in Buddhist texts—a description that is at once more philosophically interesting and more unnerving—called the three types of suffering: the suffering of pain, the suffering of change, and the suffering of conditioning. The first is what is evoked by the word "suffering" in English: pain in the body and pain in the mind. The other two are less intuitive, and more pertinent to our moment.

The "suffering of change" does not refer to the obvious fact that things change but to a very different claim: that pleasure and pain, far from being relative categories, are qualitatively different. Feelings of pain remain painful, but feelings of pleasure eventually turn into pain; that any activity that is pleasurable will, if done long enough, become painful. The examples given in Buddhist texts are things we have all experienced: feeling cold and so going outside to sit in the sun. The feeling of warmth, initially pleasant, becomes unpleasant when it gets too hot, and one has to go back inside, where one feels the pleasure of the cool interior, before getting cold and having to go outside again. We can think of any number of examples of pleasure becoming pain: the feeling of articulate inebriation that becomes word-slurring drunkenness; the feeling of satiation at the end of a meal that, with just one more bite, becomes nausea. Many of us have likely thought how nice it would be not to have to go into campus for an entire month. After several months of this particular pleasure, it has become a form of suffering. In many ways, the admonitions to moderation, to the golden mean, to knowing when to stop, admonitions that we find throughout the wisdoms of the world, seem to certify the existence of the suffering of change.

The third form of suffering, the most subtle, the most pernicious, is called the suffering of conditioning. It means that we are so conditioned as to be susceptible to suffering in the next instant, an instant over which we have no control. The most obvious example of this is the fact that none of us can say with complete certainty that we will not die today. In the Buddhist view, there are two reasons for our irresolution. One is karma, the law of the cause and effect of actions, the idea that the things that we do in the present—good and bad—bear fruit in the form of our future experience, experiences of pleasure and of pain. The other reason is impermanence, the idea that things change, a fact that in Buddhism inspires dread. Buddhist texts speak of coarse impermanence and subtle impermanence. The first is breaking a teacup, a power outage, a lost love. More consequential is subtle impermanence, a constant process of disintegration happening at such a rapid rate that it remains invisible to our ordinary sight. The suffering of conditioning goes unnoticed by those untrained to see it. But for those with eyes to see, it is unbearable. In a particularly potent metaphor, it is said that for the foolish, the suffering of conditioning is like a wisp of wool in the palm of hand, so weightless and insubstantial that they do not even know that it is there. For the wise, the suffering of conditioning is like a wisp of wool in the eye, causing immediate pain and distraction, preventing one from doing anything else until it has been removed. It seems that many of us have a wisp of wool in our eyes these days.

The wisp of wool has consequences that are not enumerated in the Buddhist canon. It elicits all manner of questions, both consequential and banal, all expressed in the future tense. When will I return to the office? When will the children return to school? When will I see my mother again? When will I see my friends again, unmediated and unmasked? When will we meet? When will we hug? When will we kiss? Will I get sick? We ask the questions. We don't know the answers.

The wisp of wool is not the virus; the virus is a case of the suffering of pain. The wisp of wool is the fact that we have no control over the future, no matter what models we construct, no matter what scenarios we project, no matter what plans we make. It has always been that way, but we have been deceived by the illusion of continuity, believing that because things look the same, they are the same. Now the wind has blown the wisp of wool out of our hand and into our eye. We no longer feel confident speaking in the future tense.

These insights about the nature of change are said to have been set forth by the Buddha, who lived twenty-five hundred years ago. Scholars are unsure of his precise dates, speculating that many Buddhist doctrines that are traditionally ascribed to him in fact were articulated long after his death. Still, we can be fairly confident that this idea of the suffering of conditioning is at least two thousand years old. If that is the case, how can it be anything but a cultural artifact, something taught in Introduction to Buddhism?

From our study of history, we understand how the events of a particular time and place shape pronouncements about the world: how the principal author of the Declaration of Independence was a lifelong slaveholder, how Marx's theory of capital derived from the conditions of the English factory, how Freud's theory of the unconscious derived from the culture of fin-de-siècle Vienna. Those historical circumstances are more difficult to reconstruct the farther we go back in time. Such insights are particularly difficult in the case of the Buddha, where nothing that he taught was written down for three or four hundred years after his death. That does not mean that they do not derive from a particular time and a particular place. Indeed, some scholars have speculated that the Buddhist emphasis on, even obsession with, suffering suggests that there was widespread famine in northern India during his life. Yet his enumeration of the sufferings of humans—birth, aging, sickness, death, losing friends, making enemies, not getting what you want,

and getting what you do not want—somehow seems to describe our own sufferings, us, the denizens of the digital age. What follows from that?

When I teach Introduction to Buddhism, I ask the students to do something difficult. I ask them to try to simultaneously perform two mental activities: analysis and imagination. Analysis is what we do as scholars. It allows us
to make connections and uncover causes that are not immediately evident,
to see, for example, evidence of the role of gender and social class in so many
Buddhist doctrines, to see, in other words, that pronouncements about the
timeless are made in time. But if we rely only on analysis, we prevent ourselves from seeing, or at least imagining, what it is about this tradition that
has inspired millions across Asia for two millennia, to imagine, for example,
what it would be like to believe in rebirth and how that would change the
sense of who we are, and who others are. But something seems different now,
especially for those who thought they had some shield against suffering. We
no longer need to imagine what it would be like to believe that we are subject
to radical change in the next moment. The inability to speak in the future
tense with any confidence is no longer an ancient Buddhist doctrine.

Now that the stakes are high, the Buddhist claim that we ultimately have
no control over the next moment seems, for want of a better word, to be true.
Yet to acknowledge the truth of a religious claim is taboo. It is something
that scholars of the humanities are taught not to do; all truth claims are to be
understood in their social, political, and cultural context. This is particularly
the case in the study of religion. In the American academy, the discipline of
religious studies is relatively recent, emerging after the Second World War.
It evolved on the model of the divinity school and the seminary, where Prot-
estant and Catholic clergy are trained. Indeed, it was common in the early
years of departments of religious studies that a number of faculty would
be ordained ministers. Even for them, however, it was important to draw a
line between apologetics and arguments, between theology and philology,
between religion and religious studies. And yet, in this year of the plague, the
line between professing and praying has become difficult to discern. A doctrine of Buddhism—a religion long condemned by Christian missionaries as
a form of idolatry—seems somehow to be true. And this discomfiting fact in
turn seems to be evidence of the truth of yet another Buddhist doctrine: the
suffering of change.

If we are to concede, or at least to imagine, that Buddhism might be right
about this, what are we to do? It is not, as some might expect, that we should
"live in the moment." This idea belongs not to the time of the Buddha but to
the New Age. For the Buddha, impermanence meant that there is nothing to

rely on in this world, that the ground is constantly falling away beneath our feet. It meant that there is constant change, and that change is ultimately beyond our control. For the Buddha, the suffering of conditioning meant that our only refuge is a changeless place, which he called nirvana, and which is not a place at all. The order of monks and nuns that he established began as an ascetic movement, made up of those who had renounced the world, taking vows of celibacy and forbidden from engaging in agriculture or commerce, so that they could devote their lives to the search for liberation. This is not something that most of us can do today, nor is it something that most Buddhists have done over the centuries. They have remained in the world, providing support to monks and nuns in hope of a better rebirth as a result of their charity, the wisp of wool remaining in their hands.

For those with the wisp in their eye, the future is not a time of hope but a time of horror. That horror can be avoided by recognizing that it is not just the earth that is disintegrating beneath our feet. Our bodies and our minds are disintegrating, not because we are growing old, getting sick, and dying of a disease but because we are only a series of moments, coming into existence and passing out of existence, a particular concoction of thoughts, sensations, and feelings, each changing all the time. For those with eyes to see, nothing in the mind or body lasts more than a blink of the eye. One fifth-century text describes this constant disintegration as like raindrops falling onto a stone courtyard during a downpour, each drop exploding as it strikes the ground.

This wisp of wool that is the suffering of conditioning raises a host of questions about personal identity, about the meaning of self. If nothing lasts longer than an instant, then, in a sense, there is no future for us. And there is no future for us because there is no us. Identity, for which so many have suffered in so many ways for so long, turns out to be an illusion. As soon as we recognize that we do not exist in the way that we have always imagined, that we do not exist in the way that we imagine ourselves in this year of politics and plague, then the future, and all the horror that it holds, will end. Then, at long last, there will be no more need for statements, declarative or interrogative, expressed in the future tense.

But what are we to do in the meantime? The fact that there is no self does not mean that there is no love, defined in Buddhism as the wish that others be happy. The fact there is no self does not mean that there is no compassion, defined in Buddhism as the wish that others be free from suffering. Indeed, it is the realization that we don't exist as we think we do that makes love and compassion possible. It is the realization that there is no self that makes it possible to dedicate our selfless selves to the liberation of others.

# CHAPTER 7

# COVID Diary

## Hands, Nets, and Other Devices

*James Cogswell*

### COVID DIARY: HANDS

As an artist, I live to make things, especially through the forming of materials with my own hands in the tangible, physical space within which I experience my own body and which I understand my self to inhabit. I use making as a form of thinking.

Figure 7.1. *Approaching Storm*, 2020. Sumi ink, shellac ink, walnut ink, watercolor, gouache, acrylic over digital drawing printed on paper, 30″ × 22″.

Making, for me, is a way of learning about the world and a way of learning about myself, a way of situating my self in the world among others. My making is essentially an investigative practice. What I make is the residue. What I make is always inflected by others, by what has transpired moments or millennia in the past in the constantly slipping Now that we inhabit together.

Hands are reminders of the constructed world and the laborers responsible for bringing it into being. We use hands as a form of communication to shape and express our inner states. They have limitless narrative potential. They give us away, revealing what we would prefer to keep to ourselves. Hands teach us to feel and to reason, to count and to indicate. Hands give us agency, as creators but also as destroyers. They give symbolic form to our willingness to act in the world. Hands can suggest both power and exchange— the raised fist and the clasp.

In the early days of the pandemic, as the world shrank around my sheltered isolation, connection evoked contagion. Points of contact with the world, my breath and my touch, were points of vulnerability. To move about in the world and to act within it was to become exposed.

On our winter academic break in New Mexico, I watched the approaching storm and responded with my hands. Two days after returning to campus in Ann Arbor, we went into lockdown.

Figure 7.2. *Hands 1*, 2020. Sumi ink, shellac ink, walnut ink, salt, watercolor, gouache, acrylic over digital drawing printed on paper, 10.5″ × 11″.

Figure 7.3. *Hands 2*, 2020. Sumi ink, shellac ink, walnut ink, salt, watercolor, gouache, acrylic over digital drawing printed on paper, 10.5″ × 11″.

Figure 7.4. *Hands 3*, 2020. Sumi ink, shellac ink, walnut ink, salt, watercolor, gouache, acrylic over digital drawing printed on paper, 9.5″ × 10.5″.

## COVID DIARY: NETS AND OTHER DEVICES

In the 1960s and 1970s, the Greek-Cypriot filmmaker Michael Cacoyannis cinematically adapted three tragedies by Euripides dealing with the Trojan War and its aftermath. At the time of their original staging, Athens was pursuing brutal wars of imperial ambition, among them an expedition to Sicily. Through his films based on those plays, Cacoyannis spoke to the turmoil resulting from the struggle for power and ideological dominance in Greece in his own time. In May 2020, I was scheduled to fly to Greece to install an adhesive vinyl frieze responding to this trilogy at the Michael Cacoyannis Foundation in Athens. My project was conceived three years earlier during the height of the immigration crisis in the Aegean, civil wars in nearby Syria and Iraq, and the deteriorating treatment of immigrants to the United States driven by the arrogant policies of our own leaders. While the COVID travel ban has forced a postponement of my installation, global events since early 2020 have only enlarged its narratives.

*Vinyl Euripides* thematically builds on the cinematic restaging of *Electra* (1962), *The Trojan Women* (1971), and *Iphigenia* (1977)—retold using my own vocabulary of images. *The Trojan Women* dwells on the enslavement of the women of Troy after the destruction of their city. In *Electra*, the murder of victorious Agamemnon after his return from Troy unleashes a chain reaction of violent revenge. *Iphigenia* explores the prequel to the war, Agamemnon's sacrifice of his daughter to expedite the sailing of his bloodthirsty invasion force. In all three films strong female protagonists face violence perpetrated by powerful men.

The making of Cacoyannis's three films coincided not only with civil conflict in Greece but also with international outrage over the spectacle of violence unfolding in Vietnam. Cacoyannis's native Cyprus was being partitioned after a bloody civil war. Feminist resistance to persistent injustice was being voiced with increasing urgency. In responding to Cacoyannis's adaptations I follow a long tradition of restaging these tragedies to expose the human cost of disastrous policies and individual actions—the suffering of war, the uncertainties of migration and exile, the squandering of life for the ambitions of the powerful.

In his films, Cacoyannis adapted ancient dramatic narratives that were themselves adaptations of even earlier stories. In like manner, to construct the images for *Vinyl Euripides* I hybridized fragments of objects and images from both the modern and the ancient world, many found in archaeological museums in Athens and Delphi as well as the Kelsey Museum of Archaeology in Ann Arbor. I plundered hands from paintings and sculptures at the University of Michigan Museum of Art—a Madonna and Child, Judith with the head of Holofernes, Esther petitioning Xerxes, the Unmerciful Servant, Vishnu, Plains Indians attacking a wagon train, a wounded lieutenant attending to the expiring General Wolfe—historical artifacts repurposed for current dilemmas.

In May 2020, on the verge of completing my project, those dilemmas unpredictably shifted. Instead of flying to Athens, I found myself driving to sanctuary in New Mexico. In my studio there I turned again to Euripides, searching for bearings within the ensuing sequence of pandemic days, firestorms in the West, civil unrest following the murder of Black citizens by our police, and the demands for a national reckoning.

The first three images of the present collection are directly adapted from individual panels of the vinyl narrative intended for Athens. The rest of the paintings are also, though more indirectly, under the spell of that project. The colors evoke the terra-cotta of the ancient vases I have been studying, and reflect the naked strata of enduring earth visible in the mesas, canyons, and arroyos beyond my windows. They are the colors of blood and rust, the alchemy of water, minerals, and fire. The funeral pyre of hands from *Vinyl Euripides* became even more starkly relevant in our altered circumstances, as did the grief of Hecuba at the destruction of her city, the murder and enslavement of her children. In another image an invasion force leaps joyfully forward on its mission of plunder, released to its grim destiny by the public murder of a young woman, abetted by her father's greed, deceit, and fumbling.

Although I painted in spectacular isolation while sequestered in the mountains of northern New Mexico, news of our struggling world was never far off. The hands, nets, monuments, seas, and Delphic devices of indeterminate purpose found in these paintings each bear their own histories and associations. My painted conversation with Cacoyannis and Euripides continues, and one day *Vinyl Euripides* will find its home in Athens. I have been spending a lot of time with Euripides.

Figure 7.5. *The Trojan Women: Pyre*, 2020. Sumi ink, shellac ink, salt, watercolor, gouache, acrylic over digital drawing printed on paper, 30″ × 22″.

Figure 7.6. *The Trojan Women: Hecuba's Grief*, 2020. Sumi ink, shellac ink, salt, watercolor, gouache, acrylic over digital drawing printed on paper, 30″ × 22″.

Figure 7.7. *Handheld Device*, 2020. Sumi ink, shellac ink, salt, watercolor, gouache, acrylic over digital drawing printed on paper, 30″ × 22″.

Figure 7.8. *Old News*, 2020. Sumi ink, watercolor, acrylic over digital drawing printed on paper, 30″ × 44″.

# CHAPTER 8

# Social Distances in Between

## Excerpts from My COVID-19 Diaries

### *Amal Hassan Fadlalla*

"Why did this pandemic take so many people by surprise here in America?" asked Amina, a friend from New York whom I've known for many years.[1] Since February 2020, when most Americans suddenly became part of the global world they had previously only consumed from a distance, Amina has not let a single week pass without calling to check on me. "Why do people think this has not happened here before, that this disease has come from somewhere else? But what do I know? I am an African immigrant, and Africa has always been the source of blame." Amina's serious questions often interrupt our casual conversations. And she is right. For the many years I have lived in this country, which I now call my second home, outbreaks of diseases such as HIV/AIDS or Ebola have often been blamed on foreign countries, alien races, or different bodily practices; in the worst racist scenarios, the "dark continent" receives the lion's share of blame. But this time, COVID-19 seems to have given Africa a break. Now it is the Chinese or the "white-but-not-quite" bodies of Europeans, like Italians, that have become the target of distancing, racism, and alienation. To hear in some news media that the disease spread like wildfire in China and Italy because of Chinese people's "bizarre eating habits" and Italians' crowded living arrangements, stemming from their close kinship relations, calls to mind widely held perceptions that linked previous disease outbreaks to Africans' innate physical, cultural, and moral behaviors. Today's new prejudices pin the pandemic to a particular race and place and describe it as creating a "new normal," without interrogating how this "new normal" is shaped by old discriminatory practices.

Like Amina, I begin this diary by asking why this pandemic took so many people by surprise in America. Why are some of us oblivious to history? Maybe the answer lies in my mother's insightful phrase: people forget what they want to forget and remember what they want to remember. In her words, forgetting becomes an act in its own right, an act of writing history in one's own terms. In another more complicated scholarly interpretation, forgetting becomes an act through which those in power have maintained the status quo for so long by simply rewriting history in order to perpetuate their divisive gender, race, and class ideologies. This sort of hegemony normalized colonialism in the past through rhetoric and missions of healing and saving in most of the colonized world, including Africa. It continues today through the ideological pursuits of neoliberal global capitalism and its engrained politics of meritocracy and ranking human lives. In order to engage Amina's unsettling questions, I reflect on my own personal experience as a transnational woman, locked down in Ann Arbor, Michigan, during the social distancing measures meant to curb the spread of the disease. I will use the tropes of walking and gardening to show how I interpret the meanings of social distancing, forgetting, conformity, and resistance. In so doing, I interrogate the emerging constructs of normality and humanity and the meanings they denote for those Americans long battling the normalized violence of sexism, racism, and xenophobia. Walking and gardening during this pandemic have not been leisurely activities that I have used in order to escape or bury my head in the sand; rather, I have used both as deliberate acts of reflecting, connecting, and remembering.

## INTERROGATING THE "NEW NORMAL": WHAT IS SOCIAL DISTANCE IF YOU LIVE IN BETWEEN?

The months of March through July have been catastrophic in the scale of death from the pandemic worldwide and the anxieties this has brought on families, especially those whose members are scattered all over the globe.[2] As someone living in between, meaning as a dual citizen of the Sudan and the United States, I can attest to the sense of vulnerability, fear, and panic that has left its mark on my transnational family and me. For the first time, I am experiencing a global health crisis in the United States rather than in the Sudan, and I have had to reckon with the construction of the "new normal" and the meaning of social distance from the perspective of a global citizen. My sister Niemat, who lives in Khartoum, Sudan, called me one day in March. Like Amina, her conversations strengthen me and help me see multiple perspectives. She convinced me, with a hint of humor, that the term "social distancing" needs to be revisited.

Sudan endured tremendous changes last year. A successful revolt led by young men and women toppled the thirty-year dictatorship of President Omar al-Bashir in April 2019. A new transitional government has been instated to prepare the country for a democratic transition after a three-year term. With the arrival of COVID-19, the new minister of health, Akram Altom, faced great challenges getting his lockdown messages across. He inherited a failed health system, gutted out by stringent neoliberal policies of privatization and international economies of debts and sanctions. In these circumstances, many Sudanese met the imposed social distancing measures (*tabaʿad ijtimaī*) with acceptance, while still other segments of the population either resisted or did not know how to deal with them. For instance, remnants of the old Islamist regime have dubbed the minister and members of the transitional government as "communists" who are against Islam and its teaching of prayer and togetherness. However, Sudanese living in remote areas and those struggling to make ends meet either don't receive the government messages or are caught between the pandemic and keeping their families afloat.

For my sister, who grapples with Sudan's daily changing realities as she tries to care for family members at home and abroad, the concept of social distancing is not new. Her awe for modern technologies, like WhatsApp and Zoom, which help bridge our already existing social distance, inspired her to search for a new alternative term. At the end of our conversation, we both agreed on "enhanced social distancing" as a term that captures the reality often forgotten by so many of us: that the new normal is not really new.

I use "enhanced social distancing" here to highlight myriad other social boundaries and divisions that we have normalized, embodied, and taken for granted over the years. Divisions along family lines, gender lines, ethno-racial lines, and national and transnational lines are not natural; they have been constructed and adopted through social and political routines, rituals, and policies that continue to fragment people and communities across the globe. Isn't racialization a form of social distancing? What about xenophobia, gender-based violence, and police brutality? Don't they all stem from deep forms of cultural and political logics, agendas, and policies that create boundaries among people in the name of racial and gender supremacy and imaginary scaling of civility and humanity? Some of us have not taken these norms for granted and have attempted to mitigate their impact by building counter-publics and platforms for learning, protesting, and resisting. Even so, the reality is that we are still ruled by these norms.

This is why when a crisis like COVID-19 takes us off guard, these normalized disparities come at us with a vengeance. This moment of enhanced social distancing, therefore, must be situated in the gendered, racist, and classist world we still inhabit. The fact that COVID-19 has brought this ugly world right in front of our doorsteps, with no guises or embellishments, is testament to the degree with which some of us have normalized the segregation of the past and the present. The violence inherent in these disparities now manifests in the death of so many people, most of whom are brown, poor, immigrants, homeless, incarcerated, and/or seniors living in nursing homes.[3] Therefore, the enhanced social distancing, which I use to interrogate the new normal here, is perpetuated by supremacist ideologies that distance governments from the immediate concerns of their own marginal citizens. In other words, I draw attention to a form of political distancing that has worked itself softly, and at times violently, in the daily lives of the working poor and racialized others, through different forms of policing and invasive neoliberal policies that continue to widen the gap between the haves and have-nots. While the neoliberal global capitalist narrative insists on distancing humans from one another by ranking and scaling them, some of us continue to refuse and resist these forms of violence and social distancing. We prefer *remembering* as a source of power to *forgetting* as an act of domination.

## FEELING THE PAIN OF OTHERS:
## INTIMACY AND CLOSENESS DURING A PANDEMIC

The injustices and health disparities so many took for granted, especially when conspiracy theorists denied the existence of COVID-19 in the first place, are inextricably linked to the "old normal": the social divisions and distancing measures already in place. Not until the disease entered communities or killed a close friend or relative did many people begin to realize the impact of the pandemic. Indeed, the construction of social proximity and distance play important roles in how people feel the trauma, pain, and suffering of others. These mechanisms of stratification have long structured our feelings, our values, and the meanings of humanity: for example, immediate family first, relatives second, friends third, neighbors fourth, and so on.

Certainly, I am no exception when it comes to how I relate to the suffering of others. Just watching the news or checking statistics provided by the various new COVID-19 visualizer apps does not elicit the same depth of emotion as when I learn how my own network of family and friends have been impacted. Thus, when my niece Shereen, who lives in Khartoum, called me one day in May to tell me that one of her best friends, Raba'a, died of COVID-19 after giving birth at age thirty-five, I wondered about the various stories, pain, and trauma hidden behind the mounting mortality statistics worldwide. "She is the one who used to advise us on Facebook to wear masks and adhere to social distancing measures. What happened? How could she have died so quickly and so easily? Was it related to her pregnancy?" These are some of the many questions that my niece kept asking as she sought solace while mourning her young friend with me over WhatsApp.

The stories my youngest sister Ihsan told me about her experience treating COVID patients also brought the pandemic closer to me in ways I had not imagined. Ihsan moved with her husband and children to Saudi Arabia a couple of years ago because, like many Sudanese doctors, she bore the brunt of being a medical professional in her own country, Sudan. Neoliberal polices imposed by the al-Bashir regime left the health sector in terrible condition. Consequently, many doctors decided to leave the country for better jobs abroad. But my sister had never imagined facing a pandemic in a foreign country when she decided to leave. When Saudi Arabia began to relax the strict lockdown measures toward the end of April, the country saw dramatic increases in COVID-19 cases.[4]

My sister's stories of how the "monster virus wreaks havoc on the bodies of young and old patients" in the ICU attest to the physical and emotional burdens doctors and health staff have experienced. Often when I called Ihsan, I could see dark blemishes on her face, resulting from the face shield she had to wear at work. She communicated more sad stories to me when I insisted on knowing the overall situation. One day, they lost a young woman who had just given birth, an immigrant man in his fifties, and another young man who everybody thought would make it. She sent a picture of herself in personal protective equipment (PPE) to show me how well doctors are taken care of there, but this did not ebb my anxiety (see figure 8.1). Instead, it confirmed to me that the burden medical workers shoulder, especially in countries where care for medical staff is limited, is heavy and shared by their proximate social networks as well. These personal experiences augmented my perception of the impact of the disease and consequently magnified my feelings of entrapment due to my living away from my immediate family network. They also showed how the pandemic makes visible the different ways we attempt to reinterpret our intimacy, humanity, and closeness in highly digitized global public networks.[5]

Figure 8.1. *Shadows: Living in Between* Image 1: Shadows, Walking in Between, Ann Arbor, USA; Image 2: Bridging Clouds, Khartoum, Sudan (Photo courtesy of Shereen M. Omer, used here with her permission); Image 3: Shadows, Walking in Between, Khartoum, Sudan (Photo courtesy of Shereen M. Omer, used here with her permission); Image 4: The View from Pauline Boulevard: Thank You Healthcare Workers; Image 5: Virtual Closeness during a Pandemic (Photo courtesy of Ihsan Hassan Fadlalla, used here with her permission).

WALKING AS AN ACT OF REMEMBERING:
INTIMACY AND DISTANCE REINTERPRETED

In the Sudan, the act of leaving a place is often expressed in the idiom of walking, as in she/he has left a place or has walked away (*mashat, masha*).[6] In my
household back home, we understood the act of our separation from our family as "walking away," and my sister Neimat added to it the phrase "walking
in the world" (*mashiyyin fi aldunia*). She has married and thus "walked away,"
as have my other siblings who have left our household, the country, or both.
Walking in this context is an act of simultaneous distancing and connecting,
especially when we all walk back home in the summer to temporarily meet,
even for a few months, as undivided family members.

Inspired by these idioms of going back and forth (*almashia wa aljayyia*),
I have always found walking to be a liberating act through which to achieve
both physical and mental well-being. Nothing relieved the tension and anxiety I experienced during this pandemic more than my routine walks at
the end of every busy and stressful day. Wandering has been a habit that
has sustained me and lifted my spirit ever since I was a child. And with
wandering came my love for nature. I remember that when I was a child,
I forced my father to grow a small area of grass in our backyard so I could
play in it. In that little green spot, I imagined different worlds made up of
little creatures and insects, which I often named or turned into humans.
They traveled distances, threw parties, and sometimes moved in long lines
like trains. In this fairy-tale world, ants were my favorite insects, until one
day I was bitten by one and ran crying to my mother, complaining about
the treacherous nature of the little creature. But my mother's explanation
was convincing: I must have, unknowingly, stepped on the ant's nest. Small
things also feel pain, even those we do not see; this is how I learned not to
pester little things, because they can fight back.

Walking helps me remember these cherished memories. Somehow it
builds my resilience to face the reality of living between different worlds. For
instance, it helps me remember that I have built a home away from home:
a place that I can always walk away from and come back to for shelter and
security. Walking in Ann Arbor this COVID-19 summer has also helped me
pay more attention to homes with neatly groomed lawns and front gardens,
mostly designed and nurtured by women. I would, at times, stop and say hello
and commend the work. Oftentimes short conversations would ensue and
result in exchanges of ideas about nature and gardening. But in my desperate
attempts to "bridge the distance," talking to some neighbors has also resulted
in silence or hesitant responses. Nonetheless, these hour-long walks, weather

Figure 8.2. *Walking as an Act of Remembering* Image 1: Clover on "Walkie-Talkie" Purse; Image 2: Washtenaw Dairy, Ice Cream Shop; Image 3: Trefoil on "Walkie-Talkie" Purse; Image 4: Enjoy Your Walk, Sidewalk Chalk Art. Photo by author.

permitting, have always made me appreciate my home and the small garden I designed in its backyard. They enabled me to reflect on privilege and disparities and to observe the new emerging spaces that may allow us to examine the past and the present.

## WALKING *HALAFA* STYLE:
### THE MAKING AND UNMAKING OF NORMALITY AND HUMANITY

Walking is also a nomadic act. My routine walks this summer have also reminded me of the time I spent working in Eastern Sudan for my master's

and doctoral projects. Eastern Sudan, or the Red Sea region, is mostly inhabited by the Hadendowa-Beja groups, whose nomadic traditions continue to
lend insights into their daily practices, especially for those who have recently
settled in the outskirts of cities and towns. I have been remembering them
because the *new* normal ignores the deep history of their practices, as social
distancing measures have been part of their cultural norms during times
of disease outbreaks and other social vulnerabilities. These norms, such as
quarantining, changing routes, or masking during illness, were all measures
required to protect the health and well-being of both the individual and community. The Hadendowa give these sets of rules or logic practices the term
*halafa*, which means to reverse in order to amend harm, ward off evil, inspire
healing, and restore health.

*Halafa* binds harm, healing, and sacrifice together in one complex term
that explains a host of ills and how to avert them: a pharmakon-like idea, if
you will, that explains sickness and harm based on the logic of social proximity and distance. Familiar bonds of kinship and togetherness can be disrupted
by mysterious ailments brought to the community through acts of crossing
physical and body borders, including walking back and forth. To reverse certain ailments, sick people are advised to take different routes than the ones
they took when they fell ill. For instance, a woman who has just given birth is
considered vulnerable to harm brought from outside the community, which
can be transmitted through body orifices, limbs, and fluids. Therefore, she
has to be secluded for forty days until she and her child regain energy and
health. Certainly, these rules have been carried over from past practices of
health and well-being, including how to protect against disease outbreaks
and epidemics. People have then given them different meanings and continued to remember them through embodied ritual practices over the years.[7]

As I contemplated the meanings of *halafa* measures this summer, I
thought of the stories of the two women who died shortly after childbirth
that my niece and sister had shared, and of the vulnerability of pregnant and
postpartum women in general. Although there is no evidence that COVID-19
directly impacts pregnancy outcomes, the CDC warns of increased risk for
pregnant and postpartum women.[8] Thus, COVID-19 and distancing measures have added pregnant women to other risk categories and disrupted
their birth plans in the United States and elsewhere.[9] Isolation from loved
ones during pregnancy, childbirth, and what were supposed to be the magi-
cal first months of parenthood; reduced access to in-person health care; and
the heavy weight of constantly fearing for the health of one's unborn child
or infant have had tremendous emotional and physical impacts on women
across the globe.

Walking in Ann Arbor this summer has also brought these memories of walking *halafa* style to mind. Changing directions or lanes in order to leave a six-foot distance for runners or other passersby felt similar at times to the practices of *halafa*. Unlike *halafa*, however, the practice of social distancing in the United States felt nothing short of a humanitarian act that citizens took upon themselves in order to counteract the delayed response of accountable institutions. Except for the have-nots, who gave up on the trickling effects of global neoliberal capitalism long ago, the logic of practice, such as *halafa*, which helps explain and even avert realities of marginality, destitution, and vulnerability, often serves as the norm.

## REIMAGINING HUMANITY:
## THE BUS, THE ENVIRONMENT, THE HUMAN

"I walk to remember and take the bus to run errands," I once explained to Amina, who could not understand why I insist on walking and resist owning a car. "It will help you move around, and now with this pandemic, it will also be safer for you," she insisted. Why should I? After all, I have managed very well and found alternatives to having a car. To me, owning a car means succumbing to a monolithic capital-driven understanding of mobility. I remember telling Amina once that I always dreamed of a different Ann Arbor: a beautiful landscape crisscrossed by rail tracks, facilitating the movement of colorful commuter trains connecting us to nearby towns and cities such as Ypsilanti, Detroit, Dearborn, Flint, and beyond. This is perhaps why I fell in love with commuter trains in Chicago and Boston and some European towns I visited a couple of years ago. But whenever I relay this fantasy to some of my close friends in Michigan, their humorous responses often come with a caveat: "Dream on. You live near Motown, the cradle of the car industry." Of course I know this fact; it was in one of the geography textbooks I studied during my formative school years in the Sudan. But I also realize that there is no harm in reimagining various norms and different modes of human interactions.

In short, I do not own a car because the many cars already in the world result in a combination of noise, pollution, and debt: an argument that might sound extreme to many but is very convincing to me. Maybe because I learned early on that if I abuse the environment, it will bite me. In addition, I favor buses and trains because they give me a different sense of community and togetherness, as well as remind me that there are other worlds out there, with other human beings guided by different norms. Most importantly, they remind me that our public sphere is not completely overtaken by the often-normalized neoliberal policies of privatization and individual achievements. During the pandemic, the bus system was rearranged to cope with "the new normal." Essential transportation workers make sure that handrails are sanitized and seating adheres to social distancing. Above all, passengers are required to wear face masks, and bus services are rendered free of charge for those who can't afford to pay in such difficult economic times. To protect drivers, passengers must enter through the middle door, unless somebody in a wheelchair needs assistance. Of course, I wish the bus ran more frequently, especially on weekends, but there is always the option to take a taxi or ride-share when I need to get somewhere quickly.

To me, taking the bus means supporting the public system and those who run it. It means seeing different faces and encountering people who may not have the means to afford a car: working-class people, indebted students, and less affluent retired seniors. For example, I often ride the bus with an elderly brown woman whom I call Tina. Tina always drags a cart full of her belongings with her on the bus, often talking loudly to someone, perhaps an imaginary friend. Nevertheless, I have observed that she is always very conscious of her whereabouts. Tina's presence in this public space, therefore, reminds us that many people must make sacrifices in order to cope with normalized disparities and structural violence. It invites us to reimagine new spaces of human interaction that expand our ideas of care, health, and compassion. This requires refusal tactics that contest normalized forms of silencing and oppression. Only then can we realize promises of social justice in our homes, neighborhoods, and public spaces and institutions.

ECHOES OF REVOLUTION:
SOCIAL DISTANCE, SOCIAL JUSTICE (DISTANT JUSTICE)

Living through the Black Lives Matter (BLM) protests that resumed after the killing of George Floyd by the police in Minneapolis on May 26, 2020, felt like déjà vu to me. Last summer, I could not go to the Sudan because of the turbulent political situation there. From December 2018 to June 30, 2019, I observed from my home in Ann Arbor the massive protests that toppled President Omar al-Bashir. Young women and men came out in droves, turning the streets of cities and towns into theaters of resistance as they proclaimed their chants and marches in the language of walking forward (*namshi mashi*) and coming out (*nihna maraqna*). This summer, despite the pandemic, BLM protesters made a difficult decision: they marched against both the old and

Figure 8.3. *The Bus, The Environment, The Human* Image 1: "Go the Distance," Blake Transit Center; Image 2: Social Care, Essential Transportation Workers; Image3: Social Distance Inside the Bus; Image 4: Social Distance Seat, Blake Transit Center. Photos by author.

new normal, with some of their slogans stating, "Racism is a deadly virus too." They were obviously choosing social *justice* over social *distancing*: they came out to resist the calculated techniques, methods, and practices of "distant justice" that have crippled the lives of African Americans in this country for centuries.

In Khartoum, protesters did the same on June 30, 2020. They went out en masse, despite strict social distancing regulations, to commemorate the sacrifices of those who had died the year before, to pay homage to their coming back to the streets, and to pressure the transitional government to deliver on their demands of justice, equality, and restitution.[10] These protests remind us that endemic inequities and discrimination are at the center of national and transnational struggles for justice. A new generation of youth feel that the impacts of sociopolitical distancing and their consequent outcomes of racism, violence, and disparities are becoming too ruthless to ignore. They are walking ahead and pushing forward, demanding a different kind of present and a more promising future.

## BLURRED VIRTUAL CONNECTIONS: ZOOMING INTO THE FUTURE

For many Sudanese last year, both Ramadan and the two Eids were times of mourning and grief because of the militaristic violence that took the lives of so many young people during the revolution.[11] This year, these occasions were far from joyous due to the pandemic.[12] Many families experienced isolation, death of family members and friends, and continued economic hardship. But new technologies have always come to the rescue, connecting us as we deal with the hardships of the present and think about how to walk ahead toward a better future. Last year, WhatsApp was the major platform through which I connected with friends and interlocutors during the revolts, and I utilized it to send both Ramadan and Eid greetings to family, friends, and colleagues. This year, as many discovered Zoom, new technologies have captured the attention of a new generation of young people who are being schooled online during the pandemic. Instead of through WhatsApp, I received Zoom invitations from my young nephews and nieces who planned our family meet-and-greet during Ramadan and the Eids. I enjoyed their funny comments as they tried to hide their smiles while watching their aunt struggle with new technology. They belong to a new generation of youth who are becoming savvy, high-tech learners and comfortable users of new media platforms. I often remind them that someone must have thought about the

Figure 8.4. *Echoes of Revolution* Image 1: In this House We Believe, Sidewalk Chalk Art; Image 2: Unmasking: We Can't Breathe; Image 3: "Revolution Cemented," Graffiti Street Art, Khartoum, Sudan (Photo courtesy of Ghasan M. Hassan Fadlalla, used here with his permission). In this image artists paint excerpts from the revolution's popular slogans and chants, such as *Sabinaha*, "We will cement the revolution," on street pavement. This one is a version of the aforementioned popular slogan painted on a street close to my family's neighborhood in Khartoum, translation is mine; Image 4: Say their Names, Graffiti Street Art.

future years ago in order to make this option available to us today. These new technologies are not ideal—they take away so much from our intimate face-to-face communication—but they enable us to bridge physical distance and see and hear each other wherever we go. Yet again, we should remember that these technologies are not equally accessible to everyone. My nephews and nieces agree.

New technologies also sensationalize serious matters, often at the expense of deep understanding of the histories of communication, discrimination, and divisions that continue to shape our present realities.[13] That the public reacted to the video of George Floyd's killing as if racial bias and the culture of police violence started with his death is just one example of how these isolated snapshots do not connect the past to the present to help us envision a just future. In a similar way, due to the misrepresentations by new technologies and social media, the Sudanese revolution has often been compared to the Arab Spring, without regard to the history of Sudanese protests and how the recent revolution was similar to or different from them. Moreover, to be surprised that COVID-19 would take a heavy toll on us in the United States and to blame it on others is yet another example of how mainstream communication has grossly disregarded the history and politics that have shaped this particular moment. To forget is to embody supremacist assumptions that some groups are invincible and immune to global catastrophes, created by the very power that reproduces such supremacy. We ought to remember that these supremacist ideas continue to distance us from the suffering and struggles of "others." In all of these events, conformity, refusal, and resistance have shaped the ways we think about our human existence.

We saw all of these responses during the pandemic in America and elsewhere. At the same time, we saw many among us make sacrifices that illuminated humans' abilities to care, give, and resist. We saw doctors, nurses, and other health care providers working tirelessly in hospital wards. We saw people in communities across America and other parts of the world mobilizing resources to help those in need. In many cities, for instance, we saw humanitarianism come back to America in full force, as many community organizations stepped up to make masks, donate PPE, and collect and distribute food to the needy.[14] In my own work, I have written about humanitarianism as an institutional form built on ideas and histories of charity and community mobilization, often practiced outside the purview of states and governments. Since the 1990s, however, most humanitarian work and deployment have been directed toward conflict zones in Africa and the Middle East, even though charities in America continued to exist. The politics of humanitarianism during the COVID-19 pandemic has shed light on the federal government's inability to respond quickly and effectively, resulting in a reliance on governors and citizens to enact social distancing measures. Citizens took it upon themselves to embody and carry out the new regulations. By citizens, I mean those who did not believe the pandemic was a hoax and did not come out armed to protest their governors' decisions, such as in the case of Michigan.[15] I consider these embodied responses to be humanitarian acts because they center the human as an active, responsible, and agentive citizen in times of disasters and in absence of accountable institutions.

SIGNS OF RESISTANCE: THE GARDEN—AREN'T WE ALL HUMANS?

During my frequent walks this COVID-19 summer, I have seen the landscape of my neighborhood altered in many ways. At the onset of the lockdown, parks were abandoned and filled with warning signs, their green grass interlaced with more dandelion and clover than I had ever seen. From time to time, I also noticed masks and gloves carelessly discarded, perhaps signaling boredom and fatigue. Throughout the onerous routines of the new regulations, however, the human continued to emerge in many creative ways. Those who tended gardens and front lawns brought nature back to counter the oppressive ways we treat our environment. Many neighbors turned their yards into resistance spaces as well. Signs thanking essential workers adorned many front yards during the early months of the lockdown. These were added to old ones, such as the "One Human Family: We Support Refugees and Our Muslim Neighbors" signs that contest xenophobia and the Muslim ban.[16] More slogans responding to later developments during the pandemic included "We Support That Woman from Michigan," a response to criticism levied against the governor of Michigan, Gretchen Whitmer,[17] and "Neighbors for More Neighbors" and "Diversity and Inclusion," which call for more community building and diversity in our neighborhoods and institutions.

When the BLM protests broke out this summer, neighbors also adorned their front yards, windows, and sidewalks with strong messages such as "Black Lives Matter," "Color Is Not a Crime," and "We Can't Breathe." In June, after the relaxation of lockdown measures, I could sense small changes all around me: a young man began frequenting the park to fly his kite, more neighbors started celebrating birthdays on their front lawns, and aromas of baked goods filled the evening air. The evening hours, when breezy, dry air, settled in, somehow reminded me of Khartoum's summers, when we used to sit outside in the yard to chat and relax after a long day. It is that dry, desert breeze in Khartoum that comes with unique aromas of frankincense, spicy tea, coffee, and doughnuts to cool the extreme dry heat of the day. There is nothing like it in Ann Arbor, of course, but some days felt similar, especially when I stopped to take a glimpse of people's shadows in the sun. I remembered doing this with playmates back home when I was a kid.

As I walked and remembered, shadows of people I met during various chapters of my life would come to me, mesmerize me. I felt like I was walking through a neutral space comforted by sounds, tastes, and aromas: doves and crickets, sharp cheddar and *kisra*, wet grass and incense.[18] I reached a state of transcendence, where the place could have been anywhere unless I was reminded otherwise: a house with an American flag flying by its side or a person who stopped me to ask where I was from. Then I decided to stop to take a deep breath at a cozy, familiar place before the end of my walk. In June, my favorite ice cream shop, Washtenaw Dairy on South Ashley, opened its doors, serving people with social distancing measures in place. It has always been one of the stops that reminds me, I am here. I bought my favorite, cappuccino-vanilla: a way to cool down and taste a familiar flavor of a place before walking back home.

And there is another comforting place: my neighbor's garden on Pauline. I stop by and say hello whenever she is out tending her garden. Angel is in her sixties, I believe, and she once told me that she was born in the Philippines. She, like so many of us, has multiple roots. Each one of them is stronger than the roots of the trees in her beautiful front yard, which she continues to feed and nourish. "Do you want some flowers?" she asked with her mask on. "Of course, I'd love some," I responded, standing six feet or more away from her, wearing my commodified African print bandana. In the age of articulation, I suppose we can add different meanings to these already fabricated signs of identity. This particular print grounded me a little during this difficult time, especially since I could not find masks in the stores at the onset of the lockdown. I wandered with my thoughts while my neighbor went in to get her clippers. I picked a few white clovers from her lawn and stuck them onto the front of my little "walkie-talkie" purse. In it, I keep a small pack of paper tissues, a little bottle of hand sanitizer, and my cell phone, which I answer when necessary. Angel's house is not far from mine. It was at the end of my walk that day, and I ended up heading home carrying a bunch of rosy peonies and a few violet-blue alliums in my hand.

She made my walk!

Thank you essential workers, friends, neighbors, and members of my close and extended families.[19]

### Notes

1. All names in this essay are real, except for Amina and Angel, whose names have been altered for privacy reasons.

2. See World Health Organization Coronavirus Disease (COVID-19) Dashboard at https://covid19.who.int/?gclid=EAIaIQobChMIroen54mA6wIVzsDACh2Uewv5EAAY ASAAEgJHBPD_BwE, accessed August 2, 2020.

3. Monica Hopper, Anna Nápoles, and Eliseo Pérez-Stable, "COVID-19 and Racial/ Ethnic Disparities," *JAMA Network* 323.24 (May 11, 2020): 2466–2467, https://jamanetw ork.com/journals/jama/fullarticle/2766098

4. Sarah Dadouch, "Saudi Arabia, Other Gulf States Reimpose Strict Measures after Coronavirus Cases Spike during Ramadan, *Washington Post*, May 20, 2020, https:// www.washingtonpost.com/world/middle_east/saudi-arabia-and-other-gulf-states -reimpose-strict-measures-after-coronavirus-spikes-during-ramadan/2020/05/20/e2 4bb7c8-99df-11ea-ad79-eef7cd734641_story.html

5. All images in these collages are organized to be viewed from right to left, unless explained otherwise. Also, photographs from Khartoum, Sudan, are marked as such. All other photographs were taken by the author during the summer of 2020 in Ann Arbor, Michigan.

6. Other verbal variations include the following: we are walking away (*mashiyyin*), or we are ready to leave or walk away (*namashi*).

7. See my in-depth analyses of *halafa* logic in *Embodying Honor: Fertility, Foreignness and Regeneration in Eastern Sudan* (Madison: University of Wisconsin Press, 2007).

8. See CDC website for "If You Are Pregnant, Breastfeeding, or Caring for Young Children," updated June 25, 2020, https://www.cdc.gov/coronavirus/2019-ncov/need -extra-precautions/pregnancy-breastfeeding.html

9. Adrianna Rodriguez, "'Heartbreaking': Moms Could Be Separated from Their Newborns under Coronavirus Guidelines." *USA Today*, March 26, 2020, https://www .usatoday.com/story/news/health/2020/03/26/pregnant-women-covid-19-could-sep arated-babies-birth/2907751001/

10. After the Sudanese revolution successfully toppled President Omar al-Bashir in April 2019, protesters continued to sit-in in front of the military headquarters in Khartoum, demanding the resignation of the remaining members of the regime. However, on June 3, 2019, militias associated with the regime cracked down on the sit-in, killing, injuring, and arresting many youths. This attempt to take over power was met with more resistance in the streets, however. Protesters mobilized in larger numbers and took to the streets again on June 30. This move forced the military establishment to agree to the demands of protesters, and a transitional government that consists of both military and civilian members is now in place. For more details, see my opinion piece, "Sudan Protest: Narratives of Violence and the Power of the Internet," *Africa Up Close*, July 26, 2019, https://africaupclose.wilsoncenter.org/author/amal-fadlalla/

11. Muslims celebrate two religious holidays: *'aid alfitr* and *'aid aladha*. The former comes after Ramadan (the fasting month), and the latter coincides with the pilgrimage to Mecca.

12. According to WHO, as of October 31, 2020, Sudan's statistics showed 13,804 reported infection rates and 837 deaths from the disease. However, the country lacks

wide-range testing and communication about the prevalence of the disease. See World Health Organization Coronavirus Disease (COVID-19) Dashboard at https:// covid19.who.int/?gclid=EAIaIQobChMIroen54mA6wIVzsDACh2Uewv5EAAYASAAE gJHBPD_BwE, accessed August 2, 2020.

13. Amal Hassan Fadlalla, "State of Vulnerability and Humanitarian Visibility on the Verge of Sudan's Secession: Lubna's Pants and the Transnational Politics of Rights and Dissent," *Signs* 37.1 (2011): 159–184. See also *Branding Humanity: Competing Narratives of Rights, Violence, and Global Citizenship* (Stanford: Stanford University Press, 2019).

14. For example, see David Sands, "These Detroit Grassroots Groups Are Stepping Up to Help Kids during the COVID-19 Pandemic," Model D, April 7, 2020, https://www .modeldmedia.com/features/covid19-grassroots-solutions-040720.aspx

15. Meagan Flynn, "Chanting 'Lock Her Up,' Michigan Protesters Waving Trump Flags Mass against Gov. Gretchen Whitmer's Coronavirus Restrictions," *Washington Post*, April 16, 2020, https://www.washingtonpost.com/nation/2020/04/16/michigan -whitmer-conservatives-protest/

16. William Roberts, "US House Approves Bill Reversing Trump's 'Muslim Ban,'" Al Jazeera, July 22, 2020, https://www.aljazeera.com/news/2020/07/house-poised-vo te-reversing-trump-muslim-ban-200721235927974.html

17. See Sands, "These Detroit Grassroots Groups."

18. *Kisra* is a Sudanese popular delicacy flatbread. It is usually very sour and thin in its texture, akin to the Ethiopian *injera*.

19. A special thank-you to my neighbor-turned-friend Lauren Mohn for reading this piece. Her close reading and valuable comments and suggestions added much to the ways I thought of, organized, and improved this essay. Thanks are also due to Yasmeen Berry for her work on the video and photo collage.

# PART III

# Grieving

# CHAPTER 9

# Grief and the Importance of Real Things during COVID-19

*Suzanne L. Davis*

## THE POWER OF REAL THINGS

"Hey lady, is this real? I mean, *really* real?" the sixth-grader touring the Kelsey Museum of Archaeology asks me during a pre-COVID-19 visit.[1] She and her classmates are intrigued, but skeptical. When told that, yes, everything around them is *really* real, the kids are surprised, then excited. Suddenly the fieldtrip is more than an outing away from school; this stuff is the real thing.

From talking with many museum visitors I know that "Is this stuff real?" is one of their most frequent questions. It's so common that an answer appears on the Kelsey's FAQs web page. In a world that prizes smartphones and high-tech virtual experiences, the survival and display of real artifacts from our ancient past is unexpected and extraordinary to many people. As soon as the question is answered in the affirmative—yes, it's real—visitors' attention sharpens. Historical objects—really real things—are powerful; they spark our imaginations and serve as touchstones, deepening our understanding of ourselves and the world around us.

The Kelsey Museum's collection focuses on the ancient Mediterranean and Middle East, and the exhibitions feature objects that are roughly fifteen hundred to five thousand years old. As such, they offer an opportunity for an exciting form of tourism—points of connection to both different places and different times. Yet the items people focus on are not the grand marble portraits of emperors, busts of gods, or recreations of ancient monuments. Instead, visitors linger over the quotidian and recognizable: sandals that look like your pair at home, coins, wine cups and garlic cloves, earrings, and toys. Kids especially love the mummy of a young boy, secreted in a dim grave-like niche, and the small mummies of a cat and a bird. These items forge a sense of both connection and distance: they drank wine from wonky glass goblets;

their money looks a lot like ours; these toys are boring compared to the ones at home; they had cats, but mummified them. Ultimately, the takeaway seems to be that these are the things of people like us. They lived long ago and far away, but the experience of being human connects us.

As a conservator, someone who preserves others' ancient treasures and trash, I have a strong sense of this connection. Charged with an item's care, I inspect it closely, noticing small things: the fingerprint left by the potter, one wobbly brushstroke, wear in the fabric where the owner's elbow must have rubbed. I know the artifact's weight and how it feels in the hand.

After leaving campus in March 2020 to comply with Michigan governor Gretchen Whitmer's "Stay Home: Stay Safe" executive order, I felt a profound sense of loss and isolation. Predictably, and like many people, I grieved the planned trips that could not be taken, missed the friends and family now too far away to visit, and mourned the weekly dinners and fellowship previously shared with friends closer to home. Less expected was how much I missed the objects in the Kelsey Museum's collection. The idea that they were waiting quietly in the dark museum, unappreciated, was upsetting; now, I felt, was a time when we all needed to see them. Because ancient artifacts do more than offer escapism through time-travel-style tourism; they are also grounding. The sense of connection to people who came before you, who lived and loved and suffered can be comforting, inspiring, and even provocative.

Ideas about objects and our connections to them might seem trivial in the face of a generation-defining global pandemic, but our relationship with material culture is important. The pandemic has spotlighted long-standing crises in our country: health disparities suffered by Black, Indigenous, and Latinx Americans; dangers to immigrants and asylum seekers fleeing climate change and violence; and the devastating effects of the criminal justice system on nonwhite citizens. The world was a brutal place before COVID-19, and the virus has intensified negative consequences for the most vulnerable. Historical artifacts—and sometimes an awareness of their absence—can help us make sense of this brutality, acknowledge grief, and find hope in the world.

## THREE THINGS

To be alive now, in the time of COVID-19, is to live in a stressful and lonely state of exception. Contact with people outside one's own household is limited, and simple, everyday activities like a quick trip to the store now require personal protective equipment and seem fraught with danger. Every day more people are infected, and death and hospital admission rates rise and fall and rise again with no end in immediate sight. As I have struggled to process feelings of loss and loneliness—and to nurture hope and some semblance of peace—in this anxious new existence, my thoughts have repeatedly turned to three objects important in my own life: a painted limestone grave marker in the collection of the Kelsey Museum; a cardboard box taped shut for shipping in 1948 and never reopened, now in my father's office; and a fork with a wood handle and three spindly steel tines that I use on a daily basis. These three things have helped me understand and, in some cases, manage my emotional reactions to challenges posed by the pandemic. Although the objects are, on the surface, very different, all three commemorate individual people. Each artifact encodes trauma and loss, but is also a mechanism for remembrance—becoming a vessel for specific stories of the collective brutality and beauty of life.

## Grave Marker

This object is a carved and painted funerary stela, or stone tablet, from Roman Egypt. Dating to the late second century CE, it depicts a young man named Nemesion. Facing the viewer, Nemesion stands with his hands upraised in a position of prayer. He has curly black hair, reddish skin, plump cheeks, and wears a tunic topped by a draped toga. Surrounded by an elaborate architectural frame, he is also flanked on both sides by jackals, animals sacred to Anubis, the ancient Egyptian god of the dead. The inscriptions tells us that he died at age twenty-four in the month of Hathur (November), although the year is not given. The limestone is now worn and the paint faded, but this gravestone would once have been very brightly colored.

Nemesion's stela is one of hundreds of similar stone markers from a necropolis—literally, a city of the dead—outside the ancient, living town of Terenouthis (modern Kom Abou Billou). When the University of Michigan excavated Terenouthis in 1935, only a fraction of the original burial ground remained; most of the graves had been destroyed by farmers who removed the ancient tombs' mudbricks for use as fertilizer (a ruthless but common historic practice). But one small area in the southeast corner of the cemetery was untouched, and from this spot more than two hundred ancient grave markers were recovered. Many were brought to the Kelsey Museum in Ann Arbor, while others were retained by the Cairo Museum in Egypt.[2] When the COVID-19 shutdown began on campus, several of these objects were in the conservation lab for an ongoing research project. As the months of off-

Figure 9.1. Funerary stela of Nemesion. The stela is made from carved and painted limestone and dates to the late second century CE. Measurements: 38.7 cm high, 30.4 cm wide, 10.7 cm thick. University of Michigan Excavations at Terenouthis, Egypt, 1935; field number 10-X; KM 21052. Photo courtesy of the Kelsey Museum of Archaeology, University of Michigan.

campus work ticked slowly by, Nemesion and the many others depicted on the stelae stayed in my mind.

Although described by scholars as "rudimentarily executed," and of "low artistic standard," the stelae are favorite objects for many people who work at the museum. Made to commemorate individual people, the gravestones are deeply personal and—almost two thousand years after they were made— they remain acutely relatable, reflecting our enduring desire to mourn and remember those we have lost. In shape, the stelae look much like grave markers in any cemetery today but, unlike a modern gravestone, they are carved with a full-figure image of the deceased. These images make the stelae immediately interesting; Nemesion looks like someone we could know. When first made, the stelae were decorated with a lifelike palette of paints and, in contrast to our modern, monochrome funereal expanses of marble and granite, the Terenouthis cemetery would have been a kaleidoscopic landscape of color in the desert outside the town.

The stelae's carvings are similarly lively; the people are obviously individuals, with varied facial features and hairstyles. Usually they appear wearing formal Roman dress, in draped togas or robes. The person's name, age at death, and date of death are usually written beneath the figure. Frequently the deceased is shown, like Nemesion, in a standing prayer position. Other times people recline on couches, with a banquet placed on a table before them. Sometimes they stand or sit in boats, a safe form of travel to the afterlife. Some individuals are shown standing, with one hand raised above a small altar. Animals with religious significance are often included: jackals, snakes, and falcons. Together and singly, the Terenouthis stelae indicate a culturally diverse population: clothing and furniture appear to be Roman, architectural motifs and inscriptions are Greek, religious iconography is strongly influenced by ancient Egyptian traditions, and individuals' names are Greek and Greek-Egyptian hybrids.

If the stelae are "crude," they are also special for their very ordinariness. Made for nonroyal and non-elite people, they depict ordinary Egyptians of all ages and come from a burial ground located on the edge of what was probably a very ordinary town. Only a few inscriptions mention occupations, but in the Kelsey's collection these indicate a linen merchant and in the Cairo Museum collection a water carrier, condiment seller, and hieroglyph carver.

Many inscriptions speak to the character of the deceased:[3]

Athenarion, devoted to her children, loving her husband, fond of her
   brother, a most worthy person, aged about 22 (?) years old. Epeiph 2.
   Be of good cheer!

Athenodoros, devoted to his children, friendly, pious, about 47 years old.
   Be of good cheer!

Artemas, son of Koureus, who is without grief, was worthy and devoted
   to his wife, children, and friends. Farewell. Aged 49.

Although the phrasing is formulaic, the inscriptions still manage to carry emotional weight. The finality of "Farewell," is poignant. "Without grief," is frequently included to comfort those left behind, as is the upbeat instruction for the reader, "Be of good cheer!" But the most frequently inscribed phrase states that death came too soon. This is used for people of all ages, from young children to those who lived comparatively long lives.[4]

Herakleides, who died before his time, about 3 years old.

Sarapous, daughter of Euanthes, died before her time, childless, devoted to her husband, fond of her sister, fond of her friends, about 14 years old.

Nemesion, son of Theanous, who has died before his time, was devoted to his children, worthy. Farewell. Age 32. Year 8, Hathur 9.

Achilleis, daughter of Ptolemaios, who has died before her time, 82 years old, worthy, noble, a cheerful person, having departed life in good fortune. Year 8, Phamenoth 2.

If these inscriptions reveal anything about the lives of the deceased, it is that they were probably difficult. The ages of wives—Sarapous at fourteen, and one scholar suggests Athenarion was really twelve—give serious pause to the modern reader. Certainly, most lives were short by today's standards. Achilleis, who died at eighty-two, is an outlier; child mortality was high and, based on the inscriptions, the average age at death in Terenouthis was twenty-eight years for women and thirty-seven years for men.

Yet in the early days of the COVID-19 shutdown, when I thought of the people of Terenouthis and their gravestones, the emotion I felt most keenly was jealousy. Despite the hardship of life in second-century Egypt, Terenouthis seemed to me to be a real community, a town where neighbors would know each other's names, where family members and childhood friends lived close by, and where the baker would know how many loaves to give you each day without being told. As the COVID-19 lockdown stretched from weeks into months, this kind of community was something I craved.

Like many of my University of Michigan colleagues, I am not from Ann Arbor, nor even from the Midwest. My family and oldest friends live far away. As an atheist, I do not belong to a religious institution. Childless, I lack the local friendships many parents develop with others who have children of the

Figure 9.2. Archival photograph from Terenouthis, 1935, showing a barrel-vaulted tomb with a stela in situ. KM 574. Photo courtesy of the Kelsey Museum of Archaeology, University of Michigan.

same age. But these were, in medical speak, preexisting conditions unrelated to COVID-19. If anything, the pandemic made my oldest and strongest ties stronger, as I called and scheduled video chats more frequently. What had changed were the weak ties. There were no more casual chats with colleagues and acquaintances on campus, no more friendly small talk with the checkout clerk at the market, or the bus driver, or the people at the yoga studio. All of these small, seemingly inconsequential interactions were gone. And, it turns out, these weak ties matter enormously in creating a sense of community and of belonging.[5]

An obvious solution would have been to recreate these small moments outside, at a safe distance, with the neighbors. But my neighborhood was not a naturally friendly space. Built ad hoc from the 1920s to the 1960s, it lacks a unified plan or architectural style and is occupied variously by an enormous range of people, from university students renting shared houses, to young families, to elderly singletons. Although I know a few people on my block, it was not the kind of neighborhood where people met up in the park and talked, or even stopped to chat while out for an evening walk.

At the same time, the word "community" was appearing everywhere. Michigan's "Stay Home" order aimed to prevent "community spread" of the virus, and signs on store windows asked shoppers to wear face coverings to protect "our community." There were "community resources" and "community mobility" reports available online, and state and local governments were developing "community mitigation" strategies. But in the neighborhood where I lived, I had little sense of belonging to a real community.

Each day, and often more than once a day, I walked a mile-and-a half-loop through the streets around my home. Prior to COVID-19, I had done this as a way to clear my head and wind down after a day at work. Now I did it to get out of the house. As I walked, I compared my neighborhood to Terenouthis. Somewhat morbidly, the shapes and arrangements of the houses reminded me of the pyramid- and barrel-roofed tombs in the ancient cemetery. I wondered, if my neighbors died from COVID-19, what would be inscribed on their tombstones? I had no idea. I didn't even know their names. Nemesion and Athenarion were more familiar to me than the couple who lived on the corner.

But what, exactly, prevented me from moving through my streets with the same confidence and familiarity Nemesion would have had in his? I had not known my neighbors since birth, as he might have, but there was no reason I could not know them now. Imagining myself a long-established resident of a small and ancient town, I began to cheerfully greet everyone I encountered, as if this were a normal practice in our area. People seemed surprised at first, but most also seemed pleased.

Figure 9.3. Archival photograph from 1935 showing pyramid and barrel-vaulted tombs in the cemetery at Terenouthis. A stela can be seen inside tomb #5. KM 565. Photo courtesy of the Kelsey Museum of Archaeology, University of Michigan.

As the pandemic continued through the summer, I greeted more and more people. Suddenly everyone seemed to be walking regularly. Chairs appeared on front porches and stoops and, sometimes, in the middle of front yards. If someone acknowledged my wave and verbal greeting, I would venture a little more, complimenting their flower beds or asking how they were doing. Most were eager to talk. I heard not only about flower-garden care, but also about the sadness of missed high-school graduations, worries about jobs, the difficulties of working with a toddler at home, new hobbies, and exercise regimens for family pets.

Before long, I could recognize my neighbors: this woman was worried about her teenaged son; that father always drank a glass of water on his front porch at 11:00 a.m. as a break from the chaos inside his house; this man had made a makeshift artist's studio in his garage; that retired couple were newly dedicated to gardening; this woman had the elderly corgi. Although I do not always know the names of these people, I do—eleven months into the pandemic—have a much stronger sense of belonging to the social landscape of my neighborhood. At a time when it is easy to feel isolated, this matters to me. And I am not sure that I would have engaged with my neighbors in this way without the inspiration of a centuries-old grave marker from a small town in ancient Egypt.

### Cardboard Box

While thinking about the Terenouthis stelae helped me acknowledge loneliness and connect with my community, a different funerary artifact has helped me think about COVID-19 and the continuing loss of individual lives. It is an unprepossessing box made from thick cardboard, now yellowed with age. Roughly square, it measures about ten inches by nine inches and is three inches high. Its three-pound weight feels surprisingly heavy for its size. A paper shipping label pasted to the top states that it contains a US flag associated with Staff Sgt. Larry R. Cooper, and the return address indicates St. Avold, France, which is home to the Lorraine American Cemetery, a site holding the graves of more than ten thousand US servicemen. A radio operator on a B-17 Flying Fortress, Cooper—my great uncle, known to the family by his middle name, Ray—was killed at age twenty-six while flying a mission over Dessau, Germany, in 1944. After his military funeral four years later, the flag draped over his coffin was folded and placed in this box, which was then taped shut with thick, black tape and mailed to his parents.

This box was on my mind in May 2020 as Memorial Day approached, and

Figure 9.4. The unopened cardboard box containing the flag from Staff Sgt. L. Ray Cooper's military funeral in 1948. Measurements: 25 cm wide, 21.5 cm wide, 9 cm high. Photograph courtesy of Ray Davis.

I spent the holiday weekend talking to two of Cooper's nephews: my father, Ray (named for Cooper), and his cousin Mike. These nephews were born a few months after Cooper was killed, so they never met their uncle, but the family's grief over his death lingered through their childhoods.

Cooper, who was born in 1917, was the youngest surviving child in a family of seven (a sister, born in 1918, died from the influenza pandemic that year). Handsome and fun-loving, he was the favorite of both his parents and his older siblings. He was working as a journalist when war broke out in 1941. After enlisting, he trained for two years before spending nine months "in theater" with the 401st Bomber Group of the Eighth Air Force. A good brother, he wrote his siblings regular letters. After he deployed, the letters instructed his siblings to keep this fact from their mother. The missing-in-action report would, therefore, have been an especially unpleasant shock to his parents. His plane was shot down on May 28, 1944, in what was later described as the roughest mission the 401st experienced during the war.

The United States had more than four hundred thousand military fatali-

Figure 9.5. Photograph of Ray Cooper prior to deployment. A typed note at top reads, "Wonder where I am going Bellair Florida May 1943." Photo scan courtesy of Ray Davis.

ties in World War II, and the 401st suffered especially heavy casualties, with more than twenty-six thousand killed. Worldwide estimates of World War II deaths include fifteen million military personnel and more than forty-five million civilians.[6] In other words, in what was a global landscape of death and destruction, Cooper's death was unexceptional.

COVID-19 is a different kind of world war, but there are disturbing parallels in how it is discussed. Doctors and nurses have been described as "soldiers" and "frontline" workers who are "battling the enemy" and "fighting the good fight." The chaos and trauma in emergency departments during the pandemic have been compared to military combat medicine. Just as in a military conflict, "essential services" often seem to equate to expendable lives. The "essential worker" category is huge and diverse, including not only medical personnel but all the support staff who keep hospitals clean and functioning, as well a vast array of people in other professions from transportation to agriculture to construction and more. By and large, these people do not have a real choice about whether or not to go to work, and most did not enter their careers expecting the job to be deadly. Simple strategies to protect them from infection—like N95 respirators for medical personnel, and face coverings for everyone else—have been in short supply, not prioritized, and actively discouraged.

In Indigenous and Black communities—two cultural groups that have historically suffered, and continue to suffer, significant harm at the hands of federal, state, and local governments—deaths are, unsurprisingly, significantly higher. Although officials have expressed alarm at the disparate rates, this alarm has not translated into additional resources to help disadvantaged communities cope. Instead, some leaders have suggested that community members have only themselves to blame.[7] Meanwhile, there has been a clear message from others—both political leaders and medical ethicists—that the deaths of older Americans are unfortunate, but acceptable.[8]

Eleven months into the pandemic, more than thirteen million people have been infected in the United States and nearly three hundred thousand have died.[9] Worldwide, there have been more than sixty-one million cases and almost 1.5 million deaths.[10] Collectively, we seem to be becoming inured to the continuous death toll. Increasingly, the societal message seems to be: this danger is now commonplace and quotidian; deaths are unavoidable; a certain loss of life must simply be accepted. There is even an idea that we should return to a pre-pandemic mode of living in order to create "herd immunity," a state achieved when a high percentage of a population is immune to a pathogen. Usually this is reached through vaccination but, in this case—with COVID-19 vaccines not yet in distribution—it would be achieved through infection, killing millions of people in the process. Proponents of this course demonstrate a callous willingness to sacrifice others' lives.

There is a shocking lack of empathy in almost all of the discourse around COVID-19, and perhaps this is because our national narratives rarely consider the stories of those left behind. Instead, the focus is on the medical professionals at the heart of the "fight," while worthwhile COVID-19 obituary projects, like the one being conducted by the *New York Times*, focus on the accomplishments and contributions of the deceased. In the United States, populist stories about World War II focus on the same things—both for individuals and collectively. They talk about the race to defeat a terrible foe, the courage and sacrifice of combatants, and military ingenuity and strategy. Far less common are the painful stories of those on the home front: the Japanese American citizens in internment camps; the women working in factories while also single-parenting; the men who were designated 4-F (rejected for service); and the families of the service people who were killed.

By 1944, combat deaths must have seemed commonplace in the United States and maybe even acceptable and worthy to many people; necessary sacrifices in the service of a greater goal. This was not the feeling in Cooper's household. When he was posthumously awarded the Air Medal and the Purple Heart, his parents and surviving siblings wanted none of it. They were notified that a colonel and an army photographer would be coming to present the medals and a letter from President Roosevelt. The intention was that these honors should be given to the next of kin, but with the senior Coopers unwilling to participate in the ceremony, the duty passed to the only other blood relative available, Cooper's young niece, Susan. About four years old at the time, she was the child of his brother Frank, who was away fighting in the Pacific. Susan's mother dressed her smartly in corduroy overalls and a ruffled blouse, told her she would meet "two nice men from the war department," and instructed her to "listen very carefully to what they say, so you can tell us about it later." The resulting photograph shows Susan alone in her grandparent's living room with Colonel Oliver Stout.

Three years after the war ended, the flag came, arriving by mail in its sturdy box. Not only did Cooper's parents refuse to open this, they did not want it in their house. Like the medals, it was given to Frank's family. When she was a little older, Susan's father showed her the unopened box and the medals again, explaining why they were important. He also told her that when he died, he did not want a flag on his casket. To him, this was an honor that should be reserved for those killed in action.

This, of course, is the intended function of objects like these. They are meant to celebrate and recognize the lost service member, and typically they are prominently displayed. Special cases are made to showcase the folded flags of those killed in action, with places to display their medals above or below. In our family, however, the flag remains sealed in its box. This is not for any grand ideological reason, like an objection to World War II or war itself, but because the family did not want a visible reminder of their loss. Today, the box resides on the back part of the desk in my father's office, where it does now serve a commemorative function; seeing the box each day reminds him of his extended family. First-person knowledge of Cooper has passed out of living memory, but the grief surrounding his death lingers. Occasionally a young cousin will suggest the flag be unboxed, but my father and his cousins—now the family elders—cannot bring themselves to do it. Remembering how upset their parents and grandparents were by the medals and the flag, they chose, each time, to simply keep them.

During COVID-19, the box with Cooper's flag is important to me not because of ideas about heroism or valor or fighting seemingly unwinnable battles. What matters to me is the weight of the grief—for just one person.

Figure 9.6. Susan Cooper with Colonel Stout at the presentation of Ray Cooper's Purple Heart and Air Medals. Photocopy scan courtesy of Ray Davis.

Cooper was not especially accomplished or connected. He never married or had children. His obituary is ridiculously short. But his family's grief was so powerful that it successfully communicated itself through two subsequent generations. And this is what I think is missing from most of the accounts of COVID-19 deaths; the raw grief of those left behind. How it feels when you can't say goodbye, when you don't know what the death was like, when your loved one's body sits in a refrigerated truck for weeks because funeral homes are too busy, when you can't hold a proper funeral. How deeply the loss of even one individual hurts families, friends, and communities.

Deaths from COVID-19 are preventable. Death after death, inexorably piling one on top of the other as if in a never-ending funeral pyre, should not feel normal. If we shared stories of grief and loss more readily, there might be more empathy and more helpful action. For me, at least, whenever I find the arguments about allowing bars to reopen or not requiring and enforcing face-coverings starting to seem more reasonable, I remember Cooper's funeral flag. Seventy-six years after his death, it remains untouched in its box from St. Avold.

### Fork

Like the first two objects, the fork is an artifact of mourning and remembrance, even though it is a utilitarian item with no funereal associations. Small and very old, it has three carbon-steel tines prone to rust and a wood handle dark with age and missing pins. Yet despite its antique status, the fork receives regular use in my kitchen. I like it as a tiny but strong whisk and because it fits well in my small hand. But I use it preferentially to other kitchen tools primarily because it connects me to my mother, grandmother, and great-grandmother; it is passed from one woman to the next when she sets up her own household.

When I hold the fork, I remember my predecessors' strength and perseverance. My great-grandmother's husband left her with a young child (my grandmother), whom she raised alone while working as a nurse. My grandmother's first child died during a long breech birth, and she suffered from rheumatoid arthritis for much of her life. But I also like to remember that both women loved to have a good time. My great-grandmother was an accomplished hostess, famous for meals that continue to live in family legend. My grandmother was a musician, a coloratura soprano with a wicked sense of humor, who chose not to pursue a promising career in opera so she could devote herself full time to raising three children. The fork is a physical

Figure 9.7. Family fork made of carbon steel with a wood handle. Measurements: 18.5 cm long, 2 cm wide, 1.6 cm high.

connection to these women; when I use it to beat eggs for an omelet or mix milk into biscuit dough, we share both the tool and the activity through space and time. I love the fork best for the daily sense of tangible connection to my own mother, who, thankfully, is still living but is too far away and too at-risk from COVID-19 for me to visit.

In the absence of any national strategy during the COVID-19 pandemic, I have decided that when it comes to my own household decision-making, the most capable adult I know—my mother—is in charge. Like her foremothers, my mom is a tough nut. When I was homesick and missing her during my freshman year in college, she said, "Well, you'll have to get over it. How do you I think I feel? My mother is dead." When I split with a serious long-term boyfriend, she said, "Good riddance. He was too polite. You never knew what he was thinking." After meeting the man I married, a second-generation Italian American who offered a small touch of diversity to our extremely WASP-y family, she said, "This is good. Fresh blood." When I struggled to conceive, she said, "You know, if I had to do it over I probably wouldn't marry or have children. It's not as great as everyone says it is." Wait, *what?*

My mom is the Anthony Fauci of our household because, in addition to her no-nonsense approach to life, she is a medical microbiologist. About COVID-19 she has said, "We are making this much worse than it needs to be." My mother has no patience for time-wasting or inefficacy. The rejection

Figure 9.8. Photograph from 1972 showing four generations of mothers and daughters who have used the fork. Clockwise from upper left: Don Davis, Pauline Hevener, Bertie Madison, and Suzanne Davis. Photograph scan courtesy of Don Davis.

of science and failure of leadership on the pandemic to date drives her crazy, but she remains calm and practical. "Just use your common sense," she tells me when I call to ask various COVID-19 freak-out questions. "What will I do when I can't ask you anymore?" I said during one call, referring not so much to COVID-19 as to, well, *all* the times I want her advice, which are frequent. "You'll figure it out," she replied.

If you have a good relationship with your parents, and if they are reasonably functional humans, their lives and perspectives provide some level of road-mapping for your own. The tangibility of the fork reminds me to consider the problem or question from my mother's or grandmothers' viewpoints. It is an effective tool, for both cookery and mental health. I feel lucky that my household possesses not only the fork but also my mother-in-law's enormous, ancient, meat-slicing knife and her carving board. These items are cherished more than most objects we possess, because they connect us not only to our mothers but also to their daily and weekly rituals. When I am struggling to make a decision or direct my life, I often ask myself: who do I want to be in this situation? Frequently, these women and how they have lived point the way.

Our family is fortunate to have been able to pass important items like these from one generation to the next. The health disparities highlighted by COVID-19 are linked to enormous wealth gaps between whites in the United States and Black, Latinx, and Indigenous Americans. Although income inequality is widely recognized as a problem, public awareness of the impact of race on families' ability to accumulate wealth remains low. Complex systems of discrimination severely disadvantage nonwhite Americans, and these, building on a long history of colonization, genocide, and slavery, create persistent barriers to families' ability to accumulate and transfer wealth, including historic objects.[11] The inability to retain meaningful objects is true, too, for refugees and asylum seekers. My fork and carving knife may seem like small potatoes when considered in the larger economic landscape, a space that includes measurable indicators linked to well-being—things like home-ownership, household wealth, health care, jobs, and earnings. But objects are, nevertheless, important. They preserve memories and tell stories. They are source materials for understanding and creating identity.

Disconnection from your history is not a small thing. In the United States, centuries of illegal acquisition and retention of Indigenous American objects have been only partly redressed by the Native American Graves Protection and Repatriation Act. Today, huge collections of Indigenous cultural material reside outside Native control. As a result, tribal museums like the Ziibiwing Center in Mount Pleasant, Michigan, accomplish much of their exhibition narratives with contemporary Indigenous objects and replicas because they have limited access to the originals produced by their ancestors.[12]

If the absence of real things can reflect historic trauma, so, too, can their creation. In 1942, the Japanese American artist Chiura Obata was an influential faculty member of the University of California, Berkeley. He had emigrated to the United States in 1903 and was in his fifties when he and his family were sent first to the Tanforan temporary detention center in San Bruno, California, and later to the Topaz War Relocation Center in Topaz, Utah, as part of the mass incarceration of Japanese Americans during World War II. While illegally detained, Obata produced more than two hundred paintings and sketches. This body of his work documents the indignities of life in the camps, but also serves as a testimony to his lifelong appreciation of beauty and the natural world. A highly productive artist, Obata's career spanned most of the twentieth century. Today, exhibitions of his work create opportunities for others to learn the personal story of a Japanese immigrant and to acknowledge and remember a painful period in history.[13]

It is too early to know what kinds of material culture might survive to embody the experience of COVID-19, but one crazy-making intangible cultural marker is the saying, "We're all in this together." This expression is repeated constantly, reflecting a profound misunderstanding of just how different Americans' individual circumstances are. As the previous examples attest, human history is not shared so much as lived side by side, with our experiences delineated by factors outside our control. While I can draw strength and comfort from an object in my family for at least four generations, other families struggle to survive economically. Indigenous American objects are now largely claimed by non–Native Americans, and other examples of cultural appropriation abound; Nemesion's funerary stela—of such interest and comfort to me in Ann Arbor—was removed from Egypt during a period when colonial rule supported large-scale excavation and export of that country's cultural heritage.[14] Obata's artwork, meanwhile, preserves his experience of illegal incarceration. We all want to know and draw strength from our histories, and objects can help us do this. They can also help us see, grieve, and develop empathy for how wildly different those histories are.


GRIEF, ACCEPTANCE, AND OBJECT LESSONS

One of the many unnatural things about life during COVID-19 is the absence of shared grief. Funeral and memorial gatherings are prohibited in most places, making it harder to mourn those who have died and creating a prolonged postponement of the catharsis these gatherings bring. Meanwhile, many of us still seem to be stuck in a totally irrational place of either pretending the virus does not exist or assuming it will not affect us. Research on loss and grief posits five main stages of emotion: denial, anger, bargaining, depression, and acceptance.[15] In terms of our collective grief around the tragedy of COVID-19, most of us seem to be lodged somewhere in the first four (I experience all four almost daily). Acceptance has been harder to achieve, possibly because most of us are grieving in isolation.

While I am separated from many of the people and activities I love and cherish, the three objects described in this essay have helped me acknowledge, accept, and understand my own feelings of loss. They have also prompted me to reflect on my values and sharpened my understanding of what matters to me at a difficult time. These three real things function as a form of auxiliary memory, connecting me to the experiences of those who came before me and offering insight and perspective. They are tools for understanding and, in this case, for acceptance and coping.

If individuals can choose objects as things to think with, and things to grieve with, so too can societies. In the United States, a transformative social justice movement is occurring at the same time as the COVID-19 pandemic. In response to the ongoing deaths of Black Americans at the hands of police, there have been massive public protests seeking criminal justice reform. But the movement has also called into question problematic monuments in public spaces. In many cases, these are Jim Crow–era statues that were purposefully erected to perpetuate ideas of white supremacy.[16] As we grapple with how to treat these monuments—deny, as some would like to do, that they are racist? destroy them? recontextualize them? remove them?—we are thinking primarily about what we do not want in our public spaces. As with COVID-19, most of us are somewhere in the first four stages of grief. If we can acknowledge and accept the truth of the pain and exclusion these monuments represent, we can ask the next and more hopeful question: what *do* we want?

If we recognize that objects and artwork can be powerful tools—connecting us to other people, places, times, and ideas—then we can carefully and thoughtfully choose what to include in our public and private spheres. We can ask: What do we value? Who do we want to be, in this moment and in the months and years to come? Whose stories do we need to hear? What do we need to grieve and what do we want to remember?

Life during COVID-19 is stressful, confusing, lonely, and sad. The real things that surround us can, however, be tools for reflection. They can help us process feelings of grief and loss and, if understanding and inspiration come as a result, they may also help us find new paths for the future.

## Notes

1. University of Michigan Kelsey Museum of Archaeology, https://lsa.umich.edu /kelsey
2. Hooper, *Funerary Stelae.*
3. Hooper's catalog of the stelae lacks page numbers, but these three translations come from entries 178, 93, and 112, respectively.
4. In Hooper's catalog these are entries 54, 58, 21, and 189.
5. Blau and Fingerman, *Consequential Strangers.*
6. National WWII Museum, "Research Starters."
7. Goldstein, "Analysis."
8. Fernandez and Montgomery, "Texas Tries to Balance"; Churchill, "On Being an Elder"; Miller, "Why I Support Age-Related Rationing."
9. Centers for Disease Control and Prevention, "Coronavirus Disease 2019."
10. *New York Times,* "Coronavirus Map."
11. Tippet et al., "Beyond Broke"; Kraus, Rucker, and Richeson, "Americans Misperceive Racial Economic Equality"; Hamilton and Logan, "Wealth Equality."
12. Ziibiwing Center of Anishinabe Culture and Lifeways, http://www.sagchip.org /ziibiwing/, accessed April 4, 2021.
13. Obata and Hill, *Topaz Moon.* An online gallery of Obata's artwork can be seen on the Smithsonian American Art Museum's web page for the exhibition *Chiura Obata: American Modern,* https://americanart.si.edu/exhibitions/obata, accessed April 4, 2021.
14. Stevenson, *Scattered Finds.*
15. Kübler-Ross, *On Death and Dying.*
16. Hayter, "Confederate Monuments."

## References

Blau, Melinda, and Karen L. Fingerman. *Consequential Strangers: The Power of People Who Don't Seem to Matter—but Really Do.* New York: Norton, 2010.
Centers for Disease Control and Prevention. "Coronavirus Disease 2019 (COVID-19) in the U.S." Centers for Disease Control and Prevention. November 28, 2020. https:// www.cdc.gov/coronavirus/2019-ncov/cases-updates/cases-in-us.html.
Churchill, Larry R. "On Being an Elder in a Pandemic." Hastings Center. April 13, 2020. https://www.thehastingscenter.org/on-being-an-elder-in-a-pandemic/.
Fernandez, Manny, and David Montgomery. "Texas Tries to Balance Local Control

with the Threat of a Pandemic." *New York Times*, March 24, 2020, sec. U.S. https://
www.nytimes.com/2020/03/24/us/coronavirus-texas-patrick-abbott.html

Goldstein, Lauren. "Analysis: Black Communities Have Been Hit Hard by the Coronavirus. Some Think Black Americans Are to Blame." *Washington Post*, May 14, 2020.
https://www.washingtonpost.com/politics/2020/05/14/black-communities-have
-been-hit-hard-by-coronavirus-some-people-think-they-are-blame/

Hamilton, Darrick, and Trevon Logan. "Why Wealth Equality Remains out of Reach
for Black Americans." The Conversation. 2019. http://theconversation.com/why
-wealth-equality-remains-out-of-reach-for-black-americans-111483

Hayter, Julian M. "Confederate Monuments Are about Maintaining White Supremacy."
*Washington Post*, August 3, 2017.

Hooper, Finley Allison. *Funerary Stelae from Kom Abou Billou*. Ann Arbor, MI: Kelsey
Museum of Archaeology, 1961.

Kraus, Michael W., Julian M. Rucker, and Jennifer A. Richeson. "Americans Misperceive
Racial Economic Equality." *Proceedings of the National Academy of Sciences* 114.39
(2017): 10324–31. https://doi.org/10.1073/pnas.1707719114

Miller, Franklin G. "Why I Support Age-Related Rationing of Ventilators for Covid-19
Patients." Hastings Center. April 9, 2020. https://www.thehastingscenter.org/why
-i-support-age-related-rationing-of-ventilators-for-covid-19-patients/

National WWII Museum. "Research Starters: Worldwide Deaths in World War II."
https://www.nationalww2museum.org/students-teachers/student-resources/res
earch-starters/research-starters-worldwide-deaths-world-war. Accessed August
11, 2020.

*New York Times*. "Coronavirus Map: Tracking the Global Outbreak." Sec. World. https://
www.nytimes.com/interactive/2020/world/coronavirus-maps.html

Obata, Chiura, and Kimi Kodani Hill. *Topaz Moon: Chiura Obata's Art of the Internment*.
Berkeley, CA: Heyday Books, 2000.

Kübler-Ross, Elisabeth. *On Death and Dying*. London: Routledge, 2009.

Stevenson, Alice. *Scattered Finds: Archaeology, Egyptology and Museums*. London: UCL
Press, 2019.

Tippett, Rebecca, Avis Jones-DeWeever, Maya Rockeymoore, Darrick Hamilton, and
William Darity Jr. "Beyond Broke: Why Closing the Racial Wealth Gap Is a Priority
for National Economic Security." Duke University Center for Global Policy Solutions, May 2014. https://globalpolicysolutions.org/wp-content/uploads/2014/04
/Beyond_Broke_FINAL.pdf

# CHAPTER 10

# Looking Backward in Order to Look Forward

## Lessons about Humanity and the Humanities from the Plague at Athens

*Sara Forsdyke*

COVID-19 has resulted in an alarming number of deaths, but also in an alarming rise in levels of social distrust. Citizens are buying guns at record rates. A militia group in Michigan attempted to kidnap the governor. Conspiracy theories abound as faith in our institutions erodes. How did we reach this point, and how might we emerge from this crisis with our trust in one another restored or even strengthened? Perhaps surprisingly, the humanities can provide some answers.

One such resource is the ancient historian Thucydides's account of the plague that took place in Athens in 430–428 BCE. This plague, which was probably a strain of typhus, killed more than a third of the population of Athens, including its wise and charismatic leader, Pericles. Thucydides, who contracted the plague himself, was not only the first to recognize the phenomenon of immunity, but also described the social consequences of a pandemic in horrifying detail. From Thucydides's vivid and disturbing account, we not only develop our capacity to empathize with the suffering of our fellow human beings but can recognize the potentially catastrophic effects of such events on society. Indeed, Thucydides's shocking portrayal of a total societal breakdown can spur us to devise ways to anticipate and avoid such a devastating outcome. One clear lesson is that societies must reinforce institutions of social cohesion that build bonds of familiarity and trust between citizens in order to survive the disruptions caused by pandemics.

Thucydides notes that the plague was more widespread and more fatal than anyone could remember in the past. Previously healthy individuals were suddenly stricken with fever, inflammations, and vomiting. Coughing followed and then outbreaks of lesions on the skin. Victims suffered an unbearable sensation of internal heat that made them unable to tolerate even the thinnest of linen clothing. They were also struck by such a powerful thirst that some threw themselves into cisterns around the city that were used to catch rainwater. Regardless of these efforts, however, the afflicted were unable to quench their thirst, or to rest or to sleep, such was their torment. After seven or eight days, the sickness spread to their intestines and they suffered extreme diarrhea, from which they often perished. Thucydides writes that the suffering caused by the disease was almost beyond the power of words to describe, and indeed almost too painful for human nature to endure.

Yet more horrifying than his description of the disease itself is his account of the breakdown of social norms of behavior. Since neither doctors nor appeals to the divine proved effective against the disease, the Athenians gave up hope and exhibited behaviors that would not previously have been tolerated. Some neglected to care for the sick, even if the afflicted were their own relatives. The bodies of the dead were left to rot in the streets or were thrown on the funeral pyres that had been built for others. Lawlessness broke out since no one expected to live long enough to be brought to trial and "a much severer sentence hung over them." Scariest of all was the emergence of a new code of behavior that reversed the normal meanings of ethical terms: the good and the useful were now redefined as the pleasurable and the profitable. Indeed, no one was eager to do what was right anymore since it was unclear if one would perish before attaining this noble goal. In sum, Athens descended into chaos as a result of the overwhelming nature of the disaster.

It is worth noting that Thucydides was a literary artist of consummate skill and that he certainly embellished his account of the plague for emotional effect. Indeed, after the plague subsided, Athens continued to lead an alliance of city-states in a war against its great rival Sparta and even launched a massive invasion of Sicily. Athens lost the war and the invasion was repelled, but nevertheless it is apparent that the Athenians were not completely at the mercy of the Spartans because of the plague. Yet Thucydides's account raises an important question: if the relatively small and unified city-state of Athens could experience such social breakdown, what chances are there for our large and divided nation? More importantly, we might ask what we can do to avoid or mitigate such an unraveling.

Just before he describes the plague, Thucydides paints a glowing portrait of the Athenians united under the charismatic leadership of Pericles. In a speech given to commemorate those Athenians who fell in the first year of the war with the Spartans, Thucydides presents Pericles as explaining to the Athenians the reasons for the greatness of Athens. Foremost among those reasons is the democratic political system. Not only does such a system serve the good of the many rather than the few, but it offers both equal political rights and equality before the law to all. In addition to political freedom, Pericles notes, the Athenians are free and tolerant of one another in their private lives. It should of course be acknowledged that the Athenian democracy did not grant full political rights to women and accepted slavery as well as the presence of a large group of noncitizen foreigners. Yet it was arguably because of the blend of freedom and equality among citizens—and Pericles's ability to unite them around these ideals—that the Athenians were able to weather the twin disasters of war and plague.

How do we measure up against democratic Athens? Our system is called a democracy, yet does it serve the good of the many as opposed to the few? Far from it. The current pandemic has further exposed the glaring inequalities in education, health, employment, wealth, and almost any other measure of well-being. In principle we enjoy equal political rights, but voting is made difficult by our failure to register voters automatically, and equality is undermined by gerrymandering. Equality before the law? The injustices of the criminal justice system, let alone the ongoing atrocities of policing, belie any claim we might make to granting all citizens the equal protection of the law. While it might be said that we have achieved a high level of freedom in our private lives, it has left us isolated and unable to come together to solve our common problems. Rather we are more divided and gridlocked than ever.

One way to redress these problems is through enlightened leadership, such as that of Pericles, who was able to unite citizens around a common vision and values. While there are many examples of such leadership in America today at the local and state level, there is a gaping absence of it at the national level, as the twin epidemics of COVID-19 and racism have glaringly exposed. In addition to uniting the Athenians around their shared democratic values, Pericles spoke of the richness of Athenians' cultural life, their openness to the world, and the robustness of their culture of debate and deliberation, "which served not as an obstacle to action, but a necessary preliminary step to action." The absence of such inspiring leadership in the White House could not be any more apparent than in Trump's focus on blaming foreigners for the virus, his criticisms of governors for their sensible responses to a public health emergency, or his treatment of peaceful demonstrators as enemy combatants. Instead of leading, he dodges responsibility. Instead of raising us up, he lowers us down. Instead of uniting us, he divides us.

But what can we do besides replace a morally bankrupt leader with a more enlightened one, as we have now done? One of the answers that Thucydides provides is to focus on creating bonds of familiarity and trust between citizens that can help societies withstand great national (or global) catastrophes. Besides his portrait of the Athenians united under Pericles's leadership, Thucydides provides a vivid portrait of what happens in states riven by factions in which there is little social trust. In such situations, Thucydides writes, partisans of each side seek to win the advantage over their adversaries at whatever cost and previous standards of behavior—moderation, consideration of all sides of a question, and willingness to compromise—are abandoned. Such was the situation in many ancient Greek city-states, where bloody civil wars broke out between democrats and oligarchs, and extremists on both sides took violent revenge on their opponents whenever they gained the upper hand.

How can we build trust in a nation of our great size and diversity? Education is surely one answer, and providing universal access to a quality education is one way to prepare citizens for reflective and constructive engagement in our common future. And the humanities should be a central part of that education. Historical and imaginative literature can help us recognize our common humanity and allow us to see patterns in our own behaviors and in society at large that are too close up to perceive or too raw to acknowledge directly. It develops our capacity for empathy and gives us perspectives on our connections to other human beings. In other words, it creates mutual understanding and the ability to cooperate with others towards common ends.

But how can we continue to build and reinforce trust between citizens after they have finished their formal education? Americans used to enjoy a rich associative life, as the great French observer of early American democracy, Alexis de Tocqueville, famously observed. With the growth of our nation and the acceleration of the pace of modern life, we have all too little time to come together to listen to one another or engage in a common activity. One promising effort to address this gap in our collective lives is Eric Lui's Citizen University, which in 2016 initiated a series of community discussions across the country where citizens from all walks of life come together to engage with one another around topics of common concern. Known as "Civic Saturdays," these meetings usually begin with a meditation on a historical or literary text that can inspire us to live up to the full meaning of what it means to be a citizen of a democracy.

By focusing on a text by a "dead white male from a European tradition" in this essay, I do not mean to diminish or marginalize resources from other cultural traditions that can help us navigate our collective future. In fact, the Greeks did not think of themselves as "white" and had much deeper connections historically to the cultures of the Middle East and North Africa than to (later) Western Europe. The text of Thucydides's history itself was likely preserved via the great library at Alexandria in Egypt, and a mosaic of him was laid in Jaresh, Jordan, in the third century CE. The appropriation of the Greeks into a "Western" tradition is a product of the modern era. But that is another story.

Regardless, texts from ancient Greece are just some of many historical and cultural resources from all over the world that can help put the present moment in perspective and reorient ourselves around a shared vision of the future. The humanities, in all their breadth and diversity, are needed in these times more than ever. As Thucydides himself wrote, the things that happened in the past will happen again in similar ways, given human nature. In these times, we need the humanities to help gird ourselves against the challenges of today, so that we hang together rather than allow things to fall apart.

# CHAPTER 11

# Protests, Prayers, and Protections

## Three Visitations during COVID-19

*William A. Calvo-Quirós*

As the COVID-19 pandemic spreads all over the world and the fears of its immediate and long-term effects define the lives of millions of people forced into lockdown, a resurgence of religious practices and rituals for healing is also taking place. Innumerable private and public acts of piety, such as virtual masses, rosaries, and Zoom religious events, have populated the news. From Pope Francis's short peregrination (on March 15, 2020) near the Church of San Marcello in Rome, defying in part the Italian government's shelter-in-place ordinance, to visit the shrine of "a famous crucifix that believers claim helped to save Romans from the plague in 1522";[1] to the emotional aerial blessing travels of the Virgen de Los Angeles, the patroness of Costa Rica, that for two days (March 21–23, 2020) was carried out over the country in a helicopter to allow Catholic believers to see her without leaving their quarantine homes,[2] Catholics worldwide are using their religion and spirituality to deal with the challenges created by the COVID-19 health crisis, and for some, even the fears of the end of times.

Popular devotions and practices requesting divine protection and intervention have fused with those sanitary rituals implored by civil and medical authorities. Holy water, saint prayers, as well as hand sanitizers and face-masks with religious images are working all together. Furthermore, despite the evidence that social distancing is essential for controlling the pandemic, many Catholic congregations in the United States requested exemptions from the stay-at-home orders on the grounds of their religious freedom.[3] Some even held religious public services against local, state, and the Vatican's ordinances. These events show again the intersections/clashes between religious and secular life, and indicate how people are trying, in many different ways, to give sense and meaning to their realities through faith during the pandemic. People under the threat of COVID are not only emphasizing old forms of religious piety, but also adapting and reconfiguring them, sometimes creating new spiritual practices, as a way to connect across different forms of Catholicism. This essay explores three distinct but overlapping Catholic religious practices during COVID, where race, class, gender, and age differences are negotiated or even contested.

Spiritual rituals for healing and protection are not new, nor are they expressions exclusive to the West or Christianity. Yet during this pandemic, many public and collective religious and spiritual practices have been modified to accommodate the closure of holy sites and churches. They have not only provided a human face to the drama of everyday survival during COVID-19, but also allowed the believers to engage in the performativity of faith within the intimacy of their own homes, without the need to leave their shelter-in-place to visit a holy site or a church. They provided a flexible, customizable, mobile, and decentralized experience of the divine that remained personal, intimate, and simultaneously profoundly collective.[4] In broader terms, the resurfacing of religious practices during the COVID-19 health and social crisis should be understood within a historical continuum that connects the present with previous "pestilences." Furthermore, it illustrates how the boundaries between institutional, dogmatic, and vernacular religiosity are never static but somewhat flexible and always changing.

In the United States and the rest of the world, the Catholic experience is defined deeply by social factors like gender, location, class, wealth, and so on. Catholic membership, in broader terms, happens at many different levels and is expressed in different degrees of intensity. Some identify themselves as practicing Catholics, attend liturgical services, and define their politics and life expectations on strict religious precepts. At the same time, there are those whose Catholicism is determined more on cultural grounds; they may engage in Catholic piety practices based only on familiar, cultural, or ethnic affiliations. The Catholic Church is more than its administrative and hierarchy bodies, exemplified by the Roman Curia, the pope, bishops, and cardinals. Still, it is also composed of thousands of well-organized religious orders, local priests, and laypeople. In broader terms, it is not a homogenous organization, as there are many "types" of Catholics. As expected, they don't always agree, even on essential matters about health practices, gender, race, or immigration issues. I subtitled this chapter "Three Visitations" because I want to explore three different religious experiences and ways people connect across various forms of Catholicism during or because of the COVID-19 pandemic. They manifest how social tensions around race, class, and gender become amplified and negotiated but again entangled and contested as people engage with the spiritual for protection, comfort, and social change during a period of crisis and transformation.

## "THE BODY OF CHRIST CAN'T BREATHE"

Under this phrase, written on a board and carried by a parishioner at St. Columba Catholic Church of Oakland, California, its members protested[5] what they described as the systematic "sin of racism" inside the Catholic Church.[6] On June 28, 2020, the event was part of the many Black Lives Matter protests during the COVID-19 pandemic in the United States. The same day, a very different discourse took place in another Catholic church. Father Theodore Rothrock, the pastor of St. Elizabeth Seton parish, located at the Diocese of Lafayette-in-Indiana, in a bulletin to his community, described the Black Lives Matter protesters as "maggots and parasites at best" and "serpents in the garden." Such opposite and contradictory points of view have long existed simultaneously within the terrains of the Catholic Church, but the complications of the COVID moment have stirred and revealed, one more time, the complicated and turbulent intersections between race and religion in place in the United States.

The phrase "The Body of Christ Can't Breathe" describes and connects two essential components for the organizers. The exhortation evokes George Floyd's death on May 25, 2020, the forty-six-year-old African American man who died from asphyxiation after being pinned down by the knee of an Anglo police officer, Derek Chauvin, in Minneapolis, Minnesota. Transcripts of the incident show that Floyd told the officer, "I can't breathe" more than twenty times before he passed out and eventually died. This police brutality event sparked protests across the United States and the world, like the one carried out by the parishioners at St. Columba Catholic Church.

Simultaneously, the St. Columba's group calls to attention a central component of the Roman Catholic faith: the presence of the Mystical Body of Christ. This concept is rooted in Saint Paul's teachings to the first Christian communities, located in what is now known as Turkey. The letter describes the church and all Christ-followers as members of a spiritual body,[7] in which Christ is "the head of [t]his body, the Church."[8] They also invoked another episode where Jesus declared, "Whatever you did for one of these . . . , you did for me."[9] In other words, for Catholics and other denominations, Christ is presented as a unifying collective experience shared by the members of the church, where the harm to one is harm to all.

The phrase's radical power emerges by connecting the parishioners' experience of racial oppression and their desire for social change as part of the ethos of Christianity and Catholicism. If the church is genuinely interconnected as a single spiritual body, therefore, the oppression and pain experienced by internal and social racism toward some of its members affects,

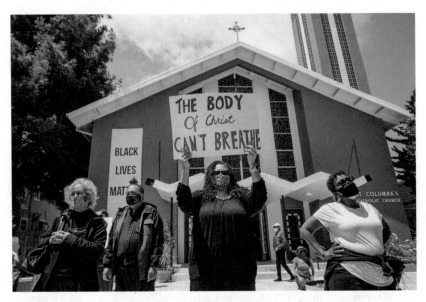

Figure 11.1. "The Body of Christ Can't Breathe." Parishioners from St. Columba Catholic Church in Oakland, Calif. Protests on Sunday, June 28, 2020. Photo by Brandon Tauszik, *The San Francisco Chronicle.*

delays, and compromises the church's moral stands and the fulfillment of God's intended plan, as understood by Christians. As strategically constructed by this Catholic group, it is not just Floyd dying by asphyxiation. It is Christ himself who cannot breathe. Here the protesters called to our attention that Christ himself (as manifested in them, as part of his spiritual body), in agony, dying by unnatural causes. They call for change by deploying their inherent rights as members within that institution, putting their lives on the front line, not just by reporting the crime and the possibilities of retaliation and further discrimination, but also by exposing themselves to the COVID-19 infection.

The recognition of the intersections between racism and Christian faith within pulpits, churches, and places of worship in the context of the United States is not new. Martin Luther King Jr., both a reverend and a civil rights leader, eloquently described these intersections: "I think it is one of the tragedies of our nation, one of the shameful tragedies, that . . . Sunday morning [service] is one of the most segregated hours, if not the most segregated hours, in Christian America."[10] As described here, the paradoxical challenge is that places of worship can be both spaces where racial discrimination can be implemented and institutionalized, and simultaneously, for many, spaces meant to promote collective change toward a more just society. For example, the Sanctuary Movement began in the 1980s as a religious response to the US government's refusal to grant asylum to Central American refugees fleeing civil wars and violence in the region. At the pinnacle of its development, the Sanctuary Movement comprised over five hundred religious groups and congregations from a range of Christian denominations, including Roman Catholics, Lutherans, Presbyterians, Baptists, Quakers, as well as Jews and non-denominational activists. Today, in the context of the Black Lives Matter and the Me Too Movement, a more secular version of the Sanctuary Movement has emerged toward the inclusion of cities and universities as they organize nationally to protect undocumented migrants, in particular Dreamers.[11]

There was also, of course, a more literal meaning to the sign the protesters were holding. The protests around Floyd's murder happened during a pandemic defined, ironically, by a pathogenic death that happens via asphyxiation. The disease attacks people's respiratory system, making it tough to breathe and get oxygen. Death by COVID-19 occurred, for the most part, due to inflammation of the lungs, pulmonary embolism, or even strokes. But just as the case of Floyd demonstrated the disproportional killing and incarceration of people of color in the United States, COVID-19 infection and death also disproportionately affected poor, migrant, and communities of color, in both cases because of the long-standing consequences of social inequality. Floyd, himself, had COVID at the time of his death.

Furthermore, even prevention of COVID-19 was tainted by these legacies. Many in these communities fell under the designation of "essential workers," which became synonymous with "disposable" because of the disproportionate level of exposure, lack of preventive measures at work, and the limited possibilities to stay home.[12] In other words, what we are witnessing here is the manifestation of a long-term slow death of people of color by the unnatural causes of systematic racism.

The St. Columba community were not just Catholics; they were also members of the United States' social body. Their intervention cannot be reduced to only racism in the pulpits. Still, by extrapolation, it intervenes as part of the larger protest movement taking place during the pandemic. Their "Can't Breathe" includes all other forms of oppression that have compromised not only their spiritual body as members of the Catholic Church, but the body of society as a whole. It engages with the larger project of trying to dismantle patriarchy, sexism, homophobia, nationalism, classism, xenophobia, and so on.

(UN)MASKING FAITH DURING A PANDEMIC:
THE POLITICS OF FACIAL MASKS

On one occasion in the middle of the pandemic, while I was attending service at Saint Thomas, one of the two Catholic parishes close to my house in Ann Arbor, Michigan, I was struck by the priest's request as I approached him for communion. He wanted me to take my face mask off before I received the Eucharist.[13] I noticed that everyone waiting in line had taken their masks off, and I was the only person still wearing one, also one of the few persons of color within a majority of white parishioners. I was accustomed to the common practice of receiving communion in my hands. The priest did not want to give me communion until I removed it. It was unclear to me how much he cared about my well-being. Because I felt pressure from him and the people waiting, I took my face mask off. For this priest, as he implied during his sermons, the use of masks was very much tied to a larger discourse about religious freedom and state interventions. This priest was not alone; the resistance to wearing face masks became a central element of tension among many conservative religious groups.

Moreover, wearing masks also became a marker in popular discourses of masculinity and freedom. Paramilitary groups protested Michigan's pandemic orders, and some of their organizers planned to kidnap the state governor to protest her COVID safety policies.[14] Again, it is crucial to recognize how we cannot disassociate secular and religious spaces as isolated entities, but rather they are profoundly interconnected. For example, the discourses about innate race and male superiority that permeate secular spaces are also circulated within religious-based groups.

The wearing (or not wearing) of masks reflected more than mere health requirements. It was demonstrated in religious and political events alike. The then-US president's refusal to wear one, recommend their use, or recognize their efficacy as a preventive health measure did not escape the media, which consistently criticized and discussed his behavior, including the undertones about masculinity's performance.[15]

Masks became venues to manifest religious beliefs and define faith spaces. They were elevated and transformed from mere medical personal protective equipment (PPE) into spiritual amulets, reliquaries of faith, and public billboards of religiosity and people's politics. For some Catholics in the United States, face masks emerged during the pandemic as a venue to express their faith publicly by wearing images of the Virgin Mary, popular saints, and angels. I saw the first mask of this kind on one of Saint Thomas's parishioners. When I asked her, "Why are you wearing an image of Our Lady of Guadalupe on your mask?" she said, "Mary is everywhere. Why not? She can also be in [*sic*] our masks. She is looking after us. She is protecting me. I am a proud Catholic." Recognizing that I, like her, was also a Latino, she added, "Es nuestra cultura," it is our culture.[16] Then, she sent me to check out a Latino-based online store from Los Angeles, where she was originally from. Under the slogan "Wear your Mexican heritage with pride," the company, Charro Azteca, claims to be owned by "first-generation Mexican-Americans, . . . [a] family operated company [that] understands how proud you are of your Mexican roots here in the U.S."[17] The company sells an array of clothing products and accessories targeting established Mexican immigrants and Mexican Americans, including a vast number of facial masks, a few of them with the images of the Virgin of Guadalupe and Saint Jude the Apostle. Here the boundaries between race, religiosity, and the consumption of religious symbols and iconography that have been extracted from their spiritual context are blurred and not always well defined. Here cultural affiliation not only is consumed, but becomes both a central identifier and a marketing strategy of the company. Moreover, wearing a Mexican-inspired mask is presented as cultural "pride."

As Charro Azteca explains, the impact of COVID-19 on labor became a factor in the production and marketing of the mask since "Many of our workers in Mexico have been affected by the lockdown. Unfortunately, they had to stop making boots, sombreros, belts, sandals, etc . . . So we had many of them turn their design work into masks."[18] By pointing out this reality, the company asserts that the purchase of a mask becomes more than just a proud cultural statement; it is also a way for US customers to feel that they are helping workers affected by the pandemic, workers who are—as Charro Azteca describes—"Mexican artesanos," Mexican craftsmen and women, most likely poor Indigenous workers. In other words, the customers were to believe that their purchase will help, at least indirectly, the quality of life of the *artesanos*. It was unclear to what extent this was verifiable. Here the consumption of religion and the marketing of culture are deeply juxtaposed.

Moreover, the company openly refers to their *charro*, or Jalisco, heritage, connecting two essential elements. The region of Jalisco has been one of the most important "exporters" of migratory labor into the United States for most of the last century, and it was also the center of the Cristero War, a religious conflict following the Mexican Revolution, between the local Catholics and the secular Mexican state between 1926 and 1929. Here religion, politics, migration, and the *charro* aesthetics collate.

Charro Azteca was not, by any means, the only company selling Catholic-

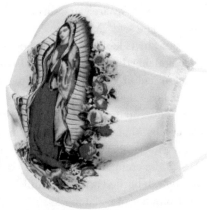

Figures 11.2, 11.3, and 11.4. Different Catholic-inspired masks and face coverings. From left to right: "Focus on me not the Storm" by PapiChulo (Etsy.com); "Virgin Mary Face Mask" by Charro Azteca (CharroAzteca.com); "St. Michael Catholic Archangel" by Beltschazar (Etsy.com).

inspired masks during the pandemic; global digital megaplayers like Amazon and eBay, as well as decentralized craft-market places like Etsy, capitalized on the intersections of fears, health care needs, and popular religiosity. The first two companies distanced themselves from any open descriptions of the religious nature of the products they sold. Yet Etsy, with its emphasis on local craft products, was more relaxed and unapologetic about the religiously inspired character of these products. Moreover, Etsy, via providers named Blessed Catholic, Global Church Miracles, Catholic Marks, Theotokos, Grace Thru Faith Gifts, and Devine Designs, provided highly specialized, customizable masks for Catholic-specific events like baptisms, first communions, confirmations, and weddings. There were also customized masks for funerals, but those tended to emphasize more pan-religious motifs, focusing on the individual's remembrance.

Most Catholic-inspired masks focused on displaying religious imagery such as saints, angels, crosses, rosaries, and so on. Some of them combined these images with messages such as "Catholic since 33 AD" or utilized religious icons with phrases attributed to spiritual figures as inspirational quotations. For example, there were masks featuring the face of Saint Father Pio with the words "Pray, Hope and Don't Worry" or with the image of the Virgin of Guadalupe with the text "Let Not Your Heart Be Disturbed," referring to a phrase allegedly given to Saint Juan Diego when the Virgin of Guadalupe appeared to him in Mexico in 1531. Other face coverings carried more subtle messages by merely displaying a white cross on a black background or just the text "Phi 4:13," referring to an epistle written by the apostle Paul to the early Christian communities in Philippi (modern Fílippoi) Greece. The epistle's reference reads, "I can do all this through him who gives me strength."[19] Other masks display more generic Christian exhortations such as "Faith over Fear," "There is power in the name of Jesus," and "Jesus Saves." Playing on the word "essential" used during the pandemic to describe workers who were crucial for the sustaining of the nation, a mask reads, "Jesus is essential: Yesterday, Today & Forever." Via these masks, it became evident that, under the imminent possibility of biological death, for some believers religion provided a referential anchor to understand the precarious circumstances surrounding their vulnerability. For them, the end of the body may be imminent, but saving their soul was essential.

There were also masks with explicit references to biblical passages that were intentionally reinscribed to help believers overcome the turbulent times created by the COVID-19 health crisis, even within the context of the social unrest. These masks portray images of a storm or the end of times, with Christ extending his hand and looking into you; the mask has the phrase "Focus on me, not the Storm," referring to the passage where the apostles are out on a fishing boat in the middle of a storm and Jesus appears to them and calms the storm. Another mask depicts Christ's crucifixion with the phrase "Public Display of Affection" in a large font, followed by a Bible passage that reads, "'God demonstrates his own love for us in this: While we were still sinners Christ died for us' Romans 5:8."[20] Most of these masks evoked predictable narratives about the performance of masculinity, in this case by the use of dark and black tones, bold fonts, rough nature settings, and the perpetuation of hypermasculine representations of Jesus Christ.

The emergence and popularization of these hypermasculine theme masks during the pandemic cannot be disassociated from the many expressions of social tensions and unrest that built up for decades and manifested during the lockdown, for example, tensions around race relationships and police profiling, the perpetuation/elimination of historical monuments, and the immigration debates. For many, these events were framed collectively as omen signs of the apocalyptic times they were witnessing. For them, the world was under siege, and not just because of COVID-19. As defined by some right-wing groups, a "Cancel Culture Movement"[21] against (Anglo-Saxon) America's values, history, and unquestionable exceptionality was underway. An emphasis on hypermasculine national narratives about an imaginary homogeneity ethnostate accompanied these discourses.[22] Here, specific state-sanctioned masculinity models merged with faith so that facial masks became tools to broadcast gender and nationalist ideology.

As exemplified in the masks' aesthetics, being a Christian man was presented as synonymous with being strong, self-assured, faithful, and tacitly heterosexual. These elements were not limited to the representation of Jesus Christ as a "strong man," but also by the hypermasculinization of the archangel Michael depicted in many of the masks. For many Catholics, Saint Michael is traditionally understood as the highest commander of God's celestial army against fallen angels and evil. Therefore, he is depicted as a soldier in armor or shield, often bearing a lance directed to the Devil or Satan, very similar to the popular image of Saint George slaying a dragon and differentiated only by the wings. His devotion, and particularly the prayer to Saint Michael, has become a staple element within traditionalist and conservative branches of Catholicism, which see him as a protector "against the malice and snares of the devil . . . Satan and all evil spirits who prowl about the world, seeking the ruin of souls."[23] The masks' images emphasize a hypermasculine Saint Michael, both at the symbolic and semiotic level, indeed as a protector and defender against a pathogenic virus and other types of "evils" in the world that try to create change and threaten normativity.

I don't see these particular religious masks as simply personal protective equipment (PPE) but as conduits of religious and masculine ideology about the safety of both the individual and collective social bodies. Here the figures of Jesus, Saint Michael, and Saint George, all as mirror images of the same hypermasculine subject, exemplified the use of the old trope that normalizes a particularly narrow type of masculinity, one that is essential for the perpetuation of an ethno-nation, which therefore must be emulated, protected, and safeguarded for the sake of the state. In this case, the masks work both as sanitary and ideological devices within the consumption of pious religiosity.

## VISITATION FRIDAYS: CREATING HUMAN CONNECTIONS VIA ZOOM

On Friday, March 27, 2020, almost three weeks into the Italian lockdown and just a week before the beginning of Holy Week, Pope Francis emitted an *Urbi et Orbi* ("to the city [of Rome] and the world"), a kind of unique and solemn moment of prayer to the world, and in this case, for those affected by the coronavirus. Following tradition, the event came with a plenary indulgence, or a particular spiritual grace, for those people who, as Holy See Press Office director Matteo Bruni explained, engaged in praying for "the end to the epidemic, [and the] relief for those who are suffering"[24] or who had died because of it. Almost immediately, people around the world started many virtual prayer groups, including rosaries. I got invited by my friend Paula, a social worker specializing in gerontology, to participate in one of these. It started informally as a regular rosary with people coming and going. Within a few weeks it became a regular group of around twenty-five to thirty people who met daily via Zoom for prayer at 5:00 p.m. This group is made of people I have met through my research about the church, a few friends, their mothers, and their colleagues. The format has always been the same: for the first minutes people share their prayer intentions, and then we voluntarily divide the praying segments among the participants. In the second half of the meeting, we pray the rosary.

Most of the participants are retirees who are living independently or in retirement communities. Because of their age and living situations, many are at high risk, are isolated, and have minimal socialization possibilities during the COVID-19 pandemic. In the beginning, we spent a lot of time resolving technical issues, and the learning curve was intense. Over time, our virtual rosary has emerged from being just a prayer group to being a way to build community and support each other during this unprecedented time.

As the weeks went by, the group evolved into a more personal daily event. Several men came to the group, but they did not stay, so I became, for the most part, the only man attending, and I was probably also the youngest person. We did not have a lot in common, not just because of our age differences, as some of them are older than my parents, but also because I am single, and most of them have been married with children. Furthermore, we did not all share the same political views during a fraught election year, and we do not belong to similar cultural, racial, or class groups. Nevertheless, we have connected with each other due to our shared sense of humanity, fears, perplexity about the pandemic, and deep desire for change. I had never prayed the rosary consistently, but the daily meeting with "the rosary ladies" has become one of the most critical and consistent events for me during the lockdown.

The first minutes of the rosary, when people express their petitions and ask for prayers, is a profoundly human and vulnerable space. People have prayed for their troubled children and grandchildren, for their friends in nursing homes, for the different catastrophes and calamities worldwide beyond religious affiliation, such as the Beirut explosion[25] or the fires in California.[26] People have asked for prayers for those who have lost their jobs because of the lockdown, for successful surgeries, and for loved ones in recovery. We have prayed for family members experiencing drug addiction, depression, and racial violence. After months of our daily meetings, we have become closer and have started to remember each other's petitions . . . even when one of us cannot attend. We have also reminded each other of our intentions if we happen to forget them. When one of the older members unexpectedly stopped attending, we all became worried and contacted her retirement home to be sure she was safe. She was in the hospital, and we prayed for her every day until she came back. We were so happy when we saw her again.

During these weeks, we followed the tragedy of the niece of one of the attendees, whose entire family had contracted COVID-19 in the Philippines. The young mother was in a coma. We prayed for a miracle that did not happen. Her niece eventually died, leaving behind a little daughter. We suffered together from the news. We prayed for Venezuela, as the family of one of us has been living there during the pandemic and under deplorable national health conditions.[27] We have been praying to celebrate a friend's family who was able to adopt a child after years of struggling with Italy's bureaucracy. In many ways, each other's intentions and worries have become collective. They prayed with me for my mom as we got news of an anomaly in her breast. They prayed for my book as I dealt with months of delays with my press because of COVID-19. I never experienced so much vulnerability about the everyday reality of death as during these pre-rosaries. The list of people in need was always massive. We have started to bring petitions from people who are not attending the group: for a colleague whose mother is sick and going through chemotherapy, for another faculty member whose boyfriend was filming a documentary in a dangerous region of the world, and for a junior scholar scared because of a recent cancer diagnosis and upcoming tenure decision.

We have helped and supported each other, but we have also clarified and shared resources about the pandemic, challenging each other to verify media information. Indeed, we are all humans trying to survive collectively. In simple words, we have been brought together by our vulnerability during a pandemic, and it has been a common religious practice that glued us together, as a group of strangers, supporting each other, in the middle of a storm. It has become a recurrent practice to read a daily COVID-19 solidarity prayer, as it reflects the members' desires for a more just and caring world in the context of the pandemic: "For all who have contracted coronavirus . . . For those who are particularly vulnerable . . . For all who experience fear or anxiety . . . For affected families who are facing difficult decisions between food on the table or public safety . . . For those who do not have adequate health insurance . . . For those who are afraid to access care due to immigration status, we pray for recognition of the God-given dignity of all."[28]

As time has gone by and little details about each participant have emerged, it has become evident that there is a rich and unique story that needs to be told and preserved behind each person. With Paula, we discussed the possibility of beginning an oral history project with these participants.[29] We proposed the idea to the whole group, and they agreed. In Catholic fashion, we called it "Visitation Fridays," as we all gather together and interview a different person every Friday after the rosary. The introductory descriptive text reads, "We call this space *Visitation Friday*, remembering the encounter of Mary and her cousin Elisabeth. Consequently, we see this as a place to meet as friends that care for each other deeply. . . . So let us just have a good time together."[30]

Following a podcast format, I designed a logo, and we chose a song for the introduction, by the international all-women group, Gen Verde.[31] The lyrics read, "I know you are not me / You have your own story / But if I make yours mine / We'll see the whole world shine . . . / Together we are strong / And if we walk as one / The revolution has begun."[32] We selected it because it recognizes each other's unique experiences and desires to work together toward change.

Because we were already connected and familiar via Zoom, it has been easy to record each interview. With members' permission, we created a private YouTube channel for them. In this way, each person has been able to store, download, and easily share their stories with their own families, independently of their distance. We defined a set of questions common to all participants. We ask them about their life experience growing up and then identify one particular event that had stayed and marked them. Recognizing their elder status, we then ask what they wish someone had told them about life, when they were young. And what advice would they say to someone more youthful who is just starting out in this adventure we call life? In the pandemic context, we have asked them how they were living these days.

Each experience has been precious and rich, as each person has described the many difficulties and victories during their lives, from their migration to the United States, to meeting their partners, to the death of loved ones, and the different changes experienced as they have moved from one stage of life to the next. Each interview has illustrated the power of resiliency of these women in a world that has changed dramatically for them. As feminists have pointed out, the women in this Zoom rosary manifested a unique women's epistemic point of reference, a standpoint[33] that has allowed them to see beyond particular events and toward a larger life-project. In this case, religiosity and faith have provided them with a narrative that, like a "golden thread,"[34] has connected their lives' events and given them continuity in such a way that even, as they have explained it, the unexpected nature of the pandemic has been lived as one more page of a book written day by day. They have exemplified a resilience that keeps them going, even now in the afternoon of their journey. Every week we interviewed a new person. Following their desires, we are now including other people they wanted to invite, specifically some of their friends in their retirement communities.

I remember the moment vividly when one of our oldest interviewees, who suffered severe health conditions, informed everyone during one of the Visitation Friday segments that she and her family had just been diagnosed with COVID-19 a few days before. As she continued the interview, we were all afraid that this might be the last chance we would have to hear her life experience. Therefore, we recorded it with the most profound sense of respect, honor, and reverence, as she was prepared to live well this new moment of her life, ready to do, as she said, "God's will."[35] After her interview, as has become our common practice, we opened the microphone to everyone, and they started sharing personal stories about their decades of interaction with her. Here they spontaneously created a space to say "Thank you," to remember a long life lived together and to accompany each other during these turbulent times. I believe that this was not the product of fate or the result of our interview skills; no, this was an expression of their own long lives caring for each other.

I have understood how the Zoom virtual rosary and Visitation Fridays have been more than a pious religious practice or a depository of people's oral histories; they manifest the importance of faith in people's lives, especially during a period of crisis and change. Furthermore, these two digital host spaces have served as a chronicle of a different narrative about what has been happening during the COVID-19 pandemic, one that is not just about death but about people living, surviving, and resisting, about their struggles dealing with isolation and the many mechanisms humans can create to flourish and connect even during the tragedy of a lockdown. As the mass media focused on the catastrophe created by COVID-19 in retirement communities around the United States, we were fortunate to see, and to experience, how people were reinscribing the virtual to make human connections, to remember, and to walk together, even during the COVID-19 pandemic. They remind us that behind each person there is an unrepeatable, unique, and precious experience and that loving and caring for each other remains the most potent force, even when confronted with our human fragility and vulnerability, especially under the threat of imminent death.

## CONCLUSION: BEYOND THE DEATHLY VISIT OF A VIRUS

The emergence and proliferation of religion and pious practices, as well as the resignification and consumption of religious objects during the COVID-19 crisis, is not surprising, as they illustrate how faith, as a malleable device, adapts and changes accordingly to the reality and needs of people, especially during times of crisis. For us, it is particularly relevant to assess how race, gender, and the performance of masculinity intersect with religiosity. These events also illustrate how, in some cases during COVID-19, religious and sanitary practices were juxtaposed within the discourses of national unity and the fantasies of a homogeneous ethnostate. Furthermore, it demonstrates that despite the assertions of a secular nation, the United States is defined by the normativity of Christianity, in its institutions and ethos.

By the time I am writing this conclusion, very rapidly, several of the women involved in the Visitation project have become seriously ill because of COVID-19 or other health complications related to their age. Some have been forced to stop attending because of their condition. Some have died. Each passing has been hard and personal, as we have spent these last months together. The day that one of them died, we listened to one of her recordings of the rosary. It was so moving and personal as we celebrated her life. We will always treasure and honor our time together, knowing that love and care for each other have brought us together despite our differences and distance, especially during a time where it seems that everything was "vanity of vanities."[36] Remaining anchored to our vulnerability and desire to connect and care for each other during the tragedy of COVID-19 represented one of the most important lessons of being humans at this time.

Certainly, COVID-19 is about death, but it is also, as in the case of Visitation Fridays, about the desire to live, and the many ways people, despite the tragedy of the pandemic, have tried to thrive, to fulfill their lives, to move a different society forward, to create meaningful connections, and to be human also via the spiritual, the ethereal, and the intangible. For the most part, the events described in this piece have been about the instinctive desire to keep breathing, fighting for the last gasp of air, even when the weight of oppressive death is on your neck.

## Notes

1. Delia Gallagher, "Pope Francis Prays for a Coronavirus Miracle at 'Plague' Crucifix Church," *CNN*, March 16, 2020, https://www.cnn.com/2020/03/16/europe/pope-francis-prayer-coronavirus-plague-crucifix-intl/index.html

2. Juan Fernando Lara Salas, "Virgen de los Ángeles Cierra este domingo vuelo para inspirar esperanza y Fortaleza frente al COVID-19," *La Nación*, March 21, 2020, https://www.nacion.com/el-pais/servicios/virgen-de-los-angeles-sobrevuela-pais-para/NGBNHGWCLJEIVO6E3REFJMZOB4/story/

3. Ian Millhiser, "Texas Pastors Demand a 'Religious Liberty' Exemption to Coronavirus Stay-at-Home Order," *Vox.com*, April 1, 2020. This and all subsequent quotations from Millhiser's sources are my own translation.

4. Frank Graziano, *Cultures of Devotion: Folk Saints of Spanish America*, 2nd ed. (New York: Oxford University Press, 2007), 11.

5. Otis R. Taylor Jr., "Oakland's Black Catholics Demand Action," *San Francisco Chronicle*, July 2, 2020, https://www.sfchronicle.com/bayarea/otisrtaylorjr/article/Oakland-s-Black-Catholics-demand-action-15380957.php?utm_campaign=CMS+Sharing+Tools+%28Premi%E2%80%A6

6. Bailey Loosemore, "Black Catholics for Justice March against 'Ugly Sin of Racism' in Downtown Louisville," *Louisville Courier Journal*, August 15, 2020, https://www.courier-journal.com/story/news/local/2020/08/15/louisville-protests-black-catholics-march-against-systemic-racism/5583939002/

7. 1 Corinthians 12:27, *The Catholic Study Bible: The New American Bible* (New York: Oxford University Press, 2013), 1617. Subsequent biblical citations are from this version.

8. Colossians 1:18.

9. Matthew 25:40.

10. Martin Luther King Jr. "Meet the Press, with Ned Brooks" *NBC*, April 17, 1960, in *The Papers of Martin Luther King, Jr.*, vol. 5: *Threshold of a New Decade, January 1959-December 1960*, ed. Clayborne Carson, Tenisha Armstrong, Susan Carson, Adrienne Clay, and Kieran Taylor (Berkeley: University of California Press, 2005), 435.

11. Dreamers are undocumented immigrants brought to the US as minors.

12. Don Bambino Geno Tai, Aditya Shah, Chyke A Doubeni, Irene G Sia, and Mark L Wieland, "The Disproportionate Impact of COVID-19 on Racial and Ethnic Minorities in the United States," *Clinical Infectious Diseases* 72.4 (February 26, 2021): 703–706; Matt Simon, "Your Income Predicts How Well You Can Socially Distance," *Wired*, August 5, 2020, https://www.wired.com/story/your-income-predicts-how-well-you-can-socially-distance/

13. There are two Catholic parishes within walking distance of the University of Michigan: Saint Mary's Newman Center and Saint Thomas Apostle. They are located within one mile from each other, but they cannot be more different in their styles, cultures, and constituencies. The Newman Center serves, for the most part, the always-revolving student community; it is run by Jesuits. Meanwhile, Saint Thomas, as the oldest Catholic church in the city, established in the 1840s, is a diocesan parish targeting a deeply conservative community. I live very close to Saint Thomas, but I am affiliated with Saint Mary and its more contemporary ethos. During the pandemic, both churches closed. However, as the restrictions started to be lifted, Saint Thomas was the first one, following the guidelines of the diocese of Lansing, Michigan, to offer full services. "A Plan to Gradually Restore," Diocese of Lansing, May 27, 2020. https://www.dioceseoflansing.org/coronavirus

14. Sara Sidner and Elizabeth Joseph, "'Just Cap Her': Texts and Video Reveal Details of the Alleged Domestic Terror Plot to Kidnap Gov. Whitmer," *CNN*, October 19, 2020.

15. Rick Noack, "Trump's Resistance to Face Masks, Even While He Is Infected with Coronavirus, Sets Him apart from Other World Leaders," *Washington Post*, October 7, 2020, https://www.washingtonpost.com/health/2020/10/07/trump-coronavirus-face-masks-world-leaders/

16. Saint Thomas parishioner, interview by the author, August 21, 2020.

17. "Virgin Mary Face Mask," *Charro Azteca*, https://charroazteca.com/shop/accesories-2/mexicanadas/masks/virgin-mary-face-mask-with-filter/

18. "Virgin Mary Face Mask."

19. Philippians 4:13.

20. Romans 5:8.

21. Aja Romano, "Why We Can't Stop Fighting about Cancel culture," *Vox.com*, August 24, 2020, https://www.vox.com/culture/2019/12/30/20879720/what-is-cancel-culture-explained-history-debate

22. Alexandra M. Stern, *Proud Boys and the White Ethnostate: How the Alt-Right Is Warping the American Imagination* (Boston: Beacon Press, 2019), 55.

23. Irene Nowell, OSB, *101 Questions and Answers on Angels and Devils* (Mahwah, NJ: Paulist Press, 2010), 41.

24. Courtney Mares, "Pope Francis to Give a Special Urbi et Orbi Blessing amid Coronavirus Pandemic," *Catholic New Agency*, Vatican City, March 22, 2020, https://www.catholicnewsagency.com/news/pope-francis-to-give-a-special-urbi-et-orbi-blessing-amid-coronavirus-pandemic-35831?utm_source=feedburner&utm_medium=feed&utm_campaign=Feed%3A+catholicnewsagency%2Fdailynews+%28CNA+Daily+News%29&utm_term=daily+news

25. "Beirut Explosion: What We Know So Far," *BBC News*, August 11, 2020, https://www.bbc.com/news/world-middle-east-53668493

26. Tim Stelloh, "California Exceeds 4 Million Acres Burned by Wildfires in 2020," *NBC News*, October 4, 2020, https://www.nbcnews.com/news/us-news/california-exceeds-4-million-acres-burned-wildfires-2020-n1242078

27. Moises Rendon and Lucan Sanchez, "Covid-19 in Venezuela: How the Pandemic Deepened a Humanitarian Crisis," *Center for Strategic and International Studies*, September 23, 2020, https://www.csis.org/analysis/covid-19-venezuela-how-pandemic-deepened-humanitarian-crisis.

28. https://mycatholic.life/catholic-prayers/a-prayer-for-healing-and-hope/#solidarity

29. In order to protect confidentiality, I avoided full names of people, and the article was shared with the group.

30. This is the text of the introduction to each episode of Visitation Friday.

31. For more information about the group, check its website at https://www.genverde.it/

32. Gen Verde, "Wave of Love," track 4 on *From the Inside Outside*, composed by Nancy L. Uelmen and Sarah G. McAllister, P.A.F.O.M., 2018, compact disc, https://www.genverde.it/contents/shop/from-the-inside-outside-eng/

33. Patricia Hill Collins, *Black Feminist Thought: Knowledge, Consciousness and the Politics of Empowerment* (New York: Routledge, 2000).

34. Chiara Lubich, *Essential Writings: Spirituality, Dialogue, Culture* (Hyde Park, NY: New City, 2007), 87.

35. Visitation Fridays, personal interview, October 16, 2020.

36. Ecclesiastes 1:2–11.

# CHAPTER 12

# Soliloquous Solipsism*

*Melanie Tanielian*

---

* The full set of images for this project is available at:
https://melanietanielian.myportfolio.com/

This chapter includes the captions for all images in the project, though it only includes a
selection of the images.

Figure 12.1. Isolation Mood . . . Day 15#EmbodyingSolitude

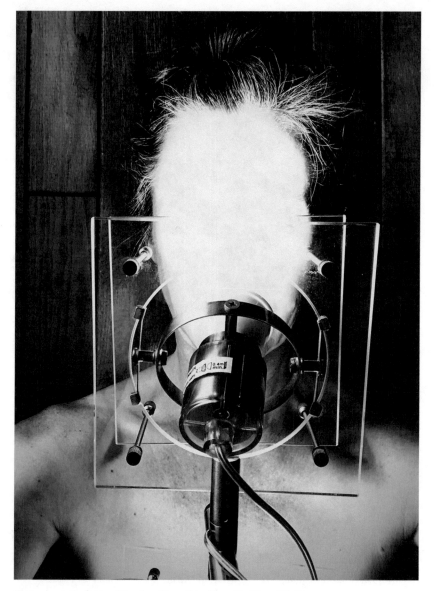

Figure 12.2. Isolation Mood . . . Day 16#20YearsNotHeardNotSeen

Isolation Mood . . . Day 17 #GardenChairMagic

Isolation Mood . . . Day 18 #NotReadyToDrown

Isolation Mood . . . Day 19 #TheyKnewThenWhyNotNow

Isolation Mood . . . Day 20 #IGotThis

Isolation Mood . . . Day 21 #ZoomIsMakingMeWantAFacelift

Figure 12.3. Isolation Mood . . . Day 22#TooFullOnHeSays

Isolation Mood . . . Day 23 #WickedShadows

Figure 12.4. Isolation Mood . . . Day 24 #ClosetMoments

Isolation Mood . . . Day25 #ExtremeDrama

Isolation Mood . . . Day 26 #CakeCoverAccident(CCA)

Isolation Mood . . . Day 27 #LaundryNet

Isolation Mood . . . Day 28 #BillseesTomWaits

Isolation Mood . . . Day 29 #toomuchSnow&MilitiasinApril

Isolation Mood . . . Day 30 #SureImighthaveDoneIt

Figure 12.5. Isolation Mood . . . Day 31 #NoWayOutofHubisShop

Isolation Mood . . . Day 32 #BasementIndustry

Isolation Mood . . . Day 33 #ClubQuaratine

Figure 12.6. Isolation Mood . . . Day 34 #Itmaynotmatter

Figure 12.7. Isolation Mood . . . Day 35 #ItClearlyDidNotMatter

Isolation Mood . . . Day 36 #NOWater

Isolation Mood . . . Day 37 #It'sgoingswimmingly

Isolation Mood . . . Day 38 #PerformingSolo

Isolation Mood . . . Day 39 #Bubblegina

Isolation Mood . . . Day 40 #Flamingo?

Isolation Mood . . . Day 41 #Benchbrace

Isolation Mood . . . Day 42 #Marked

Isolation Mood . . . Day 43 #Nullified

Isolation Mood.. . . . .Day 44 #forgottenInk

Isolation Mood . . . Day 45 #RoadkillisReal

Figure 12.8. Isolation Mood . . . Day 46 #isolationexhaustion

Isolation Mood . . . Day 47 #trytobreath

Isolation Mood . . . Day 48 #wheretobe

Isolation Mood . . . Day 49 #ThereisnoAncestryHere

Isolation Mood . . . Day 50 #ItMayBePossessed

Figure 12.9. Isolation Mood . . . Day 51 #whatelseistheretodo?

Isolation Mood . . . Day 52 #SELFCARE

Figure 12.10. Isolation Mood . . . Day 53 #BarelyHUMAN

Isolation Mood . . . Day 54 #Monstrousfeminine

Isolation Mood . . . Day 55 #Academia

"There was a time when I was sick of words. I could not make them do a thing I wanted. I wanted to be a painter or musician. I wanted a wordless medium."[1] These are the words of Neela Vaswani. Her words resonated like none other, since, like her, I was nauseated by words. The thought of populating a page, a computer screen, a Twitter feed, or even a text message with words was revolting. In search of a medium of communication, I felt that not even Hamlet's exclamation "Words, Words, Words!" could tempt more than a hollow emptiness, echoing in nothingness, a haunting perhaps. In short, words stalled at the perimeter, taunting an unreceptive historian.

## WORDS TO EXPLAIN WORDLESSNESS

In the spring of 2020, I found myself to be a historian without words: none to be read, none to be contemplated, and none to be written. As journalists colored in the global map with shades of orange and red, scientists prescribed tests, masks, and sanitary vigilance, historians—my dear colleagues—raced to what they know best. From comparisons of COVID-19 to the Spanish flu, the legacies of the politics of mask wearing, to historical studies of loneliness and boredom, historians mobilized their craft to understand the current moment. I should have led the pack. My expertise, as a historian of the modern era, after all, is in the study of severe moments of crisis. I have written a book about a world at war and an entire chapter on the spread of diseases and public health measures that failed thousands of people. Death: I was primed for researching, recounting, revising, and ultimately retelling stories of it. But this spring I not only lost the race, but the sound of the starting gun propelled me into darkness. My humanness, like a smartphone losing its battery power one tiny percentage point at a time and diminishing its screen's pixels, turned pitch black. Grief immobilized years of training in narrating historical deaths with the sole political goal of historical justice, historical accuracy, and meaning making of the historical. And, *no*, it was not communal grief, as might be expected in times of a global pandemic. If it was that, then I see how the historian self might have wandered into the familiar stories of losses, losses that could be painted in an empathetic anecdote or visualized in a fancy computer-generated graph. It was not the kind of grief that could be abstracted. It was also not a loss that had resulted from the virus, but rather one that had sat patiently in opacity.

As time froze, distraction ceased, and God went away on business, personal grief hurled his voluptuous arms around my shoulders and took hold without me recognizing him there and then. I sat in silence for hours, the mind racing through the past as if chased within a dream by an unknown enemy. In the most visceral moments, he shook me physically. On easy days masculine grief made my skin crawl. On others, I would fall off the edges of the world. At times, I would stand my ground and loiter in a memory no matter how overwhelmingly sweet or putrid. Convulsion. The sensation of what I came to recognize as a lingering and ignored loss was profoundly physical.

## #PASSAGE AND POSITION

The medium I was searching for, hence, had to be able to visualize the strange and unfamiliar physicality that the sensation of letting grief in demanded. But as words exited and the body entered stage left, it—the wordless medium I longed for—could not simply shift the representational frame from the written to the visual. There was more that it needed to be able to convey, because—as Brian Massumi writes—the body is deserving of its name because "It *moves*. It *feels*." Both movement and sensation had to be captured to respect the grieving body. How inadequate my choice would be is clear only now. At the time, I knew that if I were to attempt to unpeel grief's heavy sweaty palms one fleshy moist finger at a time—throw him off my shoulders or at the very least view him differently, maybe as poet Nancy Cross Dunham suggests, to see him as "*a friend . . . who will lightly lay a hand / on my shoulder / when tears come in the dark*" (wait—I actually hate that image)—it would take agility not to be "swallowed up in the transitional infinity."[2] I have to interject here. Theory is fun and all, productive too sometimes, but as a historian I'm all too well aware that it obscures too, obfuscates, abstracts, and redeploys as resolved insight that unsettles the theoretician. So let's settle this. Transitional infinity is the possibility, or better impossibility, of attending to the infinite points on a line. Massumi uses Zeno's philosophical arrow to explain. I think repeating it here is helpful. Zeno sees the arrow as traveling on a linear path along a trajectory "made up of a sequence of points or positions that the arrow occupies one after the other." Zeno would caution of the dilemma that between every point on this flight path there are an infinite number of intervening points. But to a historian this image is nothing but a gross simplification, as the points in any given story don't neatly align along a chronological continuum—a line. They scatter obstinately in clusters and disobedient constellations or disappear entirely from the record. I would posit that the finite number of memories and combinations or inventions thereof do much the same. Attending to and dwelling in the endless amalgamations of recollections, it's impossible to get to the end, naturally. Motion, Massumi writes, hence is impossible. Since one would find oneself stuck in a swamp of the past or implode in the realm of possibilities of fabrications. The body, this body, resisted that vision. It was not going to be swallowed up in the infinite. It fought hard. On the other end of the spectrum sits the illusion that grief has distinct and definite stages. It might be a useful therapeutic heuristic to think of it that way, but the linear is not productive when the body moves *and* feels. Stages necessitate displacement from one form of being to the next. With progress being principal, "movement [then] is entirely subordinated to the positions it connects."[3] It also implies resolution, and there may be that for some, but somehow I have the feeling that grief will stick around. So while it may neither be described as imploding in infinity nor as believing in the reality of stages as there were no traces of unimaginative beginnings and ends, how to communicate the *in between* was what was at stake.

Without words, I attempted to document the process of revising, reforming, reducing, restraining, regurgitating, and releasing grief, that is, that which defined *being human* for me at that moment. What was at hand was a cranky smartphone—one that would shut down abruptly during conversations, dialed emergency at random, and the gigabytes of which were still cluttered with what was lost. But with all good intentions, the resulting hashtagged images could only be a reductive representation of the process of *being human* situated in the paradox of passage and position. As the body moved—let's face it, in a space of privileged confinement—it is clear that a photograph could only be a naive attempt to capture a process of movement and sensation that inhabited the body that was finally allowed to be affected by a string of losses of a past. This might actually be the crux of the matter. As someone who might be described by historian Jill Lepore as a "historian who loves too much," namely that historian who sits in awe staring at a handwritten note, caresses a lock of hair that slipped from a love letter written a century ago, who goes to sleep thinking of her historical subject dodging Ottoman military officers by hiding in his aunt's home, I could not sit in reverie of my own past.[4] I determined it was lost, as those (a father, a husband, a daughter) who could provide a point of reference were either gone or absent. I lost my past. I was lost as a historian. My craft had failed my own past.

#PERSONAL AND YET SO IG PUBLIC

As my usual medium, that is, writing, signaled publication—visibility and in some form—the loss of words seemed to render me *invisible*. Solitude generally is not an uncomfortable state of being for the historian. She works alone and embraces hours of quiet. But invisibility is different and it felt disconcerting, disorienting really. But here it was, invisibility dominated the first fifteen days of self-isolation. But again the body resisted. As it moved and felt, it demanded to be seen. As I focused the lens on it, a desire grew for display. My Instagram—previously populated mainly with cat pictures and a handful of vacation shots—became the site of a dark display that sought validation. Populating it daily may not have been so different from the incessant narcissist selfie snapper's urge to find approval from the world. A *New York Times* article from April declared "Nude Selfies are Now High Art" and explored how people sought to break their isolation and the government-imposed sexual dry spell.[5] The exchange of "carefully posed, cast in shadows, expertly filtered" nudes apparently was a thing on encrypted apps. I can see the value. At the same time, my motivation to make that which was so intimately personal so public was neither about crafting a perfect beautiful self along the lines of the narcissist, who at least in part, seeks "a grandiose self-presentation that is motivated by the need to regulate self-esteem."[6] Nor was it about providing anyone a stimulus for self-pleasure (not that I have control over that) or my own unmet sexual needs. *So why this personal display?* Clearly the images, and I feel slightly uncomfortable about this, are self-involved, indulgent of my experience and clearly imposing on my social media network, as the algorithm populated some of my friends' daily feed. At the same time, they were representative of a different past, not the one I had lost, but the one I had muted. A past that valued the creative and was full of self-expression— loud, boisterous really. As I am writing this I realize that the domineering male influences, the ones I was mourning, had also been the ones who had demanded censorship. Proper behavior, adherence to the code of conduct in a household of silence, cultural norms that prohibited the sharing of family or relationship problems with even the closest of friends, all had stifled self-expression and necessitated an incomplete form of *being human*. Unmuted in solitude, a soliloquy of the self took form but unlike in the past, it would not be confined to an inner dialogue that had caused years of insomnia and an incessant consumption of Benadryl. It found community and assurance in a small group of friends and strangers who assured me that whatever it was, no matter how dark, how beautiful, how staged, how trite, how obnoxious, how naive, how profound, the unmuted self was fine. It was deserving; it was after all *being human.*

## Notes

1. Neela Vaswani, "Words, Words, Words," *Appalachian Heritage* 42.1 (2014), https://www.questia.com/magazine/1G1-377575489/words-words-words

2. Brian Massumi, *Parables for the Virtual: Movement, Affect, Sensation* (Durham, NC: Duke University Press, 2002), 2.

3. Massumi, *Parables for the Virtual*, 3.

4. Jill Lepore, "Historians Who Love Too Much: Reflections on Microhistory and Biography," *Journal of American History* 88.1 (2001): 129–144.

5. https://www.nytimes.com/2020/04/24/opinion/sunday/covid-nude-selfies.html?searchResultPosition=1

6. Christopher T. Barry, Hannah Doucette, Della C. Loflin, Nicole Rivera-Hudson, and Lacey L. Herrington, "'Let Me Take a Selfie': Associations between Self-Photography, Narcissism, and Self-Esteem," *Psychology of Popular Media* 6.1 (2017): 49.

# PART IV

## More Waiting/Sheltering

# CHAPTER 13

# Finding Home between the Vincent Chin Case and COVID-19

*Frances Kai-Hwa Wang*

1

First I heard from the high schoolers at Chinese School that all their parents were stocking up on rice and bottled water.

Then I heard about the fights breaking out in the California Costcos. Don't mess with Asian Aunties.

Weeks later, the rest of America went crazy for toilet paper.

But I am the child of immigrants. So while y'all were #quarantinebaking sourdough bread, I was sprouting bean sprouts, grinding soy milk, coagulating tofu from scratch, sewing masks. Old School.

2

Asian students say coronavirus is spreading discrimination at Michigan State University | Lansing State Journal

Coronavirus graffiti at park leaves Asian American woman "scared, frustrated" | Royal Oak Tribune

Local groups respond to aggression against the Asian community | WZZM Grand Rapids

3

When I first came for grad school, the only thing I knew about Michigan was that this was where Vincent Chin was killed. And I was afraid.

27 years old. Chinese American. A bachelor party. A baseball bat.

"It's because of you little . . . that we are out of work," said the white autoworker.
"These aren't the kind of men you send to jail," said the judge.
A $3,000 fine.
All these years I have lived in Michigan, I have held it at arm's length, felt like I did not belong, waited for the day I could finally return home.
Then I learned about all the people who came together across differences of race and ethnicity demanding justice for Vincent Chin, the people who still speak out to defend others today, the people who would craft a new answer to the question Vincent Chin's mother asked, all those years ago,
"What kind of law is this? What kind of justice?"


4


Chinese Americans in Michigan donate more than 200,000 masks, supplies | Detroit Free Press
Michigan leaders encourage reporting of anti–Asian American hate crimes amid COVID-19 | WWMT West Michigan
Opinion | Hate has no home in Michigan, especially in coronavirus crisis | Bridge Magazine


5


As the hashtags surge #StopAAPIHate #washthehate #IamNotAVirus #hateisavirus #StandAgainstHatred,
And Big Gretch starts trending,
I feel, for the first time in all these years, like I belong here. Like I am not alone here. Like this can be home here.
Even as the last snowstorm of the season sweeps in.
But in choosing to call this place home, we have to make this home for all of us, all our communities. (#Asians4BlackLives #FlintWaterCrisis #RunWithMaud #JusticeForGeorgeFloyd #JusticeForBreonnaTaylor)
What will you do to create community, the Beloved Community, where no mother ever has to ask, "What kind of law is this? What kind of justice?"

# CHAPTER 14

# Caged with the Tiger King

## The Media Business and the Pandemic

*Daniel Herbert*

In March 2020, large swaths of the United States shut down in response to the spreading COVID-19 pandemic. Office buildings emptied, universities sent students home, and virtually all spaces where groups of people congregate closed—including nearly all of the country's movie theaters. The *Hollywood Reporter* stated on March 16 that the three largest chains were closing, representing more than fifteen hundred locations and nearly twenty thousand movie screens.[1] By that point major franchise films, including the latest James Bond film, *No Time to Die*, had already postponed their release in theaters.[2] Many films also halted production during this time, including *Mission Impossible 7*, while in mid-March Disney postponed production on a live-action adaptation of *The Little Mermaid*.[3] Actor Tom Hanks, widely regarded as an amicable and accessible movie star, humanized the threat posed by the virus when he announced on March 11 via Instagram that he and his spouse, actress Rita Wilson, had tested positive for COVID-19. Hanks called on others to treat the virus seriously, making an appeal to caution and reason that contrasted with the voices of denial, racism, and xenophobia that also swirled within the larger public discourse about COVID-19.

Although stories like these may initially seem inconsequential within the larger context of the COVID-19 pandemic, they are noteworthy in at least two respects. First, they show that, along with other business sectors in the United States, the American entertainment industry has been affected in complex ways by the pandemic. Given that the film and television business generates over $100 billion annually, this is no small matter simply in terms of economics. Second, in light of the noticeable publicity the media business attracted related to COVID-19, it appears that the media business was also an important touchstone for Americans' *cultural* understandings of the pandemic. If nothing else, the numerous stories that connected the popularity of Netflix's *Tiger King* to our new socially distanced conditions illustrate how entertainment media and conceptions of COVID-19 overlapped with one another in significant ways. As we imagined how we might conduct ourselves and find relief and even pleasure in a world where public and group interactions appeared threatening, our use of home entertainment—and the business that enables it—seemed more important than ever.

Through the spring, summer, and early fall of 2020, the American movie business strained to adapt to the confusing and rapidly changing social and economic situation. Yet for all that media business contended with a deep rupture in its traditional way of doing business, specifically its reliance upon movie theaters, Hollywood's emerging reaction to the pandemic entailed some important extensions of historical trends, specifically the increasing reliance upon digital streaming and video-on-demand. Did *Tiger King* really offer a picture of Hollywood's "new normal"? With so many people trapped at home, watching whatever oddball programming they could find, how would movie culture change amid the pandemic? Certainly, social life in the United States is so heterogeneous, stratified, and unevenly experienced that it would be foolhardy to make sweeping claims about "American media culture" as though that were a single or uniform entity. Yet we might take disparity and fragmentation as generalized cultural conditions and, further, understand that Hollywood has worked to engage such a fragmented culture for some time. From this perspective, it becomes clearer that some elements of the American entertainment media industry were *already* structured in such a way as to address audiences affected by COVID-19.

But in order to fully understand the significance of the new dominance of digital delivery for film and television, it helps to look at how the pandemic affected Hollywood in a holistic way. It is conventional to divide the film and television business into three interdependent areas—production, distribution, and exhibition/retail—and the production sector of Hollywood has certainly *not* benefited from the pandemic. Commercial film and television productions are generally expensive, labor-intensive affairs that bring an array of workers into project-based teams that typically work in close proximity with one another. These are not conditions that naturally militate against the transmission of a virus. And because movies are so expensive and time-constrained, shutting down a production that is already in progress is extremely undesirable. Yet that is precisely what happened in spring 2020.

In the face of the widespread halt in production, Hollywood's unions and guilds worked quickly to create safety guidelines for returning to in-person work.[4] In addition to asking that cast and crew observe social distancing measures, wash their hands, and use personal protective equipment (PPE) like masks, a white paper released by the Alliance of Motion Picture and Television Producers called for the creation of a new position, a "Designated COVID-19 Compliance Officer," to be placed on every production. This compliance officer would be responsible for overseeing "physical distancing, testing, symptom monitoring, disinfecting protocols, and PPE education," among other duties.[5] Despite such efforts, filmmaking remained troubled by the pandemic. When *Jurassic World: Dominion* resumed production after a four-month hiatus, for example, the producers implemented new safety measures that placed an additional $5 million on the film's already enormous $200 million budget. The production also had to change a planned location shoot after several crewmembers tested positive for COVID-19.[6] Even worse in some ways was *Songbird*, a pandemic thriller produced by Michael Bay, who is known for making films with spectacular scenes of cataclysmic destruction. The union that represents actors and other performers, SAG-AFTRA, issued a "do not work" order to the film because its producers had been unclear about safety protocols.[7] Although the union retracted the order after the producers clarified the precautions, the situation generated negative press for what may have already seemed an ill-considered project. In the greater context of COVID-19, film and television production hardly constituted an "essential" industry comprising "first responder" labor. Yet due to the logistics, economics, and organizational structures of media production, this area of the industry was profoundly strained, threatening the longer-term commodity chain for entertainment media.

The pandemic hit the movie theater business—a crucial end point to that commodity chain—even harder than it did media production. Moreover, the disruption caused to movie theaters brought into stark relief the way in which the entire movie business has been fundamentally structured by the theatrical market. With the vast majority of theaters closing at least for a time, a number filed for bankruptcy and an estimated 150,000 movie theater employees were furloughed.[8] Over the course of the summer, industry professionals made multiple forecasts about when theaters might reopen; these projections consistently proved overly optimistic and plans to reopen were repeatedly pushed back. Many theater chains did reopen to various extents in late August and early September, but still faced significant challenges. Part of the problem was that regulations regarding social distancing have been so disparate on a state-by-state level.[9] Compounding this regional variation, different theaters and chains devised their own safety measures. Some require masks; others do not. Some require social distancing; others merely make recommendations. Different theaters allow for different numbers of viewers and theater capacities.[10] If we take it that "the theatrical experience" is not just central to Hollywood's business model but is also an important aspect of contemporary movie culture, then it is clear that the pandemic is drastically reshaping this culture.

Still, theater chains were encouraged by indications that audiences were excited to go back to theaters. A survey from late August found that 74% of respondents would be willing to attend movie theaters within the next month and that only 15% planned to wait until there was a COVID-19 vaccine before returning to a theater.[11] Yet, even with theaters open, there was the issue of the movies themselves. Simply put, there were almost no new movies playing in theaters. In late August, for example, the only notable new film to be released was the modestly budgeted thriller *Unhinged*, which earned around $4 million in its opening weekend.[12] Although the film's producers found this performance satisfactory in light of the situation with the pandemic,[13] such revenue is not nearly enough to produce a blockbuster success. In these conditions, it became clear that the Hollywood studios were loath to release major movies in theaters until a vaccine is released and audience comfort levels return to normal.

In fact, the crisis for theaters points toward COVID-19's impact on movie distribution more generally, an area of the media business that has responded quite dynamically to limitations created by the pandemic. Distribution is the primary function of the Hollywood studios; in addition to the work of circulating movies to theaters and television screens, movie distribution also entails market research, advertising, licensing, and many more activities that are largely done by a bureaucratic labor force in offices and cubicles. Thus, on the human level, COVID-19 unsettled film and television work in much the same way as it did other white-collar service industries; many studio employees began working from home and strained to find ways to maintain workflow and productivity. But as a general industrial process, distribution took fascinating turns over the course of 2020, a number of which pointed toward new opportunities for the business as well as notable trends in audiences' cultural habits and behaviors.

Because even under normal circumstances the theatrical market, or "window," is limited to a handful of movies per weekend, Hollywood studios create calendars to optimize the distribution of films over the course of a year. Holiday weekends are big events, of course, and studios release horror films and Oscar contenders consistently in the fall, for instance. Thus, studios scrambled to adjust their schedules as the pandemic continued to threaten the theatrical market into summer 2020 and beyond. Many films had their theatrical release postponed multiple times, including the super-hero movie *Black Widow*, originally planned for May 11 but pushed to November 6, and postponed again to May 2021. Such delays kicked off a cascade of additional postponements, as the precious shelf space of opening weekends grew scarcer. Like falling dominos, films got pushed farther and farther into a future presumed to be unaffected by COVID-19. Many films have been rescheduled for 2022, while others have been pushed back indefinitely.[14]

Such rescheduling also unsettled the home video business, which has historically followed the theatrical window. The traditional market for "packaged media," consisting of DVD and Blu-ray rentals and sales, had been declining for more than a decade when the pandemic made the situation even more precarious. Family Video, which is the only major video store chain remaining since Blockbuster and Hollywood Video went bankrupt about a decade ago, had to close over 450 stores for as long as ten weeks during the pandemic.[15] Although Family Video stores reopened as restrictions were loosened on businesses, the company faced a secondary predicament due to a shortage of upcoming rental titles as a result of the lack of films being distributed to theaters.[16] Redbox, which operates nearly forty thousand automated video-vending machines in front of retail business across the country, warned customers to wash their hands and disinfect DVDs in the early phase of the pandemic,[17] then later began offering "touch free" use of its kiosks.

The virus did not affect all parts of the home video market in the same way. Because they sell groceries among other types of goods, big-box retail chains like Target and Wal-Mart were deemed "essential businesses" and remained open even under the strictest social distancing regulations. Stores like these continued to sell DVDs and Blu-Rays throughout the pandemic and thus remained active sites for the flow of tangible video commodities. Some reports even suggest that Walmart's DVD sales increased in the early phases of the pandemic.[18] Smaller operations found creative ways of maintaining business during the pandemic. Bull Moose, for instance, is a small, independently owned chain of stores in Maine and New Hampshire that sells music CDs, books, and DVDs. During the stay-at-home mandate during the pandemic, Bull Moose was able to maintain its business by taking orders over phone and internet, allowing customers to pick items curbside. Bull Moose also used social media to sell merchandise, conducting auctions on Facebook Live.[19] These online events proved so successful that the company plans to continue holding them after in-store business resumes.[20]

Bull Moose's small-scale use of the internet during the pandemic signals the larger, even macro-scaled aspect of the contemporary media business that has been an area of important activity during the pandemic: digital media distribution and delivery. This area of the media business has been, in fact, incredibly dynamic for more than a decade, following Netflix's launch of its subscription video-on-demand (SVOD) streaming service in 2007 and Amazon's Prime Video service in 2011. Online video earned over $10 billion in 2016, surpassing for the first time DVD and Blu-ray rental and sales revenue, which stood at around $8 billion that year.[21] As of mid-2020, Netflix remained the biggest of the SVOD services, with over 60 million subscribers in the United States and over 180 million worldwide.[22] Amazon Prime Video had around 100 million subscribers in the United States alone and over 150 million worldwide, while US-based Hulu had 30 million subscribers.[23]

Several major players entered this already considerable SVOD sector in the period directly leading up to the COVID-19 pandemic. Technology giant Apple launched Apple+ TV in November 2019 and quickly attained 33 million subscribers.[24] Also in November, the Walt Disney Company continued its perpetual expansion by launching the Disney+ SVOD service and amassed more than 50 million subscribers by May 2020.[25] Finally ( for the moment, anyway), AT&T subsidiary WarnerMedia launched the HBO Max streaming portal on May 27, 2020, months into the ongoing pandemic, and had over 4 million users by the end of June.[26]

Anecdotes about the supposed viral popularity of *Tiger King* aside, it does appear that the pandemic directly affected the streaming video business. Multiple studies and news stories examined how social distancing practices and shelter-in-place orders were impacting people's media consumption. One report from early April stated, "Netflix Inc., Hulu and the like are expected to get a boost from the extra couch time resulting from social distancing," and cited a survey that showed that 20% of respondents planned to subscribe to a new streaming service despite the fact that many had lost their jobs.[27] Subsequent reports indicated that SVOD services like Netflix did, in fact, enjoy a "pandemic peak" in March and April.[28] One study found that people doubled their average hourly use of streaming services during the pandemic to more than four hours of viewing per day.[29] Netflix acquired nearly sixteen million new users in the first months of 2020, the company's largest quarterly increase.[30] One reported called this a "mind-boggling subscriber addition,"[31] while a spokesperson for Netflix stated with a strange mix of munificence and apparent smugness, "We are fortunate to have a service that is even more meaningful to people confined at home."[32] The company continued this growth as the pandemic continued, garnering an additional ten million new subscribers in the second quarter of the year.[33]

Other Hollywood companies worked strategically to exploit digital media delivery in response to the lack of a theatrical market. Of these, Universal Pictures acted especially quickly and aggressively in making new movies available as video-on-demand "premium rentals." In late March, one could rent Universal's *Bloodshot* (2020), *The Invisible Man* (2020), and *Emma* (2020) on Amazon or Apple TV for around $20—only a few weeks after their release in theaters. Universal also released the animated kids' film *Trolls World Tour* on April 10, the same day the film was released in the limited number of theaters that remained open at that time. Doing so created a bit of a scandal within the industry, as prior to the pandemic, theater chains refused to carry movies from any studio that released major films directly on digital platforms.

Disney reacted to the pandemic by speeding up the release of several movies through the Disney+ streaming service, including the blockbusters *Frozen II* (2019) and *Star Wars: Episode XI—The Rise of Skywalker* (2019). The rushed digital release of these popular franchise films helped distinguish Disney's SVOD service during this unusually competitive moment. As with Netflix, company spokespeople made statements that aimed to deflect their apparent opportunism. Disney CEO Bob Chapek, for example, tried to create parallels between the narrative of *Frozen II* and the pandemic, stating that "the themes of perseverance and the importance of family are messages that are incredibly relevant during this time, and we are pleased to be able to share this heartwarming story early with our Disney+ subscribers to enjoy at home."[34]

The universalizing invocations of "family" and "home" in this statement conform to the kind of ideological work typically done by so many Disney films, programs, theme parks, and products, which overlook or aim to strategically incorporate issues of social difference in the process of providing escapist pleasures. To be sure, many Americans have suffered dramatically as a result of the COVID-19 pandemic, and these struggles and tragedies have been exacerbated by social inequities structured by racial, gendered, and class disparities. (It needs to be noted, also, that streaming platforms responded directly to the Black Lives Matter movement and the protests against racial injustice in the summer of 2020 by creating new African American and/or Black-themed generic categories and featuring them prominently on their home pages. The complexities and contradictions of such social justice branding and marketing deserve more serious consideration than can be done here, unfortunately.) For many others, social and economic conditions make streaming entertainment media out of reach or irrelevant. Such differences in social identities and lived experiences make it impossible to tidily connect strategies and practices

within the entertainment business and "media culture" more generally. Nevertheless, we might think, somewhat accurately, that the widespread use of digital streaming services in the spring and summer of 2020 illuminates something
important and powerful about Americans' desire or even need for escape from
the pandemic, socially distanced from one another but connected intimately
with a variety of electronic screens.

This presumption certainly appears to be driving the business decisions
of multiple Hollywood companies regarding streaming media during this
time. It might be a stretch to say that COVID-19 provided a "right place, right
time" scenario for companies like Netflix, but the pandemic has encouraged companies to experiment with digital video release patterns that may
not have otherwise occurred until years in the future. Disney, for instance,
released *Mulan* directly to Disney+, charging $30 to home viewers (in addi-
tion to the monthly subscription fee), circumventing movie theaters entirely
after the film's theatrical release had been delayed several times in the spring.
Although the results of this experiment appear to be mixed at best, it highlights how a vertically and horizontally integrated media corporation like
Disney is shifting gears to rely more heavily on its streaming capabilities in
the face of the continuing pandemic.

Even more unconventional is a deal made between Universal Pictures and
the AMC theater chain.[35] The two companies announced that they came to
an agreement that allowed Universal to release its films via digital delivery
only seventeen days following their theatrical release. In return, Universal
agreed to pay an unknown percentage of its revenue from the digital market
to AMC, so as to keep AMC from boycotting future Universal releases. This
highly unusual agreement defies the historical time frame for the theatrical
window and yet has the potential to maintain something of the theatrical
business even while distributors adjust to meet consumers' desires for home
entertainment. Perhaps more drastically, near the end of 2020 Warner Bros.
announced that it would release all of its movies in 2021, including "tent-
pole" blockbusters like *Dune* and *The Matrix 4*, on the HBO Max service on
the same date that it released films in theaters. This move entirely upends
the exclusivity of the theatrical market for major Hollywood films, which has
been the status quo since the creation of the home video market in the 1970s.
One report referred to Warner Bros.' action as "surprising" and "shocking,"[36]
while another stated that it portended a "looming apocalypse" for the theatrical exhibition business.[37] Although Warner Bros. made it clear that it only
intended to follow this practice for a single year, the company will certainly
use this as an opportunity to evaluate how to maximize the use of its propri-
etary streaming platform.

Indeed, experiments like these have the potential to reshape the American entertainment media business beyond the pandemic, encouraging adjustments in audiences' behaviors and habits. As this short assessment has shown, COVID-19 has unsettled the entire film and television business, and it will likely remain disrupted for the foreseeable future. Film and television producers and laborers will continue to struggle to find ways to make media in a safe and healthy way. In all likelihood, this means that media production will occur more sporadically and with unexpected interruptions as well as additional costs related to COVID-19 safety measures. The theatrical exhibition business will continue to be highly irregular due to regional variations in physical distance regulations and localized conditions. This unpredictability will significantly alter the way Hollywood releases feature films, in terms of schedule, market (theatrical vs. home video), and even the types of movies released in different markets. The temporary "winners" of the industrial situation created by the pandemic are the digital streaming services, which are able to exploit existing content libraries, as well as any new films and programs that are produced under these circumstances, by making them available directly to people's homes.

To be sure, such alterations in the industry have been years in the making, and the pandemic largely exacerbated and accelerated this process. Amid these industrial changes, however, it is important to reflect on how media culture will change and adapt as well. I do not hold any notions that public movie viewing in theaters provides some communal social formation that is crucial to democracy, that the loss of movie theaters somehow threatens a social fabric. But I do think that the sweeping dominance of streaming film and television, as an everyday practice by individuals and small groups in relatively isolated conditions, should call our attention to the ways in which we are already "socially distanced" from one another. The industry is presently responding to a social world of increased fragmentation and isolation as effects of the pandemic, but fragmentation and isolation are certainly not new phenomena. In this context, we might worry about being stuck with whatever movies and programs get pushed down the digital pipes: an endless flow of *Tiger King* and other programs we might never watch if they weren't so easily accessible and we weren't so eager for distraction and unexpected enjoyment. We might also consider, though, how the streaming media practices encouraged and enabled by industrial changes are bound up in other processes of social division. The challenge moving forward is to understand how these two concerns relate to one another.

## Notes

1. Pamela McClintock, "AMC, Cinemark Close All U.S. Theaters as Cinemas across the Country Go Dark amid Coronavirus," *Hollywood Reporter*, March 16, 2020, https://www.hollywoodreporter.com/news/amc-theatres-close-all-locations-as-cinemas-us-go-dark-1285012

2. Alex Ritman and Pamela McClintock, "'No Time to Die' Release Delayed Due to Coronavirus Outbreak," *Variety*, March 4, 2020, https://www.hollywoodreporter.com/heat-vision/bond-movie-no-time-die-delayed-due-coronavirus-1282170

3. David McNary, "'Mission: Impossible 7's' Italy Shoot Delayed Due to Coronavirus," *Variety*, February 24, 2020, https://variety.com/2020/film/news/mission-impossible-7-production-italy-delayed-coronavirus-1203513612/; Nick Romano, "Disney Halts *The Little Mermaid* and Other Film Productions over Coronavirus," *Entertainment Weekly*, March 13, 2020, https://ew.com/movies/the-little-mermaid-production-halted-coronavirus/

4. David McNary, "Unions, Studios Release Back-to-Work Guidelines amid COVID-19 Pandemic," *Variety*, June 1, 2020, https://variety.com/2020/film/news/unions-studios-coronavirus-back-to-work-guidelines-1234622181/

5. Industry-Wide Labor Management Safety Committee Task Force, "Proposed Health and Safety Guidelines for Motion Picture, Television, and Streaming Productions during the COVID-19 Pandemic," Alliance of Motion Picture and Television Producers, June 1, 2020, 13, https://www.sagaftra.org/files/sa_documents/IWLMSC%20Task%20Force%20White%20Paper%206-1-20.pdf

6. Naman Ramachandran, "'Jurassic World: Dominion' Scales Back Malta Shoot after Coronavirus Outbreak," *Variety*, August 19, 2020, https://variety.com/2020/film/global/jurassic-park-malta-shoot-coronavirus-1234739834/

7. David McNary, "SAG-AFTRA Issues Do Not Work Order on Pandemic Thriller 'Songbird,'" *Variety*, July 2, 2020, https://variety.com/2020/film/news/sag-aftra-issues-do-not-work-order-on-pandemic-thriller-songbird-1234697446/

8. Jake Coyle and the Associated Press, "After Four-Month Drought, Movie Theaters Beg Studios: Release the Blockbusters," July 23, 2020, https://fortune.com/2020/07/23/movie-theaters-open-release-date-new-films-coming-out-when-blockbusters-tenet-mulan-a-quiet-place/

9. "NATO COVID-19 State Government Relations Report: Reopening, Relief & Recovery," National Alliance of Theater Owners, August 19, 2020, https://www.natoonline.org/wp-content/uploads/2020/08/8-19-2020-NATO-COVID-19-State-Government-Relations-Report-1.pdf

10. Tom Brueggeman, "All Movie Theaters Have New Safety Guidelines, but They Vary Widely by State," *IndieWire*, August 6, 2020, https://www.indiewire.com/2020/08/movie-theaters-safety-guidelines-vary-by-state-1234577599/

11. "As Theaters Reopen, Confidence in Moviegoing Grows and Safety Measures Are a Must According to New Atom Tickets Survey," *CelluloidJunkie.com*, August 20,

2020, https://celluloidjunkie.com/wire/as-theaters-reopen-confidence-in-moviegoi
ng-grows-and-safety-measures-are-a-must-according-to-new-atom-tickets-survey/

12. Ryan Faughnder, "Box Office: 'Unhinged' Debuts with $4 Million in First Big Test of Moviegoing in the Coronavirus Era," *Los Angeles Times*, August 23, 2020, https://www.latimes.com/entertainment-arts/business/story/2020-08-23/box-office
-return-unhinged-coronoavirus

13. Faughnder, "Box Office."

14. "Here Are All the Movies and TV Shows Affected by Coronavirus," *New York*, August 2020, https://www.vulture.com/2020/08/here-are-all-the-movies-and-tv-sho
ws-affected-by-coronavirus.html

15. Matthew McCormick, email to author, July 30, 2020.

16. McCormick, interview by author, May 12, 2020.

17. Benjamin VanHoose, "Is It Safe to Use Redbox during the Pandemic? What to Know about Disinfecting Your Movie Rentals," *People*, April 16, 2020, https://people.com/movies/is-it-safe-to-use-redbox-during-the-pandemic-what-to
-know-about-disinfecting-your-movie-rentals/

18. Hannah Sparks, "Walmart Reports Increase in Sales of Tops, Not Pants, during the Coronavirus Lockdown," *New York Post*, https://nypost.com/2020/03/27/walmart
-reports-increase-in-sales-of-tops-not-pants-during-coronavirus-lockdown/

19. Mick Pratt, head of Bull Moose marketing and promotions, interview by author, 12 May 2020.

20. Pratt, interview by author.

21. "The State of Home Entertainment: 2017 Edition," S&P Global Market Intelligence, December 2017, 6.

22. Steven Zeitchik, "Netflix Adds a Whopping 16 Million Subscribers Worldwide as Coronavirus Keeps People Home," *Washington Post*, April 21, 2020, https://www.wa
shingtonpost.com/business/2020/04/21/netflix-adds-whopping-16-million-subscrib
ers-worldwide-coronavirus-keeps-people-home/

23. Don Reisinger, "Amazon Prime's Numbers (and Influence) Continue to Grow," *Fortune*, January 12, 2020, https://fortune.com/2020/01/16/amazon-prime-subscripti
ons/

24. Audrey Conklin, "Streaming Services by the Numbers," *FoxBusiness.com*, May 4, 2020, https://www.foxbusiness.com/lifestyle/streaming-services-cost-users

25. Gene Del Vecchio, "Disney Plus Has the Potential to Become a $30 Billion Giant in Only 5 Years," *Forbes*, May 11, 2020, https://www.forbes.com/sites/genedelvecchio
/2020/05/11/disney-plus-has-the-potential-to-become-a-30-billion-giant-in-only-5-y
ears/#3ef207bf34a3

26. Todd Spangler and Cynthia Littleton, "HBO Max and HBO Have 36.3 Million Subscribers, Up 5% from End of 2019, AT&T Says," *Variety*, July 23, 2020. https://variety
.com/2020/digital/news/hbo-max-subscribers-subscribers-q2-att-1234714316/

27. John Fletcher, "Kagan Survey How Coronavirus Has Already Changed Media Consumers," *spglobal.com*, April 1, 2020, https://www.spglobal.com/marketintelligen

ce/en/news-insights/blog/kagan-survey-how-coronavirus-has-already-changed-me
dia-consumers

28. Erik Gruenwendel, "Report: Netflix, Hulu Usage Declined as COVID-19 Quarantine Measures Relaxed," *MediaPLayNews.com*, June 25, 2020, https://www.mediap
laynews.com/report-netflix-hulu-use-declined-as-covid-19-quarantine-measures-rel
axed/

29. Gruenwendel, "Report."

30. Jon Swartz, "Netflix Has Biggest Quarter with Nearly 16 Million New Subscribers Signing On," *Marketwatch.com*, April 22, 2020, https://www.marketwatch.com/sto
ry/netflix-adds-more-than-15-million-new-subscribers-stock-rockets-higher-2020-04
-21

31. Trefis Team, "Netflix Subscriber Growth 2x Expectations; Good News or Peak?," *Forbes*, April 28, 2020, https://www.forbes.com/sites/greatspeculations/2020/04/28
/netflix-subscriber-growth-2x-expectations-good-news-or-peak/#5a5b45c83ea1

32. Zeitchik, "Netflix Adds 16 Million Subscribers."

33. Aric Jenkins, "Netflix Q2 Earnings: Stock Plummets as Ted Sarandos Is Named Co-CEO," *Fortune*, July 16, 2020, https://fortune.com/2020/07/16/netflix-q2-earnings
-2020-stock/

34. Bruce Haring, "'Frozen 2' Gets an Earlier-Than-Expected Release on Disney+ to Keep the Kids Amused," *Deadline.com*, March 13, 2020, https://deadline.com/2020/03
/frozen-2-gets-an-earlier-than-expected-release-on-disney-to-keep-the-kids-amused
-1202883148/

35. Brent Lang and Rebecca Rubin, "Universal, AMC Theatres Forge Historic Deal Allowing Theatrical Releases to Debut on Premium VOD Early," *Variety*, July 28, 2020, https://variety.com/2020/film/news/universal-amc-theatres-historic-deal-windows
-1234718737/

36. Rebecca Rubin and Matt Donnelly, "Warner Bros. to Debut Entire 2021 Film Slate, including 'Dune' and 'Matrix 4,' Both on HBO Max and in Theaters," *Variety*, December 3, 2020, https://variety.com/2020/film/news/warner-bros-hbo-max-theaters
-dune-matrix-4-1234845342/

37. Anthony D'Alessandro, "Would Cinemas Be Hypocritical Playing Warner-HBO Max Movies after Continual Netflix Rebuff? Let's Count Exhibition's Headaches Right Now," *Deadline.com*, December 8, 2020, https://deadline.com/2020/12/hbo-max-thea
trical-window-exhibition-fallout-amc-cinemark-1234652501/

# CHAPTER 15

# Prosthetics for Right Now

*Nick Tobier*

I learned to make pretzels and baguettes, among other things, between March 20 and May 29, 2020, when the state of Michigan issued stay-at-home orders. We could not eat all of the baked goods we made (who really can eat eighteen bagels?) among our immediate family (but we often did).

They tasted great—really. But as satisfying as it was to make them (and eat them), the act of sharing them via a contactless front porch drop-off to neighbors, some of whom I had never really interacted with, enabled me to feel connected to a world outside of our house and beyond a screen. Our street email list in the first month of the stay-at-home order was a daily call to community. I am going to Meijer—does anybody need something? Who has yeast? I can teach some really cool physics lessons for kids. We were all at home—but we were all in this together. We lived side by side but, like children involved in parallel play, did not rely on each other for much more than greetings. The opportunity of being forced to respond to an emergency presented us with what is possible by exposing what was already present—latent generosity, the desire for connection, altruism, and purposefulness.

Neighborhood Window, a proposed window insertion, essentially a tele-scoping box, encourages social connection while keeping physical distance and provides an outlet for neighborhood sociability. This window, I reasoned, can be paired with an icon-based signal and map (physical as well as virtual) to let folks know what is on offer.

Think about what we saw—either directly or via news. Italians sere-nading one another from their balconies. New Yorkers nightly at 7:00 p.m. cheering from windows for frontline health care workers. There are scores of projects, individual efforts, and revolutionary social movements of all scales inventoried in the remarkable database Collective Action and Dis-sent under COVID.

Think about where we were in March 2020. Largely home (if you had the

Figure 15.1. *Neighborhood Window*, 2020. Enabling a social exchange as well as distribution of goods, *Neighborhood Window* simultaneously creates a distribution system while recognizing that our quotidian errands accomplish more than simply procuring goods. There are precedents for this minor renovation that opens up homes and businesses to the street—not only the drive-through takeout windows but pet doors, mail slots, milk delivery hatches, coal chutes. Photo by author.

Figure 15.2. *Visitors' Platform*, 2020. During March 2020–May 2020, the number of COVID cases was surging in southeast Michigan, particularly in Detroit. Some of the hardest-hit places were nursing homes, where to protect nurses and residents, visitors were prohibited. We delivered PPE to nurses during this time period every week, and one of the caregivers—who had lost both patients and staff—told us how isolated many of the residents felt. Unaccustomed to video calls, families whose loved ones were on the ground level were frequently seen waving, holding up their children, bringing balloons or hand-lettered signs to the windows. By deploying scissor lifts, which already have guard rails surrounding their platforms, construction projects that are on pause can lend their infrastructure to enabling face to face contact. Photo by author.

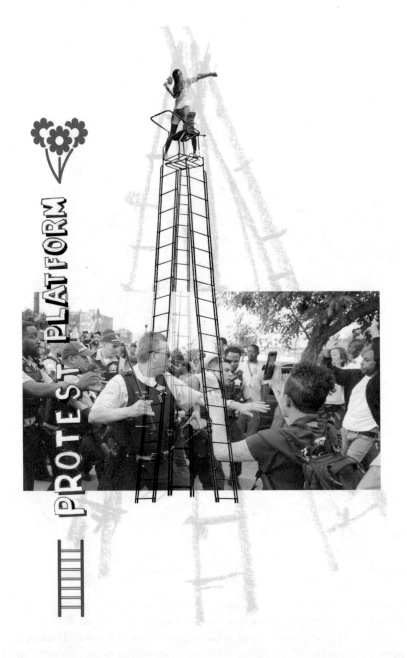

Figure 15.3. *Protest Platform*, 2020. Reclaim the Streets, a collective known best in the mid-1990s for staging pedestrian takeovers of British motorways, sets up a tripod right away at each of their actions using extension ladders lashed together, frequently topped by a massive sound system and frequently an improvisational DJ at the controls of a sound system to inspire action before the police arrive. Adapting this logic and transforming it from a disruption of vehicular activity to a protection of protestors, this elevated perch enables peaceful protestors to see a great distance—serving both as a lookout and a visible coordinator. Photo by author.

Figure 15.4. *To Protect*, 2020. Umbrellas in Hong Kong have been used quite effectively as a protection against the use of tear gas turned on peaceful protestors. Adding leaf blowers to the arsenal of household defenses against the excessive firepower deployed by authorities, protestors in Portland turned their garden tools to disperse the caustic substances away from the eyes of the marchers. To Protect transforms a bicycle into a pro-protest vehicle. Deploying a motorcycle windshield as a transparent barrier and a leaf blower mounted as a cannon, pedal-powered protectors can advance as a protective shield ahead of a line of marchers. Photo by author.

Figure 15.5. *Winter Light + Power*, 2020. Have you tried to exercise at home or on your own? Good for you. With or without Zoom or YouTube, it can be a challenge. Winter Light and Power proposes hauling out and setting up the stationary bikes that are gathering dust in a basement corner onto a covered platform for those who may prefer a little healthy encouragement (or competition) that comes with physical presence. We can use each cycle to transfer the hub and pedal power to illuminate a chandelier, creating an illuminated beacon on Main Streets, in a park, a town green, and coax each of us out of isolation—yes, even when it is cold—and into a physically distant but socially connected communal utility. Take that, SoulCycle. Photo by author.

luxury of working from home); hoarding or searching for toilet paper, yeast, flour; thrust into school closures with improvised learning plans; and watching from near and far as COVID cases surged in Detroit, Milan, and New York City while Donald Trump insisted that the virus posed no more danger than the seasonal flu. By May 2020, after witnessing the death of George Floyd, one more Black American murdered by police, individuals who had been isolated at home poured into the streets. In Minneapolis, in New York City, in Paris, and in Ann Arbor, the combined weight of racial injustice, social isolation, and pandemic anxiety collided with shared protest and public demonstrations of collective will.

In her 2009 book *A Paradise Built in Hell*, Rebecca Solnit writes of the sense of shared purpose and coincidental communities that arise in response to disasters.[1] If you haven't read it, the book chronicles the efforts of volunteers at Ground Zero post-9/11, soup kitchens in the 1906 San Francisco earthquake, workers in the Halifax Shipyard Fire, citizens in the Mexico City earthquake, and the on-the-ground relief efforts during and post Hurricane Katrina. To that list we can add the 2011 tsunami in Japan, Hong Kong democracy protests, the COVID-19 pandemic, and Black Lives Matter.

As an artist and designer whose work is devoted to public space and social interaction, for me this period instigated a series of imaginings for a near and present future that range from the exchange of goods and services to constructions that enable social protest. Over these past months, my impulse has been to toggle between two extremes—one that recognizes our daily lives as social beings and ways to enable doses of human connection, and the other that contends with the abuses of power through building platforms that enable protest and rupture. To invent new forms in response to emergency—a more precise and generative term than the language of new normal, which suggests a passivity or acceptance—is to act with urgency in the face of being separated from all that is familiar.

Our daily lives may in fact return to what they were like before our current moment—but truthfully, I hope not without willful transformation. The aftermath, ideally, of an emergency is that we emerge. Not merely come out of a disaster, but rise out of challenging circumstances into a world where we never forget what we confronted, how we found solace in the smallest exchanges and how we found our voices through shared anguish, outrage, and connection. Disaster, Solnit notes, shocks us out of slumber—but only skillful effort keeps us awake.[2]

## Notes

1. Rebecca Solnit, *A Paradise Built in Hell: The Extraordinary Communities That Arise in Disasters* (New York: Viking, 2009).
2. Solnit, *Paradise Built in Hell*, 119.

# PART V

# Resisting

# CHAPTER 16

# COVID-19's Attack on Women and Feminists' Response

## The Pandemic, Inequality, and Activism

*Abigail J. Stewart*

For two decades, the Global Feminisms Project (GFP) has interviewed feminists around the globe. In the essays that follow in Part V, we draw on the expertise of eight of the scholars who are part of the project to learn about the impact of COVID-19 on women, as well as the responses of feminist activists, in different countries. The Global Feminisms Project includes interviews with feminist activist-scholars from nine different countries: Brazil, China, Germany, India, Nicaragua, Nigeria, Poland, Russia, and the United States, and those interviews are all publicly available online.[1] (As of September 2020, interviews with participants from other countries are in process (Peru) and planned (Tanzania), and others will be added, no doubt.) The authors of these essays have worked directly on six of these interview projects (Brazil, Germany, India, Nicaragua, Nigeria, and Russia). Some essayists also come from these GFP countries (Germany, Nicaragua, Nigeria), and some come from other countries they discuss (Argentina, Turkey). From the beginning the Global Feminisms Project was envisioned as serving many different disciplines and interdisciplines (such as women's and gender studies and area studies), including but not limited to the humanities. It never aimed to "represent" women's movement activism in any complete way within a country, let alone the entire globe. Instead it aimed to document some forms of feminist activism and scholarship in those countries where feminist activist-scholars at the University of Michigan had established ties.

We encourage readers of these grouped essays to explore the website where the interviews can be accessed as videos or transcripts. But those materials cannot tell us directly about the impact of COVID-19, though they do address many aspects of gender and power, at local and global levels, before the pandemic. Moreover, we are currently creating new materials scholars can use for teaching as well as for research. All twelve projected lesson plans are currently also on the website, along with the interviews, time lines, maps, and other background information about each country.[2]

The essays in this part go beyond what is on the website to consider what the scholars associated with the Global Feminisms Project, regardless of their own national origins and different disciplines, have learned during this period about the situation of women generally, and feminist activists in particular, during this very difficult time. These scholars share three critical assets in analysis of the impact of COVID-19. First, their perspective is both global (in identifying circuits of practice and ideas worldwide) and local (grounded in particular situations). It is part of the long-standing ethos of the project to consider how global currents affect local histories and activism, while also examining how local activism and circumstances may alter global phenomena. Second, our joint analytic framework is feminist, foregrounding women's experience, and highlighting relations of power that define not only gender, but race, class, sexuality, and other social hierarchies. Finally, our methods include analysis of all forms of text, including formal and informal media, narratives, and interviews. For that reason, Part V includes separate essays addressing the impact of COVID-19 at different levels and in different national contexts. Across the essays we can see some commonalities in the impact of the pandemic, as well as some differences. A unifying theme across the essays is that the impact of the pandemic has exacerbated existing inequities within and between nations, foregrounding the importance of the relations of power and dominance that preoccupy us all. In doing that, the pandemic has made everyday life more difficult for many women worldwide, and feminist activists—alert to the new problems women face—have met the crisis head-on.

Thinking across nations, medical anthropologist Abigail Dumes discusses how scientific and medical ideas about sex/gender differences structure understanding of diseases, and specifically how they have been implicated in understanding COVID-19. Noting some recent progress in mobilizing the health research community to rectify the long exclusion of women from clinical research, and some increased recognition that both sex and gender must be considered, Dumes points out that the reports about COVID-19 (though attentive to greater *medical* impact of the illness on men), did not equally well focus on disparate effects of treatment efforts. Moreover, the efforts that have been undertaken privilege biological sex (male vs. female sex) over the different gendered roles individuals play, regardless of their biological sex (including those beyond the male-female binary). Moreover, these two concepts are clearly inadequate alone to address people's complex and intersecting social positions and relationships to power and privilege, leaving invisible the particular issues for poor women, women of color, gender and sexual minorities, and women with disabilities. If we do not examine individuals' simultaneous race-ethnicity, class, sexuality, age, and other intersections with sex and gender, our picture of the impact of both the disease and its treatments is critically limited.

In evaluating the global discussion of apparent gender differences in leadership as a factor in outcomes associated with COVID-19, psychologist Verena Klein shows that a simple focus on the head of government may obscure important issues. In particular, both the direction of causality (for example, is it that women leaders make better decisions or that countries that choose women leaders are characterized—on average—by better social circumstances for meeting the pandemic?) and gendered outcomes on the ground may be invisible. Klein points out how much, when commentators characterize women's unique responses, they rely on gender stereotypes. For example, they emphasize that women leaders are "humble" enough to listen to scientific evidence, rather than stressing their educational and occupational commitments to science, evidence, and expertise. They emphasize that their communications are caring, rather than that they are willing to be open and transparent about their actions, and stress that they are risk-averse, rather than decisive, in acting to shut down epidemic-spreading activity. This emphasis on stereotypically "feminine" qualities recycles a tired and sexist discourse precisely when at least some women leaders are demonstrating the kind of decisive, informed, and humane leadership most citizens of all countries hope for from their leaders, regardless of sex or gender! By examining these processes in the German context in particular—where Angela Merkel's leadership has been recognized, if not always for the right things—Klein shows that another layer of overwhelmingly male leadership in the country is overlooked, as is the disproportionately negative effect of the pandemic on German women workers and family members.

Analyzing the impact of global and national decision-making on the labor markets in India, sociologist Jayati Lal considers how global class and gender inequities associated with capitalism and patriarchy have formed the basis of disparate effects of the pandemic. Those women workers in the lowest-wage work, particularly the lower-status health workers, and those in the informal sector who perform caregiving and domestic work, have been among the most afflicted by COVID-19 itself, as well as by the economic dislocations of unemployment and deepened poverty. Lal emphasizes the complex entanglement of patriarchal structures and capitalism, pointing to the importance of dismantling both in order to offer solutions that can reach the poorest women in urban India.

Three essays focus on the impact of the pandemic in different Latin American contexts. Historian Sueann Caulfield, historian and women's and gender studies scholar Eimeel Castillo, and literary and cultural scholar Marisol Fila each focus on how particular government actions and failures to act in Brazil, Nicaragua, and Argentina respectively, have exacerbated existing vulnerabilities and inequities that disproportionately affect women. These include (as in India) women's increased economic vulnerability and higher exposure to COVID-19 due to caretaking labor, as well as increased risk of domestic violence and loss of access to reproductive health care. At the same time, all three note the mobilization of feminist, Indigenous, Afro-descendent, and LGBTQ activism to protect and defend the most vulnerable groups in each country.

Sueann Caulfield, in discussing Brazil's painful experience with COVID-19, reminds us that the current regime has reversed many progressive policies enacted by the previous two. As a result, Indigenous people's rights have been under threat, and critical health assistance withheld. Black feminists and Indigenous women have responded by mobilizing appropriate and necessary care for their communities. Similarly, government action prevented women of color—who are concentrated in caregiving and domestic jobs at the low-wage end of the labor force—from strengthening their union activism before COVID-19. Nonetheless, the unions representing these workers have taken strong actions to advocate for domestic workers' rights, supported by feminist scholars' analysis of the oppressive exploitation of women of color by privileged white households. In addition, Black feminist activists have organized relief for their communities and have continued their struggle for political representation. Despite these impressive efforts, not only has the virus surged uncontrolled, but so has violence against women and LGBTQ individuals, violence that is opposed by ongoing feminist activism.

Nicaragua is an interesting contrast, given its long-term government by a single authoritarian leader, Daniel Ortega. Eimeel Castillo notes that this regime has been characterized by many antidemocratic actions against protestors and electoral reforms, as well as a long-term decline in social services to the Nicaraguan population, with a high rate of exile from the country, as well as state killing of civilians and taking of political prisoners. The Nicaraguan official government response to the pandemic was very slow and highly politicized. Castillo shows that gender-based violence—already a focus of activism and concern among feminists in Nicaragua—has expanded in the context of the pandemic, not only with few sanctions for those who harm women, but in fact the release of individuals charged with femicide and rape. In this repressive and dangerous context, digital activism by feminists has expanded in an effort both to improve the legal environment for women in Nicaragua and to force the implementation of existing legal protections.

Marisol Fila discusses how the past but recent Argentine government of President Mauricio Macri created a context for the COVID-19 epidemic that included increased inequality and greater difficulty for vulnerable populations. For that reason, despite the election of the more progressive new president (Alberto Fernandez) and vice president (Christina Fernandez de Kirchner) in late 2019, the impact of the pandemic has been terrible for those with the fewest resources. Perhaps, however, some optimism about the current government's commitment to reduce inequality has fed the inspiring rise of feminist activism and Afro-descendent activism, both of which have increased during this same period. Because of the constraints on public advocacy in the age of COVID-19, the activists have taken good advantage of the opportunities afforded by the opening of public digital spaces.

In a very different region of the world, Turkey offers some parallels to the observations about the impact of COVID-19 in these Latin American contexts. Interdisciplinary women's and gender studies and psychology scholar Özge Savaş focuses on how Turkey's recent political history served to exacerbate the impact of the pandemic as a result of women's and LGBTQ individuals' already serious vulnerability to both state and domestic violence. By removing social protections (such as women's shelters and other social services to households and families) and acting to confine women's roles to traditionally defined families, the government ensured that women would be at greater risk of violence and economic privation when the inevitable and necessary COVID-19-related confinement to homes occurred. Moreover, like some other countries, the government of Turkey enacted laws to reduce prison sentences and provide prison releases, but here they specifically excluded women peacebuilders and activists, while at the same time their discourse demonized unmarried and childless women. Of course, these actions disproportionately affected Kurdish minority women. Even in this oppressive context, as in Latin America, women in Turkey have responded with social media campaigns bringing the specific conditions oppressing women and LGBTQ individuals in Turkey, and in particular among the Kurds, into view by those within and outside the country.

Finally, legal scholar and activist Abiola Akiyode-Afolabi and anthropologist Ronke Olawale explore how Nigerian women's lives have been affected by the pandemic not only in some of the same ways discussed in other essays, but also by increasing problems of access to water, sanitation, and hygiene; corruption around the distribution of care resources; and reduced attention to women's maternal and reproductive health needs. They draw on an important study of poor women's health needs and experience in this context, confirming that in Nigeria, as elsewhere, existing structural inequities were exacerbated in the face of the pandemic. Many women activists have engaged in efforts to address the basic needs of Nigerian women and families, and they have worked closely in coalitions across the country and with women activists throughout Africa. Reflecting Akiyode-Afolabi's own activist commitments, she and Olawale outline not only the terrible impact of COVID-19 for poor Nigerian women, but also an agenda for the post-COVID-19 world they imagine.

Of course, readers interested in a particular national context may be especially drawn to an essay focused on that context. But we remain committed, as a group, to core aspects of the vision of the Global Feminisms Project. These include the value of examining women's movement activism as a lens for understanding social conditions that motivate and demand it; the notion that examining local contexts in depth always illuminates and is illuminated by comparing it with other particular contexts; and the importance of considering the ways in which circumstances truly are "local" and at the same time reflect the transnational flow of ideas, materials, and people. The eight essays illustrate these themes clearly: gender, class, race, and other inequalities predated the pandemic and took idiosyncratic form in these different political and cultural contexts. But in every case the pandemic worsened the situation of the less powerful, and specifically that of women.

Certain problems arose for women consistently across different settings, though precisely how and for which women clearly varied; but issues of violence against women, and the expectation that women would sacrifice their health and employment to take care of others, were intensified everywhere, jeopardizing women's safety and well-being in particular ways. Clearly, wherever governments were particularly repressive, the problems were profoundly intensified. But even in relatively enlightened political environments, even elite women—like world leaders—were not exempt from gendered processes of devaluation and stereotyping. And the scientific process of studying the virus's impact itself was affected by the failure to attend to the disparate impact of the virus in the context of gender and other relations of social power and domination. We learn a great deal in each essay not only about the commonalities of these phenomena, but crucially about the particularities of these processes, given historical, political, and social situations. Most inspiring across these essays is the creative, courageous, and forthright way feminist scholars and activists have met the new challenges to women's lives posed by this global pandemic.

### Notes

1. Global Feminisms Project, "Interviews," https://sites.lsa.umich.edu/globalfeminisms/interviews/. Accessed April 4, 2021.

2. Global Feminisms Project, https://sites.lsa.umich.edu/globalfeminisms/. Accessed April 4, 2021.

# CHAPTER 17

# The Virus That Kills Twice

## COVID-19 and Domestic Violence under Governmental Impunity in Nicaragua

*Eimeel Castillo*

Perhaps more than any other country in Latin America, Nicaragua's self-identified left-wing government has failed its citizens, especially women, during the pandemic.[1] COVID-19 arrived after two years of continued political repression and deepening economic crisis. In April 2018, Nicaraguans went to the streets to object to the mismanagement of a wildfire in a natural reserve and the promulgation of a presidential decree reducing benefits to pensioners. While these were immediate motivations for the civil unrest, demonstrations were a reaction to rising authoritarianism and corruption. President Daniel Ortega (2007–) and his wife, Vice President Rosario Murillo, responded to widespread demonstrations in major cities with state-sponsored terrorism and by criminalizing all forms of protest.[2] Ortega, as commander in chief of police, approved the order to shoot live rounds at protesters and organized paramilitary groups to intimidate the population, which resulted in more than three hundred civilian deaths, three hundred imprisonments, and 103,000 exiles.[3] Accused of crimes against humanity by an international group of lawyers in December that year, the ruling couple has since struggled to project stability and normalcy amid the impunity and illegitimacy that have become hallmarks of their regime.[4] The scenario brought on by the pandemic has demonstrated that Ortega's political maneuvering takes precedence over protecting the lives of Nicaraguans and has illustrated how authoritarianism often augments the vulnerability of women, especially young women.[5] The impunity and lawlessness that reign in Nicaragua are key to understanding how the pandemic has worsened the already existing epidemic of domestic violence and femicide. As they document the increase in gender-based violence, women's rights activists affiliated with long-standing local organizations such as the Women's Autonomous Movement are demanding government accountability for a culture of impunity that extends to the domestic sphere.

Gender-based violence has been a major concern for women's rights activists and human-rights defenders in Nicaragua for decades. Years of grassroots organization and advocacy by a coalition of women's movements organized around the Women's Network against Violence led to the promulgation of Law 779 (Comprehensive Law Against Violence Against Women) in June 2012.[6] This law expanded the notion of violence to include its psychological and economic forms and defined femicide as a punishable crime for the first time. However, the law faced opposition from the executive. Ortega, who converted to Catholicism in 2005, gained the sympathy of the Catholic Church by forcing his party's deputies to legalize a total abortion ban in September 2006, just two months prior to the presidential elections. In line with his newly adopted Christian persona and in alliance with religious groups, Ortega prevented Law 779's full implementation.[7] A little more than a year after its approval, he ordered a reform that instituted a process of mediation between victims and abusers and established partisan councils that intervene in the legal process to "preserve the unity of the family."[8] As the state disempowered victims, domestic violence continued unabated in this country, in which more than half of Nicaraguan women who live with a male partner have experienced some form of violence in their homes.[9]

Women's rights activists from an array of local movements have denounced the government's role in worsening the situation through its responses to the pandemic. They have documented a shocking rise in violence against women, including murder, even though the regime never declared shelter-in-place orders, as most countries have. For example, Católicas por el Derecho a Decidir (Catholics for the Right to Decide), an association of laypeople supporting women's rights, which estimates that the annual number of femicides over the past five years ranged from fifty-three to fifty-eight, documented ninety-seven cases of femicide or attempted femicide in the first seven months of this year.[10] Only thirteen of these cases are being prosecuted, and 60% of the victims are women under the age of thirty-four, which indicates the particular vulnerability of young women.[11]

While activists such as Católicas director Martha Flores have pointed out that the situation of self-quarantine facilitates abuse, the proliferation of gender-based violence cannot be ascribed exclusively to longer hours in contact with abusers in the home.[12] The Observatory for Women's Lives, an organization that monitors news on gender-based violence, has noted that due to the climate of lawlessness that has reigned supreme in Nicaragua since the

2018 political crisis, abusers are committing crimes at higher rates. Activists point out that abusers are aware that the police and the judicial system are likely not to prosecute them, and that if they are convicted, they may be pardoned. The government and its institutions are devoting all their resources and attention to persecuting dissidents and applying a "politics of officialized impunity" to criminals.[13]

Moreover, the regime's discourse and actions reflect a forcefully misogynist stance. For instance, members of Católicas were outraged by Ortega's release of five hundred sexual offenders in May 2020, a measure they saw as a "legal aberration that creates an even greater lack of protection for women victims."[14] In a press release, authorities stated that the government had freed the abusers because it wanted to reunite families during "Mother's Day month." The complicity of the government has had concrete, tragic results for women: one of the released abusers assassinated his former partner, a thirty-year-old schoolteacher, in June.[15]

Activists reacted quickly as domestic violence surged during the months of the pandemic. Building on a long trajectory of grassroots collaboration among multiple feminist and women's rights groups, they continued diverse advocacy efforts that include prevention, bringing charges against perpetrators, and supporting abused women. They also initiated new services, such as a recent hotline for women seeking counsel. This work is done despite extremely adverse political circumstances, including the aforementioned inability to organize demonstrations or to express any criticism of official policies without facing charges. For example, the national police constantly harass activists from the Women's Autonomous Movement for criticizing the government's actions in regard to women's access to the law or reproductive rights.[16] It is worth emphasizing that Nicaragua is one of the few countries in Latin America, alongside El Salvador, Honduras, and the Dominican Republic, that have a total abortion ban.[17]

Social distancing measures have propelled innovative uses of digital forms of activism, with young, self-identified feminists leading the way. These feminists have developed an array of educational campaigns, including livestreaming of seminars and talks, transmission of podcasts and sketches, and the creation of digital magazines that are later distributed through social media. These efforts raise awareness not only of the importance of following international public health recommendations, in the absence of governmental guidance, but also the gender-specific dimension of the pandemic.[18]

The case of Nicaragua illustrates how quickly women's rights can erode when we add a pandemic to an already established authoritarian regime that enjoys a culture of impunity. It can also teach us about the key role that civil society organizations, such as the women's movement and feminist collectives, exercise in leading the way forward and fighting back against a political and judicial system that disregards real threats to the population, whether in the form of the epidemic of violence against women or the COVID-19 pandemic. Law 779 represents an important step in creating a legal framework within which to break the silence and prevent the innumerable forms of violence that Nicaraguan women experience in their day-to-day lives. However, there is much that needs to be done to ensure its effective implementation, and any initiative to enforce it more comprehensively would certainly require a democratic system. It is unlikely that any legislation to protect women's lives can be put into real effect if the national police do not properly enforce it, since this police force is the same institution serving as repressive tool to sustain the ruling couple. Amid this gloomy scenario, new generations of women's rights activists and feminists are leading the way and are not afraid to speak and act, despite the governmental impunity in Nicaragua.

### Notes

1. Observatorio Ciudadano Covid-19 Nicaragua, "Estadísticas de Covid-19."

2. Salinas, "Ortega declara ilegales las protestas."

3. The Interamerican Commission of Human Rights indicates that as of July 2020, there were still eighty-five civilians incarcerated as political prisoners. Mecanismo Especial de Seguimiento para Nicaragua, "Boletín Julio 2020."

4. President Ortega has been able to run for reelection indefinitely through unconstitutional electoral reforms and election fraud. In December 2018, he ordered the expulsion of the Interdisciplinary Group of Independent Experts, composed of legal experts in human rights violations, just one day before they published a report concluding that the government had perpetrated crimes against humanity. To avoid further international scrutiny, the National Assembly, controlled by Ortega's party, approved an amnesty law in June 2019.

5. Examples of the regime's response include manipulation of official records, unjustified dismissal of medical personnel, and refusal to grant entry to Nicaraguans attempting to return from neighboring countries. EFE, "Nicaragua envía policías."

6. Solís, "La Ley 779."

7. Neumann, "In Nicaragua."

8. Solís, "La Ley 779."

9. Ellsberg et al., "Candies in Hell." See also Solís, "La Ley 779." In its most recent

annual report, the Nicaraguan Institute for Legal Medicine indicates that 81% of performed medical examinations in domestic violence cases during 2018 were done to women. Instituto de Medicina Legal, "Anuario 2018," 5.

10. Numbers are undercounted, and some feminists have stated that between seventy and one hundred women are assassinated per year. Blandón, "Los feminicidios nos hablan."

11. Romero, "Violencia contra las mujeres."

12. Romero, "Violencia contra las mujeres."

13. Herrera Vallejos and Cáceres, "El desmontaje del marco jurídico."

14. Vásquez Larios, "Orteguismo liberó."

15. Red de Mujeres Contra la Violencia Nicaragua, "Boletín Informativo RMCV 4," 4.

16. Movimiento Autónomo de Mujeres Nicaragua, "Al menos 70 mujeres."

17. Nicaragua is one of the few countries in the world that prohibits abortion even when the pregnancy threatens the life of the mother or as a result of rape. The total abortion ban was approved through a reform to the penal code in September 2006 and supported by then-presidential candidate Daniel Ortega and the Catholic clergy.

18. See, for example, the social media of organizations such as Las Malcriadas and Enredadas por el Arte y la Tecnología.

## References

Blandón, María Teresa. "Los feminicidios nos hablan de la sociedad que hemos construido." *Revista Envío 427*, October 2017. https://www.envio.org.ni/articulo/5402

EFE. "Nicaragua envía policías a frontera con Costa Rica por migrantes varados." *Confidencial*, July 24, 2020. https://confidencial.com.ni/nicaragua-envia-policias-a-frontera-con-costa-rica-por-migrantes-varados/

Ellsberg, Mary, Rodolfo Peña, Andrés Herrera, Jerker Liljestrand, and Anna Winkvist, "Candies in Hell: Women's Experiences of Violence in Nicaragua." *Social Science & Medicine* 51.11 (December 2000): 1595–1610. https://doi.org/10.1016/S0277-9536(00)00056-3

Herrera Vallejos, Carmen, and Agustina Cáceres. "El desmontaje del marco jurídico que defiende a las mujeres de ser víctimas de femicidio, está provocando el aumento de sus asesinatos." Enredadas por el Arte y la Tecnología. July 2, 2020. https://enredadas.org/2020/07/02/femicidios-primersemestre2020/

Instituto de Medicina Legal (Corte Suprema de Justicia). "Anuario 2018." https://www.poderjudicial.gob.ni/pjupload/iml/pdf/Anuario_2018.pdf. Accessed August 26, 2020.

Mecanismo Especial de Seguimiento para Nicaragua. "Boletín Julio 2020." Accessed August 16, 2020. https://www.oas.org/es/cidh/actividades/visitas/2018Nicaragua/BOLETIN_MESENI_2020_07.pdf

Movimiento Autónomo de Mujeres Nicaragua. "Al menos 70 mujeres activistas y defensoras de derechos humanos han sido agredidas por policías." April 20, 2020. http://www.movimientoautonomodemujeres.org/noticias/ver/277

Neumann, Pamela. "In Nicaragua, a Failure to Address Violence Against Women." NACLA. April 28, 2017. https://nacla.org/news/2017/04/28/nicaragua-failure-address-violence-against-women

Observatorio Ciudadano Covid-19 Nicaragua. "Estadísticas de Covid-19 en Nicaragua." https://observatorioni.org/estadisticas-covid-19-nicaragua/. Accessed August 15, 2020.

Red de Mujeres Contra la Violencia Nicaragua. "Boletín Informativo RMCV 4," May–June 2020, 1–13. https://www.sidocfeminista.com/ver_archivo.php?c=14451&title=4to%20bolet%C3%ADn%20de%20la%20Red%20de%20Mujeres%20contra%20la%20Violencia&categoria=BOLETINA&id_c=1054&fbclid=IwAR2tx4DPaXKb2D99dkMB0S6UOnsG811b10i-OJN2A76F4U7HqgKxdyDrqZc

Romero, Keyling T. "Violencia contra las mujeres: 35 asesinadas en seis meses, y solo 15 feminicidas procesados." *Confidencial*, July 4, 2020. https://confidencial.com.ni/nicaragua-35-mujeres-asesinadas-en-seis-meses-y-solo-15-feminicidas-procesados/?fbclid=IwAR2ogQ9wrhLCVN9q-Lv0zxjY3C4X648_-Ndn-6pEh1B99rJ9FR8yr9yBYLU

Salinas, Carlos. "Ortega declara ilegales las protestas en Nicaragua." *El País*, September 29, 2018. https://elpais.com/internacional/2018/09/29/america/1538186460_718736.html

Solís, Azahaléa. "La Ley 779 tiene una larga historia de lucha y su reforma envía a la sociedad un mensaje muy negativo." *Revista Envío* 380, November 2013. https://www.envio.org.ni/articulo/4770

Vásquez Larios, Martha. "Orteguismo liberó a violadores de niñas y femicidas sin que estos cumplieran sus condenas." *La Prensa*, June 5, 2020. https://www.laprensa.com.ni/2020/06/05/politica/2681635-orteguismo-libero-a-violadores-de-ninas-y-femicidas-sin-que-estos-cumplieran-su-condena?fbclid=IwAR10w37XtsN-iTnQ9lR94RHgkcubjdKs8U8d3tMJZKYqSTRUDElqomfmC7c

# CHAPTER 18

# "Our Steps Come from Long Ago"

## Living Histories of Feminisms and the Fight against COVID in Brazil

*Sueann Caulfield*

Amid the horrors of the COVID-19 epidemic in Brazil, one of the few promising developments is the emergence of a diverse array of women activists at the forefront of efforts to defend vulnerable populations through direct action and political lobbying. Black feminist activists, in particular, have occupied unprecedented space in recent public discourse. Of course, these efforts cannot begin to compensate for the governmental negligence that permitted the virus to spread virtually unabated, particularly in remote rural and forested regions and poor urban neighborhoods. Since June 2020, Brazil has maintained its position as the nation with the second or third highest number of COVID-19 infections in the world.[1] Brazil's president, Jair Bolsonaro, unabashedly emulating US president Donald Trump, has denied the severity of COVID-19, dismissed the suffering of its victims and refused to mourn the dead, disseminated false information, discredited his government's public health officials, disparaged state and local leaders' efforts to stop the spread of the virus, and attended mass rallies against social distancing and face masks.[2] Bolsonaro's refusal to follow his own government's public health guidelines, even after replacing his health minister three times, led to a rebuke by the Supreme Court. As is true in the United States, the president's actions and inaction have exacerbated the disproportionate effects of the pandemic on the nation's most vulnerable populations.[3] As feminists mobilize through diffuse campaigns to support these populations, they have developed new strategies to combat deep-rooted patterns of injustice that produce this vulnerability.

Black feminist thinkers and activists frequently reference "ancestrality" and emphasize that their presence was made possible by a long history of struggle. Although a full discussion of this history is beyond the scope of this brief essay, it is important to keep in mind the dramatic reversal, after 2014, of more than a decade of unprecedented economic growth combined with federal government policies designed to eradicate poverty and promote diversity, inclusion, and equality. Under the center-left governments of Presidents Lula da Silva (2003–11) and Dilma Rousseff (2011–16), whose redistributive programs and expansion of affirmative action famously helped to lift millions out of poverty and widen access to public universities, a new generation of activists came of age. Alongside "historical" militants of the 1980s and 1990s, young people working in diverse political and cultural realms invigorated and expanded earlier Black, Indigenous, women's, LGBTQI+, and other "new left" movements, as they pressured the leftist state to make good on its yet-unfulfilled promises of justice and equality for all.

The vibrant civil society sustained during the early 2000s has evolved into multiple points of resistance under Bolsonaro, who took power in January 2019 amid a prolonged economic crisis and corruption scandal, and after participating in a right-wing cabal that impeached the nation's first female president in 2016. As Bolsonaro's responses to the pandemic have showcased his efforts to distance the state from his leftist predecessors' rhetorical, if not real, commitment to inclusionary human rights protections, these resistance forces have struggled to fill the void.

Among the earliest examples of this dynamic comes from the Amazon region, home to hundreds of Indigenous groups. In a pattern that was soon replicated throughout the country, the epidemic spiraled out of control by mid-April 2020. Bolsonaro had already endangered Indigenous peoples' hard-won, and still precarious, constitutional rights to physical and cultural survival by defunding the Indian Protection Service and removing limitations on commercial activities in Indigenous ancestral homelands. The resulting upsurge in violence and environmental devastation led human rights organizations and the government's own Public Ministry to warn of impending genocide. The arrival of COVID brought new urgency to their warnings.[4]

Pan-Indigenous organizations and local communities sprang into action, deploying national and international networks that they had developed since the 1970s to dispatch desperate calls for assistance.[5] While male leaders frequently headed outward-facing political mobilization, Indigenous women went to work locally. Building on decades of grassroots organizing focused on the creation of sewing and artisanal collectives as well as community health care and education, domestic violence, and cultural preservation, some Indigenous women cared for the sick, while others disseminated information through radio and in person, collected and distributed masks, food, and other supplies, and maintained direct communication with private and public funding organizations.[6] Existing women's networks also intensified efforts to address the specific impact of the crisis on Indigenous women. In the Amazonian Rio Negro region, for example, activists anticipated and responded to the rise in domestic violence that followed worldwide patterns by mobilizing a network that includes Indigenous women leaders, the women's police station chief, and feminist scholars at the distant University of São Paulo. They created "live" YouTube and Facebook events, reached out to at-risk women, and created and distributed pamphlets and other resources.[7]

Women have played similar roles in defense of *quilombolas*, or people who claim communal rights to lands of ancestors who had escaped from slavery. The Brazilian constitution of 1988, created in response to demands by diverse civil society organizations in the aftermath of a twenty-one-year dictatorship (1964–85), recognizes the descendants' rights to these territories, just as it recognizes Indigenous ancestral claims, but, like Indigenous communities, Black *quilombo* communities have become especially vulnerable to attack, and to the pandemic, under Bolsonaro.[8]

Although this work helped some groups to remain isolated and undoubtedly saved lives, it was impossible to coordinate without government support. It took months for congress to pass emergency legislation to protect Indigenous peoples and *quilombolas*, and the law went into effect in July 2020 only after Bolsonaro had vetoed articles calling for the provision of potable water, basic hygiene supplies, access to emergency hospital care, and food. Congress overrode many of these line-item vetoes in August, but by then the disease had already ravaged the Amazon region and spread to Indigenous groups throughout the country.[9] While government officials denied reports of the disproportionate impact on Indigenous peoples, a study published by a respected research institute found that Amazonian Indigenous people died at rates that were 20% higher than among the region's general population and 150% higher than that of Brazil as a whole.[10] As COVID quickly spread throughout the country, Indigenous organizations continued to report on its underreported toll among their diverse peoples and on the devastating loss of elders who had played crucial roles in their people's cultural and linguistic survival.[11]

When the COVID crisis surged in urban areas, it laid bare the disproportionate vulnerability of women of color, who are overrepresented in low-wage, informal, and caretaking labor.[12] Domestic work—the single largest occupational category for women in Brazil and the lowest paid—is performed almost entirely by women (94%), about 65% of whom are Black or brown.[13] In the early 2000s, expanding social and educational opportunities for women had reduced the supply of domestic workers, resulting in rising wages, new visibility for a struggling union movement, and, in 2013, a much-celebrated constitutional amendment that recognized domestic workers' rights under federal labor law. These gains were reversed in the years that followed, when conservative governments slashed social programs and workers' benefits and the economic crisis swelled the ranks of older women workers who perform an array of domestic and caretaking work informally. These conditions made domestic work one of the highest-risk occupational categories in Brazil in relation to COVID-19.[14]

Domestic workers' vulnerability gained widespread public attention when the first COVID death was reported in Rio de Janeiro on March 17. The victim was Cleonice Gonçalves, a sixty-three-year-old Black housekeeper. Gonçalves's employer had fallen ill upon return from vacationing in Europe, but sent Gonçalves home only when the housekeeper herself showed symptoms. Gonçalves carried the virus to her small hometown, where she died at a public hospital that lacked facilities to care for her.[15]

Gonçalves' death sparked emotional appeals by individual domestic workers and their children, imploring employers to do the right thing by releasing domestic workers with pay.[16] The Public Ministry issued a "technical note" with the same recommendation, but without any enforcement mechanism.[17] Some employers complied voluntarily. Celebrities posted YouTube tutorials on how to wash dishes or run a vacuum cleaner.[18] Mounting deaths of domestic workers around the country, however, and the endangerment of their families and communities, underscored the peril of relying on employers' benevolence. As municipal authorities debated whether domestic work constituted "essential service" during lockdowns, many employers insisted that their employees continue working, while 39% dismissed domestic workers without pay.[19] Although congress passed an emergency unemployment fund in April, many domestic workers reported that they feared risking future employment if they refused their employers' requests to come back to "help out." Those who held legal contracts could collect unemployment only if their employers chose to furlough them during the crisis. Many reported that rather than release them, their employers insisted that they shelter in place together, whether or not they had formerly "lived in."[20]

An avalanche of complaints by domestic workers to union offices and other organizations has brought new visibility to a decades-old movement for domestic workers' rights. As they work to address abuses and lobby for broader state action, activists such as Luíza Batista, president of the National

Federation of Domestic Workers (FENATRAD), have helped to place domestic work at the center of national discussions of class, racial, and gender injustice. In interviews and "live" internet discussions, Batista has argued that the pandemic has fortified the "slavocratic heritage," magnifying historical patterns of inequality and disregard for Black lives that are specific to Brazil, the last country in the Americas to abolish slavery (in 1888).[21] Similarly, Maria Izabel Monteiro Lourenço, head of the Domestic Workers Union of Rio de Janeiro, pointed out that Bolsonaro's opposition to the constitutional protection of domestic servants' rights as a congressman in 2013, and his refusal to enforce these rights as president, perpetuate the legacy of slavery within Brazilian households by naturalizing servitude and reinforcing employers' feeling of entitlement.[22] Commenting on these dynamics, Monique Evelle, a prominent young Black feminist activist and intellectual whose mother was a domestic worker, noted sarcastically that "the middle class hasn't yet been notified" that slavery ended more than 130 years ago.[23]

Keila Grinberg, one of Brazil's most respected historians of slavery, supports this analysis with archival evidence. In an indictment of her white, liberal, middle-class peers who whine that they "need" their maids, she compares them to nineteenth-century slaveholders who considered slavery a "necessary evil." For Grinberg, the expectation that domestic workers risk their lives to serve middle-class families epitomizes the ways white privilege devalues Black lives, fueling the endemic violence against the Black population that white liberals claim to oppose. Grinberg reveals that her consciousness of her own white privilege was raised by Black colleagues, students, and activists in personal interactions, just as Black voices collectively transformed public discourse on race over the past two decades.[24]

Similar analyses by these four different advocates for domestic workers reflect the impact of this transformation within feminist discourse. Back in the 1970s and 1980s, when many Black activists felt alienated by white-led feminist organizations, they created their own. Today, Black feminist groups such as Geledes ( formed in 1988) and Criola (1992), now well-established nongovernmental organizations (NGOs), have played a central role in developing feminist responses to COVID and inspiring young activists. Interpreting the Black Lives Matter movement in the Brazilian context, where police murder Black youths at a much higher rate than in the United States, they place the COVID crisis within a long history of genocidal public policies against Indigenous and Afro-descended populations that have expanded under the Bolsonaro regime. In the same breath, they reference ancestral sources of strength.

"Our steps come from long ago" (*Nossos passos vêm de longe*), a phrase coined in a 1994 Criola publication, has become a mantra for Black feminists, one that connects their work to generations of Black women who fought for their people's survival.[25]

An example of this work is The Time Is Now, a relief project created by a coalition of Black feminist organizations that pressured the government to distribute emergency aid to poor communities in Rio and São Paulo while collecting donations and sending young activists to distribute essential supplies and services to families.[26] Black feminist organizations also joined several other feminist and social justice NGOs to protest the gutting of state programs to combat domestic violence. When Bolsonaro's supporters in congress delayed a bill to restore the programs (until July 7), and when Bolsonaro personally denounced and demoted Ministry of Health officials who supported reproductive and sexual health care services, these feminist organizations led online protests and mobilized their own programs to support women.[27] Finally, Black feminist organizations have supported local initiatives to fight COVID as part of a longer struggle for political representation. An example is the Marielle Franco Institute, named for the Black feminist city councilwoman in Rio de Janeiro who was murdered in 2018. The institute has registered hundreds of local grassroots COVID relief organizations in an effort to identify and support potential women, Black, or poor candidates for public office. By channeling the outpouring of solidarity in poor communities into electoral politics, the institute hopes to populate post-pandemic governing bodies with "many Marielles," ensuring that disadvantaged populations are represented and the struggle for justice continues.[28]

Although many of these campaigns provided essential services, created a sense of solidarity with vulnerable groups, or pressured the state to act, feminist and other civil society efforts could not hope to compensate for the state's refusal to develop a coordinated national defense strategy. As predicted by international organizations—in studies that were well publicized in Brazil—violence against women surged, and women and LGBTQ individuals lost reproductive and sexual health care.[29] Meanwhile, social gatherings and pro-Bolsonaro rallies defied public health measures, while popular support for the president rose temporarily as a result of the emergency unemployment assistance, demonstrating that solidarity was far from universal.

Feminists persist nonetheless, following steps begun long ago.

## *Notes*

1. All websites cited in this chapter were accessed on August 30, 2020. "Cumulative Cases," *Johns Hopkins University & Medicine Coronavirus Resource Center*, November 28, 2020, https://coronavirus.jhu.edu/data/cumulative-cases. As is true worldwide, a higher proportion of those infected in Brazil are women (54%), but more men have died (58%).

2. Monica Yanakiew, "Tropical Trump," *Al Jazeera*, November 27, 2020, https://www.aljazeera.com/economy/2020/11/27/tropical-trump-where-will-brazils-bolsonaro-stand-with-biden; Mauricio Savarece, "Brazil's Bolsonaro Rejects COVID-19 Shot, Calls Masks Taboo," *ABC News*, November 28, 2020, https://abcnews.go.com/International/wireStory/brazils-bolsonaro-rejects-covid-19-shot-calls-masks-74428885

3. FIOCRUZ, "Populações vulneráveis," *FIOCRUZ, Covid-19*, https://portal.fiocruz .br/populacoes-vulneraveis; Vitória Régia da Silva, "Pessoas trans e LGBT+, negras e indígenas estão mais expostas ao impacto da covid-19, aponta pesquisa," *Gênero e Número*, June 29, 2020, http://www.generonumero.media/lgbt-coronavirus/

4. Dimitrius Dantas, "Bolsonaro é denunciado em tribunal internacional por incitação a genocídio indígena," *O Globo*, November 28, 2019, https://oglobo.globo.com /brasil/bolsonaro-denunciado-em-tribunal-internacional-por-incitacao-genocidio -indigena-24106314; "ISA Report at the UN Denounces High Risk of Genocide of Isolated Indigenous Peoples," *Instituto Socioambiental*, February 28, 2020, https://www .socioambiental.org/en/noticias-socioambientais/isa-report-at-the-un-denounces -high-risk-of-genocide-of-isolated-indigenousIndigenous-peoples; "MPF quer direito a resposta para indígenas em 'live' e Twitter de Bolsonaro," *Correio Braziliense*, March 12, 2020, https://www.correiobraziliense.com.br/app/noticia/politica/2020/03/12 /interna_politica,833856/mpf-quer-direito-a-resposta-para-indigenas-em-live-e-twi tter-de-bols.shtml; Rubens Valente, "'A proposta do governo Bolsonaro ao índio é o genocídio,' diz subprocurador," *UOL Notícias*, April 19, 2020, https://racismoambiental .net.br/2020/04/20/a-proposta-do-governo-bolsonaro-ao-indio-e-o-genocidio-diz-su bprocurador/; Conselho Indigenista Missionário, "A ameaça de genocídio que paira sobre os povos indígenas isolados no Brasil," *CIMI.org.br*, July 7, 2020, https://cimi.org .br/2020/07/ameaca-genocidio-paira-povos-indigenas-isolados-brasil/

5. "COVID-19 e os povos indígenas, banco de iniciativas," *Instituto Socioambiental*, August 20, 2020, https://covid19.socioambiental.org/; "Emergência indígena, dados covid 19," *Articulação dos Povos Indígenas do Brasil*, August 19, 2020, http://emergenci aindigena.apib.info/dados_covid19/

6. Ricardo Verdum, *Mulheres indígenas, direitos e políticas públicas* (Brasília: Inesc, 2008); Juliana Radler, "À frente de campanha, mulheres indígenas do Rio Negro dão voz e corpo à luta contra a Covid-19," *Instituto Socioambiental*, July 22, 2020, https://www.socioambiental.org/pt-br/noticias-socioambientais/a-frente-de-campa nha-mulheres-indigenas-do-rio-negro-dao-voz-e-corpo-a-luta-contra-a-covid-19

7. Juliana Radler, "Covid-19: Mulheres indígenas do Rio Negro lançam campanha de arrecadação," *Instituto Socioambiental*, April 29, 2020, https://www.socioambiental

.org/pt-br/noticias-socioambientais/covid-19-mulheres-indigenas-do-rio-negro-lanc
am-campanha-de-arrecadacao; "Mulheres indígenas: O sagrado da existência e a cura
da terra," *Articulação dos Povos Indígenas do Brasil*, August 1, 2020, http://apiboficial
.org/2020/08/01/mulheres-indigenas-o-sagrado-da-existencia-e-a-cura-da-terra/

8. "Negras, índias e quilombolas lutam contra a Covid-19," *Jornal do Comércio*, July
20, 2020, https://www.jornaldocomercio.com/_conteudo/cadernos/empresas_e_ne
gocios/2020/07/747596-negras-indias-e-quilombolas-lutam-contra-a-covid-19.html;
"4.504 quilombolas contaminados pela COVID-19," *Coordinação Nacional de Articulação das Comunidades Negras Rurais Quilombolas*, August 28, 2020, http://conaq.org
.br/; "Racismo: 'Se a gente não morre de covid, morre na ponta do fuzil,' diz conselhei-
ra de saúde," *Rede Brasil Atual* (blog), June 17, 2020, https://www.redebrasilatual.com
.br/cidadania/2020/06/racismo-se-a-gente-nao-morre-de-covid-morre-na-ponta-do
-fuzil-diz-conselheira-de-saude/

9. Oswaldo Braga de Souza, "Congresso derruba vetos presidenciais a plano
emergencial para indígenas e quilombolas," *Instituto Socioambiental*, August 19, 2020,
https://www.socioambiental.org/pt-br/noticias-socioambientais/congresso-derru
ba-vetos-presidenciais-a-plano-emergencial-para-indigenas-e-quilombolas

10. "Secretário nega que mortalidade por covid-19 seja maior entre indígenas,"
*Agência Senado*, August 8, 2020, https://www12.senado.leg.br/noticias/audios/2020
/08/secretario-nega-que-mortalidade-por-covid-19-seja-maior-entre-indigenas;   Instituto de Pesquisa Ambiental da Amazônia, "Mortalidade de indígenas por covid-19
na Amazônia é maior do que média nacional," *IPAM.org.br*, June 21, 2020, https://ip
am.org.br/mortalidade-de-indigenas-por-covid-19-na-amazonia-e-maior-do-que-me
dias-nacional-e-regional/

11. Letícia Mori, "Morte de anciãos indígenas na pandemia pode fazer línguas in-
teiras desaparecerem," *BBC News Brasil*, August 29, 2020, https://www.bbc.com/portu
guese/brasil-53914416

12. Instituto Brasileiro de Geografia e Estatística, *Síntese de Indicadores Sociais*,
*Estudos & Pesquisas* 40 (2019): 31, https://biblioteca.ibge.gov.br/visualizacao/livros/li
v101678.pdf

13. Instituto Brasileiro de Geografia e Estatística, *Síntese de Indicadores Sociais*,
19–26, 40; Luana Pinheiro et al., "Vulnerabilidades das trabalhadoras domésticas no
contexto da pandemic de COVID-19 no Brasil," *Nota Técnica* (UN Women and Instituto
de Pesquisa Econômico Aplicada, June 2020), 7, http://repositorio.ipea.gov.br/bitstre
am/11058/10077/1/NT_75_Disoc_Vulnerabilidades%20das%20Trabalhadoras%20D
omesticas.pdf

14. Instituto Brasileiro de Geografia e Estatística, *Síntese de Indicadores Sociais*, 19;
Pinheiro et al., "Vulnerabilidades das trabalhadoras domésticas."

15. Gram Slattery and Rodrigo Viga Gaier, "A Brazilian Woman Caught Coronavirus on Vacation: Her Maid Is Now Dead," *Reuters*, March 24, 2020, https://www.reute
rs.com/article/us-health-coronavirus-rio-idUSKBN21B1HT

16. "Pela Vida de Nossas Mães (@pelavidadenossasmaes)," Instagram, https://
www.instagram.com/pelavidadenossasmaes/; Marques Travae, "After the Death of a

Maid Who Contracted Covid-19 Working for Her Employer Returning from Italy, Children of Domestic Workers Call for Their Paid Leave," *Black Women of Brazil*, March 26, 2020, https://blackwomenofbrazil.co/after-the-death-of-a-maid-who-contracted-covid-19-working-for-her-employer-returning-from-italy-children-of-domestic-workers-call-for-their-paid-leave/

17. "Coronavírus: Ministério Público do Trabalho faz orientações sobre o trabalho doméstico," *iDoméstica* (blog), March 19, 2020, https://blog.idomestica.com/4314/coronavirus-ministerio-publico-trabalho-recomendacoes-trabalho-domestico/

18. "Maitê Proença faz tutorial de faxina durante isolamento," *Contigo!*, March 25, 2020, https://contigo.uol.com.br/noticias/famosos/maite-proenca-faz-tutorial-de-faxina-durante-isolamento-dar-valor-a-quem-faz.phtml; Rodrigo Lara, "Sem perrengue," *UOL Notícias*, July 5, 2020, https://www.bol.uol.com.br/noticias/2020/07/05/sem-perrengue-esses-21-tutoriais-vao-salvar-sua-vida-na-quarentena.htm

19. "Coronavírus no Brasil: 39% dos patrões dispensaram diaristas sem pagamento durante pandemia, aponta pesquisa," *BBC News Brasil*, accessed August 30, 2020, https://www.bbc.com/portuguese/brasil-52375292

20. Fábio Massalli, "Suspensão de contrato ou redução de jornada vale para domésticas," *Agência Brasil*, August 4, 2020, https://agenciabrasil.ebc.com.br/economia/noticia/2020-04/suspensao-de-contrato-ou-reducao-de-jornada-vale-para-domesticas; "Trabalhadoras domésticas têm o direito de se proteger do coronavírus," *Fenatrad*, March 16, 2020, https://fenatrad.org.br/2020/03/16/trabalhadoras-domesticas-tem-o-direito-de-se-proteger-do-coronavirus/

21. Lola Ferreira, "Entrevista: 'A "Casa Grande" não consegue passar sem a servidão das pessoas negras,'" *Gênero e Número*, June 5, 2020, http://www.generonumero.media/casa-grande-domesticas-servidao-miguel/

22. "Trabalhadoras domésticas e a Covid-19," *Fenatrad*, May 20, 2020, https://fenatrad.org.br/2020/08/21/02902/

23. Monique Evelle, "A escravidão acabou: Só falta avisar à classe média," *Desabafo Social*, March 13, 2015, http://desabafosocial.com.br/blog/2015/03/13/a-escravidao-acabou-so-falta-avisar-a-classe-media/

24. Keila Grinberg, "Letras sensatas: A revolução começa em casa," *Época*, July 2020, https://piaui.folha.uol.com.br/materia/letras-sensatas-revolucao-comeca-em-casa/

25. Gabriel Cabral, "A cor dos 100 mil mortos," *Negrê* (blog), August 11, 2020, https://negre.com.br/a-cor-dos-100-mil-mortos-covid-19-e-a-populacao-negra/; Silier Andrade Cardoso Borges, "As ruas e a Covid-19: Novas e velhas expressões das desigualdades sociorraciais durante a pandemia," *Geledés* (blog), July 11, 2020, https://www.geledes.org.br/as-ruas-e-a-covid-19-novas-e-velhas-expressoes-das-desigualdades-sociorraciais-durante-a-pandemia/; "Nossas Vidas Importam: A pandemia da COVID-19 afeta a todos e todas, mas de formas diferentes," *Anistia Internacional Brasil*, //anistia.org.br/campanhas/nossas-vidas-importam/; Fernanda Carneiro, "Nossos passos vem de longe," in *O livro da saúde das mulheres negras: Nossos passos vêm*

*de longe*, ed. Jurema Werneck et al. (Rio de Janeiro: Pallas; Criola; Global Exchange, 1994); Jurema Werneck, "Dialogues for Democracy with Jurema Werneck," interview by Juliana Góes and Elizabeth Hordge-Freeman, July 20, 2020, video, https://www.democracybrazil.org/dialogues-for-democracy

26. "Agora é a hora: Mulheres negras no enfrentamento à pandemia," *Criola*, accessed August 30, 2020, https://criola.org.br/onepage/agora-e-a-hora/

27. CEFEMEA et al., "Nota de Repúdio," June 6, 2020, https://sxpolitics.org/ptbr/wp-content/uploads/sites/2/2020/06/Nota-Tecnica-MS_Cfemea_Curumim_SPW_assinaturas_11_05_17h.pdf; "Geledés no Enfrentamento ao Coronavírus—PLPs em Ação!," *Geledés*, April 6, 2020, https://www.geledes.org.br/geledes-no-enfrentamento-ao-coronavirus-plps-em-acao/

28. "O amanhã começa hoje," *Instituto Marielle Franco*, accessed August 30, 2020, https://www.institutomariellefranco.org/

29. Marina Teodoro, "Negligência do Estado atrasa combate à violência doméstica," *Terra*, August 21, 2020, https://www.terra.com.br/noticias/brasil/negligencia-do-estado-atrasa-combate-a-violencia-domestica,d6b6144eb0c676ae186d1a3e5655f8d8vpjq7dkx.html; "Estado de SP registra 62 casos de violência doméstica por dia pela internet durante quarentena," *Geledés*, August 14, 2020, https://www.geledes.org.br/estado-de-sp-registra-62-casos-de-violencia-domestica-por-dia-pela-internet-durante-quarentena/

# CHAPTER 19

# Making Sense of Sex and Gender Differences in Biomedical Research on COVID-19

*Abigail A. Dumes*

Until thirty years ago, sex didn't matter in biomedical research. In the United States, the founding of the National Institutes of Health's Office of Research on Women's Health and the Society of Women's Health Research (SWHR) in 1990 marked the emergence of biomedical interest in "biological sex differences" and an attendant call to approach sex as a biological variable by including women in clinical research and "disaggregating" biomedical data by sex. Prior to this, and the 1993 NIH Revitalization Act, which "mandated that, if relevant, women and minorities be included in clinical research trials,"[1] participants in clinical trials were almost exclusively white men.[2] However, as Miller et al. observe, "It was not until 2001 when the Institute of Medicine (IOM) asked the question 'Does Sex Matter?' that sex and gender were considered as two variables forming the basis of individualized medicine."[3] Since then, and with the formation of organizations such as the International Society of Gender Medicine in 2006 and the Sex and Gender Women's Health Collaborative in 2012, some biomedical physicians and scientists have begun to include sex *and* gender within the same field of analysis, a shift from (what came to be known in the mid-1990s as) "sex-based biology" to "sex- and gender-based medicine" (SGBM).[4] Even still, after three decades of effort, proponents of sex-based biology and SGBM argue that there is still too little attention to sex—and to sex *and* gender—within biomedical research.

Enter the novel coronavirus SARS-CoV-2 that causes COVID-19, a disease that kills more men than women, at the same time that, in the United States, it has hospitalized and killed Black, Hispanic, and Native Americans at higher rates than White Americans,[5] making clear that "racism, not race, is a risk factor for dying of COVID-19."[6] Perhaps yet another novel feature of this virus is that, less than a year into its pandemic presence, the amount of attention given to COVID-19's sex and gender dimensions has already been relatively significant. Although there's too little data at this point to know why, it *is* important to note the emphasis on "relatively." As Griffith et al. observe, "Results from the randomized, controlled Adaptive COVID-19 Treatment Trial, which tested remdesivir as a therapeutic agent for the treatment of COVID-19, showed a 4-day difference in time to recovery between the treatment group and the control group, but the study did not provide explicit information on sex-based efficacy or adverse reactions."[7] Griffith et al. also observe that "an immunologic sex difference may exist in the mitigation of COVID-19, yet 86% of participants enrolled in clinical trials of immunotherapies (eg, tocilizumab) are men."[8] However, as Womersley et al. point out, "Even the fact that some countries are considering sex as an important factor in covid-19 outcomes is a significant improvement when compared with the norm of non-sex-disaggregated data collection for other infectious and chronic diseases."[9] In an effort to understand why more men than women die from COVID-19, some scientists have focused on immunological differences,[10] while others have focused on hormonal differences.[11] Still others have issued calls for the importance of "collecting sex-disaggregated data" about COVID-19.[12] And trials that administer hormones to men with COVID-19 have already been launched.[13]

In *Inclusion: The Politics of Differences in Medical Research*, sociologist Steven Epstein suggests that, when it comes to sex-based biology research, "not only do the accounts that privilege the biological often deflect our attention from the social organization of gender relations, but sometimes such accounts also serve to naturalize the conditions of gender inequality that in and of themselves may be bad for women's health and well-being."[14] In light of Epstein's observation, the biomedical attention that *has* been given to both sex (e.g., immunological and hormonal differences) *and* gender (e.g., social patterns in health behaviors such as hand washing and smoking) in the context of COVID-19 seems particularly noteworthy. By March 2020, *The Lancet* had published a comment piece by the Gender and COVID-19 Working Group that called on "governments and global health institutions to consider the sex and gender effects of the COVID-19 outbreak."[15] And in April 2020, it published an editorial that described how the "success of the global response [to COVID-19] . . . will depend on the quality of evidence informing the response and the extent to which data represent sex and gender differences" and that "obscuring sex and gender differences in treatment and vaccine development could result in harm."[16] There have also been commentary[17] and review articles that examine the "impact of sex and gender on COVID-19" in the United States[18] and Europe.[19] And Global Health 5050, an "initiative to advance action and accountability for gender equality in global health," has dedicated an entire resource site to "Sex, Gender and COVID-19."

More recently, on June 24, 2020, Harvard's GenderSci Lab launched a COVID Project, which, in its "US Gender/Sex COVID-19 Data Tracker" and other features,[20] follows feminist social neuroendocrinologist Sari van Anders's use of "gender/sex" as "an umbrella term for both gender (social-ization) and sex (biology, evolution)" that "reflects social locations or iden-tities *where gender and sex cannot be easily or at all disentangled*" (emphasis mine).[21] In following van Anders's lead, the GenderSci Lab has found that, by bringing gender and sex into the same field of analysis, the analysis is not complete without also "aggregating"—or analyzing the intersectional impli-cations of—sex and gender's relationship to race, class, and ethnicity, among others. As the lab's directors observe in a June 24, 2020, *New York Times* op-ed, "What's Really behind the Gender Gap in COVID-19 Deaths?," "To be sure, sex-linked biology may play a role in the development of some chronic diseases, but always in complex interaction with class, race, or ethnicity, and gender-related variables."[22] And in a blog post, its members conclude that "lack of intersectional data with variables such as comorbidities, occupation, race, age, institutional living environment, and other variables hinders efforts to analyze disparities in gender/sex outcomes."[23] In the end, it seems, the road to fully understanding COVID-19 and addressing its disparities in health out-comes leads back to what Black feminist activists and scholars have been arguing since the late 1970s: that gender/sex should always be analyzed in intersectional—or, in the context of biomedicine, "aggregate"—relationship to all other dimensions of social oppression.[24]

### Notes

1. Miller et al., "Embedding Concepts," 194.
2. Women remain underrepresented in clinical trials, particularly in the research areas of HIV/AIDS, chronic kidney disease, and cardiovascular disease. See Feldman et al., "Quantifying Sex Bias."
3. Miller et al., "Embedding Concepts," 195.
4. Epstein, *Inclusion*; Madsen et al., "Sex- and Gender-Based Medicine."
5. Khazanchi et al., "Racism, Not Race." In capitalizing "White," I follow Eve L. Ew-ing (2020), who argues that capitalization attends to the "specificity and significance of Whiteness" and helps to dismantle "its seeming neutrality" and "power to maintain its invisibility." See also Painter (2020) and Appiah (2020).
6. Wallis, "Why Racism, Not Race, Is a Risk Factor."
7. Griffith et al., "Men and COVID-19," 42.

8. Griffith et al., "Men and COVID-19," 43.
9. Womersley et al., "Covid-19," 1.
10. Scully et al., "How Biological Sex Impacts"; Takahashi et al., "Sex Differences in Immune Responses."
11. Grandi, Facchinetti, and Bitzer, "Gendered Impact of Coronavirus Disease."
12. Sharma et al., "Sex Differences in Mortality."
13. Richardson and Shattuck-Heidorn, "Introducing the GenderSci Lab."
14. Epstein, *Inclusion*, 254–255.
15. Wenham, Smith, and Morgan, "COVID-19," 847.
16. *The Lancet*, "The Gendered Dimensions of COVID-19," 1168.
17. Griffith et al., "Men and COVID-19."
18. Walter and McGregor, "Sex- and Gender-Specific Observations."
19. Gebhard, Regitz-Zagrosek, and Neuhauser, "Impact of Sex and Gender."
20. Richardson and Shattuck-Heidorn, "Introducing the GenderSci Lab."
21. van Anders, "Beyond Sexual Orientation," 1181.
22. Shattuck-Heidorn, Reiches, and Richardson, "What's Really behind the Gender Gap."
23. Danielsen, Rushovich, and Tarrant, "Highlights."
24. "Intersectional Feminism"; Smith, "Black Feminism and Intersectionality."

## References

Danielsen, Ann Caroline, Tamara Rushovich, and Mimi Tarrant. "Highlights from the GenderSci Lab's US Gender/Sex Covid-19 Data Tracker." Blog post, June 24, 2020. https://www.genderscilab.org/blog/covid-data-highlights
Epstein, Steven. *Inclusion: The Politics of Difference in Medical Research*. Chicago: University of Chicago Press, 2007.
Feldman, Sergey, Waleed Ammar, Kyle Lo, et al. "Quantifying Sex Bias in Clinical Studies at Scale with Automated Data Extraction." *Journal of American Medical Association Network Open* 2.7 (2019): e196700. https://doi.org:10.1001/jamanetworkopen.2019.6700
Gebhard, Catherine, Vera Regitz-Zagrosek, Hannelore K. Neuhauser, Rosemary Morgan, and Sabra L. Klein. "Impact of Sex and Gender on COVID-19 Outcomes in Europe." *Biological Sex Differences* 11.1 (2020): 29. https://doi.org:10.1186/s13293-020-00304-9
"The Gendered Dimensions of COVID-19." Editorial in *The Lancet* 395.10231 (April 11, 2020): 1168. https://doi.org/10.1016/S0140-6736(20)30823-0
Grandi, Giovanni, Fabio Facchinetti, and Johannes Bitzer. "The Gendered Impact of Coronavirus Disease (COVID-19): Do Estrogens Play a Role?" *European Journal of Contraceptive and Reproductive Health Care* 25.3 (2020): 233–234. https://doi. org: 10.1080/13625187.2020.1766017
Griffith, D. M., et al. "Men and COVID-19: A Biopsychosocial Approach to Understanding Sex Differences in Mortality and Recommendations for Practice and Policy Interventions." *Preventing Chronic Disease* 17 (2020): 200–247.

"Intersectional Feminism: What It Means and Why It Matters Right Now." UN Women. July 1, 2020. https://doi.org/10.1016/S0140-6736(20)30823-0

Khazanchi R., C. T. Evans, and J. R. Marcelin. "Racism, Not Race, Drives Inequity across the COVID-19 Continuum." *Journal of American Medical Association Network Open* 3.9 (September 25, 2020): e2019933. https://doi.org:10.1001/jamanetworkopen.2020.19933

Madsen, Tracy, et al. "Sex- and Gender-Based Medicine: The Need for Precise Terminology." *Gender and the Genome* 1 (2017): 122–128.

Miller, Virginia M., et al. "Embedding Concepts of Sex and Gender Health Differences into Medical Curricula." *Journal of Women's Health* 22.3 (2013): 194–202.

Richardson, Sarah S., and Heather Shattuck-Heidorn. "Introducing the GenderSci Lab COVID-19 Project." Blog post, June 24, 2020. https://www.genderscilab.org/blog/covid-intro

Scully, E. P., J. Haverfield, R. L. Ursin, C. Tannenbaum, and S. L. Klein. "Considering How Biological Sex Impacts Immune Responses and COVID-19 Outcomes." *Nature Reviews Immunology* 20.7 (2020): 442–447.

Sharma, Garima, Annabelle Santos Volgman, and Erid D. Michos. "Sex Differences in Mortality from COVID-19 Pandemic: Are Men Vulnerable and Women Protected?" *Journal of the American College of Cardiology: Case Reports* 2.9 (2020): 1407–1410.

Shattuck-Heidorn, Heather, Meredith W. Reiches, and Sarah S. Richardson. "What's Really behind the Gender Gap in COVID-19 Deaths?" *New York Times*, June 24, 2020. https://www.nytimes.com/2020/06/24/opinion/sex-differences-covid.html

Smith, Sharon. "Black Feminism and Intersectionality." *International Socialist Review* 91 (2011).

Takahashi, T., P. Wong, M. Ellingson, et al. "Sex Differences in Immune Responses to SARS-CoV-2 That Underlie Disease Outcomes." *Nature* 588 (August 26, 2020): 315–320. https://doi.org/10.1038/s41586-020-2700-3

van Anders, Sari M. "Beyond Sexual Orientation: Integrating Gender/Sex and Diverse Sexualities via Sexual Configurations Theory." *Archives of Sexual Behavior* 44 (2015): 1177–1213.

Wallis, Claudia. "Why Racism, Not Race, Is a Risk Factor for Dying of COVID-19." *Scientific American*, June 12, 2020. https://www.scientificamerican.com/article/why-racism-not-race-is-a-risk-factor-for-dying-of-covid-191/

Walter, Lauren A., and Alyson J. McGregor. "Sex- and Gender-Specific Observations and Implications for COVID-19." *Western Journal of Emergency Medicine* 21.3 (2020): 507–509. https://dx.doi.org/10.5811%2Fwestjem.2020.4.47536

Wenham, Clare, Julia Smith, and Rosemary Morgan. "COVID-19: The Gendered Impacts of the Outbreak." *The Lancet* 395.10227 (2020): 846–848. https://doi.org/10.1016/S0140-6736(20)30526-2

Womersley, Kate, et al. "Covid-19: Male Disadvantage Highlights the Importance of Sex Disaggregated Data." *British Medical Journal* 370 (2020): m2870.

# CHAPTER 20

# Digital Encounters from an Intersectional Perspective

## Black Women in Argentina

*Marisol Fila*

On December 10, 2019, Alberto Fernandez and Cristina Fernandez de Kirchner became president and vice president of Argentina, bringing to an end the conservative regime of President Mauricio Macri (2015–19).[1] The new government promised to resume the progressive social and economic policies of the previous center-left governments of Nestor Kirchner and Cristina Fernandez de Kirchner (2003–15), which had brought improved living conditions for the most vulnerable sectors of society and worked toward the implementation of human rights policies, social and economic relief plans, and the support and promotion of public education, health, and culture.[2] Macri's government had abandoned these policies, and his four-year term saw a rise in employment and drop in production and consumption, pushing almost 1.5 million Argentinians into poverty.[3] Gender disparities also increased under Macri. Currently, women continue to suffer higher levels of unemployment and job insecurity than men.[4] Those who experience intersecting forms of oppression, such as trans, Afro-Argentine, Indigenous, and migrant women, are even more economically vulnerable.[5]

Globally, the emergency created by COVID-19 has had a disproportionate impact on the most vulnerable populations.[6] The Argentine sociologist and feminist Karina Bidaseca affirms that throughout Latin America, the pandemic has deepened class, gender, and ethnic-racial inequalities in almost every realm of public and private life, including the domestic sphere, health centers and hospitals, and work, education, and political participation.[7] Studies also show that the rates of gender-based violence, femicides, and anti-trans violence have been increasing since the beginning of 2020.[8]

In Argentina, the gender-differentiated impact of COVID-19 is evident in the data on Emergency Family Income (IFE),[9] a program created by the

Argentine state to soften the impact of the economic crisis caused by the pandemic among the most economically vulnerable sectors.[10] Among the nearly nine million beneficiaries, 55.7% are women.[11] Women are especially vulnerable not only because they form the majority in informal employment, but also because they face greater obstacles to entry into the labor market and are responsible for housework and childcare.[12] As the feminist economist Mercedes D'Alessandro[13] affirms, women dedicate triple the amount of time to these tasks that men do.[14]

Gender inequality has been vigorously denounced over the past decade in Argentina. Women have organized and protested against the multiple inequalities that run through social life, increasingly from an intersectional perspective.[15] Evidence of the rising visibility of organized feminism in Argentina are the Ni Una Menos[16] movement and the Campaña Nacional por el Derecho a un Aborto Legal, Seguro y Gratuito[17] (National Campaign for the Right to Legal, Safe, and Free Abortion). Ni Una Menos started in 2015 as a grassroots feminist movement against gender-based violence and has spread across several Latin American countries.[18] Similarly, the campaign for abortion rights and its green bandana have become a symbol of women's resistance in many Latin American and European countries.[19] The demands for reproductive rights and an end to gender-based violence have exhibited the new characteristics of the Argentine feminist movement. Younger generations are taking leadership roles and generating new methods of struggle that combine forms of activism that span from the streets to social media.[20] Similarly, debates on women's rights have been increasingly visible in mainstream media over the past few years, and women's presence in academia and government has expanded.[21] The current government recently created the Dirección de Economía, Igualdad y Género[22] (Office of Economy, Equality, and Gender) within the Ministry of Economy, which aims to reduce existing gender gaps in the economic sphere.

Persistent gender inequality exacerbates the historical and structural inequalities that negatively impact the Indigenous, Afro-descendant, and LGBTQI populations. Unfortunately, as Karina Bidaseca observes, to date, there is no statistical data on how the pandemic has affected these groups, and the mainstream media has largely ignored them.[23] Diverse groups of Afro-Argentine women, however, have responded vigorously to the crisis, drawing attention to the particular experiences of historically marginalized subjects. One illustration of these responses was the activities carried out within the framework of July 25, the Día Internacional de la Mujer Afrolatina, Afrocaribeña y de la Diáspora (International Day of Afro-Latin, Afro-Caribbean, and

African Diasporic Women). This commemoration was established in 1992 after a meeting in the Dominican Republic of more than four hundred women from diverse Latin American countries to mark the struggle and denounce the conditions faced by Afro-descendant women in the region.[24] In Argentina, the city of Buenos Aires established July 25 as Afro Women's Day in 2012.[25]

Like feminists, Afro-Argentines have gained visibility over the past decade and achieved recognition by the Argentinian state in 2013, when November 8 was officially designated as the National Day of Afro-Argentines and Afro Culture.[26] The date marks the birth of María Remedios del Valle, an Afro-Argentine soldier known as "Mother of the Motherland" who participated in the independence wars of 1810–18.[27] Afro-Argentine women played an important part in this recognition. and a few years ago, in 2018, the Commission for November 8 created its own gender area. The strength gained from the inclusion of a gender area in the commission and the initiatives that the area generated in these past two years[28] led to another recognition of the contributions of Afro-Argentine women to Argentine identity. In September 2020, the Ministry of Culture launched a series of open national competitions for artists and writers to submit portraits, poetry, cartoons, short documentary films, and songs that recognize the figure of María Remedios del Valle and the role of Afro-Argentine women in the history of Argentina and Latin America.[29] Afro-Argentine women have also been active in both the Afro-Argentine and feminist movements, with a growing presence in the National Women's Marches and the National Women's Encounters.[30] The growing visibility of the Afro-Argentine movement and of Afro-Argentine women in particular is remarkable for Argentina, whose national imaginary erases the history, contributions, culture, and presence of Afro-descendant and Indigenous groups.[31]

The lockdown prevented Afro-Argentine women from gathering in person in 2020 but demonstrated their ability to generate alternative mechanisms of expression and reflection on the condition of being a Black woman in Argentina, and specifically on the impact of COVID-19. Through events transmitted via streaming or posts on social media,[32] interviews published in Black feminist digital magazines,[33] and other forms of digital communication, Afro-Argentine women denounced the disproportional impact of the pandemic on essential care and service workers, domestic workers, and those who participate in the informal labor market. Interestingly, the shift to a virtual space generated the possibility of holding meetings, panels, and other events that brought together Afro-Argentine women from all over Argentina. An example is the panel "Mirando la realidad desde la intersección: Afrofeminismos en Argentina"[34] (Looking at Reality from the Intersection: Afro-Feminisms in Argentina), held through YouTube and organized in conjunction with the Ministry of Women, Gender, and Diversity.[35] This national dialogue could not have occurred at the local demonstrations that have taken place in recent years. Likewise, the possibility of documenting these encounters and events by recording them and posting the videos on social media, blogs, and websites contributes to the creation and maintenance of a public archive of present and historical struggles and experiences of racialized groups, experiences that have been silenced by the hegemonic narratives of national identity.[36]

Finally, the possibility that digital space opened for communication not only at a national but also at an international level has been another of the salient elements of the commemoration of July 25 during the pandemic. Groups of Afro-Argentine women exchanged experiences and reflections on their situation with groups of other Afro-Latin American women,[37] highlighting the particularities of being a Black woman in Argentina, where society's gaze locates Black female bodies as foreigners,[38] while also building networks of shared experiences with Afro-descendant women across the Americas, and in a close dialogue with the antiracist manifestations that have been happening worldwide over the last few months.[39]

The economic, social, political, and health crisis generated by the pandemic has undoubtedly fallen with greater force on Argentina's most vulnerable groups. However, it has not prevented action, reflection, and struggle by organized women's groups and, in particular, as I have tried to outline in these few pages, by collectives that have developed intersectional and transnational perspectives. These collectives seek to make visible struggles and demands that are specific to local contexts and social imaginaries, while at the same time recognizing experiences and realities shared throughout Latin America and around the world. Finally, the shift to a digital space, to a virtuality that in other circumstances saturates and distorts information and realities, in this case has supported the creation of networks of transnational feminist struggle and a public archive of historically silenced voices and experiences.[40]

### Notes

1. Goñi, "Argentina Election." All internet sources in this essay were accessed on August 25, 2020.
2. Londoño and Politi, "In Argentina Election."
3. D'Alessandro et al., "Las brechas."

4. Women earn on average 29% less than their male peers, a gap that widens in the informal sector, reaching 35.6%. See D'Alessandro et al., "Las brechas."

5. For instance, in the city of Buenos Aires, 65% of transgender people rent rooms in hotels or pensions, 3.6% are homeless, and only 9% have formal employment. See Ni Una Menos, "Sabias que en la CABA el 65% de las travesties y trans."

6. United Nations, "Everyone Included"; Kendi, "Stop Blaming Black People"; Code Switch, "Ask Code Switch"; Grupo de Trabajo CLACSO Feminismos, resistencias y emancipación, "Pandemia y postmandemia."

7. CLACSO, "Encuestas sobre el impacto."

8. Grupo de Trabajo CLACSO Feminismos, resistencias y emancipación, "Pandemia y postmandemia."

9. Argentina.gob.ar, "COVID-19."

10. The IFE applies exclusively to unemployed workers in the informal labor market, domestic workers, or independent workers. See Argentina.gob.ar, "COVID-19."

11. Peker, "Mercedes D'Alessandro."

12. Peker, "La desocupación."

13. Mercedes D'Alessandro is the current director of the Dirección de Economía, Igualdad y Género (Office of Economy, Equality and Gender) within the framework of the Ministry of Economy and author of the book *Economía Feminista* (*Feminist Economics*) (2018). See Mercedes D'Alessandro, https://mercedesdalessandro.com/

14. Peker, "Mercedes D'Alessandro."

15. Collins, "No es feminismo sin interseccionalidad"; Rociosileo, "¿Qué es el feminismo interseccional?"

16. Ni Una Menos, http://niunamenos.org.ar/; Ministerio de Cultura Argentina, "A cinco años."

17. Campaña Nacional por el Derecho a un Aborto Legal, Seguro y Gratuito, http://www.abortolegal.com.ar/

18. Medley, "5 Things I Learned."

19. Montañez, "El pañuelo verde"; Caselli, "Birth of a movement"; Amnesty International, "The Green Wave."

20. Peker, *La Revolución de las hijas.*

21. Struminger, "Ni Una Menos"; Iglesias, "Tercera convocatoria nacional."

22. Dirección de Economía, Igualdad y Género, https://www.argentina.gob.ar/economia/igualdadygenero

23. CLACSO, "Encuestas sobre el impacto."

24. Race and Equality, "So That Our Voices Are Heard"; UNESCO, "July 25th."

25. Legislatura Ciudad Autónoma de Buenos Aires, "Conmemoran el día internacional."

26. Argentina.gob.ar, "Día nacional de los afroargentinos."

27. Ministerio de Cultura Argentina, "El 8 de noviembre."

28. Since the creation of the gender area in the Commission for November 8, Afro-Argentine women have been organizing a series of encounters, panel discussions,

workshops, and talks on the history of Afro-Argentine women and their participation in the building of the Argentine state. The figure of María Remedios del Valle has been a central component of these events. See more in Area de Genero Comisión 8n, Facebook page, https://www.facebook.com/areadegenero

29. Ministerio de Cultura Argentina, "Participá en las convocatorias."

30. Similarly, Afro-Argentine activist women from the gender area of the Commission for November 8 called for a stronger and more active participation of Afro-Argentine and Afro-indigenous Argentine women at the Segundo Encuentro Plurinacional de Naciones, Pueblos e Identidades Indígenas, Afrodescendientes, Migrantes y Diversidades (Second Plurinational Meeting of Indigenous Nations, People and Identities, Afrodescendants, Migrants and Diverse Identities). At the meeting, to be held between November 21 and 23 of 2020, the gender area is offering a series of workshops on Afrodescendant and Afro-Indigenous feminisms in Latin America. See Segundo Encuentro Plurinacional de Naciones, Pueblos e Identidades Indígenas, Afrodescendientes, Migrantes y Diversidades, Facebook page, https://www.facebook.com/EncuentroPlurinacional and "Segundo Encuentro Plurinacional de Naciones, Pueblos e Identidades Indígenas, Afrodescendientes, Migrantes y Diversidades," Area de Genero Comisión 8n, Facebook, November 18, 2020, https://www.facebook.com/areadegenero/photos/193128102272560

31. Alberto and Hoffnung-Garskof, "Racial Democracy"; Briones, "Mestizaje y blanqueamiento."

32. Maga_Arteafro, "Mirando la realidad"; Mesaafrocordoba, "VI encuentro de mujeres Afroamericanas"; Biblioteca del Congreso, "Charla online Identidad afroargentina"; Mesaafrocordoba, "El sabado 25 de julio."

33. Schweizer, "¿Es Buenos Aires una ciudad racista?"

34. Ministerio de las Mujeres, Géneros y Diversidad de la Nación, "Mirando la realidad"; Ministerio de las Mujeres, Géneros y Diversidad, "#ConstruirAgenda Afrofeminismos en Argentina"; 8ngenero, "Dia de las mujeres."

35. Ministerio de las Mujeres, Géneros y Diversidad, https://www.argentina.gob.ar/generos

36. Andrews, *Afro-Argentines of Buenos Aires*.

37. Jornadasfeminismoposcoloniales, "Resistencias feministas."

38. 8ngénero, "Mujeres y diversidades afro."

39. 8ngénero, "Emancipa Live"; Temwa Gondwe Harris, "Racismo Insidioso"; Mesaafrocordoba, "VI encuentro de mujeres Afroamericanas."

40. Department of Global Communications, United Nations, "UN Tackles 'Infodemic'"; PanAmerican Health Organization, "Understanding the Infodemic."

### References

8ngenero. "Dia de las mujeres Negras y afros." Instagram photo. July 25, 2020. https://www.instagram.com/p/CDEkQ34AyU-/?utm_source=ig_web_copy_link

8ngenero. "Emancipa Live: Feminismo antirracista en Latinoamérica." Instagram photo. July 26, 2020. https://www.instagram.com/p/CDHgJ5rAH81/?utm_source =ig_web_copy_link

8ngenero. "Mujeres y diversidades afro." Instagram photo. July 25, 2020. https://www .instagram.com/tv/CDFkUbAgnw4/?utm_source=ig_web_copy_link

Alberto, Paulina, and Jesse Hoffnung-Garskof. "Racial Democracy and Racial Inclusion: Hemispheric Histories." In *Afro-Latin American Studies: An Introduction*, edited by Alejandro de la Fuente and George Reid Andrews. Cambridge: Cambridge University Press, 2020.

Amnesty International. 2019. "The Green Wave." https://www-amnesty-org/en/latest /campaigns/2019/08/the-green-wave/

Andrews, George Reid. *The Afro-Argentines of Buenos Aires, 1800–1900*. Madison: University of Wisconsin Press, 1980.

Area de Genero Comisión 8n. "Segundo Encuentro Plurinacional de Naciones, Pueblos e Identidades Indígenas, Afrodescendientes, Migrantes y Diversidades." Facebook, November 18, 2020. https://www.facebook.com/areadegenero/photos/1931 28102272560

Argentina.gob.ar. "COVID-19—Ingreso familiar de emergencia." https://www.argenti na.gob.ar/justicia/derechofacil/leysimple/emergencia-sanitaria-covid-19-ingreso -familiar-de-emergencia

Argentina.gob.ar. "Día nacional de los afroargentinos y la cultura afro." November 16, 2019. https://www.argentina.gob.ar/noticias/dia-nacional-de-los-afroargentinos -y-la-culturaafro#:~:text=Esta%20fecha%2C%20que%20se%20conmemora,el%20r econocimiento%20de%20sus%20derechos.

Biblioteca del Congreso. "Charla online identidad afroargentina: Día Internacional de la Mujer Afrodescendiente." July 15, 2020. https://bcn.gob.ar/servicios/cursos-vir tuales/charla-online--identidad-afroargentina--dia-internacional-de-la-mujer-afr odescendiente

Briones, Claudia. "Mestizaje y blanqueamiento como coordenadas de aboriginalidad y Nación en Argentina." *Runa* 23 (2003): 61–88.

Caselli, Irene. "The Birth of a Movement: How Activists Are Winning the Battle to Make Abortion a Right." *The Correspondent*, February 7, 2020. https://thecorrespon dent.com/277/the-birth-of-a-movement-how-activists-are-winning-the-battle-to -make-abortion-a-right/36669679101-ad3c0da9

Code Switch. "Ask Code Switch: The Coronavirus Edition." May 13, 2020. https://www .npr.org/2020/05/12/854977002/ask-code-switch-the-coronavirus-edition

Collins, Joan. "No es feminismo sin interseccionalidad." *Afroféminas*, March 3, 2019. https://afrofeminas.com/2019/03/03/no-es-feminismo-sin-interseccionalidad/

Consejo Latinoamericano de Ciencias Sociales (CLACSO). "Encuestas sobre el impacto de la pandemia en las mujeres." May 28, 2020. https://www.clacso.org/encuest as-sobre-el-impacto-de-la-pandemia-en-las-mujeres/

D'Alessandro, Mercedes, Victoria O'Donnell, Sol Prieto, and Florencia Tundis. "Las brechas de género en la Argentina Estado de situación y desafíos." Ministerio de

Economía Argentina, Secretaria de Política Económica, Dirección Nacional de Economía, Igualdad y Género. https://www.argentina.gob.ar/sites/default/files /las_brechas_de_genero_en_la_argentina_0.pdf

Department of Global Communications, United Nations. "UN Tackles 'Infodemic' of Misinformation and Cybercrime in COVID-19 Crisis." March 31, 2020. https://www .un.org/en/un-coronavirus-communications-team/un-tackling-%E2%80%98info demic%E2%80%99-misinformation-and-cybercrime-covid-19

Goñi, Uki. "Argentina Election: Macri Out as Cristina Fernández de Kirchner Returns to Office as VP." *The Guardian*, October 28, 2019. https://www.theguardian.com/wo rld/2019/oct/28/argentina-election-macri-out-as-cristina-fernandez-de-kirchner -returns-to-office-as-vp

Grupo de Trabajo CLACSO Feminismos, resistencias y emancipación. "Pandemia y postmandemia: Economía para la vida." *Boletín Miradas y horizontes feministas* 1.1 (August 2020). https://www.clacso.org/boletin-1-miradas-y-horizontes-feminis tas/

Iglesias, Mariana. "Tercera convocatoria nacional por #NIUnaMenos Con globos ne-gros y cintas violetas, una multitud marchó contra el machismo." *Clarín*, June 3, 2017. https://www.clarin.com/sociedad/niunamenos-arranco-marcha-congreso -plaza-mayo_0_H15h_FlMb.html

Jornadasfeminismoposcoloniales. "Resistencias feministas en tiempos de pandemia racializada." Instagram photo. May 31, 2020. https://www.instagram.com/p/CA2C HkwgF48/?igshid=rappj1rb30tf

Kendi, Ibram X. "Stop Blaming Black People for Dying of the Coronavirus." Coura-geous Conversation, April 14, 2020. https://courageousconversation.com/stop-bla ming-black-people-for-dying-of-the-coronavirus/

Legislatura Ciudad Autónoma de Buenos Aires. "Conmemoran el día internacional de la mujer Afrodescendiente, Afrocaribeña y de la Diáspora." July 25, 2018. https:// www.legislatura.gov.ar/_post_old.php?ver=7215#:~:text=El%2025%20de%20julio %20de,de%20la%20Legislatura%20de%20la

Londoño, Ernesto, and Daniel Politi. "In Argentina Election, Leftists Savor Victory over Incumbent." *New York Times*, October 27, 2019. https://www.nytimes.com/20 19/10/27/world/americas/argentina-election-results.html

Maga_Arteafro. "Mirando la realidad desde la intersección: Afrofeminismos en Argen-tina." Instagram photo. July 22, 2020. https://www.instagram.com/p/CC9owakAIK c/?igshid=1sr3dzsjdpu7q

Medley, Magdalena. "5 Things I Learned at Argentina's #niunamenos March against Femicide." Amnesty International. July 14, 2016. https://www.amnestyusa.org/5-th ings-i-learned-at-argentinas-niunamenos-march-against-femicide/

Mesaafrocordoba. "El sabado 25 de julio, celebramos el Día Internacional de las Mu-jeres Afroamericanas." Instagram photo. July 27, 2020. https://www.instagram.com /p/CDJxAFfjqDc/?utm_source=ig_web_copy_link

Mesaafrocordoba. "VI encuentro de mujeres Afroamericanas en Córdoba." Instagram

photo. July 21, 2020. https://www.instagram.com/p/CC6_Ihkj8Zj/?igshid=1np1ao
gy3trj0

Ministerio de Cultura Argentina. "A cinco años de un grito arrollador: 'Ni una menos.'"
https://www.cultura.gob.ar/a-5-anos-del-ni-una-menos-vivas-nos-queremos
-9091/

Ministerio de Cultura Argentina. "Participá en las convocatorias para reconocer la
figura de María Remedios del Valle." https://www.cultura.gob.ar/maria-remedios
-del-valle-valiente-capitana-9620/

Ministerio de Cultura Argentina. "Por qué el 8 de noviembre es el Día Nacional de los
afroargentinos." https://www.cultura.gob.ar/por-que-el-8-de-noviembre-es-el-dia
-nacional-de-los-afroargentinos-y-de-la-cultura-afro_5054/

Ministerio de las Mujeres, Géneros y Diversidad. "#ConstruirAgenda Afrofeminismos
en Argentina." YouTube video. July 23, 2020. https://www.youtube.com/watch?v=
KmAFzNMF-pk

Ministerio de las Mujeres, Géneros y Diversidad de la Nación. "Mirando la realidad
desde la intersección: afrofeminismos en Argentina." Facebook. July 23, 2020.
https://m.facebook.com/MinGenerosAR/photos/a.117691039744299/1804288001
37189/?type=3&source=57&__tn__=EH-R

Montañez, Camila. "El pañuelo verde: Símbolo de Resistencia de las mujeres." International Planned Parenthood Federation. March 21, 2019. https://www.ippfwhr.org
/resource/el-panuelo-verde-simbolo-de-resistencia-de-las-mujeres/

Ni Una Menos. "Sabias que en la CABA el 65% de las travesties y trans." Instagram
photo. July 22, 2020. https://www.instagram.com/p/CC9dpKHgb-j/?igshid=1a7xd
ics5n46x

PanAmerican Health Organization. "Understanding the Infodemic and. Misinformation in the Fight against. COVID-19." 2020. https://iris.paho.org/bitstream/handle
/10665.2/52052/Factsheet-infodemic_eng.pdf?sequence=5

Peker, Luciana. "La desocupación y el trabajo no pago suben para las mujeres: Jefas de
casa full life, pero gratis y sin descanso." *Infobae*, June 12, 2020. https://www.infob
ae.com/sociedad/2020/06/12/la-desocupacion-y-el-trabajo-no-pago-suben-para
-las-mujeres-jefas-de-casa-full-life-pero-gratis-y-sin-descanso/

Peker, Luciana. *La revolución de las hijas.* Buenos Aires: Paidós Argentina, 2019.

Peker, Luciana. "Mercedes D'Alessandro: 'El IFE evitó que haya entre 2 y 4 millones
de nuevos indigentes y la mayoría de las beneficiarias son mujeres.'" *Infobae*, July
20, 2020. https://www.infobae.com/sociedad/2020/07/20/mercedes-dalessandro-
el-ife-evito-que-haya-entre-2-y-4-millones-de-nuevos-indigentes-y-la-mayoria-de
-las-beneficiarias-son-mujeres/

Race and Equality. "So That Our Voices Are Heard and Included! Today We Commemorate the International Day for Afro-Latino, Afro-Caribbean, and Diaspora Wom-
en." https://raceandequality.org/english/so-that-our-voices-are-heard-and-inclu
ded-today-we-commemorate-the-international-day-for-afro-latino-afro-caribbe
an-and-diaspora-women/#:~:text=July%2025%20marks%20the%20International
,and%20sexism%20in%20the%20region

Rociosileo. "¿Qué es el feminismo interseccional?" *Escritura Feminista,* December 12, 2017. https://escriturafeminista.com/2017/12/12/que-es-el-feminismo-intersecci onal/

Schweizer, Melina. "¿Es Buenos Aires una ciudad racista?" *Afroféminas,* July 25, 2020. https://afrofeminas.com/2020/07/25/es-buenos-aires-una-ciudad-racista/

Struminger, Brenda. "Ni Una Menos: Miles de mujeres marcharon al Congreso, esta vez con el aborto legal como principal reclamo." *La Nacion,* June 4, 2018. https:// www.lanacion.com.ar/sociedad/ni-una-menos-comenzo-una-nueva-marcha-esta -vez-con-el-aborto-legal-como-principal-reclamo-nid2140827

Temwa Gondwe Harris, Suzanne. "Racismo insidioso." *Agrupación Xangô,* July 23, 2020. https://agrupacionxango.wordpress.com/2020/07/23/racismo-insidioso/

UNESCO. "July 25th: International Afro-descendant Women's Day." http://www.catedr aeducacionjusticiasocial.org/internacional-afro-descendant-womens-day/

United Nations. "Everyone Included: Social Impact of COVID-19." https://www.un.org /development/desa/dspd/everyone-included-covid-19.html

# CHAPTER 21

# The Media Discourse on Women-Led Countries in the COVID-19 Pandemic

## Using Germany as an Example

*Verena Klein*

At the beginning of the COVID-19 pandemic, particularly in English-speaking countries, a debate was sparked about whether women-led countries were dealing better with the crisis. On the basis of selected newspaper articles, the present essay aims to depict the media discourse surrounding female leadership in the pandemic with a special focus on Germany, a woman-led country.

In early April 2020, *Forbes* magazine headlined: "What do countries with the best Coronavirus responses have in common? Women Leaders."[1] Indeed, there is one study showing that countries with women leaders, namely Finland, Germany, Iceland, Taiwan, Norway, Denmark, and New Zealand, have a six times lower coronavirus death rate than countries led by men. This result remains, even when comparing matched pairs of female- and male-led countries.[2] But how can this trend be explained?

Boiling down the overall themes observed in the media coverage about why countries led by women handled the crisis better,[3] there are three main themes:

1. Women leaders listen to advice (e.g., using varied information sources, having the humility to listen to expert opinions);
2. Women leaders are empathic, compassionate, and caring (e.g., using social media messages, honest communication); and
3. Women leaders are risk-averse (e.g., they imposed early lockdowns).

However, the picture is of course more complicated. Women leaders are unfortunately still a small sample, given that only 15 of the 193 United Nations countries have women in charge. Putting this power disadvantage in a humorous, if disillusioned, way, one article noted: "Whenever Merkel has attended a G20 meeting during her 14 years as chancellor of Germany, she has rarely faced a line for the ladies' toilet."[4]

Media outlets have discussed other factors besides the small sample size that limits the generalizability of this phenomenon. For instance, "It's also possible that this isn't about female leaders but about the kind of country that chooses a woman to lead it."[5] Here the question of causality arises: do countries perform better during the pandemic *because* they have women in charge, or do countries have women leaders *because* they were already performing better in terms of important contextual factors (e.g., lower rates of sexism, more diversity).[6]

A different theme dominated the discussion that addressed the question of whether male leadership styles saturated by ego, overinflated masculinity and populism, as observed in Russia, the United States, and Brazil, have become obsolete.[7] Lewis (2020), for instance, concluded: "It's not that women leaders are doing better. It's just that strongmen are doing worse."

It is not surprising that the above-mentioned characteristics of female and male leadership revolve very much around gender stereotypes. Drawing from social psychological theories, in most societies women are expected to display a communal orientation (e.g., warmth, nurturance, sensitivity to others), whereas men are expected to display agentic traits (e.g., entitlement, assertiveness, dominance).[8] Gender stereotypes, therefore, produce certain expectations or norms for behavior (i.e., how women and men should behave). Stereotypes guide behavior and can function as self-fulfilling prophecies through which societal expectations produce behavior that confirms them.[9] That said, gender stereotypes perpetuate the status quo when it comes to gender inequality. The same is true when it comes to the public discussion of gendered leadership styles. In view of that, it is critical that the media debate has been dominated by the perspective that women leaders perform better because of their stereotypical female characteristics (i.e., female leaders are empathic, humble, and risk-averse). This ignores the fact that women leaders might have acted as they did because of other qualities that go beyond typical gender stereotypes.

If we focus specifically on the situation in Germany, Angela Merkel, who is currently considered the most powerful woman in the world, is a scientist and holds a PhD in quantum physics. We note that Germany, led by Merkel, did a great job in tackling the pandemic. "Thanks to extensive testing from the outset, plenty of intensive care beds, and the chancellor's periodic forthright reminders that Covid-19 was 'serious—so take it seriously.'" Merkel named the pandemic the "greatest challenge" since 1945—and lamented every death as that of "a father or grandfather, a mother or grandmother, a partner."[10]

As a possible consequence of Merkel's training as a scientist, the German approach in developing a coronavirus policy was characterized by considering different sources seriously, including epidemiological models, evidence from countries such as South Korea that had already successfully established an effective testing strategy, and data from health care providers.[11] In other words, as Helen Lewis pointed out in her *Atlantic* piece: "Her leadership style is more influenced by her scientific background than by her second X chromosome. (Although, of course, how she is perceived and treated is definitely influenced by her gender.)"[12]

Interestingly, the debate on women's versus men's leadership was not especially prominent in the German media landscape. Instead, what was discussed was how the *pandemic threatens women's emancipation*. Recently, the Hans Böckler Foundation published a study showing that the pandemic revealed traditional gender roles: women are more likely to reduce their work hours than men, while their proportion of care work continues to grow. Although the consequences of the pandemic hit women harder than men, decision-makers in dealing with the crisis in Germany are primarily men. The working group on the relaxation of lockdown measures of the German National Academy of Sciences Leopoldina, to give an example, consisted of twenty-four men and two women. By the same token, one study examined the gender distribution of experts in media presence showing that in TV formats, one in five experts was female (22%), and 7% in news outlets.[13]

Merkel has always struggled to label herself a feminist, and her legacy is not particularly known for pushing gender equality forward.[14] For years she was the head of the Christian Democratic Union, a center-right party, with only 19.9 % parliamentary seats occupied by women (only the ultra-right party Alternative für Deutschland has fewer female members of the parliament). Recently a debate has been rekindled about implementing a quota for women in leadership positions. Noting this fact is not intended to diminish the success of Merkel's government in dealing with the pandemic, but rather to challenge the view that women leaders are necessarily supportive of establishing feminist policies, in times of a pandemic or in times without an additional external threat.

Although the material used for this essay has without doubt its limitations (i.e., newspaper articles do not provide data to establish causality), what conclusions can be drawn from the media debate surrounding gendered leadership styles in the pandemic?

First, women leaders may have done a better job than male leaders in managing this pandemic, but causality seems to be nebulous. It remains, for instance, unclear if female leadership made countries successful in tackling the pandemic, or countries that vote for women leaders already have better social conditions to deal with a threat such as the COVID-19 pandemic.

Second, female leaders may have performed better than male leaders because of qualities that are not stereotypically female, although that is what the discourse is pointing to. For instance, Angela Merkel's leadership style during the pandemic can be better attributed to her scientific background and knowledge than to the stereotypical portrayal of women as humble listeners that dominated the media coverage.

Third, a focus on overall outcomes may overlook important negative outcomes for women within even those countries. As the situation in Germany demonstrates, focusing just on female leadership risks disregarding perpetuated gender inequalities in political and social participation as well as the negative outcomes of the pandemic, especially for women.

### Notes

1. Wittenberg-Cox, "Countries with the Best Coronavirus Responses."
2. Garikipati and Kambhampati, "Women Leaders Are Better."
3. Henley and Roy, "Are Female Leaders More Successful"; King, "Women Are Better Leaders"; Kristof, "What the Pandemic Reveals"; Taub, "Why Are Women-Led Nations Doing Better"; Wittenberg-Cox, "Countries with the Best Coronavirus Responses."
4. Lewis, "Pandemic Has Revealed the Weakness."
5. Kristof, "What the Pandemic Reveals."
6. Chamorro-Premuzic and Wittenberg-Cox, "Will the Pandemic Reshape Notions."
7. Leonhardt and Leatherby, "Where the Virus Is Growing Most"; Kristof, "What the Pandemic Reveals."
8. Koenig and Eagly, "Evidence for the Social Role Theory."
9. Ellemers, "Gender Stereotypes."
10. Henley and Roy, "Are Female Leaders More Successful."
11. Miller, "Secret to Germany's COVID-19 Success"; Taub, "Why Are Women-Led Nations Doing Better."
12. Lewis, "Pandemic Has Revealed the Weakness."
13. Knöfel and Voigt, "Medienpräsenz in der Coronakrise."
14. Kray, "Angst for dem F-Wort"; Schultheis, "World's Most Powerful Woman."

# References

Chamorro-Premuzic, Tomas, and Avivah Wittenberg-Cox. "Will the Pandemic Re-shape Notions of Female Leadership?" *Harvard Business Review*, June 26, 2020. https://hbr.org/2020/06/will-the-pandemic-reshape-notions-of-female-leadership

Ellemers, Naomi. "Gender Stereotypes." *Annual Review of Psychology* 69 (2018): 275–298.

Garikipati, Supriya, and Uma Kambhampati. "Women Leaders Are Better at Fighting the Pandemic." *Voxeu*, June 21, 2020. https://voxeu.org/article/women-leaders-are-better-fighting-pandemic

Henley, Jon, and Eleanor Ainge Roy. "Are Female Leaders More Successful at Managing the Coronavirus Crisis?" *The Guardian*, April 25, 2020. https://www.theguardian.com/world/2020/apr/25/why-do-female-leaders-seem-to-be-more-successful-at-managing-the-coronavirus-crisis

King, Michelle. "Women Are Better Leaders: The Pandemic Proves It." CNN, May 5, 2020. https://www.cnn.com/2020/05/05/perspectives/women-leaders-coronavirus/index.html

Knöfel, Ulrike, and Claudia Voigt. "Medienpräsenz in der Coronakrise, Männer erklären, wie systemrelevant Frauen sind." *Der Spiegel*, May 28, 2020. https://www.spiegel.de/kultur/corona-krise-und-medienpraesenz-maenner-erklaeren-wie-systemrelevant-frauen-sind-a-d5fb4b50-4236-4dd6-b850-7770f56dded0

Koenig, Anne M., and Alice H. Eagly. "Evidence for the Social Role Theory of Stereotype Content: Observations of Groups' Roles Shape Stereotypes." *Journal of Personality and Social Psychology* 107.3 (2014): 371–92. https://doi.org/10.1037/a0037215

Kray, Sabine. "Angst for dem F-Wort (Fearing the F-word)." *Die Zeit*, June 23, 2017. https://www.zeit.de/kultur/2017-06/feminismus-angela-merkel-gleichstellung-10nach8

Kristof, Nicholas. "What the Pandemic Reveals about the Male Ego." *New York Times*, June 13, 2020. https://www.nytimes.com/2020/06/13/opinion/sunday/women-leaders-coronavirus.html

Leonhardt, David, and Lauren Leatherby. "Where the Virus Is Growing Most: Countries With 'Illiberal Populist' Leaders." *New York Times*, June 2, 2020. https://www.nytimes.com/2020/06/02/briefing/coronavirus-populist-leaders.html

Lewis, Helen. "The Pandemic Has Revealed the Weakness of Strongmen." *The Atlantic*, May 6, 2020. https://www.theatlantic.com/international/archive/2020/05/new-zealand-germany-women-leadership-strongmen-coronavirus/611161/

Miller, Saskia. "The Secret to Germany's COVID-19 Success: Angela Merkel Is a Scientist." *The Atlantic*, April 20, 2020. https://www.theatlantic.com/international/archive/2020/04/angela-merkel-germany-coronavirus-pandemic/610225/

Rudman, Laurie A. "Self-Promotion as a Risk Factor for Women: The Costs and Benefits of Counterstereotypical Impression Management." *Journal of Personality and Social Psychology* 74.3 (1998): 629–645.

Rudman, Laurie A., and Kimberly Fairchild. "Reactions to Counterstereotypic Behavior: The Role of Backlash in Cultural Stereotype Maintenance." *Journal of Personality and Social Psychology* 87.2 (2004): 157–176. https://doi.org/10.1037/0022-3514.87.2.157

Schultheis, Emily. "Is the World's Most Powerful Woman Finally a Feminist?" *New York Times*, January 13, 2019. https://www.nytimes.com/2019/01/30/opinion/angela-merkel-feminism.html

Taub, Amanda. "Why Are Women-Led Nations Doing Better with Covid-19?" *New York Times*, May 15, 2020. https://www.nytimes.com/2020/05/15/world/coronavirus-women-leaders.html

Wittenberg-Cox, Avivah. "What Do Countries with the Best Coronavirus Responses Have in Common? Women Leaders." *Forbes*, April 13, 2020. https://www.forbes.com/sites/avivahwittenbergcox/2020/04/13/what-do-countries-with-the-best-coronavirus-reponses-have-in-common-women-leaders/#6e3e18413dec

CHAPTER 22

# Coronavirus Capitalism and the Patriarchal Pandemic in India

## Why We Need a "Feminism for the 99%" That Centers Social Reproduction

*Jayati Lal*

Contagious diseases do not cause social breakdown; they merely reveal the ways in which society is already broken.

—Mark Bould, "The Virus Has Seized the Means of Production"

It is by now widely acknowledged that the COVID-19 crisis has exacerbated social inequalities. Words and phrases that reflect the diversity of work experiences during the pandemic slowdown—such as "essential workers," "Zoom," and "work from home," or WFH—populate our lexicon and permeate popular consciousness alongside the old standbys "laid off" and "unemployed." The disparate effect of the coronavirus on women workers has also deepened gender inequalities globally,[1] revealing how the burdens of care work, and especially childcare, which falls disproportionately on women, limit their ability to work full time, increase their likelihood of being laid off, and hamper their recovery from unemployment. The effects of the pandemic recession on women's unemployment have been so pronounced in the United States[2] that economists are now referring to this recession as a "shecession."[3] And because the industries most affected by the pandemic closures (leisure, hospitality, and education) are those in which women of color predominate in low-wage jobs, the pandemic has hit those who are least able to weather job loss and uncertainty the hardest.[4] Finally, women are overrepresented in "frontline" service work in nursing, airlines, teaching, food services, and retail, which also puts them in the front lines of the pandemic and at greater risk of exposure to the virus.[5]

The new "visibility" of care work has been a central media narrative throughout the pandemic. Ironically, the gendered effects of the pandemic have done more to advance the goal of making women's unpaid domestic and care work visible and valued than decades of feminist activism was able to accomplish—from the Wages for Housework Campaign in the 1970s[6] to the A Day without Women Strike for International Women's Day in March 2017 (https://www.weforum.org/agenda/2017/03/day-without-women-interna tional-womens-day-gender/). And yet the COVID-19 crisis has also revealed existing fault lines in mainstream "one percent feminism"[7] that ignores the plight of working-class and poor women, whose labor in underpaid domestic and care work underwrites the professional accomplishments of middle- and upper-class women.

There have been many comparisons between coronavirus and the Spanish flu in 1918 that killed an estimated 1% to 2% of the human population. Mike Davis draws attention to a little-discussed aspect of the Spanish flu, which is that close to 60 percent of global mortality in that pandemic occurred in India because a famine coincided with a major drought, causing widespread starvation among the poor, making them more susceptible to viral infection. It was the British colonial policy of forced grain exports from India, secured by "brutal requisitioning practices," that caused the famine. Just as colonialism "preconditioned" many more Indians to die in the Spanish flu, capitalism has preconditioned the vulnerability of specific marginalized groups to the coronavirus. Any vision for a feminist post-pandemic future must address these structural inequalities of globalized capitalism on a platform of transnational feminist solidarity. This is not just because viruses that do not respect borders require an "international public health infrastructure," as Davis notes,[8] but also because, as the similar effects of the pandemic across variously structured capitalist patriarchies has shown us, coronavirus *is* capitalism, and the pandemic *is* patriarchal. This necessitates investments in the *social infrastructure* of capitalism that will entail the recognition, valuation, and support of the paid and unpaid gendered labor of social reproduction.[9]

The Indian government's response to the pandemic amplified these trends, transforming a health crisis into a humanitarian disaster. My aim here is to trace the effects of the government's response to COVID-19 on women workers and their alignments with pre-pandemic gender inequalities that are rooted in the structures of capitalist patriarchy. Since fighting the pandemic's effects will require a transnational, intersectional, feminist vision that centers women's care work and social reproduction labor in any policy for the post-pandemic economic recovery, understanding how it was reconfigured is an important first step. I focus on three areas of work in which the pandemic has exacerbated existing inequalities of gender, race, class, caste, sexuality, and religion—and which historically rely on women workers: community health care, paid domestic work, and unpaid housework.

As coronavirus infections peaked in the early hot-spot locations in China, Italy, and Spain at the beginning of 2020, lockdowns, shelter-in-place, and stay-at-home orders aimed at shutting down public activity to limit the movement of people and hence the virus quickly followed. According to the University of Oxford's COVID-19 Government Response Tracker, India's draconian lockdown was among the strictest in the world.[10] When India's prime minister, Narendra Modi, declared a "complete coronavirus lockdown" of the country for twenty-one days on March 24, 2020, effective midnight that day and without any prior warning, millions of rural migrants who work in cities earning daily wages were stranded with no means of transportation to return to their homes.[11] Factories closed, schools and malls were shuttered, and transportation was shut down, including city and interstate trains and buses. Migrants and daily-wage workers in the informal sector, who often live at their workplaces in construction sites and in factories, or in shared rented accommodations in working-class slums and *jhuggi-jhopri* squatter settlements, lost both their livelihood and housing in one fell swoop. Facing evictions, and with no immediate means of earning subsistence wages, jobless migrant workers and their families took to the roads in an epic mass movement of people across the country, in some cases walking hundreds of miles to their homes.[12] Journalists reported hearing hauntingly similar stories from most returning migrants, who said that "they had no choice but to return to their homes, even if it risked passing the virus on to their village."[13] Among the first wave of migrants were the casually employed working poor, who earn daily wages at or below subsistence levels and live at the edge of precarity.[14] In some cases, such as in construction and hotel work, the layoffs and closures affected workers who were let go with unpaid back wages, forcing an immediate decision to leave their city.[15]

Between disease and hunger, it was, as another reverse migrant noted, no choice at all: "We're stuck . . . either we stay and die, or leave and die."[16] In India, the alternatives were not between weighing the danger to public health (saving lives) with the calamity of an economic downturn (saving livelihoods), just as it is not a choice for millions of American "essential workers" who continue to work in frontline, low-wage jobs through the pandemic. Rather, as economists discussing India's lockdown in the online magazine *The India Forum* put it: "Because India is so poor and because her [sic] occupational structure so unamenable to being shifted online, it is a question of *lives versus lives*."[17]

Chaotic efforts by the government to provide buses for the migrants were woefully inadequate and could not service the estimated thirty million who were all trying to flee their city at the same time.[18] Those who were able to get seats were packed into buses, and later trains, that were filled beyond their capacity without regard to "social distancing." Others, who set off on foot, faced hunger and exhaustion, and their slow march home was followed by grim stories of gruesome accidents,[19] starvation, and death.[20] They also faced harassment and beatings by police,[21] including forced returns and interrupted journeys when they were barred from crossing state borders or exiting their cities to conform to the lockdown. Meanwhile, the government proved itself to be quite capable in organizing transport via special flights for overseas workers stranded in China, Iran, and Italy.[22]

The lockdown, Arundhati Roy notes, "worked like a chemical experiment that suddenly illuminated hidden things. As shops, restaurants, factories and the construction industry shut down, as the wealthy and the middle classes enclosed themselves in gated colonies, our towns and megacities began to extrude their working-class citizens—their migrant workers—like so much unwanted accrual."[23] It strains credulity that this vast class of informal migrant workers, who work in or for almost every middle- and upper-class home in India, were a "long invisible class of people" that were brought "into the national spotlight" by the lockdown.[24] It is instead undoubtedly the case that they have been hiding in plain sight—*made* invisible by the popular press and treated as inconvenient truths that could be ignored by their middle-class employers and policymakers. Perhaps all it took was a photograph of a distraught man crying on the side of the road,[25] which was widely circulated on social media, to pierce this bubble of willful ignorance and complacent blindness to the daily tableaus of poverty displayed on city streets.

The gendered nature of the pandemic and its unequal effects on women globally[26] have been widely reported in the media.[27] According to recent reports by the International Labour Organization, women workers are disproportionately affected by the health crisis, since a large proportion of women work in sectors that have been severely impacted by the crisis.[28] Furthermore, and compounding these effects, is the fact that women are also more likely to be informal workers in these hard-hit industries and are therefore already exposed to greater risk during the COVID-19 crisis.[29] In India, Dalits, tribal groups, and Muslims are also disproportionately concentrated in low-wage and informal sector work, which puts them at greater risk of falling into poverty.[30] According to a recent study, COVID-19 has resulted in Dalits being three times more likely to lose their jobs than upper-caste workers.[31] While many informal workers are endangered during the pandemic because of their reliance on various forms of public labor, transgender persons are an especially vulnerable group since they rely on work such as "begging, sex work and ritual functions" that all entail social contact.[32]

Women were also disproportionately affected by the lockdown in India, as a significant majority of women workers—close to 95 percent—are employed in the informal sector, which was worst hit by the pandemic closures.[33] A study conducted in 2017 found that, because they need to balance their paid work with unpaid care work, poor women are limited to work in the informal sector due to the proximity of this work to their homes. In urban slums, this means that poor women work in precarious jobs in a range of occupations that are "low paid, irregular, unsafe jobs with little or no job security."[34] According to a survey done by the news agency IANS in mid-May, two months into the lockdown, a quarter of the population was either being laid off or was already without work, with more women than men losing their jobs.[35] The same survey found that job losses were higher among the lowest-paid workers and in semi-urban areas where industrial jobs in factories are more likely to be located, extending the daily-wage worker migrant joblessness crisis into the relatively privileged class of "permanent" or contractual blue-collar workers.

The setbacks for women workers who are laid off from such jobs, especially for single women migrating from rural areas to work in factories, for whom the opportunity to work is often a hard-won freedom wrested from parental control, are likely to have long-term economic consequences for an entire generation of women, as there may be no possibility of them returning to work in the future. There are predictions that India's coronavirus economy may lead to an increase in arranged marriages as families seek to counter their economic losses by ensuring their daughter's future financial stability through such alliances.[36] Younger, school-age girls who left school during the lockdown have been forced to work at manual daily-wage jobs to help their indebted, unemployed parents and may never return to complete their education.[37]

One specific category of workers affected by the coronavirus crisis globally has been that of health workers. According to a recent World Bank study, women make up a large segment of health workers—as much as 70% of the health workforce across 104 countries.[38] Since women are much more likely to be nurses than physicians—eight out of ten nurses are women, according to the same study—they carry greater risks as frontline health workers in their exposure to the virus. In India, women comprise 83.4% of nurses and 38% of all health workers.[39] In response to the pandemic, the government mobilized its woefully underpaid 3.5 million women community health workers to become frontline responders against COVID-19.[40] Comprising Anganwadi workers in community childcare centers, ASHAs (accredited social health activists) at the village level, and auxiliary nurse midwives, health workers were not supplied personal protective equipment (PPE) as they fanned out door-to-door to help distribute food, screen for and provide information on the virus, track migrants on their journeys home, undertake contact tracing, report those suspected of being COVID positive, and help to get the sick to medical centers.[41] Faced with this impossible list of tasks, and despite their success in stemming the rate of infection in high-density areas such as the slums of Dharavi in Mumbai and in the state of Kerela,[42] they have predictably suffered COVID-19-related illness and deaths. Although these workers were publicly "celebrated" with pot-banging by the quarantining middle class at Modi's request, in the early stages of the pandemic, when fear and ignorance about the transmission of the virus reigned, health workers were also attacked in public, evicted by their landlords, and harassed by their neighbors as potential vectors of contagion. By August, thousands of women health care workers went on strike, demanding better pay, including insurance and risk allowances and the regular payment of their monthly wages, as well as safety equipment such as proper protective gear during the pandemic.[43]

At the same time that the migrant crisis was unfolding, unemployed urban slum-dwellers faced devastating consequences of Modi's lockdown as they were sequestered in their working-class neighborhoods, imprisoned in their homes, and monitored by overzealous police when they violated the quarantine to seek work or food.[44] As Roy notes, "The lockdown to enforce physical distancing had resulted in the opposite—physical compression on an unthinkable scale. This is true even within India's towns and cities. The main roads might be empty, but the poor are sealed into cramped quarters in slums and shanties."[45] Having withdrawn into their gated communities and fortress-like homes, urban elites championed the lockdown and continued to maintain strict confinement rules even as the government began loosening restrictions. As Ruchir Sharma reported in his article, "The Rich Love India's Lockdown" for the New York Times, this support for the lockdown was driven by the fear of contagion that "millions of illiterate Indians will pour into the streets and superspread the disease."[46]

In his recent review of outbreak narratives in contagion-themed films in light of the current pandemic, "The Virus Has Seized the Means of Production," the cultural critic Mark Bould suggests that "wet market" serves as a metonym for "a dangerous, disease-ridden, feudal past whose filthy touch sullies our sanitary modernity," a colonialist trope that reverberates through our current pandemic political discourse. In like fashion, the liminal bodies of unhygienic, dirty, urban slum-dwellers and rural migrant "superspreaders" are expelled as Other to the rational order of the planned city—the concrete high-rise condos, gated apartment buildings, and luxurious bungalows in green neighborhoods with their air-conditioned domestic interiors sealed to the heat, dust, pollution, and disease—securing it as "home" to India's rich and middle-class urban elite. Like the "wet market," slum-dwelling superspreaders "signify urban poverty and seem somehow premodern, like they should have been left behind in the sticks, not brought into the city to bubble away, threatening to spill over."[47] And yet many Indian households could not function without them.

The pandemic has woven the weft of viral contagion into the warp of ritual caste purity, translating the hygienic practice of "social distancing" during the pandemic to heightened fears of contagion. Dalits, who are more likely to be poor, informal workers, are more vulnerable both to the virus because of their work and to increased caste discrimination during the pandemic.[48] Dalit return migrants faced renewed caste discrimination in their village quarantine centers and when searching for work at their villages, where caste and coronavirus comingled in the "double stigma of coming from a lower caste and having travelled from New Delhi where the coronavirus is spreading."[49]

The lockdown also brought an immediate halt to the daily influx of the vast army of household employees that middle-class Indian households rely on to enable their homes to function.[50] The cooks, nannies, maids, gardeners, sweepers, drivers, guards, and other slum-dwelling workers who comprise the public-private nexus of bourgeois domesticity are typically migrant workers from poorer states. Among these workers, it is "maids," or domestic workers, who are the most ubiquitous household workers in India, as they are employed across the social ladder, including in lower-middle-class households. It is also common for upper-middle-class households to have several domestic workers for different tasks, such as for mopping and cleaning, cooking, and childcare.[51] There are an estimated fifty million domestic workers in India,[52] many of whom are Dalit or from other disadvantaged castes and tribal minority groups.[53] The National Domestic Workers Movement, which rejects the terms "maid" and "servant" in favor of "domestic worker," estimates that 90% of domestic workers in India are women. They also note the intertwining of caste and class identities for domestic workers in India: "The stigma linked to domestic work is heightened by the caste system, since tasks such as cleaning and sweeping are associated with the people belonging to the 'so-called' low castes."[54]

It should therefore come as no surprise that domestic workers have been the site of considerable pandemic anxiety since their bodies breach the threshold between the diseased-public and hygienic-private worlds during the quarantine. As with domestic workers globally,[55] they have also been among the worst affected among household workers, with some news sites reporting that a majority were being let go without wages in the first few months of the pandemic.[56] By the end of April, one month into the lockdown, 83% of domestic workers who were surveyed in Delhi by the Institute of Social Studies Trust reported facing "severe to moderate economic crises in their families."[57] A majority (54%) of respondents to the survey, which was conducted among part-time, full-time, and live-in domestic workers in Delhi, reported that they were unable to collect their salaries due to restrictions imposed by the lockdown.

The specific attention that this group of workers received in local governmental policies points to concerns about their breaching the divide between slums and middle-class homes, and hence their potential for spreading COVID-19, while also highlighting their importance to the routine functioning of domestic life in India. Early in the pandemic, and prodded by the government, it seemed as though some employers were willing to pay their domestic workers despite the ban on them working.[58] Other employers were either not able or willing to do so, claiming, "No work, no pay" for the duration of the lockdown. This economic vulnerability of women domestic workers during the pandemic has been a global trend; the International Labour Organization estimates that 72% of domestic workers globally were at "significant risk" of losing both jobs and incomes as a result of the lockdown and lack of social security measures.[59]

Even after the restrictions were eased, and domestic workers were willing and eager to come back to work to resume earning, residents welfare associations (RWAs), which function like co-op boards, but on a larger scale of neighborhood or housing community, were empowered by local governments to ban the entry of maids into the colonies and neighborhoods that they controlled.[60] Meanwhile, India's National Centre for Disease Control put the onus on workers and went so far as to issue an advisory for urban slums in June,[61] urging domestic workers to request "exemptions" from work for two weeks to curb the spread of coronavirus, failing which, they "should practice proper handwashing with soap and water at and after work." By then, having spent months without household help, many women employers were willing to fight their RWAs to get their maids back to work despite the threat of contagion.[62] Other employers reportedly asked their part-time or full-time women domestic workers who were either single or living alone "to move in with them for the duration of the lockdown period," which some did, in order to save on food costs.[63]

Throughout these machinations, there seems to have been little concern for the welfare of domestic workers or their families. While promoting sanitation practices such as handwashing for domestic workers aims to protect their employers, domestic workers expressed concerns about the risks posed to their own health, "by frequent exposure to employers in their homes," which could only be addressed by delaying their return to work and the provision of personal protective supplies rather than just soap and hand sanitizer.[64]

Domestic workers are among the lowest-paid domestic staff, especially compared to male-dominated occupations such as drivers and cooks, which often means that they must work in several households simultaneously to earn a living wage.[65] In attempting to mediate residents' desire for their domestic workers' return with concerns for public health, one local government went so far as to suggest that RWAs should limit their work to a single household,[66] displaying a callous disregard for the economic reality of domestic workers, while privileging employer-households' safety.

The pandemic has also affected live-in and "full-time" domestic workers,[67] who are more frequently single, young migrant women who obtain room and board with their wages.[68] While their wages have remained stable during the lockdown,[69] in the absence of part-time domestic workers who come for specific jobs and a few hours a day, live-in and full-time domestic workers are asked to take over their chores, thereby intensifying their already considerable workload.

Perhaps more than any other issue, the health crisis has exposed gender inequalities in the unpaid housework and care work in families, a burden that falls disproportionately on mothers, wives, and daughters relative to men and boys. With school closures and work-from-home (WFH) policies in place, there have been countless reports of how the additional burdens of care have fallen on women's shoulders.[70] This comes as no surprise when women were spending two to ten times more time on unpaid care work than men globally in the "pre-pandemic" world.[71] In India, women's unpaid care work is three times the global average, as they take on 9.6 times more unpaid care work than men.[72] Spending over three-quarters of the workday—close to six hours on average—on unpaid care work[73] severely limits women's ability to enter into full-time paid work, which then traps them into lower-paid, intermittent, and part-time work.[74] Another consequence of this unequal care work burden is that women in India also suffer from a sleep deficit, with over 71% women sleeping less than their husbands because of household chores.[75]

For middle- and upper-class professional working women in India, the solution to this inequality has been to hire domestic workers, whom Ikita

Punit refers to as "the middle-class Indian wife's women-at-arms." But the pandemic also revealed how the Indian family's "unspoken sexism" had merely been papered over with hired domestic help. As she notes, "The equalising agent's—the maid—sudden disappearance from the Indian middle class is making way for the return of archaic and debilitating gender roles."[76]

In working-class domestic workers' households during the lockdown, a majority of women reported increased demands on their time for domestic work, and only 14% received assistance from their husbands.[77] In younger, well-off professional couple's households where both partners are now WFH, there have been reports of an incipient move toward gender equality and the emergence of a "reformed" masculinity among househusbands who are contributing more to housework and childcare than they did when both spouses were working outside the homes.[78] There is likely no change in rich households, regardless of the work status of women, as they rely on live-in domestic workers and nannies who have not been displaced during the lockdown and have therefore maintained their pre-pandemic gender regimes of domestic labor.

In an article for *The Atlantic*, "The Coronavirus Is a Disaster for Feminism," Helen Lewis expressed the same worry as Punit: that the coronavirus pandemic's school closures and workplace stay-at-home measures, which have forced childcare back into the home from the paid economy, will return gender roles to the 1950s and be a setback for feminism: "Dual-income couples might suddenly find themselves living like their grandparents, one homemaker and one breadwinner." And further, Lewis fretted, "Across the world, women's independence will be a silent victim to the pandemic."[79] Punit and Lewis are both pointing to what Arlie Hochschild referred to as the "stalled revolution" over thirty years ago.[80] Hochschild argued that women's entry into the workforce, including into historically male-dominated fields, promised revolutionary change toward gender equality. However, since men neither took up work in fields that had been historically dominated by women, nor did they help with domestic chores that occupied women's "second shift" at home, the gender revolution was one-sided, and thus the feminist revolution was stalled. Likewise, when working women hire domestic workers to look after their kids or to do their housework in order to be free to work, they do not undo gender inequality so much as reconfigure it in a cascading "global care chain" of paid and unpaid care work transnationally outsourced down the income ladder.[81] Revolution stalled.

In unmasking the significance of women's unpaid work of social reproduction in capitalism—of care work, childcare, kin work, and domestic work—the coronavirus crisis has foregrounded the uncomfortable truth that feminism's stalled revolution is still with us. Social reproduction entails "the array of activities and relationships involved in maintaining people both on a daily basis and inter-generationally."[82] Although the work of cleaning, cooking, feeding, and caring in the domestic sphere reproduces workers in capitalism and is therefore "productive" labor that generates value and indirectly contributes to profits, it is unpaid work when it is privatized in the family, viewed as the voluntary emotional labor of caring, and wrapped in the ideology of familialism.[83] By encoding gender into the circuitry of capitalism through the unpaid labor of housewives and children who are *made* dependent on the historically higher "family wage" of a male breadwinner and concomitant lack of public provision for childcare, the mystification of social reproduction as "women's work" conjoins capitalism with patriarchy.[84] Palriwala and Neetha refer to this as the ideology of *gendered familialism*, which, they suggest, is central not only to "the dynamics of care practices in India," but also to public discourse and policy, "which reiterates care as a familial and female responsibility and works to devalue and diminish the dimensions of care."[85]

Framing care work as social reproduction enables us to see more clearly the links between the work of low-wage health workers and domestic workers on the one hand, and the unpaid labor of housewives, mothers, and even children on the other hand, as both forms of work—in and out of the labor market, paid and unpaid—are constructed as "women's work" through the gendering of care across class lines. Although the lockdown has increased the burden of care work, and especially childcare, for employed parents of all social classes because of school and workplace closures, and has made the issue more visible, the classed gender gaps in social reproduction that have been magnified during the pandemic are a constitutive aspect of patriarchy in capitalism. While feminists have rejected ahistorical and universal conceptions of patriarchy that glossed over differences of class, race, caste, sexuality, religion, and other co-formations of identity and power, globalized capitalism has shaped the COVID-19 pandemic as patriarchal, heightening intersectional gender inequalities in social reproduction that are at the heart of capitalism. This accounts for the similar gender effects of the pandemic across geographic locations, and across social classes, especially in terms of women's increased care work. For feminism to remain relevant in the postpandemic world, it must confront and address the devalued, underpaid, and unpaid work of social reproduction systemically, at the social level, rather than supporting individual solutions at the household level that liberate middle-class women from domesticity by exploiting working-class and low-wage women workers as their domestic substitute—for example, by fighting for policies such as universal childcare and state-mandated minimum wages for domestic and care workers, along with the recognition of and support for their unionization.

Drawing parallels to her earlier work on disaster capitalism, Naomi Klein uses the term "coronavirus capitalism" to refer to the ways in which companies and people exploit, profit from, and are complicit in creating disasters.[86] In the United States, the coronavirus crisis has already demonstrated how federal aid aimed at small businesses to fund worker furloughs and hold off layoffs was disproportionately funneled by banks to their big clients—large companies with deep pockets—rather than the small business for which they were intended. India's $260 billion relief package is similarly biased, as "only a fraction of this came as extra handouts for the poor, with the majority instead devoted to tiding over businesses."[87] Modi used the pandemic as an opportunity to raise money for a fund called "PM Cares," which is set up as a private trust with no accountability or oversight as to how it will be spent.[88] Likewise, there was political capital to be gained by the Trump administration's denials of the impending pandemic and Modi's crackdown on migrants. Rather than seeing the pandemic as a state of exception and as social interregnum, a more emancipatory narrative of the pandemic would be to chart it as "coronavirus capitalism"—as a form of disaster capitalism in the present—which would "lift contagion out of the past and into the circuits of capital where it belongs."[89]

How do we disrupt this model of business as usual? Not just to make it through the pandemic to rebuild what's been lost, but to break from the past and decommission the existing gendered circuitry of capitalism? In *Feminism for the 99%: A Manifesto*, Cinzia Arruzza, Tithi Bhattacharya, and Nancy Fraser lay out a vision for the future that is especially resonant for these times. Writing before the pandemic, they claim in Thesis 4: "What we are living through is a crisis of society as a whole—and its root cause is capitalism."[90] A crisis, they note, is not just a time of suffering, which is what we are seeing now on an epic scale. Rather, it "is also a moment of political awakening and an opportunity for social transformation" (18). Highlighting the need to revalue women's unpaid domestic and care work, their understanding of social reproduction (Thesis 5) points a way forward toward an emancipatory post-pandemic feminist future: "Gender oppression in capitalist societies is rooted in the subordination of social reproduction to production for profit. We want to turn things right side up" (20). Doing so would *value* frontline and care workers as essential workers and pay them accordingly, while also valuing and supporting social reproduction in the unpaid domestic and care economy.

In a recent interview with the *Washington Post*, cofounder and executive director of the National Domestic Workers Alliance, Ai-jen Poo, expressed optimism that the pandemic may have already begun this transformation. When asked whether she thought that there would be "a new appreciation in our society for domestic workers, caregivers—as with essential workers across the board—coming out of this crisis," Poo's response was hopeful: "There has to be. There already is. I mean, the number of people who are recognizing caregivers and grocery workers for the first time is a transformative shift in our culture. *And there's no going back. You can't unsee things.* So it's really the opportunity of a lifetime to transform the way we support workers and value care . . . my hope is that this cultural shift will catalyze a transformative policy shift that actually puts the safety net and the care infrastructure in place that we've always needed."[91]

In their feminist manifesto, Arruzza et al. correctly twin "political awakening" with opportunities for "social transformation."[92] The cultural recognition of essential and care workers that Poo speaks of is just a first step in this long battle. To move to the stage of crafting transformative policies that encode this revaluation in the currency of capitalism will take active feminist struggle and organizing, which will be made more difficult amid the economic austerity that is likely to emerge in the post-pandemic world.

There are two immediate consequences of the care economy that may hinder the development of a radical anticapitalist feminist realpolitik, and the politicization of women essential workers in particular, in the short run. First, the double shift of paid work and unpaid care work leaves overworked and sleep-deprived women, especially low-wage essential and care workers, little "spare" time for political activism. As a form of "depletion through social reproduction,"[93] this limits their potential politicization and mobilization as members of a collective movement. Second, the "gendered familialism" of social reproduction is not just a top-down ideology reflected in state policies that consign care work to women's private, familial responsibilities.[94] It is also a form of cultural capital for women whose labor is otherwise devalued and hence too a powerful site for their identification as gendered subjects of domesticity and motherhood. Both tendencies have the potential to forestall the development of feminist political subjects who are able and willing to challenge capitalist patriarchy to make political claims for the recognition and valuation of their labor and their rights as paid and unpaid care workers.

Perhaps a greater stumbling block to a radically democratic post-pandemic feminist future lies in the politicization of middle-class and rich women on issues of social reproduction. Whether their renewed appreciation for domestic workers will translate into political actions of cross-class, gender-based solidarity remains in question. At a minimum, this will require the practice of active *unforgetting*—to bear witness and hold on to memories of the widespread suffering and loss that the pandemic has engendered—and the willingness to act on pandemic-induced revelations on the significance of "variegated" forms of social reproduction across time, geography, and social space.[95] Rhetorical calls for a "feminism for the 99%" thus need a clear articulation of the political demands that this places on privileged middle- and upper-class women, from stay-at-home mothers who are housewives to working professionals and academic feminists, to act against their perceived self-interest in solidarity with the multitude of women who, like them, are devalued by the contingent configurations of social reproduction in capitalist patriarchy. At the very least, and against a pessimism of the intellect, we must assert an optimism of the will as a precondition for this feminism. At the very least, we can hope that the personal awakening about women's vulnerabilities and labor in domestic and care economies across vastly different locations such as India and the United States might engender resonant cross-class empathetic connections that are a necessary precondition for any politics of solidarity.

Notwithstanding these obstacles to women's politization, building such a political community is not outside the reach of feminist organizing. Among competing feminist visions of the post-pandemic future, we need to fight for a socialist feminism that locates social reproduction as central to the revolutionary transformation of society.[96] In doing so, this radical "feminism for the 99%" will necessarily address the entanglements of nation, race, class, caste, sexuality, and gender that structure capitalist relations of social reproduction rather than settling for gender equality within these systemic inequalities. The pandemic offers us the opportunity to harness the new visibility of reproductive labor and societies' collective "insight" on the value of care workers toward a utopic radical feminist vision of the future: "Historically," Arundhati Roy writes, "pandemics have forced humans to break with the past and imagine their world anew. This one is no different. It is a portal, a gateway between one world and the next. We can choose to walk through it, dragging the carcasses of our prejudice and hatred, our avarice, our data banks and dead ideas, our dead rivers and smoky skies behind us. Or we can walk through lightly, with little luggage, ready to imagine another world. And ready to fight for it."[97]

CODA, MAY 2021:

The devastating second wave of the pandemic that is unfolding in India brought a seven-fold surge in COVID-19 infections in just five weeks between late March and April as weddings, large political rallies for a few key state-level elections, and a month-long religious gathering attended by an estimated 3.5 million pilgrims spread newer more virulent virus strains of COVID-19 across the country.[98] While Modi boasted of India's vaccine-manufacturing capabilities and touted improvements in health-infrastructure to battle COVID in early January as the first wave ebbed, by mid-April, a mere 1.3% of Indians had been fully vaccinated.[99] Unlike the milder first wave, which devastated poor city-based migrant workers who were pushed to return to their villages with just four hours' notice following Modi's sudden and complete national lockdown, this wave has reached beyond the poor and entered into middle class and rich homes.[100] As impersonal statistics on infection rates and deaths have transformed into personal stories of afflicted family members in the media, it seems that everyone has been affected by the pandemic by just one degree of separation.[101]

Instead of waiting to be ejected, this time, city-based poor migrants fled the city for their village in anticipation of being trapped without any means of transportation, which spread the virus from urban to rural areas, where, for all practical purposes, there are no functional health services.[102] Instead of acting decisively on the incontrovertible data regarding rising COVID-19 infection rates and deaths, this time, stung by a backlash against the first lockdown and in the thrall of potential electoral wins, Modi and his ministers actively encouraged and participated in super-spreader events with large gatherings of unmasked people.

By early May, the numbers of fully vaccinated people had inched up to a mere 2%.[103] In the deadly arithmetic of the pandemic, those at the top among the 99% are no longer protected from the consequences of decades of government disinvestment and privatization in healthcare. Medical staff and hospital beds are woefully insufficient in both government and private facilities, while blood, drugs, PCR tests, PPE, oxygen, and oxygen canisters are simply no longer available, including on the black market, while prices have predictably soared.[104] Forced to scramble for scarce medical resources and to care for sick family members themselves, rich Indians are encountering the inaccessibility of necessary goods and services that the poor routinely confront because they cannot afford them. And as family members and live-in domestic workers have succumbed to COVID, employers are forced to care for their sick care workers.

The common plight of the rich and poor across urban and rural areas in this deadly second wave underscores how, in addition to the class-based exploitative care-chains that stall the gender revolution when well-off women hire poorer women to care for their homes and kids, India's care economy has also historically relied on passing the costs of social reproduction from urban to rural areas via the cyclical and generational replacement of older workers who return to their villages when they are sick or used-up, while a new crop of younger rural workers migrates to the cities to replace them. The care crisis that we are witnessing during the pandemic highlights the urgent need for systemic changes in the provision of care. This should entail not only a gender revolution in the private sphere—the redistribution of care and domestic work within families to address gender inequities—but it must also address the social costs of gendered care regimes in the public sphere, including the lack of workplace benefits for parental leave, the dearth of public childcare and eldercare provisions, the absence of minimum wages for privatized care work, and inadequate social security and health benefits for care workers. Such public welfare expenditures to mitigate the effects of the patriarchal pandemic can easily be funded by progressive taxation on the profits of the 1% from coronavirus capitalism. In a period when the wealth of Indian billionaires reportedly grew by 35% during the lockdown, and the increased wealth of just the top eleven of these billionaires during the pandemic could fund the health ministry of India at its current budgetary levels for ten years,[105] surely this is a good place to start.

## Notes

1. Morse and Anderson, "COVID-19 Crisis Is Exacerbating Gender Inequality."
2. Alon et al., "Impact of the Covid-19 Crisis."
3. Gupta, "Some Women Call This Recession a 'Shecession.'"
4. Gupta, "Some Women Call This Recession a 'Shecession'"; Holpuch, "The 'Shecession.'"
5. Paskin, "Women Are Bearing the Brunt."
6. Federici, *Wages against Housework.*
7. Burnham, "Lean In."
8. Davis, "Mike Davis on Coronavirus."
9. Hall, "Social Reproduction."
10. India Today Web Desk, "India Implements Strictest Lockdown."
11. Suri, Gupta and Kottasová, "Modi Orders Complete Lockdown."
12. Jha, "These Gut-Wrenching Photos."
13. Mahaprashasta and Srivas, "Ground Report."

14. Chishti, "Explained."
15. Slater and Masih, "World's Biggest Lockdown."
16. Slater and Masih, "World's Biggest Lockdown."
17. Ray, Subramanian, and Vandewalle, "India's Lockdown."
18. Chishti, "Explained."
19. BBC, "India Coronavirus Lockdown."
20. Scroll Staff, "Covid-19."
21. Asthana, "Amidst a Lockdown."
22. Slater and Masih, "World's Biggest Lockdown."
23. Roy, "The Pandemic Is a Portal."
24. Perrigo and Bagri, "How the Pandemic Is Reshaping India."
25. PTI, "Wanted to See His Dying Son."
26. Grown, "Coronavirus Live Series."
27. Evans, "How Will COVID-19 Affect Women"; Paskin, "Women Are Bearing the Brunt."
28. International Labour Organization, "ILO Monitor," 5th ed.
29. International Labour Organization, "ILO Monitor," 5th ed., 9.
30. Centre for Equity Studies, "Labouring Lives"; Srivastava, "Has Coronavirus Brought Caste Discrimination Back."
31. Sahoo, "Lockdown Hit More Workers."
32. Sen, "Coronavirus."
33. International Labour Organization, "ILO Monitor," 2nd ed.
34. Sengupta and Sachdeva, "Double Burden of Women," 2.
35. IANS, "Women, People."
36. Schultz and Raj, "For Indian Women."
37. Perrigo and Bagri, "How the Pandemic Is Reshaping India."
38. Boniol et al., "Gender Equity."
39. Anand and Fan, "Health Workforce in India," 9.
40. Bhowmick, "Millions of Women Volunteers."
41. Scott, Javadi, and Gergen, "India's Auxiliary Nurse-Midwife."
42. Altstedter and Pandya, "Mumbai Slum"; Varma, "Foot Soldiers."
43. PTI, "ASHA, Anganwadi."
44. Centre for Equity Studies, "Labouring Lives."
45. Roy, "The Pandemic Is a Portal."
46. Sharma, "The Rich Love India's Lockdown. For the Poor It's Another Story."
47. Bould, "Virus Has Seized the Means."
48. Ray, Subramanian, and Vandewalle, "India's Lockdown."
49. Srivastava, "Has Coronavirus Brought Caste Discrimination Back."
50. Pokhareln and Bellman, "How Much Do Indians Pay."
51. Banerjee, "Women and Their Childcare Needs," 22.
52. Ghosh and Bikhu, "Impact of COVID-19," 3.
53. Anti-Slavery International, "India."
54. National Domestic Workers Movement, "Issues of Domestics," 1.

55. International Labour Organization, "ILO Monitor," 5th ed., 10.

56. India.com News Desk, "Amid COVID-19 Scare."

57. Ghosh and Bikhu, "Impact of COVID-19."

58. Kalra, "Coronavirus."

59. International Labour Organization, "ILO Monitor," 5th ed., 10.

60. Akhtar, "Residents' Associations in a Fix."

61. Gupta, "Some Women Call This Recession a 'Shecession.'"

62. Punit, "Social Distancing."

63. Ghosh and Bikhu, "Impact of COVID-19."

64. SEWA Bharat, "Gendered Precarity," 4.

65. Pokhareln and Bellman, "How Much Do Indians Pay."

66. Kalra, "Coronavirus."

67. Kalra, "Coronavirus."

68. National Domestic Workers Movement, "Issues of Domestics," 2.

69. Ghosh and Bikhu, "Impact of COVID-19."

70. Simon, "Women and the Hidden Burden."

71. Ferrant et al., "Unpaid Care Work."

72. Addati et al., *Care Work.*

73. Organisation for Economic Co-operation and Development, "Employment."

74. Ferrant et al., "Unpaid Care Work."

75. Singh, "Gender Mender."

76. Punit, "Social Distancing."

77. Ghosh and Bikhu, "Impact of COVID-19."

78. Singh, "Gender Mender."

79. Lewis, "The Coronavirus Is a Disaster for Feminism."

80. Hochschild, *Second Shift.*

81. Hochschild, "The Nanny Chain."

82. Glenn, "Social Construction and Institutionalization," 133.

83. Bhattacharya, "What Is Social Reproduction Theory"; Federici, *Wages against Housework.*

84. Hart, "Capitalist Patriarchy"; Federici, "The Making of Capitalist Patriarchy."

85. Palriwala and Neetha, "Stratified Familialism," 1049.

86. Klein, "Coronavirus Capitalism."

87. Perrigo and Bagri, "How the Pandemic Is Reshaping India."

88. Komireddi. "How Modi Turned Covid-19 into a Cash Machine."

89. Bould, "Virus Has Seized the Means."

90. Arruzza, Bhattacharya, and Fraser, *Feminism for the 99%*, 16.

91. Ottesen, "New Economic Austerity," emphasis added.

92. Arruza, Bhattacharya, and Fraser, *Feminism for the 99%.*

93. Rai, Hoskyns, and Thomas, "Depletion," 88.

94. Palriwala and Neetha, "Stratified Familialism," 1066.

95. Bakker and Gill, "Rethinking Power, Production, and Social Reproduction."

96. Federici, *Wages against Housework.*

97. Roy, "The Pandemic Is a Portal."
98. Public Broadcasting Service, "COVID-19 Is out of Control in India."
99. "India Is Struggling with a Catastrophic Second Wave."
100. Bhowmick, "What India's COVID-19 Crisis Means for Narendra Modi."
101. Khullar, "India's Crisis Marks a New Phase in the Pandemic."
102. Kutty, "Second COVID Wave Has Breached Urban-Rural Divide."
103. Ellyatt, "India Is the Home of the World's Biggest Producer of Covid Vaccines."
104. "India Is Struggling with a Catastrophic Second Wave."
105. Dutta and Sardar, "The Inequality Virus—India Supplement 2021," 2.

## References

Addati, Laura, Umberto Cattaneo, Valeria Esquivel, and Isabel Valarino. *Care Work and Care Jobs: For the Future of Decent Work*. Geneva: International Labour Organization, 2018. https://www.ilo.org/global/publications/books/WCMS_633135/lang--en/index.htm

Akhtar, Sadia. 2020. "Residents' Associations in a Fix over Allowing Domestic Helps, Walks." *Hindustan Times*, May 4, 2020. https://www.hindustantimes.com/gurugram/residents-associations-in-a-fix-over-allowing-domestic-helps-walks/story-p28hLpHudhOUIBldUcVGgJ.html

Alon, Titan, Matthias Doepke, Jane Olmstead-Rumsey, and Michèle Tertilt. "The Impact of the Covid-19 Crisis on Women's Employment." Econofact Network, Fletcher School, Tufts University. *Econofact* (blog), August 27, 2020. https://econofact.org/impact-of-the-covid-19-crisis-on-womens-employment

Altstedter, Ari, and Dhwani Pandya. "The Mumbai Slum That Stopped the Virus." *Bloomberg.com*, October 8, 2020. https://www.bloomberg.com/features/2020-mumbai-dharavi-covid-lockdown/

Anand, Sudhir, and Victoria Fan. "The Health Workforce in India." Human Resources for Health Observer Series No. 16. Geneva: World Health Organization, 2016.

Anti-Slavery International. "India: Domestic Workers." *Anti-Slavery International* (blog). https://www.antislavery.org/what-we-do/past-projects/india-domestic-workers/. Accessed June 4, 2020.

Arruzza, Cinzia, Tithi Bhattacharya, and Nancy Fraser. *Feminism for the 99%: A Manifesto*. New York: Verso Books, 2019.

Aschoff, Nicole. "COVID-19 Should Be a Wake-Up Call for Feminists." *Jacobin*, April 4, 2020. https://jacobinmag.com/2020/04/covid-19-coronavirus-pandemic-feminism/

Asthana, N. C. "Amidst a Lockdown, Why Must Cops Wield the Lathi with Such Impunity and Callousness?" *The Wire*, March 27, 2020. https://thewire.in/government/lathi-police-brutality-coronavirus

Bakker, Isabella, and Stephen Gill. "Rethinking Power, Production, and Social Reproduction: Toward Variegated Social Reproduction." *Capital & Class* 43, no. 4 (2019): 503–23. https://doi.org/10.1177/0309816819880783

Banerjee, Monika. "Women and Their Childcare Needs: Addressing Childcare Provisioning in India through a Gendered Lens." ISST Working Paper Series (2020)-2. New Delhi: Institute of Social Studies Trust. https://www.isstindia.org/publicatio ns/1595487848_pub_WOMEN_AND_THEIR_CHILDCARE_NEEDS_3_-_final.pdf

BBC. "India Coronavirus Lockdown: Road Accident Kills 24 Migrant Workers." *BBC News*, May 16, 2020, sec. India. https://www.bbc.com/news/world-asia-india-526 88899

Bhattacharya, Tithi. "What Is Social Reproduction Theory?" *Marxismo Critico*, October 17, 2017. https://marxismocritico.com/2017/10/17/what-is-social-reproducti on-theory/

Bhowmick, Nilanjana. "Millions of Women Volunteers Form India's Frontline COVID Response." *National Geographic*, June 1, 2020. https://www.nationalgeographic .com/history/2020/06/millions-women-volunteers-form-india-frontline-covid-19 -response/

Bhowmick, Nilanjana. "What India's COVID-19 Crisis Means for Narendra Modi." *Time. com*, May 7, 2021. https://time.com/6046580/india-covid-19-middle-class-modi/

Bond-Theriault, Candace. "COVID-19: A Black, Queer, Feminist Grounding and Call for Self and Community Care." *Ms. Magazine*, March 26, 2020. https://msmagazi ne.com/2020/03/26/covid-19-a-black-queer-feminist-grounding-and-call-for-self -and-community-care/

Boniol, Mathieu, Michelle McIsaac, Lihui Xu, Tana Wuliji, Khassoum Diallo, and Jim Campbell. "Gender Equity in the Health Workforce: Analysis of 104 Countries." Working Paper 1: WHO/HIS/HWF/Gender/WP1/2019.1. 2019. Geneva: World Health Organization. http://www.who.int/hrh/resources/gender_equity-health _workforce_analysis/en/

Bould, Mark. "The Virus Has Seized the Means of Production." *Boston Review*, May 8, 2020. https://bostonreview.net/arts-society/mark-bould-virus-has-seized-means -production

Burnham, Linda. "'Lean In' and One Percent Feminism." *Truthout*, March 26, 2013. https://truthout.org/articles/lean-in-and-one-percent-feminism/

Centre for Equity Studies. "Labouring Lives: Hunger, Precarity and Despair amid Lockdown." New Delhi: Centre for Equity Studies. 2020. http://centreforequitystud ies.org/wp-content/uploads/2020/06/Labouring-Lives-_Final-Report.pdf

Chishti, Seema. "Explained: How Many Migrant Workers Displaced? A Range of Estimates." *Indian Express*, June 8, 2020. https://indianexpress.com/article/explain ed/coronavirus-how-many-migrant-workers-displaced-a-range-of-estimates-644 7840/

Davis, Mike. "Mike Davis on Coronavirus: 'In a Plague Year.'" *Jacobin*, March 14, 2020. https://jacobinmag.com/2020/03/mike-davis-coronavirus-outbreak-capitalism -left-international-solidarity

Dutta, Mayurakshi, and Sucheta Sardar. "The Inequality Virus—India Supplement 2021." Oxfam Briefing Paper. New Delhi: Oxfam India, January 22, 2021. https://

www.oxfamindia.org/knowledgehub/workingpaper/inequality-virus-india-suppl
ement-2021

Evans, David. "How Will COVID-19 Affect Women and Girls in Low- and Middle-
Income Countries?" *Center for Global Development* (blog), March 16, 2020. https://
www.cgdev.org/blog/how-will-covid-19-affect-women-and-girls-low-and-middle
-income-countries

Ellyatt, Holly. "India Is the Home of the World's Biggest Producer of Covid Vaccines.
But It's Facing a Major Internal Shortage." CNBC, May 5, 2021. https://www.cnbc
.com/2021/05/05/why-covid-vaccine-producer-india-faces-major-shortage-of-do
ses.html

Federici, Silvia. The Making of Capitalist Patriarchy. Interview by Andrew Sernatinger
and Tessa Echeverria. *Marxismo Critico*, February 24, 2014. https://marxismocriti
co.com/2014/02/24/the-making-of-capitalist-patriarchy/

Federici, Silvia. *Revolution at Point Zero: Housework, Reproduction, and Feminist Struggle*. Oakland, CA: PM Press / Common Notions, 2012.

Federici, Silvia. *Wages against Housework*. Bristol, UK: Power of Women Collective and
Falling Wall Press, 1975.

Ferrant, Gaëlle, Luca Maria Pesando, and Keiko Nowacka. "Unpaid Care Work: The
Missing Link in the Analysis of Gender Gaps in Labour Outcomes." OECD Development Centre, 2014. Accessed April 20, 2020. www.oecd.org/dev/development-gen
der/Unpaid_care_work.pdf

Ghosh, Anweshaa, and Ashmeet Kaur Bikhu. "Impact of COVID-19 National Lockdown on 'Women Domestic Workers in Delhi.'" Creating Momentum for Gender
Transformative Programming and Advancing Gender. Institute of Social Studies
Trust, 2020. Accessed November 29, 2020. http://www.isstindia.org/publications
/1591186006_pub_compressed_ISST_-_Final_Impact_of_Covid_19_Lockdown
_on_Women_Informal_Workers_Delhi.pdf

Glenn, Evelyn Nakano. "The Social Construction and Institutionalization of Gender
and Race: An Integrative Framework." In *Race, Gender, Sexuality, and Social Class:
Dimensions of Inequality*, edited by Susan J. Ferguson, 125–39. Newbury Park, CA:
Sage, 2013.

Grown, Caren. "Coronavirus Live Series: The Impact of the Pandemic on Women and
Girls." World Bank Live. May 15, 2020. https://live.worldbank.org/coronavirus-imp
act-pandemic-women-and-girls

Gupta, Alisha Haridasani. "Why Some Women Call This Recession a 'Shecession.'"
*New York Times*, May 9, 2020. https://www.nytimes.com/2020/05/09/us/unemploy
ment-coronavirus-women.html?utm_source=dlvr.it&utm_medium=twitter

Hall, Sarah Marie. "Social Reproduction as Social Infrastructure." *Soundings* 76 (Winter 2020): 82–94. https://doi.org/DOI:10.3898/SOUN.76.06.2020

Hart, Mechthild. "Capitalist Patriarchy." In *The Wiley Blackwell Encyclopedia of Gender
and Sexuality Studies*, edited by Nancy A. Naples, 1–5. John Wiley & Sons, 2016.

Hochschild, Arlie R. "The Nanny Chain." *American Prospect*, February 19, 2001. https://
prospect.org/features/nanny-chain/

Hochschild, Arlie R. *The Second Shift: Working Parents and the Revolution at Home*. New York: Viking Penguin, 1989.

Holpuch, Amanda. "The 'Shecession': Why Economic Crisis Is Affecting Women More Than Men." *The Guardian*, August 4, 2020, sec. Business. http://www.theguardian.com/business/2020/aug/04/shecession-coronavirus-pandemic-economic-fallout-women

IANS. "Women, People in Semi-urban Areas Bear the Brunt of Job Losses." Outlookindia.com. May 16, 2020. https://www.outlookindia.com/newsscroll/women-people-in-semiurban-areas-bear-the-brunt-of-job-losses/1836606

"India Is Struggling with a Catastrophic Second Wave." *The Economist*, April 24, 2021. https://www.economist.com/asia/2021/04/24/india-is-struggling-with-a-catastrophic-second-wave

India Today Web Desk. "India Implements Strictest Lockdown in the World, Lags in Testing: Expert." *India Today*, April 10, 2020. https://www.indiatoday.in/india/story/india-implements-strictest-lockdown-in-the-world-lags-in-testing-expert-1665604-2020-04-10

India.com News Desk. "Amid COVID-19 Scare, Domestic Help Must Refrain from Work in Urban Slums for Short Period, Says Advisory." India.com. June 17, 2020. https://www.india.com/news/india/amid-covid-19-scare-domestic-helps-must-refrain-from-work-in-urban-slums-for-short-period-says-advisory-4060143/

International Labour Organization. "ILO Monitor: COVID-19 and the World of Work. 2nd Edition." Briefing note. April 7, 2020. http://www.ilo.org/global/topics/coronavirus/impacts-and-responses/WCMS_740877/lang--en/index.htm

International Labour Organization. "ILO Monitor: COVID-19 and the World of Work. 5th Edition." Briefing note. June 30, 2020. http://www.ilo.org/global/topics/coronavirus/impacts-and-responses/WCMS_749399/lang--en/index.htm

Jha, Nishita. "These Gut-Wrenching Photos Show What Happens When a Coronavirus Lockdown Backfires." *BuzzFeed News*, March 30, 2020. https://www.buzzfeednews.com/article/nishitajha/india-coronavirus-lockdown-migrant-workers

Kalra, Richa Jain. "Coronavirus: Should Domestic Helps Be Allowed to Work? Housing Societies in Two Minds." NDTV.com, May 8, 2020. https://www.ndtv.com/india-news/coronavirus-india-should-domestic-helps-be-allowed-to-work-housing-societies-in-two-minds-2225664

Khullar, Dhruv. "India's Crisis Marks a New Phase in the Pandemic." *The New Yorker*, May 13, 2021. https://www.newyorker.com/science/medical-dispatch/indias-crisis-marks-a-new-phase-in-the-pandemic

Klein, Naomi. "Coronavirus Capitalism—and How to Beat It." *The Intercept*, March 16, 2020. https://theintercept.com/2020/03/16/coronavirus-capitalism/

Komireddi, Kapil. 2020. "How Modi Turned Covid-19 into a Cash Machine." *The Critic Magazine*, May 11, 2020. https://thecritic.co.uk/pm-cares/.

Kutty, Sushil. "Second COVID Wave Has Breached Urban-Rural Divide, with Healthcare Collapsing in India's Rural Hinterland." *National Herald*, May 18, 2021. https://

www.nationalheraldindia.com/opinion/second-covid-wave-has-breached-urban -rural-divide-with-healthcare-collapsing-in-indias-rural-hinterland

Lewis, Helen. "The Coronavirus Is a Disaster for Feminism." *The Atlantic*, March 19, 2020. https://www.theatlantic.com/international/archive/2020/03/feminism-wo mens-rights-coronavirus-covid19/608302/

Mahaprashasta, Ajoy Ashirwad, and Anuj Srivas. "Ground Report: Chaos at Anand Vihar as Buses Prepare to Take Migrant Workers Home." *The Wire*, March 28, 2020. https://thewire.in/rights/covid-19-lockdown-migrant-workers-bus

Morse, Michelle Milford, and Grace Anderson. "How the COVID-19 Crisis Is Exacer-bating Gender Inequality." *United Nations Foundation–Covid19* (blog), April 14, 2020. https://unfoundation.org/blog/post/shadow-pandemic-how-covid19-crisis -exacerbating-gender-inequality/

National Domestic Workers Movement. "Issues of Domestic Workers in India." National Domestic Workers Movement, 2016. Accessed September 4, 2020. http:// www.nd wm.org/resources/Issues%20of%20Domestic%20workers%20in%20India.pdf

Organisation for Economic Co-operation and Development. "Employment: Time Spent in Paid and Unpaid Work, by Sex." OECD.Stat. Accessed April 7, 2021. https:// stats.oecd.org/index.aspx?queryid=54757

Ottesen, K. K. "A New Economic Austerity Could Be 'as Life-Threatening as the Virus Itself,' Says Head of the National Domestic Workers Alliance." *Washington Post*, June 2, 2020. https://www.washingtonpost.com/lifestyle/magazine/economic-austeri ty-could-be-as-life-threatening-as-the-virus-itself-says-head-of-the-national-dom estic-workers-alliance/2020/05/29/ad35020a-93cd-11ea-82b4-c8db161ff6e5_sto ry.html

Palriwala, Rajni, and N. Neetha. "Stratified Familialism: The Care Regime in India through the Lens of Childcare." *Development and Change* 42.4 (2011): 1049–1078. https://doi.org/10.1111/j.1467-7660.2011.01717.x

Paskin, Janet. "Women Are Bearing the Brunt of Coronavirus Disruption." *Bloomsberg Businessweek*, March 11, 2020. https://www.bloomberg.com/news/articles/2020 -03-11/coronavirus-will-make-gender-inequality-worse

Perrigo, Billy, and Neha Thirani Bagri. "How the Pandemic Is Reshaping India." *Time*, August 19, 2020. https://time.com/5880585/india-coronavirus-impact/

Pokhareln, Krishna, and Eric Bellman. "How Much Do Indians Pay Their Many Do-mestic Helpers?" *Wall Street Journal*, May 3, 2016, sec. World. https://www.wsj.com /articles/BL-IRTB-32008

PTI. "ASHA, Anganwadi, Other Scheme Workers to Go on 2-Day Strike." *Telangana To-day*, August 6, 2020. https://telanganatoday.com/asha-anganwadi-other-scheme -workers-to-go-on-2-day-strike

PTI. "Just Wanted to See His Dying Son: Story behind Photograph of Crying Man That Shook India." Outlookindia.com. May 16, 2020. https://www.outlookindia.com/we bsite/story/india-news-just-wanted-to-see-his-dying-son-story-behind-photogra ph-of-crying-man-that-shook-india/352899

Public Broadcasting Service. "COVID-19 Is out of Control in India, Where Most Vaccines Are Made. How Did That Happen?" *PBS NewsHour*, April 27, 2021. https://www.pbs.org/newshour/health/covid-19-is-out-of-control-in-india-where-most-vaccines-are-made-how-did-that-happen

Punit, Itika Sharma. "Social Distancing from House Helps Is Exposing the Indian Family's Unspoken Sexism." *Quartz India*, March 26, 2020. https://qz.com/india/1823823/with-coronavirus-lockdown-working-indian-women-face-family-sexism/

Rai, Shirin M., Catherine Hoskyns, and Dania Thomas. 2014. "Depletion: The Cost of Social Reproduction." *International Feminist Journal of Politics* 16 (1): 86–105. https://doi.org/10.1080/14616742.2013.789641

Ray, Debraj, S. Subramanian, and Lore Vandewalle. "India's Lockdown." *India Forum*, April 9, 2020. https://www.theindiaforum.in/article/indias-lockdown

Roy, Arundhati. "The Pandemic Is a Portal." *Financial Times*, April 3, 2020. https://www.ft.com/content/10d8f5e8-74eb-11ea-95fe-fcd274e920ca

Sahoo, Priyanka. "Lockdown Hit More Workers from Lower Castes, Reveals Study by University in Haryana." *Hindustan Times*, August 4, 2020. https://www.hindustantimes.com/mumbai-news/lockdown-hit-more-workers-from-lower-castes-reveals-study-by-university-in-haryana/story-wkIfltjnSCQv8p0vE01XAP.html

Schultz, Kai, and Suhasini Raj. "For Indian Women, the Coronavirus Economy Is a Devastating Setback." *New York Times*, June 9, 2020, sec. World. https://www.nytimes.com/2020/06/09/world/asia/india-coronavirus-women-economy.html

Scott, Kerry, Dena Javadi, and Jessica Gergen. "India's Auxiliary Nurse-Midwife, Anganwadi Worker, Accredited Social Health Activist, Multipurpose Worker, and Lady Health Visitor Programs." CHW Central. April 4, 2018. https://chwcentral.org/indias-auxiliary-nurse-midwife-anganwadi-worker-accredited-social-health-activist-multipurpose-worker-and-lady-health-visitor-programs/

Scroll Staff. "Covid-19: At Least 22 Migrants Die While Trying to Get Home during Lockdown." *Scroll.in*, May 29, 2020. https://scroll.in/latest/957570/covid-19-lockdown-man-collapses-dies-halfway-while-walking-home-300-km-away-from-delhi

Sen, Priyadarshini. "Coronavirus: India's Partial Lockdown Reeks of Class, Caste Bias Leaving Socially, Sexually Disadvantaged Groups Vulnerable." *Outlook India*, March 22, 2020. https://www.outlookindia.com/website/story/opinion-coronavirus-indias-partial-lockdown-reeks-of-class-caste-bias-leaving-socially-sexually-disadvantaged-groups-vulnerable/349250

Sengupta, Sudeshna, and Shubhika Sachdeva. "From Double Burden of Women to a 'Double Boon': Balancing Unpaid Care Work and Paid Work." IDRC Digital Library. May 2017. https://idl-bnc-idrc.dspacedirect.org/handle/10625/56506

SEWA Bharat. "Gendered Precarity in the Lockdown: What the Lockdown Shows Us about the Precarity of Women Workers." May 2020. https://www.wiego.org/publications/gendered-precarity-lockdown-india

Sharma, Ruchir. "The Rich Love India's Lockdown. For the Poor It's Another Story." *New York Times*, May 30, 2020, sec. Opinion. https://www.nytimes.com/2020/05/30/opinion/sunday/india-coronavirus-lockdown-inequality.html

Simon, Madeleine. "Women and the Hidden Burden of the Coronavirus." *The Hill*, March 19, 2020. https://thehill.com/changing-america/respect/equality/488509 -the-hidden-burden-of-the-coronavirus-on-women

Singh, Rajiv. "Gender Mender: How WFH Is Demolishing Gender Roles." *Forbes India*, July 20, 2020. https://www.forbesindia.com/article/coronavirus/gender-mender -how-wfh-is-demolishing-gender-roles/60941/1

Slater, Joanna, and Niha Masih. "In India, the World's Biggest Lockdown Has Forced Migrants to Walk Hundreds of Miles Home." *Washington Post*, March 27, 2020. https://www.washingtonpost.com/world/asia_pacific/india-coronavirus-lockdo wn-migrant-workers/2020/03/27/a62df166-6f7d-11ea-a156-0048b62cdb51_story .html

Srivastava, Shruti. "Has Coronavirus Brought Caste Discrimination Back in India?" *Deccan Herald*, August 21, 2020. https://www.deccanherald.com/national/has-cor onavirus-brought-caste-discrimination-back-in-india-876055.html

Suri, Manveena, Swati Gupta, and Ivana Kottasová. "Modi Orders Complete Lock-down for 1.3 Billion People in India." *CNN.com*, March 24, 2020. https://www.cnn .com/2020/03/24/asia/india-lockdown-coronavirus-intl/index.html

Varma, Vishnu. "The Foot Soldiers of Kerala's Covid-19 Battle, 26,000 Women Who Won't Overlook Any Detail." *Indian Express*, May 5, 2020. https://indianexpress .com/article/facebook-stories-of-strength-2020/governing-the-crisis/the-foot-sol diers-of-keralas-covid-19-battle-25000-women-who-wont-overlook-any-detail-63 94687/

# CHAPTER 23

# Whose Challenge Is #ChallengeAccepted?

## Performative Online Activism during the COVID-19 Pandemic and Its Erasures

*Özge Savaş*

Pınar Gültekin's body was found inside a concrete-filled barrel in the forest five days after her disappearance on July 17, 2020.[1] The cold-blooded murderer, her ex-boyfriend, testified in court that he killed her because she refused to get back together with him. Pınar's death sparked a global social media campaign. Women in Turkey started posting black-and-white portraits of themselves on Instagram with the hashtags #ChallengeAccepted and #WomenSupportingWomen, which then caught on internationally, reaching more than six million posts. Celebrities including Khloe Kardashian, Paris Hilton, Janet Jackson, and Katy Perry posted their black-and-white portraits. The hashtags turned into a celebration of self-love and women's support for each other.[2] The global(ized) campaign quickly erased the origin story and the struggles of women against state violence in Turkey. Even the attempts to recover from this erasure participated in a more egregious form of erasure: posts were circulated worldwide explaining that "this was about *Turkish women*," homogenizing women in Turkey and completely wiping out Pınar's Kurdish identity, the struggle of Kurdish women activists against the ongoing violence of the Turkish state, and the heterogeneity of the feminist movement in Turkey. The single most important message women in Turkey wanted to convey had been buried: a call for the enforcement of the Istanbul Convention, an international treaty offering social and legal guidelines for how to decrease violence against women.

The Turkish government signed the Istanbul Convention in 2011. The Istanbul Convention, also known as the Council of Europe Convention on Preventing and Combating Violence against Women and Domestic Violence, aims to end gender-based violence by pushing governments to implement policies for prevention of violence, protection of those who experience violence, and punishment of the perpetrators. The European Court of Human Rights oversees the implementation of the Convention in the member states. Along with the Turkish state, thirty-four countries are signatories and have ratified the Convention. Turkey had the lowest number of femicides (121) reported in 2011, the year it signed the Convention. However, the number of femicides has been sharply increasing in the last decade, and the government simply stopped enforcing the treaty; in 2019 alone, men killed 474 women in Turkey. Recently, the Turkish president, Recep Tayyip Erdoğan, stated his intention to pull out of the Istanbul Convention in a renewed attempt to delegitimize the regulation by condemning it for "putting dynamite at the foundation of the family."[3] Femicide numbers in Turkey are expected to be higher in 2020 since the government introduced a stay-at-home order during the COVID-19 pandemic while keeping women's shelters closed, forcing women to stay with their abusers.

After Pınar's death, women's rights and LGBTQI+ activists across Turkey took to the streets amid the COVID-19 pandemic in opposition to the increasingly authoritarian Justice and Development Party (AKP) government, which destroyed the basic rights feminists had fought for and won.[4] The AKP government launched a $15.4 billion COVID-19 relief package to remedy the consequences of the pandemic. However, not surprisingly, the twenty-one-point stimulus package did not include any reference to gender-based policies or allocate funds to combat gender-based violence or improve women's economic situation during the pandemic.[5] From the approximately $300,000 allocated to the Ministry of Family, Labor and Social Services, it was not clear how the funds would be shared among families, unemployed people, and women. The ministry announced a $200 stimulus check for each family. However, questions about whether women who needed economic assistance qualified for this assistance remained unanswered.[6] The ministry did not take any measure or create a procedure to prevent the funds from being given to abusive spouses in domestic violence situations.

After AKP stepped into power in 2002, the Turkish state actively dismantled institutions that protected women's and LGBTQI+ rights; strategically targeted, criminalized, and suppressed women peacebuilders and Kurdish women dissidents; and confined women's role to childbirth and caring for family. One of the first attempts to confine women to family and home and to force them into care economy by the Justice and Development Party was the replacement of the title "Ministry for Women and Family" with "Ministry of Family and Social Policies."[7] The AKP government justified this change by claiming that the use of "women" or "gender" threatens traditional family values. The erasure of "women" from the name of the ministry paved the way for *not addressing* discrimination, inequality, and violence based on gender. Next, in 2018, the AKP merged the Ministry of Family and Social Policy with the Ministry of Labor and Social Services, and named it the "Ministry of Family, Labor and Social Services." With this change, women's unpaid care labor in the family has been made even more invisible, preparing for AKP's neoliberal policies to create a care economy that relied on women's labor to take care of children and elderly family while releasing the state from its responsibility to offer social welfare to its citizens.[8] Further, right-wing politicians legitimized domestic violence and femicides by victim-blaming: deeming women with no children "deficient, incomplete,"[9] and undeserving; calling unmarried women irresponsible, promiscuous, "freedom-lovers";[10] and stating that "women should not laugh out loud."[11] Under the AKP's rule, unmarried women do not count as deserving of any rights, while married women who experience domestic violence are told to stay with their abusers.

The globally embraced #ChallengeAccepted movement, with individualistic displays of self-love and empowerment, quickly became performative, erasing the stories of Pınar and other Kurdish women whose struggles are compounded by state violence and male dominance. Pınar was a twenty-seven-year-old single Kurdish woman who studied economics and wanted to be a public official. Among her siblings, she was the only one who was literate and continued her education. Before she was violently murdered, Pınar was preparing to visit her family in their village, Hizan, in Bitlis province in southeast Turkey.[12] Although we do not know much about Pınar or her family's story, we know that the Turkish state displaced Kurdish families in the 1990s as part of its assimilationist policies, forcing Kurds to live among Turkish majorities. This systemic violence has led to great discrepancies in educational attainment and economic outcomes between the Kurdish minority and the dominant Turkish majority in Turkey. Kurdish women especially have become the targets of the Turkish state's assimilationist and exploitative policies.

Over the last two decades, AKP's hostile discourse and policy changes resulted in the dismantling of institutions that advocated for women's rights. An increasing number of femicides happened simultaneously with the suppression of Kurdish dissidents and women peace activists. In 2012, the Turkish state and the Kurdistan Worker's Party (PKK) reached an agreement to start the "peace process" and put an end to the armed conflict that has been going on since the late 1970s in the predominantly Kurdish-populated southeastern provinces. However, even after a truce, in 2013, the government began to actively target women peacebuilders and the civil society organizations run by them. Between 2015 and 2017, the Kurdish provinces experienced one of the most violent episodes in history. The Turkish state committed serious human rights violations by burning more than one hundred civilians trapped in basements, and pursued a "masculinist occupation policy," in which Turkish law enforcement left writings with derogatory sexual content on walls to humiliate women; tore apart women's underwear in their bedrooms; and scattered used condoms throughout their houses.[13] About half a million Kurds were displaced, and thousands were killed in the cities of Cizre, Suruç, and Ceylanpınar. In 2018, AKP took advantage of the extended state of emergency that was declared as a result of the failed coup attempt to shut down civil society organizations and arrest women who were affiliated with Kurdish women's movement, including members of Women's Peace Initiative and Women's Freedom Assembly. These women were outspoken about the gendered nature of the ongoing conflict and violence in Kurdish villages. The AKP also shut down two of the four women's shelters run by Kurdish municipalities.

Women across the globe are bearing the brunt of the COVID-19 pandemic as they face multiple and intersecting oppressions due to inadequate (at its best) and violent government policies. In Turkey, stay-at-home orders are effectively killing women due to the absence of effective protections from domestic violence, measures for adequate economic support for families and for women, and policies for child and elder care and support that do not rely on women's labor. If those shelters remained in operation today, they could have saved the lives of women and LGBTQI+ individuals, offering much-needed protections from increased domestic violence during the pandemic. While the government's COVID-19 response provided early release to approximately ninety thousand prisoners in order to relieve the country's overfull prisons, the bill excluded "political prisoners," many of whom are women peacebuilders and activists who worked hard in advocating for women's shelters.[14] State violence against Kurds and women continues during the pandemic, exacerbating serious health risks to prisoners in Turkey's already inadequate prisons with poor hygiene standards, insufficient meals, and poor health care. Women and LGBTQI+ individuals in Turkey are in immediate need of recognition of their rights, an end to violence through enforcement of the Istanbul Convention, creation of protective measures, and release of political prisoners. In the current political climate, it is difficult to expect the authoritarian Turkish government to change its policies or stigmatizing discourse; however, a sustained domestic public demand with increased international pressure on the government to address gender-based violence during and after the COVID-19 pandemic is critical. We need feminist global solidarity without the erasure of our differences, centering the voices of those whose struggles are compounded by sexist, racist, ableist, capitalist, and xenophobic institutions.

## Notes

1. "Pinar Gultekin's Killing."
2. A similar social media campaign had become viral with the hashtag #ChalengeAccepted in 2016 to increase awareness of breast cancer and to empower women.
3. "Erdoğan Signals Withdrawal."
4. McKernan, "Murder in Turkey."
5. Bayram, "COVID-19 Salgininda Kadinlarin Guvenligi."
6. Dollar amounts in this section are based on Turkish liras (TL) at the time of writing. At the time of writing, TL 1,000 was about US$200, but in the months following, the Turkish lira lost value and TL 1,000 dropped to about US$134.
7. "Turkey: Backward Step."
8. "The Care Economy."
9. "Turkish President."
10. A recent example of this is the tweet by an AKP Istanbul councilor, Hamdullah Arvas, who legitimized the murder of Zeynep Senpinar by blaming it on her being in an "extramarital" relationship and a "freedom-lover" ("AKP Istanbul Councillor").
11. "Turkish Deputy Prime Minister."
12. Mohammed, "Family of Slain Pınar Gultekin."
13. Kurtay and Briy, "Kurdish Women's Experience."
14. Alici, Bor and Dasli, "Turkey's Missing WPS Agenda."

## References

"AKP Istanbul Councillor Legitimizes Killing of Woman by Boyfriend, Say Couple 'Was Having Extramarital Life." *Duvar English*. https://www.duvarenglish.com/topics/hamdullah-arvas/. Accessed August 25, 2020.

Alici, Nisan, G. Bor, and G. Dasli. "Turkey's Missing WPS Agenda and Implications for the COVID-19 Pandemic." May 28, 2020. https://blogs.lse.ac.uk/wps/2020/05/28/turkeys-missing-wps-agenda-and-implications-for-the-covid-19-pandemic/

Bayram, Deniz. "COVID-19 Salgininda Kadinlarin Guvenligi." May 13, 2020. https://www.catlakzemin.com/covid-19-salgininda-kadinlarin-guvenligi/

"The Care Economy." *International Labour Organization.* https://www.ilo.org/global /topics/care-economy/lang--en/index.htm. Accessed August 25, 2020

"Erdoğan Signals Withdrawal of Turkey from Istanbul Convention." *Duvar English.* August 13, 2020. https://www.duvarenglish.com/women/2020/08/13/erdogan-signa ls-withdrawal-of-turkey-from-istanbul-convention/

Kurtay, Mahir and A. Briy. "Kurdish Women's Experience of State Violence in Turkey." April 30, 2019. https://www.opendemocracy.net/en/north-africa-west-asia/kurdi sh-womens-experience-of-state-violence-in-turkey/

McKernan, Bethan. "Murder in Turkey Sparks Outrage over Rising Violence against Women." July 23, 2020. https://www.theguardian.com/world/2020/jul/23/turkey -outrage-rising-violence-against-women

Mohammed, Sarkawt. "Family of Slain Pınar Gultekin Speak of Daughter's Life." July 27, 2020. https://www.rudaw.net/english/middleeast/turkey/27072020

"Pınar Gultekin's Killing Was a Premediated Murder Say Lawyer Epozdemir." *Bianet Online.* July 28, 2020. http://bianet.org/english/women/228136-pinar-gultekin-s-k illing-was-a-premeditated-murder-says-lawyer-epozdemir

"Turkey: Backward Step for Women's Rights Abolishing Women's Ministry Harms Women's Rights Efforts." Human Rights Watch. June 9, 2011. https://www.hrw.org /news/2011/06/09/turkey-backward-step-womens-rights

"Turkish Deputy Prime Minister Says Women Should Not Laugh Out Loud." *The Guardian,* July 29, 2014. https://www.theguardian.com/world/2014/jul/29/turkish -minister-women-laugh-loud-bulent-arinc

"Turkish President Says Childless Women Are 'Deficient, Incomplete.'" *The Guardian,* June 5, 2016. https://www.theguardian.com/world/2016/jun/06/turkish-president -erdogan-childless-women-deficient-incomplete

# CHAPTER 24

# COVID-19

## Nigerian Women and the Fight for Holistic Policy

*Abiola Akiyode-Afolabi and Ronke Olawale*

### INTRODUCTION

On February 27, 2020, Nigeria recorded its first COVID-19 case. Since then, the infection rate has continued to rise rapidly in the country. As of January 1, 2021, Nigeria reported approximately 87,607 confirmed cases, 73,713 recoveries, and 1,289 deaths (Center for Disease Control, Nigeria, January 2, 2021). Like other countries, the Nigerian government declared the COVID-19 pandemic a national emergency and introduced preventive and containment measures in all the states across the country.

The negative impact of COVID-19 further exacerbates the poor condition of the populace, with women in informal sectors being the worst hit because they depend on daily earnings for their survival and that of their families. More than half of Nigerians live below the international poverty line of US $1.25 a day.[1] Women in Nigeria constitute 49.7% of the population and are the principal caregivers in families. The negative effect of COVID-19 on women's health is enormous as women continue to be at higher risk of exposure to infectious disease, which poses a threat to their general well-being. Furthermore, the COVID-19 epidemic and ensuing lockdown increased Nigerian women's vulnerability to family-based violence in a country where the preexisting rates of violence against women and girls were already high.

During the lockdown, nonprofit women's organizations in Nigeria supported vulnerable women in the country by leveraging COVID-19 into an opportunity to hold the government accountable for the spike in gender-based violence and abuse of women's health, rights, and socioeconomic needs. This essay examines the role of women's organizations in four sections. The first part looks at the role that the women's movement plays in the cultural, socioeconomic, and political context in Nigeria and how organized resistance to government ineptitude has led to increased women's participation in governance and accountability. The second section examines the COVID-19 pandemic and its impact on women; the third discusses the Nigerian government's COVID-19 response and the involvement of feminists and women's groups in developing that response. The final section proposes gender-responsive programming and policy in post-COVID-19 Nigeria.

## THE WOMEN'S MOVEMENT AND THE STRUGGLE FOR EMANCIPATION

Although women's activism in Nigeria predates colonialism,[2] their activities during the postcolonial era of state formation and transformation in Africa were auxiliary, as men dominated the continent's emancipation movements.[3] Born out of a response to the continuous struggle with varied forms of discrimination and misogyny against women and girls, feminist activism and social movements have metamorphosed into strategic organizations supporting women's and girls' rights, political participation and leadership, and governance in Nigeria. Overall, feminist and social movements have been around for over a century and are historically recognized as popular groups deployed to challenge male domination and corrupt governance.[4] In addition, the autonomy of women's organizations makes it easy for members to work together across communal identities, which, in turn, has increased their effectiveness in social struggles.

Since independence in 1960, several women's groups have been formed, in both rural and urban Nigeria, to ensure women's representation in society. Most of these women's organizations are linked to kin, ethnic, religious, or regional groups. In contrast, others are women's coalitions, like the National Council of Women's Societies, formed in 1958, and Women in Nigeria, formed in 1982. Nigerian women occupy leadership roles in all sectors of the economy. Consequently, we can argue that there is progress in achieving gender equality. Through the consistent interventions in gender equality, organizations like the Gender and Constitution Reform Network, Women Advocates Research and Documentation Center (WARDC), Legislative Advocacy Coalition on Violence against Women, and the National Coalition on Affirmative Action have advocated for change in legislation, constitution review, and the passage of the comprehensive Violence against Persons Prohibition Act. To date, seventeen states have passed legislation to stop gender-based violence against women and children in Nigeria. Similarly, women's groups in the country have played critical roles in sustaining government responses to the insurgency in northeast Nigeria and during the COVID-19 emergency.

## COVID-19 AND ITS IMPACT ON NIGERIAN WOMEN

The COVID-19 outbreak has disproportionately impacted vulnerable groups, particularly women and girls, through food insecurity, poor nutrition, ill health, unstable income and livelihoods, and weak protection.[5] Women function as household heads and are critical health care frontline responders in Nigeria, roles that place them at increased risk of infection. With schools closed and children at home during the lockdown, women are more likely to bear a significant proportion of the burden of childcare, parenting, and homeschooling, according to WARDC. Traditional gender roles also put the responsibility for the care of sick family members on women. The opportunity cost is that while men may go back to work whenever restrictions are lifted, women can only resume work when/if no one is sick in their families and schools reopen. This situation creates a loss of income, which furthers gender inequality and domestic abuse. Similarly, the amount of domestic work done by women—cooking, washing, and general housekeeping—has remarkably increased the burden of unpaid care work, thereby putting additional mental and physical stress on women. The pandemic's impact is perhaps more severe on single mothers because they have to provide care and may not have an additional income during the COVID-19 epidemic.

The COVID-19 pandemic exacerbates lingering problems of lack of access to water, sanitation, and hygiene (WASH); health services; disrupted livelihoods; and increased family-based violence—all of which, though affecting all people, have more significant consequences for women and girls. Women's maternal and sexual reproductive health needs and rights are at risk of being deprioritized during the COVID-19 lockdown, as the situation hinders their access to pre- and postnatal care.[6] Availability of safe water, sanitation, and waste management and hygienic conditions are essential for preventing the spread of COVID-19 and staying healthy. The Nigerian government's effort to improve community-based WASH facilities and waste management services and running water in households has been mostly ineffective, as millions of families are not served.

Moreover, the distribution of government COVID-19 relief (funds and food), which presumably targets the poor, is marred by corruption and politicization of the process, according to WARDC. Consequently, those at greater risk for hunger and disease remain underserved. In some states, residents state they were either unaware of such government programs or that the relief items were diverted by politicians who distributed them to their constituencies or family members.

A report by WARDC further shows the impact of COVID-19 among disadvantaged women. The report includes information on the different needs, capacities, and coping strategies of women, men, boys, and girls during a humanitarian medical emergency such as COVID-19.[7] According to the report, promoting transparency and accountability in government institutions is critical for the effective implementation of gender equality and service delivery. Women are often more dependent on essential services, such as health care, education, water, and sanitation, because of their domestic roles. Thus, corruption in essential services creates disproportionate access and negative consequences including sexual abuse for women and girls. According to one study, the girls and women most frequently sexually abused were female respondents from the Federal Capital Territory (FCT), Abuja (58.8%), Kaduna State (47.2%), and Lagos State (46.5%).[8] Female respondents in Kwara State experienced the least domestic violence (27.9%), while Kano State reported 28.4%. Among female respondents, 37.8% said they experienced sexual abuse, while 45.2% suffered domestic violence during the COVID-19 crisis.

The study revealed that about 60% of the respondents were fully engaged in childcare during the pandemic, increasing women's unpaid labor, and leading to their economic disempowerment. Additionally, accountability principles did not provide a framework for managing government services during the lockdown. There was low utilization of health care facilities during this period, which saw increased reports of mental distress. Approximately 24% of the respondents across all surveyed states said they experienced depression and feelings of hopelessness during COVID-19; 40% experienced tiredness and frustration due to the outbreak. Less than three-quarters of the respondents regularly washed their hands under running water (70.6%) or had access to materials, products, and facilities for menstrual hygiene (74%).

NIGERIAN WOMEN'S RESPONSE TO COVID-19

Since the outset of the COVID-19 epidemic, there has been an increased focus on women's leadership roles in the global response. Just as the challenges that women face are underreported, their contributions to COVID-19 responses go unacknowledged. In Nigeria, even though women were not deliberately included in government programs to contain the virus, Nigerian women have continued to organize and mobilize to provide support at different levels to alleviate social suffering. Social media offers one channel through which women organize and make their voices heard. For instance, blogs allow women to share their pandemic experiences. The lack of fairness in the distribution of government services, for example, was widely discussed in blogs. Women organized and held meetings (through Zoom and Blue-Jeans) and webinars to discuss how to contain the spread of the virus and how to support economically disadvantaged women.

WARDC conducted a series of public webinars focused on different ways that COVID-19 impacted women. Other organizations like Women's Rights Advancements and Protection Alternative (WRAPA), Women International League for Peace and Freedom, and the Women Aid Collective organized radio programs and jingles to create awareness about response mechanisms existing during the lockdown. Over 283 other women organizations across Nigeria proposed policy direction for government responses to gender-based violence. The Nigerian Women Trust Fund organized a webinar, "COVID-19 Response and Recovery: The Roles of Women Politicians," to explore women's contributions, gaps, and the need to think about gender as part of the recovery process. Members of the Federation of Muslim Women Associations, Nigeria, also hosted workshops with local leaders to advise community members and raise awareness on preventing the spread of the virus. In some states, women's groups played prominent roles in distributing food items to less privileged communities. In urban areas, women also worked to educate other women about COVID-19.

Nigerian women have built transnational coalitions with other African women's organizations. For example, the Women, Peace, and Security program hosted a webinar with its Peace and Social Change Fellowship participants that included leaders of grassroots women's organizations across Nigeria, Uganda, the Democratic Republic of Congo, Lesotho, and Sudan. Although the five participating organizations represent different political contexts in Africa, they united in expanding their approach to peacebuilding beyond armed conflicts to include common challenges in Africa, such as reproductive health, food security, and girls' and women's education. During the current global health crisis, these groups are mobilizing their communities to respond to the growing threat of COVID-19 to women and children. Their strategy offers wisdom on practical ways to care for each other, as well as reimagining societies grounded in solidarity, equity, and support systems in communities.

Another coalition of civil society organizations, under the auspices of #StateOfEmergencyGBV, emerged during the COVID-19 pandemic. Most members are part of the feminist Womanifesto WhatsApp group. This group demanded that the Nigerian government declare a state of emergency to respond to the spike in gender-based violence (GBV) during the COVID-19 outbreak. The group also organized rallies and protests and submitted a petition signed by over three hundred organizations to the Governor's Forum—a group including the governors of the thirty-six states of Nigeria—demanding that the government take immediate action to respond to GBV. Due to mounting pressure from the group, all thirty-six states' governors publicly declared GBV a national emergency. Furthermore, the National Assembly (NASS)—the Nigerian legislative body—convened three virtual meetings to address increased GBV in Nigeria. The NASS committed to supporting an increased budget for women's issues for building infrastructure across the country to respond to GBV in the post-COVID-19 era.

Organizations like Women's Aid Collectives, WARDC, Project Alert, Stand to End Rape, Initiative WRAPA, Education as a Vaccine, Mirabel Center, Dorothy Njemanze Foundation FIDA, the Women's International League for Peace and Justice, BraveHeart Initiative, CeCe Yara, Women at Risk, Action Aid Nigeria, and UN Spotlight Initiatives on Ending Violence against Women provided support for women and girls during the period of COVID-19, covering programs for prevention, protection, and responses to GBV. Some of these groups provided personal protective equipment, relief, and legal counseling and supported survivors' rehabilitation. The only women's radio station (wfm917) in Nigeria also provided free broadcasts of helplines, held several webinars, and used radio programs to create awareness of women's needs during the lockdown.

On March 24, 2020, the Nigerian government passed the economic stimulus bill to cushion the effect of COVID-19. Up to N20,000 (approximately US$50) was credited to hundreds of low-income and vulnerable households registered in the National Social Register. Then, the Central Bank of Nigeria disbursed funds to indigent citizens' accounts. A school feeding program was activated to support children from low-income households. However, because the people being served were not involved in the decision-making process, the process was fraught with a lack of transparency and accountability. Therefore, the interventions produced minimal outcomes.

CONCLUSION: POLICY OPTIONS AFTER COVID-19 IN NIGERIA

The COVID-19 pandemic has created global social and economic impacts unparalleled in human history. The disease outbreak has affected people's health, businesses, families, and the global economy and has disproportionately impacted women and the vulnerable. The coronavirus has taken a toll on Nigerian people: many have lost family members and friends, and some businesses will never reopen. Whereas the effect has led to policies that should cushion hardship for women, we must seize the opportunities that this moment provides to rebuild sustainable, inclusive, and resilient societies. The economic and social impacts of the pandemic will likely result in increased crime rates, aggression, and violence of diverse kinds. Therefore, it is essential to introduce measures that can alleviate human suffering and tackle social and economic malaise. National governments must show ingenuity by developing programs and policies that support economic growth, including boosting market interest rate reductions to ensure the financial system's highest liquidity. Governments must also prioritize and invest in programs that foster social protection and employment and guarantee access to essential services for women and other vulnerable groups during the post-COVID-19 era—and women should be part of these conversations.

*Notes*

1. Awofeso and Irabor, "Assessment of Government Response."
2. Awe, *Nigerian Women in Historical Perspective*; Abdul et al.
3. Awe, "The Role of Women."
4. Mudhai, Wright, and Musa, "Gender and Critical Media-Information Literacy."
5. Partners West Africa, Nigeria, *Impact of COVID-19 Pandemic.*
6. Women Advocates Research and Documentation Center, *Rapid Gender Analysis*; Partners West Africa, Nigeria, *Impact of COVID-19 Pandemic.*
7. Women Advocates Research and Documentation Center, *Rapid Gender Analysis.*
8. https://nigeria.actionaid.org/publications/2020/rapid-gender-analysis-impact-covid-19-households-nigeria-national-survey

## References

Abdul, M. M., Adeleke, O., Adeyeye, O., Babalola, A., Eyo, E., Ibrahim, M. T., et al. (2011). *Analysis of the History, Organisation, and Challenges of Feminism in Nigeria*. Available online at: www.nawey.net/wp-content/uploads/downloads/2012/05/Femini sm-in-Nigeria.pdf

Adegboye, Oyelola A., Adeshina I. Adekunle, and Ezra Gayawan. "Early Transmission Dynamics of Novel Coronavirus (COVID-19) in Nigeria." *International Journal of Environmental Research and Public Health* 17.9 (2020): 3054.

Aina, Olabisi Idowu, Ibiyinka Ogunlade, Oluwatoyin Olatundun Ilesanmi, and Afolabi Comfort. "Institutionalization of Gender Mainstreaming in Nigeria's Tertiary." *European Scientific Journal*, Special Issue, November 2015, 314–339.

Awe, Bolanle, ed. *Nigerian Women in Historical Perspective*. Lagos: Sankore, 1992.

Awe, Bolanle. "The Role of Women in Management in the '90s." *Journal of Management in Nigeria* 26.6 (1990): 9–13.

Awofeso, Olu, and Paul Irabor. "Assessment of Government Response to Socio-economic Impact of COVID-19 Pandemic in Nigeria." *Journal of Social and Political Sciences* 3.3 (2020): 677–686.

Ilesanmi, Oluwatoyin Olatundun. "Bridging Gender Equity Gap in Africa: A Psycho-historical Exposition of Efunsetan Aniwura." *International Journal of Psychology and Counselling* 2.3 (2010): 33–43.

Ilesanmi, Oluwatoyin Olatundun. "Gender Equity and National Development." *Journal of Applied Educational & Vocational Research* 1.1 (2006): 51–58.

Mudhai, Okoth Fred, Bianca Wright, and Aliyu Musa. "Gender and Critical Media-Information Literacy in the Digital Age: Kenya, South Africa, and Nigeria." *Journal of African Media Studies* 8.3 (2016): 267–280.

Partners West Africa, Nigeria. *Impact of COVID-19 Pandemic on Women in Nigeria: A Snapshot Study to Assess the Physical, Economic, and Social Impact of the COVID-19 Pandemic on Women in Nigeria*. 2020.

Women Advocates Research and Documentation Center. *Rapid Gender Analysis of the Impact of COVID-19 on Households in Nigeria: A National Survey*. 2020.

World Health Organization. *COVID-19 Pandemic Expands Reach in Africa*. April 2020.

World Health Organization. *State of Health in the WHO African Region*. 2018. https:// www.afro.who.int/publications/statehealth-who-african-region. Accessed April 7, 2021.

World Health Organization. *Under-Five Mortality*. 2018. https://www.who.int/gho/chi ld_health/mortality/mortality_under_five_text/en/. Accessed April 7, 2021.

# PART VI

# Not Waiting

# CHAPTER 25

# COVID-19 through an Asian American Lens

## Scapegoating, Harassment, and the Limits of the Asian American Response

*Roland Hwang*

During the COVID-19 pandemic, many have observed and written that the virus does not discriminate based on race or ethnic identity. While it is true that all of us are susceptible to the virus, it has had a disproportionate medical and social impact on racial and ethnic minorities. In the aftermath of the killing of George Floyd, Breonna Taylor, and Ahmaud Arbery, we have entered a concurrent period of examination and reflection about systemic and institutionalized racism. In addition to a public health crisis in which Black and brown people are contracting and dying from the disease with greater frequency,[1] the virus has also sparked widespread racism against people of Asian descent. I am struck by how a portion of the US population is quick to blame Asian Americans for the spread of COVID-19, playing into the "perpetual foreigner" stereotype,[2] a persistent view of Asian Americans as not quite "real" Americans. Asian Americans are presumed to be from somewhere else no matter how many generations they have been here. This scapegoating leads to a second pandemic that Asian Americans face—an epidemic of anti-Asian hate. But the othering of Asian Americans is not new. It is being choreographed and stoked by President Trump and members of his administration who call the pandemic "Chinese flu" or "Kung Flu" to pointedly stir up anti-Asian hate to activate a long history of racism.

## OTHERING THROUGHOUT HISTORY

Anti-Asian animus and violence, including the harassment and attacks stemming from the current COVID-19 pandemic, is a part of the United States' racist legacy. One only has to peruse US history to see many episodes of harassment and violence against Asians and Asian Americans, beginning as early as the 1800s. Soon after the completion of the transcontinental railroad in 1869, which was largely built off the labor of thousands of Chinese immigrants, an anti-Chinese riot sparked in Los Angeles in 1871.[3] A mob of five hundred Angelenos attacked and dragged Chinese out of their homes, and seventeen Chinese were lynched.[4] Congress passed the Chinese Exclusion Act of 1882, the first law to prevent the entry of all members from a specific ethnicity or nationality, in part, due to fear that Chinese workers were not assimilable and were bringing disease to the United States.[5] This discriminatory law left a legacy of exclusion that prevailed until its repeal in 1943. After the repeal of the Chinese Exclusion Act of 1882, only 105 Chinese immigrants were allowed into the United States until the passage of the Immigration Act of 1965. This history of immigration caps leaves Asians underrepresented in the US population; Asians comprise 60% of the world's population, yet they only comprise 6% of the US population.

Anti-Japanese sentiments reached a peak with the incarceration of 110,000 Japanese Americans in concentration camps during World War II without equal protection or due process.[6] And many Michiganders and civil rights activists recall the 1982 brutal beating and murder of Vincent Chin, a twenty-seven-year old Chinese American. The perpetrator, mistakenly thinking Vincent was Japanese, blamed him for the downturn of the US auto industry, infamously saying: "It's because of you m—— f——s we're out of work."[7] The othering of Asian Americans ebbs and flows but has been pervasive over more than a century.

For me, othering is personal. Growing up in Detroit in the 1950s, I will never forget being pulled out of a kickball circle in my elementary school playground because the teacher said, "He is a bad boy." I attribute it now to being the only Asian in the school a couple of years after the Korean War. I was often mistaken for Korean although I am ethnically Chinese. My eighth-grade shop teacher would always call me "Wing Wong" or "Ching Chong" because he was too lazy to say my name. No one else in class was derided with ethnic nicknames or called by anything but their real names. More recently, as I was on my way from the Michigan Supreme Court back to my workplace at the Department of Attorney General, a boy who looked like a high schooler in the midst of a school field trip group yelled out "Ching Chong," bringing back memories of my shop teacher. An elderly woman recently told me: "Go back to where you came from," as I entered the McNamara Federal Building in Detroit. I was born in Detroit.

It took me decades to realize these incidents were each microaggressions with macrohistories.

OTHERING NOW

President Trump repeatedly referred to the COVID-19 pandemic as the "Chinese flu," "Wuhan flu," and "Kung Flu"[8] despite advisories from the World Health Organization and the Center for Disease Control to refrain from calling diseases by an ethnic or geographic name.[9] Such phrases stoke resentment and spur people to act violently toward Asians. In February, for example, a sixteen-year-old boy in the San Fernando Valley was hospitalized after being attacked by high school bullies who accused him of having coronavirus simply because he was Asian American.[10] In March, the Cung family—including their two children, a two-year-old and a six-year-old—were attacked and stabbed at a Midland, Texas, Sam's Club by a perpetrator who thought they were Chinese and thus carrying the virus.[11] The Stop AAPI Hate Center and the media have reported many instances of Asian Americans being yelled at, spit upon, harassed, and assaulted since the onset of the pandemic.[12]

GOODWILL AS AN ASIAN AMERICAN COMMUNITY'S
FIRST RESPONSE

Goodwill on the part of the Asian American community has been a crucial way of fighting this othering. Many Asian American organizations have donated money and secured personal protection equipment, delivering thousands of masks and gowns to hospitals, nursing homes, and police departments. The Association of Chinese Americans in Detroit, for example, donated twenty-one thousand masks and one thousand gowns to forty locations, including the Detroit Police Department, the Canton Police Department, the Northville Township Police Department, and several nursing homes.[13] The Filipino American National Historical Society and We the People of Detroit procured six hundred cases of hand sanitizer to distribute to those without water in Detroit and Flint. The Philippine Association of Medical Technologists–Michigan donated money to Gleaners Community Food Bank, Capuchin Soup Kitchen, the Philippine Red Cross, and Breath of Life Foundation.[14] Through their organizations and individual generosity, Asian Americans have been part of the solution to the pandemic, though these acts of goodwill for frontline workers and first responders do not address the concurrent victimization of Asian Americans.

Diverse and broad coalition building, within and outside the Asian American community, has always been and continues to be a powerful tool. After Vincent Chin's murder in 1982, a group seated around a restaurant table formed American Citizens for Justice (ACJ) because there were no Asian American civil rights organizations to readily take up the cause of justice for Vincent.[15] That meeting blossomed into a larger movement when Asian Pacific American Advocates, at that time called Organization of Chinese Americans, joined with American Citizens for Justice. Other local organizations quickly came to the aid of ACJ. When ACJ opened up its office and had no furniture, the Anti-Defamation League Michigan donated its office furnishings. When ACJ could not get a meeting with the county prosecutor to discuss his failure to have assistant prosecutors attend the sentencing phase of a case, the Detroit Association of Black Organizations paved the way for a meeting. ACJ to this day is still involved in advocacy and civil rights education, working with the Michigan secretary of state on the census and voting access for disabled and limited-English-proficiency voters; working with Michigan United on immigrant rights; and working with Boys and Men of Color on racial inequity.

The COVID-19 pandemic demands further coalition building. Former presidential candidate Andrew Yang and Anti-Defamation League CEO Jonathan Greenblatt coauthored an article decrying anti-Asian violence and anti-Semitism.[16] Coalitions are also forming to gather data and respond to hate incidents. The Asian Pacific Policy and Planning Council, OCA, and Asian Americans Advancing Justice have created a database called Stop AAPI Hate.[17] To date, the Stop AAPI Hate database counts twenty-three hundred anti-Asian hate incidents since COVID-19 arose.[18]

## TAKEAWAYS

All of us must take action against COVID-related xenophobia. It is time to declare war against racism.[19] Individuals need to take action in response to xenophobia in the midst of the COVID-19 pandemic and beyond.[20] [21] Do not use racist or xenophobic rhetoric to refer to COVID-19. Take the opportunity to denounce anti-Asian verbiage and bigotry. In the name of bystander intervention, whenever it is safe, call out xenophobic statements. Intervene with and identify, document, and distract the perpetrator.

Know whom to contact if you see or hear something. In Michigan, the attorney general's hate crime hotline is 313-456-0200. The Michigan Department of Civil Rights tallies hate incidents that may not necessarily constitute hate crimes and can be reached at 313-456-3700.

We need to count anti-Asian hate incidents accurately and be able to take action. It is progress to have a national database that is counting anti-Asian incidents in almost real time. But counting can only do so much. It is another matter to be able to tend to victims, compensate them for their harm, file reports with the authorities, and press charges as a routine matter rather than an exception. Data gatherers must come together to find a common data criteria as the COVID-19 pandemic progresses and for all future hate crises.

We need race and ethnicity-based education. We must emphasize the fact that Asian Americans are Americans to eliminate the "perpetual foreigner" stereotype. Author Helen Zia writes that Asian Americans are "missing in history." We need to write them back in by advocating for multiethnic education. Groups like OCA–Asian American Advocates and the 1882 Project, a nonpartisan effort to address the Chinese Exclusion Laws,[22] have worked together to integrate more Asian American history content into K–12 education. While academic offerings beyond core subjects, such as ethnic studies, may be on the chopping block due to the pandemic and accompanying economic downturn, our current period of confronting systemic and institutional racism sparked by George Floyd's murder demands that we promote courses that teach about the complexities of being American in a multiethnic society. To the University of Michigan College of Literature, Science, and the Arts' credit, there is a race and ethnicity course requirement. A college-level commitment to race and ethnic studies must be sustained despite hard economic times and the federal government's absurd call for the end of diversity training at the federal level as allegedly "teaching people to hate our country."[23]

We need effective organizing for civil rights. Asian Americans still have far to go in the quest for civil rights, full societal participation, and parity with other Americans. There is power in organizing. There is a Chinese proverb that applies: a single chopstick can be easily broken, but a bundle of chopsticks cannot. In the corporate sphere, affinity groups or employee resources groups have been implemented to give people of minority groups a voice and connection. For Asian Americans, this is a step toward combating the "bamboo ceiling" and fighting for equal access to career advancement.[24] We need this type of organizing at the community, neighborhood, or grassroots level to fight for empowerment and representation.

The Asian American community needs to be organized not only at the national level, but also at the congressional, state, and local district levels. When members of Congress or other politicians make disparaging remarks against people based on their race or ethnicity, the Asian American community needs to have the capacity to collectively call them out. It is not enough to have a small number of politicians representing Asian American interests in the halls of government. There needs to be a grassroots network across the United States that has the ability to challenge xenophobic statements.

And, finally, we need Asian American unity on civil rights matters and to build coalitions beyond the Asian American community. The Asian American community is incredibly complex and diverse. On a day-to-day basis, most Asian Americans identify by their ethnic background, such as Chinese American, Korean American, Filipino American, South Asian American, and so on.[25] Asian Americans are not bound together by a common national origin, ethnicity, language, or cuisine; instead the community is bound by a commitment to seeking justice for all Asian Americans and fighting for an equal footing with all other Americans. There is a roundtable called National Council of Asian Pacific Americans that does great work, and thirty-five Asian American groups participate in the council.[26] Yet few people outside the civil rights realm have heard of the council. The Asian American community needs a bigger, more visible pulpit to raise its profile in the midst of the pandemic. It is time to unify the multitude of Asian American organizations into a more synchronous movement working in tandem with civil rights organizations to call out against the hate. Particularly in this time of COVID-19 pandemic, Asian Americans must work together and with other communities to stand up against hate.

### Notes

1. Jeff Green and Jackie Gu, "The Covid Death Rate Is Getting Worse in Majority-Black Communities," Bloomberg.com, July 13, 2020; Maria Goody and Daniel Wood, "What Do Coronavirus Disparities Look Like State By State?," NPR, May 30, 2020.

2. "What Is Perpetual Foreigner Syndrome?," Igi-global.com, https://www.igi-glo bal.com/dictionary/perpetual-foreigner-syndrome/22418, accessed April 4, 2021.

3. Sucheng Chan, *Asian Americans: An Interpretive History* (New York: Twayne Publishers, 1991), 48, 193.

4. Erika Lee, *The Making of Asian America* (New York: Simon & Schuster, 2015), 93.

5. Chan, *Asian Americans*, 53–54.

6. Angelo Ancheta, *Race, Rights and the Asian American Experience* (New Brunswick, NJ: Rutgers University Press, 2010), 30–32.

7. "It's because of you little motherfuckers that we're out of work" is the quote testified to by Racine Colwell the dancer in *United States v Michael Nitz*, No. 83-60629, (US District Court for the Eastern District of Michigan) transcript p. 226, as cited in Paula Yoo, *From a Whisper to a Rallying Cry*, New York: W.W. Norton, 2021, p 10.

8. Claire Wang, "Trump's Kung Flu Slur, Pervasive Scapegoating, Recall a Brutal Decades-Old Hate Crime," NBC News, June 23, 2020.

9. World Health Organization, "WHO Issues Best Practices for Naming New Human Infectious Diseases," May 8, 2015, https://www.who.int/publications/i/item/WHO-HSE-FOS-15

10. StopAAPIHate.com; "Bullies Attack Asian American Teen at School, Accusing Him of Having Coronavirus," CBS News, February 14, 2020.

11. "Man Accused in Sam's Club Stabbing Indicted," *Midland Reporter-Telegram*, March 30, 2020; Maria Chen, "Texas Sam's Club Stabbing of Burmese Man and Son Confirmed by FBI as Hate Crime," Next Shark, March 31, 2020; "Suspect in Sam's Club Stabbing Indicted for Attempted Capital Murder," San Angelo Live, June 19, 2020.

12. "Spit On, Yelled At, Attacked: Chinese-Americans Fear for Their Safety," *New York Times*, March 23, 2020.

13. Association of Chinese Americans, www.acadetroit.com

14. FILAMCCO newsletter, July 2020.

15. Joseph Lam, "The 1982 Killing of Vincent Chin Was the First Time Asian Americans Came Together to Fight for Justice," *South China Morning Post*, June 23, 2020.

16. Andrew Yang, "Yang & Anti-Defamation League CEO: Avoid Coronavirus Racism and Scapegoating," *USA Today*, March 20, 2020.

17. www.asianpacificpolicyandplanningcouncil.org

18. www.StopAAPIHate.com

19. Bill Hing, "Time to Declare War against Racism," *ImmigrationProfBlog*, May 29, 2020.

20. Sangsuk Sylvia Kang and Purna Kambhampaty, "I Will Not Stand Silent: 10 Asian Americans Reflect on Racism during Pandemic and the Need for Equality," *Time*, June 28, 2020.

21. Jeff Yang, "It's Time for Asian Americans to Unite in Solidarity with Black Americans," CNN, June 5, 2020.

22. 1882 Foundation Homepage, https://1882foundation.org/

23. Paul Kiernan and Andrew Restuccia, "All Federal Agencies Told to Suspend Diversity Training Programs," *Wall Street Journal*, October 4, 2020.

24. Liyan Chen, "How Asian Americans Break the Bamboo Ceiling," *Forbes*, January 20, 2016.

25. Rinku Sen, "How to Organize Asian Americans–Notes from Two Generations," Reappropriate, June 2020.

26. National Council of Asian Pacific Americans, www.ncapaonline.org

# CHAPTER 26

# The High Stakes of Blame

## Medieval Parallels to a Modern Crisis

*David Patterson*

In 589 CE, a devastating flood of the Tiber River at Rome was quickly followed by an outbreak of bubonic plague.[1] The disease killed a countless multitude, including the pope, and contemporary observers understandably sought to rationalize the catastrophe. What had caused it, and just as importantly, who was to blame? In the end, they blamed themselves: penitential processions were promptly organized, designed to cleanse the populace of sin. As the legend evolved in the later Middle Ages, it gained a miraculous conclusion. According to the *Legenda aurea*, the affair ended when the people of Rome—led in procession by Gregory the Great—witnessed the archangel Michael standing atop the eponymous Castel Sant'Angelo, sheathing a bloody sword.[2] The message was clear: God had been satisfied by collective penance, and therefore ended the bloodshed.[3] In the era of COVID-19, medieval historians can't help but be struck by the continued resonance of premodern responses to natural disasters. Like our medieval forebears, our first instinct in a time of crisis is to find somewhere to affix blame, to discover a culprit so that a remedy can be prepared. This is perhaps understandable, but history suggests that assigning blame can be a tricky and even dangerous thing.

When confronted with seemingly inexplicable natural disasters like floods and plagues, medieval people turned to some usual suspects. Sometimes they were prepared, like the admirable Romans of 589, to blame themselves—to seek remedies for their own faults and sins. This kind of self-evaluation could be individual or, as seems to have been the case in sixth-century Rome, collective: in other words, what have *we* as a community done to deserve this? In the grips of the COVID-19 pandemic, such soul-searching has touched many of us. We are able to know a great deal more about the virus afflicting us than medieval Romans were able to know about the bubonic plague; yet strikingly, the urge to self-blame often remains acute. "I gave this to my dad," was the heart-wrenching comment of one man, who (unaware) transmitted a fatal infection to his elderly father.[4] If science has expanded our understanding of the microscopic culprit, it has not let humanity off the hook.

On a collective level, such soul-searching can take the form of scolding: we keep an eye on members of our community, noting with exasperation the too-close conversations in grocery stores, the unmasked individuals in our public spaces, the small holiday gatherings of friends and family that offend our better judgment. This sort of self-criticism, whether individual or collective, can take a heavy psychological toll. Yet, lacking unanimity, it is far from cathartic, and offers no prospect of relief or of ending the pandemic. No vision of St. Michael will appear to sheath a dripping sword. We must ask ourselves what we are doing when, like the Romans of 589, we tell ourselves that we are to blame for our own predicament.

Introspective self-blame is not always palatable, so it is not surprising that in many cases medieval people were quite ready to blame others. When the Black Death began its terrifying march across southern France in 1348, some Christians—suspicious of the "Other" that lived in their midst—blamed local Jewish communities. Vicious persecutions ensued, a prelude to the horrific anti-Semitic massacres that tracked the Black Death like an ancillary plague across fourteenth-century Europe.[5] While this magnitude of hate and violence based on groundless accusations is thankfully absent today, a substantial increase in anti-Asian hate crimes has been reported in 2020.[6] An online database for reporting anti-Asian discrimination in the United States recorded 673 incidents within its first week of operation in March.[7] In subtler ways, too, the urge to blame "outsiders" still haunts us. When the International Committee on Taxonomy of Viruses (ICTV) chose "COVID-19" as the name for the new disease, it followed guidelines developed to prevent the sort of geographic stigma that attached to some previous pandemics.[8] ("Spanish flu," it turns out, was first reported in Kansas.) Yet in his stubborn refusal to use the proper medical term, Donald Trump has gleefully encouraged precisely the sort of geographic blame-game the ICTV sought to avoid. The phrase "China virus" (and the still more vulgar "Kung Flu") seem calculated to externalize and racialize the threat. Similarly, the administration's trumpeting of its border closures handily ignores the fact that by the end of January (when the earliest closures came into effect) Americans were already spreading the virus among themselves quite effectively.[9]

In Italy, where grievous infection and mortality rates during the spring gave way to a more stable situation by summer, the return of around nine hundred migrant workers (who had gone home to celebrate the Islamic holiday of Eid) caused popular uproar and was blamed for a new "spike" in infec-

338    BEING HUMAN DURING COVID

tions. For one Italian newspaper, the focus of the story became the migrants'
lack of fixed address and their alleged dishonesty in dealing with contact
tracers.[10] In parts of Canada where case numbers have remained low, some
have expressed their desire to keep it that way by vandalizing cars with nonlo-
cal license plates.[11] Unlike the horrific pogroms that accompanied the Black
Death, or the anti-Asian violence and discrimination that has plagued the
US, some level of suspicion toward outsiders may seem relatively harmless,
even rational in the midst of a pandemic. But we should always be on guard
against the urge to search for "strangers" in our midst, those onto whom we
might transfer blame.

In the Middle Ages, blame was sometimes transferred upward rather than
outward. The behavior of rulers, whose intimate connection with God meant
that their every action reverberated through Creation, could cause disorder
and upheaval in the cosmos, and thus the natural world. A bad king could
cause bad weather, poor harvests, and even plague.[12] In medieval Europe—
whose populations seldom had recourse against poor government—a concept linking earthly kingship with cosmic implications offered a critical tool
for influencing otherwise unreachable rulers. A calamitous flood or epidemic could be a sign that God disapproved of the conduct of the powerful—an especially dangerous sign because it was broadcast to all through the
medium of nature.[13] Maybe this is why royal chroniclers sometimes omitted
plagues and other calamities from their official histories.[14]

A similar impulse might lie behind the efforts of some contemporary
leaders to downplay COVID-19, deflecting blame from themselves through
misleading statements and prevarications that end up hindering effective
management of the pandemic. In early March 2020, Donald Trump infamously declared that the coronavirus pandemic was a "hoax," later clarify-
ing that he meant his opponents' critiques were, rather than the virus itself.
Later that month, sounder judgment seemed to prevail when he announced
that the United States could slow the spread of COVID-19 with fifteen days
of social distancing.[15] In the weeks and months since, the disorienting messages have proceeded fast and furious: in early April, a bizarre triumphal-
ist narrative emerged, in which other countries were "jealous" of America's
excellent coronavirus response and testing record; later in the month, calls
to "liberate" states that were scrupulously following the federal government's
own coronavirus management guidelines; and in mid-November, a multina-
tional pharmaceutical corporation's announcement about the efficacy of an
experimental immunization became a "Vaccine WIN" for President Trump.[16]
When leaders spread misinformation in the midst of a pandemic, they hin-

der effective responses both within their own governments and among citizens. While some of the president's mistruths (such as claiming credit for the Pfizer vaccine) merely induce eye rolling, others have actively caused harm. His statements have contributed to anti-lockdown protests in states experiencing severe outbreaks, and a cavalier attitude toward the administration's own public health guidelines have turned White House functions into "superspreader" events.[17]

Other countries have also witnessed dishonest and ineffective leadership in the face of the pandemic. In late March, Brazilian president Jair Bolsonaro proclaimed that lockdowns and other drastic measures were unnecessary because hydroxychloroquine—an antimalarial drug also touted by President Trump—would be a miracle cure. Despite the celebratory tone of this pronouncement, the situation in Brazil steadily slid into catastrophe (and some trials have since hinted that hydroxychloroquine may actually be harmful).[18] By mid-December, the country had recorded more than seven million cases and 184,827 deaths, even as Bolsanaro chided Brazilians for being "sissies" (*maricos*, a homophobic term) in the face of the pandemic.[19] In China, too, what is allowed to be known about the circulation of the virus aligns suspiciously with the interests of the ruling party, so that in late October it was in Xinjiang province—among a Muslim-minority population targeted by a campaign of violence and intimidation—that a regional outbreak was reported and, of course, promptly contained.[20] The incident allowed the Chinese government to blame a harassed and allegedly "diseased" minority for a new COVID outbreak, while demonstrating the efficacy and power of the state in bringing it under control.

In such cases the behavior of a virus is made a proxy of governmental competence: nature is supposed to reflect the excellence of ruling authorities. In the Middle Ages, this was a double-edged sword; if an orderly natural world indicated upright rule, then out-of-control natural disasters could reflect the opposite. We moderns, too, are capable of blaming governments for natural disasters, and not without justification.[21] In the harsh light of COVID-19, the citizens of many countries have new reasons to scrutinize their leaders. As in the Middle Ages, a natural crisis thought to be exacerbated by poor governance can be a useful indictment of the powerful. Where democracy prevails, electors can respond suitably. We cannot hope to restore cosmic order by choosing a new king, but we can at least address some of the wrongs perpetrated by a bad one.

The medieval theory of cosmic kingship, by perceiving intimate links between rulers and the natural world, focused blame on the great and the powerful. Today, particularly when it comes to COVID-19, we know that very *small* things matter, too. Utterly oblivious to politics, the submicroscopic virions of SARS-CoV-2 will spread with relentless efficiency given any opportunity. How much of the blame, then, can we apportion to nature itself, to inscrutable forces beyond our control? In the Middle Ages, calamities were sometimes attributed to shadowy natural processes, to strange movements of heaven and earth. Epidemics could arise from "corruptions of the air" that occurred mysteriously and spread illness over great distances. Among the causes of corrupt air were decaying matter, malign conjunctions of the planets, and earthquakes that released unhealthy vapors from the depths.[22] Such proto-scientific explanations coexisted with theological ones. A corruption of the air could just as easily arise from decaying morals as from decaying matter, and even mechanistic processes like the revolution of the planets were thought to have been originally set in motion by God, so that malign events occurred with (at least passive) divine sanction.

We may look askance at medieval people's attempts to explain their natural world, but we should bear in mind that our own knowledge is incomplete and ever evolving. When we blame an epidemic on natural processes that are still incompletely understood, we risk simplifying a complex web of relationships. Well before the advent of COVID-19, epidemiologists were warning that increased human encroachment into the remaining habitat of other organisms might risk the spread of zoonotic diseases, those that jump from animal to human hosts.[23] Factory farming, the live animal trade, and even climate change have all been implicated in shifting global patterns of disease. A pandemic cannot be separated from the larger ecological crises we face, and we may be justified in feeling, like some medieval commentators, that our cosmos is rather out of whack. Though we no longer blame corrupted air for epidemiological misfortunes, we continue to possess a very imperfect understanding of the complex ways diseases evolve and spread in and between animal and human populations. If we decide to blame natural processes for the present crisis, we should be humbled by the continued mystery of the world around us; by both its fragility and its potency, its ability to harm us.[24]

Of course, it would be simplistic to blame any single culprit for our current predicament. Apportioning blame is always fraught with risks of oversimplification or unfairness. Yet it isn't always fruitless when approached thoughtfully; our medieval examples show that to ponder guilt and blame is to hold a place for hope as well. When we blame ourselves, we hope to do better. When we ignorantly blame "outsiders," we expose a time-worn human urge to define "us-ness" and "other-ness," one that can with effort be resisted, and maybe even overcome. When we examine the culpability of leaders and political institutions, we join a long and healthy tradition of critiquing power. If we are so lucky, we can even oust those who have mishandled the crisis, or at least pressure them to do better. When we attribute blame to natural processes, we can seek to understand them more clearly in all their complexity. Approached without malice or ignorance, blame can be about hope as much as lamentation and flagellation, of selves and others. The archangel Michael may not appear to us, bloody sword in hand, but lately an even more miraculous vision has appeared: nurses wielding vaccines. At some point, perhaps blame can give way to hope.

### Notes

1. An allegedly eyewitness account of the flooding, plague, and procession is offered in Gregory of Tours, *Decem libri historiarum* 10.1, ed. B. Krusch and W. Levison, Monumenta Germaniae Historica [MGH] (Hannover: Hahn, 1951), 477.

2. Jacobus de Voragine, *Legenda aurea*, vol. 1, ed. G. Maggioni (Florence: SISMEL Edizioni del Galluzzo, 1998), 288.

3. Paolo Squatriti, "The Floods of 589 and Climate Change at the Beginning of the Middle Ages: An Italian Microhistory," *Speculum* 85.4 (2010): 799–826; David J. Patterson, "*Adversus paganos*: Disaster, Dragons, and Episcopal Authority in Gregory of Tours," *Comitatus* 44.1 (2013): 1–28.

4. Jon Schuppe, "'I Gave This to My Dad': COVID-19 Survivors Grapple with Guilt of Infecting Family," NBC News, May 16, 2020, https://www.nbcnews.com/news/us-ne ws/i-gave-my-dad-covid-19-survivors-grapple-guilt-infecting-n1207921

5. Samuel K. Cohn Jr., "The Black Death and the Burning of the Jews," *Past and Present* 196.1 (2007): 3–36.

6. Angela Grover et al., "Anti-Asian Hate Crime during the COVID-19 Pandemic: Exploring the Reproduction of Inequality," *American Journal of Criminal Justice* 45.4 (2020): 647–667.

7. Francesca Duong, "Disarming Racism: Students, Staff and Faculty Lead Multiple Efforts to Combat Anti-Asian Hate," *Michigan Daily*, May 20, 2020, https://www .michigandaily.com/section/campus-life/disarming-racism-students-staff-and-facul ty-lead-multiple-efforts-combat-anti

8. World Health Organization, "Best Practices for the Naming of New Human Infectious Diseases," May 15, 2015, https://www.who.int/publications/i/item/WHO-HSE -FOS-15

9. Sridhar Basavaraju et al., "Serologic Testing of US Blood Donations to Identify SARS-CoV-2-Reactive Antibodies: December 2019–January 2020," *Clinical Infectious Diseases*, November 30, 2020, https://doi.org/10.1093/cid/ciaa1785

10. Carlo Picozza and Fabio Tonacci, "Coronavirus, è allerta a Roma per 900 bengalesi rientrati da Dacca," *La Repubblica*, July 10, 2020, https://www.repubblica.it/cronaca/2020/07/10/news/coronavirus_quei_voli_dal_bangladesh_che_fanno_torna re_la_paura_a_roma-261524905/

11. Sophia Harris, "Canadian Drivers with U.S. Licence Plates Harassed by Fellow Canadians," CBC News, July 3, 2020, https://www.cbc.ca/news/business/canada-u-s -border-harassment-u-s-license-plates-banff-1.5634534

12. These dire consequences of misrule were spelled out explicitly at the Council of Paris in 829 CE (2.2, ed. Werminghoff, 669) and elsewhere.

13. It was in this spirit that the ninth-century Frankish historian Nithard concluded his account of the wars between Charlemagne's grandsons (*Historiarum* 4.7) with a lament about *natural* (rather than political) disorder, since for him they were the same thing: in the days of Charlemagne, nature had been harmonious, "But now, the elements everywhere are turned against all things."

14. Jean-Pierre Devroey, *La nature et le roi: Environnement, pouvoir et société à l'âge de Charlemagne, 740–820* (Paris: Albin Michel Littérature, 2019), 255ff. Cf. Thomas Wozniak, *Naturereignisse im frühen Mittelalter* (Berlin: De Gruyter, 2020), who points out that chroniclers sometimes recorded natural phenomena meticulously, even when no moral transgression was apparent; one never knew for sure, and perhaps later observers would be able to put two and two together.

15. Daniel Strauss and Oliver Laughland, "Trump Calls Coronavirus Criticism Democrats' 'New Hoax' and Links It to Immigration," *The Guardian*, February 29, 2020, https://www.theguardian.com/us-news/2020/feb/28/trump-calls-coronavirus -outbreak-a-hoax-and-links-it-to-immigration-at-rally; "15 Days to Slow the Spread": https://www.whitehouse.gov/articles/15-days-slow-spread/

16. Michael Shear and Sarah Mervosh, "Trump Encourages Protest against Governors Who Have Imposed Virus Restrictions," *New York Times*, April 17, 2020, https:// www.nytimes.com/2020/04/17/us/politics/trump-coronavirus-governors.html; Laurie McGinley et al., "Trump Rails against 'Medical Deep State' after Pfizer Vaccine News Comes after Election Day," *Washington Post*, November 11, 2020, https://www.wa shingtonpost.com/politics/2020/11/11/trump-angry-about-pfizer-vaccine/

17. "White House Hosted Covid 'Superspreader' Event, Says Dr Fauci," BBC News, October 10, 2020, https://www.bbc.com/news/election-us-2020-54487154

18. Ernesto Londoño and Mariana Simões, "Brazil President Embraces Unproven 'Cure' as Pandemic Surges," *New York Times*, June 13, 2020, https://www.nytimes.com /2020/06/13/world/americas/virus-brazil-bolsonaro-chloroquine.html; Joshua Geleris et al., "Observational Study of Hydroxychloroquine in Hospitalized Patients with Covid-19," *New England Journal of Medicine* 382.25 (June 2020): 2411–2418; cf. Samia Arshad et al., "Treatment with Hydroxychloroquine, Azithromycin, and Combination in Patients Hospitalized with COVID-19," *International Journal of Infectious Diseases*, July 2020, https://doi.org/10.1016/j.ijid.2020.06.099, a recent large study in Michigan that did show significant benefits of hydroxychloroquine, illustrating that scientific uncertainty also surrounds the treatment of COVID-19.

19. Antonia Noori Farzan and Miriam Berger, "Bolsonaro Says Brazilians Must Not Be 'Sissies' about Coronavirus, as 'All of Us Are Going to Die One Day,'" *Washington Post*, November 11, 2020, https://www.washingtonpost.com/world/2020/11/11/bolso naro-coronavirus-brazil-quotes/. Statistics are from the World Health Organization (available at https://covid19.who.int/).

20. "Covid-19: China Tests Entire City of Kashgar in Xinjiang," BBC News, October 26, 2020, https://www.bbc.com/news/world-asia-54504785

21. Ted Steinberg, *Acts of God: The Unnatural History of Natural Disasters in America* (New York: Oxford University Press, 2000), showed that even seemingly random and transitory "acts of God" like hurricanes can be political (rather than "natural") disasters, and that Amartya Sen's insight (based on a study of the Bengali famine of 1943) about the socially unequal effects of natural disasters has many American applications.

22. See, for example, Albertus Magnus, *On the Causes and Properties of the Elements*, trans. Irven Resnick (Milwaukee, WI: Marquette University Press, 2010), 110.

23. R. S. Ostfeld, "Biodiversity Loss and the Rise of Zoonotic Pathogens," *Clinical Microbiology and Infection* 15.1 (2009): 40–43.

24. In the social sciences, a "material turn" has lately drawn attention to the ways in which nonhuman *things* can exhibit agency, playing important roles in human social and cultural systems. On the benefits of such an approach, see Ted Steinberg, "Down to Earth: Nature, Agency, and Power in History," *American Historical Review* 107.3 (2002): 798–820.

# CHAPTER 27

# Unmuting Voices in a Pandemic

## Linguistic Profiling in a Moment of Crisis

*Nicholas Henriksen and Matthew Neubacher*

### WHAT THE WAY WE FORM OUR WORDS REVEALS ABOUT US

In August 2020, Pew Research predicted that more than half of elementary and high-school students would attend class virtually in the fall due to the pandemic, and this is only part of the picture. With workplaces, classrooms, and health care visits all pushed online, our voices have quickly become more important than ever. This rapid shift to remote communication has reduced attention to nonvocal communicative cues while simultaneously increasing the salience of the vocal elements of conversation. Poor audio quality caused by unstable internet connections or lack of webcam access can compound this issue because people must then rely more on the sound of their voice to carry their input. Since the digital divide disproportionately affects minority and rural communities, these groups now have more difficulty communicating and being heard. The result is that we find ourselves in a pivotal moment to recognize voice-dependent discrimination, known as "linguistic profiling," and to reflect on the harm that existing discrepancies in internet access produce when coupled with underlying prejudices that perpetuate inequalities in everyday life.

In any language community, speakers' accent, pronunciation, word choice, and other linguistic features (e.g., hesitations, intonation, volume) all convey social information about them, including their geographic origin, race, ethnicity, gender, and/or socioeconomic background. These quick judgments can be innocuous, such as inferring that your coworker is from the Midwest when they ask for a "pop" instead of "soda." But what happens when these linguistic clues link to stereotypes and prejudices? In such situations, the assumptions made about the way a person speaks can translate into negative assumptions about the person themselves—this is linguistic profiling.

As we navigate the continuing waves of COVID-19, it is unlikely that we will be back to face-to-face meetings anytime soon. We must thus ask ourselves: how are biases toward minority communities emphasized differently when professional communication is pushed onto virtual platforms, and are we able to delink internal bias from the content of what a speaker is telling us?

In this essay, I will provide an overview of the vast topic of linguistic profiling using current examples from the United States and will show how the pandemic may make instances of such discrimination more prevalent. In highlighting this, I aim to contextualize linguistic profiling within the long histories of inequity against minorities in the United States. Then, based on my own scholarship on the also-profiled Andalusian Spanish dialect, I demonstrate how the present crisis makes these deeply entrenched biases more obvious and offers an opportunity to create more inclusive practices.

## WHAT IS LINGUISTIC PROFILING?

Making assumptions based on speech is an integral and often positive part of communication, but when this leads to stereotyping and discrimination, those assumptions can create harm and make communication difficult for many speakers. Just as racial profiling uses people's appearance to assume their race and activate social stereotypes, linguistic profiling uses language to assume characteristics about a speaker.[1] By using auditory cues that might identify which race, ethnicity, or linguistic subgroup a speaker belongs to, listeners unintentionally activate implicit biases they hold regarding these groups, thereby leading to inequitable treatment.

Beyond this, the effects of linguistic profiling intersect with other types of bias relating to social identity. In a study by Kelly Wright,[2] housing applicants speaking African American Language (AAL)[3] or Southern American English (SAE) were less likely to be offered access to housing in the United States than speakers of mainstream US English, even when the applicants had only communicated via phone. Notably, the effect was greater for AAL speakers than for speakers of SAE, who are predominantly white.[4] A recent publication by a research team from the University of Michigan[5] reviews empirical outcomes documenting such inequalities due to language perceptions across multiple social spheres—education, employment, media, justice systems, housing markets, and health care institutions.

Of course, these issues are further complicated due to the complex history and social contexts surrounding the use of minority languages. In the case of the United States, the shadow of slavery, widespread Jim Crow policies, and centuries of structural racism provide a backdrop for many of the current race- and class-based struggles manifesting in the present time of unrest and exacerbated inequality. The resulting power dynamics, which taint our relationship with language and which position language itself as a structural element maintaining racial logics, allow for implicit bias to discredit the voices of linguistic subgroups and deny equal treatment. In the trial following the murder of Trayvon Martin in Florida, for example, Martin's friend and key witness, Rachel Jeantel, testified using AAL. Following the trial, one of the jurors reported that Jeantel was "hard to understand," with another stating that "her testimony played no role whatsoever in their decision."[6] Though she provided crucial details to the jury, having been on the phone with Martin at the time of his death, Jeantel's testimony was largely ignored during the jury's deliberations due to their unfamiliarity with Jeantel's speech patterns.[7] This is not a one-off: throughout judicial and nonjudicial environments, marginalized language varieties are often misheard, misjudged, or ignored altogether, creating an unjust power structure of language that promotes discrimination. These situations create opportunities for implicit bias to manifest and ignore underrepresented voices.

To avoid the dangers of such inequality, many speakers of marginalized dialects "code-switch" to sound like the group with more social power. Code switching describes the process of alternating between two or more languages or dialects in day-to-day life. This phenomenon is so commonplace and well understood that it is actually the premise for a popular film: in the hit movie *Sorry to Bother You*, a Black telemarketer has trouble connecting with his clients until an older operator advises him to "use his white voice." Code switching is one example of many unfair adjustments minorities make to better fit into a white-dominated culture. These problems, and the choice of whether to code-switch (if able), are intensified by COVID-19 for students and professionals alike who now rely more on their voices than ever for daily communication. However, code switching is a double-edged sword, as doing so ends up strengthening the positive associations of the prestigious dialect without legitimizing the use of the marginalized dialect in such a setting. These associations are also strengthened by the expectations of those in power. Some teachers demand the reproduction of accent-less speech from second-language students, including many Latinx youth in the United States. As a result, learners are internalizing the idea that accented English is not acceptable in any situation.[8]

In effect, linguistic profiling both reinforces and perpetuates existing prejudices and social inequalities, often hurting ethnic minorities, immigrants, and other cultural subgroups such as younger speakers or members of the LGBTQ+ community. In a period of widening social inequality, the existence of and potential increase in linguistic profiling can be especially harmful.

## LINGUISTIC BIAS AND SOCIAL JUSTICE IN 2020

Coinciding with the intensified struggle with linguistic prejudice and the litany of other issues brought on by the pandemic has been a moment of cultural reckoning about anti-Black racism. The Black Lives Matter movement has origins tied to the history of anti-Black prejudice, including linguistic prejudice. Founded in 2013 following the acquittal of Trayvon Martin's killer, Black Lives Matter aims to acknowledge the presence of systemic racism and protest the ways that anti-Black bias continues to undermine human rights, especially in the form of extrajudicial killings. Through this combined context, discussions about linguistic profiling are especially relevant and help us better understand the many ways the pandemic will change our means of communication and the judgments we make about one other.

Yet it remains impossible to determine how the intersection of the pandemic and the Black Lives Matter movement will change the way that marginalized voices are treated in the United States and abroad. The movement has greatly emphasized the role of implicit bias in widening social inequalities. Will the ongoing campaigns usher in new civil rights laws that pay legal attention to linguistic profiling? How might the role of language in the judicial system change as legal proceedings are conducted remotely, when the very existence of linguistic profiling is often denied by lawyers and police? With schools adjusting to remote and hybrid setups, how might students be treated differently when they rely more heavily on their voices to relay information or ask questions?

As we move forward in our new world of remote interaction, it is imperative that we answer such questions by understanding how linguistic profiling occurs and acknowledging implicit biases. Specifically, it will become necessary to make linguistic profiling a sustained part of the ongoing conversation about race. We must also deconstruct harmful patterns during communication, both by listening more closely to the content of *what* our interlocutors say rather than *how* they are saying it, and by normalizing other's speech through exposure and deliberate learning efforts. For example, a recent publication on bias against AAL in the transcriptions of white and some Black court reporters speaks to the importance of deliberate inclusion of marginalized speech varieties in professional training.[9] This type of training fosters familiarity for non-AAL speakers as well as destigmatization both at the internal (among AAL speakers) and external (among non-AAL speakers) levels.

## UNMUTING VOICES IN A PANDEMIC

Early in the pandemic, the Pew Research Center found that 53% of Americans believed that the internet was essential to them during the viral outbreak.[10] Their results also reveal deeper inequities: across both urban and rural areas of the United States, one-third of parents say their children rely on their cell phones to finish schoolwork due to a lack of computer access at home, a statistic that rises to 43% for lower-income parents. The same survey found that 40% of low-income parents believe their children will need to seek out public Wi-Fi to finish assignments, compared to 22% overall.[10] With both disease spread and unemployment disproportionately affecting lower-income and minority communities, reliance on strong internet access is only further weakening these communities' abilities to support themselves. The compounding effects of inadequate internet access or devices with the higher digital literacy demanded by online schools create difficult learning environments for thousands of students, especially children who do not natively speak English but are expected to learn the language with limited in-person interaction.[11] The same is true for minorities seeking medical treatment— not only are African Americans already less likely to receive quality treatment from doctors,[12] but those with poor internet access are now less able to access telemedicine services that make health care safer during the pandemic.

These technological inequities represent another intersection of linguistic prejudice with existing disparities. Therefore, conducting research into the speech cues that prime stereotypes will contribute to honest discussions of the systemic biases that are inextricably linked with nonstandard speech. Scholars in linguistics are well positioned to combine empirical findings and humanistic insights in ways that can influence social and policy change. Craft et al. (2020) highlight the importance of linguistics especially in driving some of these shifts:

> Because it is not widely believed that language is a signal of who we are, where our roots lie, or who the people are that we think of as ours, it also is not common to believe that discrimination based on language is akin to

discrimination based on identity, history, regionality, or community. This is one area in which linguists have a special role to play in the societies in which we live because we are the professionals who know these orientations to be inaccurate, and we have the skills and tools to explain how and why. (402)

It will be difficult, nonetheless, to find direct evidence for whether linguistic profiling has increased during the pandemic, especially because many people fail to acknowledge their biases or otherwise mask them. However, with the pandemic already exacerbating existing inequalities and the transition online making the sound of our voices more relevant, the conditions are ripe for more instances of linguistic profiling. I therefore encourage speakers of all language varieties to consider the situations where such bias may occur and do the work to address these forms of discrimination.

My scholarship on Andalusian Spanish offers one example of how this can happen. Although the distinction is regional rather than racial, Andalusia offers parallel examples to the United States in its demonstration of how language plays a role in propagating social inequalities. For many Andalusians, the most salient feature that sets them apart from other Spaniards is their dialect, in a similar vein that linguistic profiling in the United States often involves ethnic or regional biases deduced from judgments about speech. By understanding which linguistic elements comprise the Andalusian dialect and contribute to Andalusian identity, we can better identify instances of linguistic profiling and give legitimacy to the accent. As our digital future pushes us to rely more heavily on voices in our communications, now is the time to reflect seriously on this point.

## AN OCEAN AWAY, SIMILAR SENTIMENTS PREVAIL

Andalusia is an autonomous region in southern Spain that includes well-known cities such as Granada, Málaga, and its capital, Seville (see Figures 1 and 2). It is the most populous autonomous region of the country, governing over eight million people, and represents a contemporary vacation spot for travelers from Northern Europe. Many signature cultural icons come from Andalusia, including visual artists such as Pablo Picasso and Diego Velázquez, and poets and playwrights such as Luis de Góngora, Gustavo Becquer, and Federico García Lorca. Prior to the fifteenth century, large areas within Andalusia were ruled by North African Moors, whose legacy continues to influence local culture, particularly in some of the regional vocabulary

Figure 27.1. Andalusia is located in southern Spain. Graphic: Abby Olsen.

Figure 27.2. The eight provinces of Andalusia. Graphic: Abby Olsen.

and surviving architecture. Economically, Andalusia's rural landscape yields large exports of wine, pork, and olive oil. However, this agriculture-based commerce results in a lack of major industrial urban centers that are more common to northern Spain. Additionally, after decades-long repression and population decimation during Francisco Franco's dictatorship (Andalusia was a bastion of many anti-Franco communist and anarchist parties), weak upward mobility continues to hold back southern households from achieving higher incomes.[13]

Andalusia is not a linguistically homogeneous region. The southern provinces have variable use of *seseo* versus *ceceo* (i.e., the use of either the "s" or "th" sounds to pronounce the letters "s," "c," and "z"), in addition to various ways of producing the "ch" and "sh" sounds in words like *muchacho* 'boy' or *chorizo* 'sausage.' Furthermore, the core elements of Andalusian speech, such as eliminating the "s" at the end of words, actually represent an advanced development of Castilian Spanish, along with other linguistic innovations. Yet, due to its unconformity with Castilian Spanish, which is the prestige variety, Andalusian Spanish speakers enjoy less social value than normative speakers and are often treated as speaking an improper, poorly educated form of Spanish, which can negatively impact speakers' self-esteem and self-efficacy.[14] This is in part because the norm for what Castilian Spanish should look and sound like is established by the government agency Real Academia Española. Foreign books are typically translated into normative Castilian Spanish, even in places where a regional dialect has enough common prestige to merit a local translation of unique words or phrases. Overall, the lack of recognition of Andalusian Spanish as a valid accent continues to propagate stereotypes and harm the self-esteem of its speakers.

In addition, Andalusian speakers commonly face a variety of stereotypes attributed to the region; they can be stereotyped as lazy, unproductive, unprofessional, and self-interested.[15] While some depictions of the region show a lively and expressive populace, the imagery is also of a Spain that is rural, local, traditional, and religious, with the impression that it is less developed than the northern half of the country.[16] In many cases, readers of books or viewers of films are not explicitly told a scene is set in Andalusia; rather, the social context is made obvious through the use of the Andalusian accents by local characters.

The economic consequences of the pandemic have only heightened the social inequalities felt by Andalusians. Tourism accounts for 14% of the region's GDP, and the slowing of travel has contributed to layoffs that have affected over a quarter of the region's workers, the worst in mainland Spain.[17] Thousands of jobs in Andalusia are at risk, as myriad European countries issue stern travel warnings or require visitors returning from Spain to quarantine. In a direct parallel, the economic impact of the shutdown in the United States has also disproportionately affected minority communities: people of color are less likely to be able to telework, more likely to work in essential positions that leave them vulnerable to infection, and also more likely to work in low-wage industries that are experiencing record layoffs. Amid these challenges faced by the speakers of minority dialects, language-based stereotypes may seem minor in comparison; however, by judging speakers preemptively, their learning, employment, health care, and other needs are affected during a time of crisis. As we navigate the continuing waves of COVID-19 and remain in a remote environment, we need to give ourselves extra checks to ensure that we are not relying on bias when talking with interlocutors of different dialects or accents.

## THE ROLE OF ACADEMICS IN ADDRESSING LINGUISTIC BIAS

Now more than ever, the pandemic and the Black Lives Matter movement show how language prejudice further widens social gaps. This sentiment is echoed in Craft et al. (2020): "Linguists bear the greatest responsibility to examine not only how language functions as an object of study but also how that object interfaces with the systems our societies create" (402).[18] Since moving to remote research and teaching in March 2020, I have reflected on how I can translate my research and teaching into a form of activism in the context of current events. Essentially, across professions and specializations, there is room for everyone to meaningfully consider the implications of our work and to open space for innovation.

For my students, class discussions surrounding Andalusian speech open the door to specific conversations about what speech elements prompt stereotypes. These conversations, in my view, are essential for deconstructing the stigmas attached to marginalized varieties. To offer one example of how this has happened, in June 2020 my students and I collaborated on a project to explore the depth of linguistic stereotypes in Andalusia across Spain. In a seminar entitled "Do You Speak Andalusian?," We developed a survey about language attitudes toward Andalusian Spanish. There were two parts to our survey: first, dialect identification, and second, attribute ratings. In the first phase of the survey, we asked the participants to identify the region of Spain most associated with the pronunciation that they heard in the stimulus. The respondents overwhelmingly labeled the Andalusian pronunciations as belonging to Andalusia, showing that the dialect is easily and immediately identifiable.

In the second phase of the survey, we assessed the attitudes the listeners had toward the pronunciation of each stimulus. Our preliminary findings reveal that after hearing just one word or phrase from a speaker, Spanish listeners were more likely to rank the Andalusian pronunciations as less serious, less educated, less productive, and less urban, while ranking the Castilian pronunciations the highest on the same scales. These attitudes were shared by respondents from both within and outside of Andalusia. Somewhat unexpectedly, for some of the phonetic features that we studied, the Andalusian respondents ranked themselves more harshly than the Castilian respondents. Put differently, Andalusians seem to have heavily internalized the negative stigmas associated with their accent. Linguistic profiling is therefore not just a manifestation of implicit bias between groups but also an internal process affecting people's self-judgments.

I remind my students that you can't understand a language without understanding its culture—this includes recognizing and mitigating implicit bias. By acknowledging the implications of our research for understanding the human experience, linguists offer legitimacy to claims of negative linguistic profiling and encourage conversation around topics of bias and systemic prejudice. I emulated these goals through the aforementioned course and am compelled to advocate for more contextual education in my courses that prepare students for the social and historical background of the population groups they are studying.[19] To this end, I recently mentored a student's undergraduate thesis titled "Sound Change in Western Andalusian Spanish: An Acoustic Analysis of Phonemic Voiceless Stops," which carries out a full-scale linguistic analysis on some of the most stigmatized features of the Andalusian dialect, approaching them using the same framework that applies to any standardized dialect.

As discussed earlier in the research by Kelly Wright on AAL,[3] results like the ones from my seminar on Andalusian Spanish are not unique to a single country or area. Whereas the Spanish paradigm relates to the stereotypes assigned to a particular region, linguistic profiling in the United States can play on stereotypes rooted in its long history of racism and ethnic prejudice. As a global phenomenon, its impacts vary, but by drawing attention to findings on the Andalusian accent, I hope to build on previous research on marginalized varieties.

Other linguists at the University of Michigan similarly urge awareness of social issues through public engagement. The College of LSA dean, Anne Curzan, hosts a weekly NPR podcast called *That's What They Say*, which analyzes how the English language is changing, including dialectal pronunciation differences. As exemplified by her popular TED talk,[20] Curzan aims to make linguistics accessible to a wide audience by validating and explaining different forms of language. For example, Curzan is a strong advocate for accepting the use of the singular "they" pronoun in English.[21] Another professor, Teresa Satterfield, researches bilingualism and language variation; her public engagement occurs through local, community-based work. Specifically, Satterfield spearheads a Saturday-school education program, called En Nuestra Lengua, for children of Spanish-speaking immigrants who live in southeast Michigan.

This program helps legitimize the source accent of the Latinx community by developing academic and literacy skills in Spanish for bilingual children. In addition to fueling their academic passions, colleagues like Curzan and Satterfield are developing innovative ways to promote awareness and create positive change.

## RAISING THE STAKES

There is no perfect time to initiate conversations aimed at confronting our individual biases; we need to use our voices, power, and privilege to unapologetically advocate for equality in every communicative circumstance. Through my own scholarship and teaching on Andalusian Spanish, I aim to contribute to the legal, cultural, and social legitimacy of claims of linguistic bias, both in Andalusia and elsewhere. Trauma, bias, and stigma are deep and intergenerational, but we have power as individuals to reject these destructive cycles and choose understanding and acceptance. Examining the automatic, split-second judgments we make about a speaker may seem like an inconsequential act of protest, but as we further depend on audio-reliant communication platforms, this represents a crucial step toward continuing our evolution into a less-prejudiced society.

## *Notes*

I cowrote this essay with Matthew Neubacher, then an undergraduate student at the University of Michigan studying political science. As a research assistant at my lab, Matthew became familiar with the linguistic details of Andalusian Spanish. He is also committed to matters of diversity, equity, and inclusion at the University of Michigan and looks forward to contributing to data-driven conversations around social justice. The content reflects multiple years of collaboration between Matthew and me in the Speech Production Lab.

1. John Baugh, "Linguistic Profiling," in *Black Linguistics: Language, Society, and Politics in Africa and the Americas*, ed. Sinfree Makoni, Geneva Smitherman, Arnetha F. Ball, and Arthur K. Spears (New York: Routledge, 2003), 155–168. Routledge, 2003. For additional information, see Baugh's most recent TEDx Talk, around 5:18, "The Significance of Linguistic Profiling | John Baugh | TEDxEmory," *TEDx Talks*, 28 June 2019, https://www.youtube.com/watch?v=GjFtIg-nLAA

2. Kelly E. Wright, "Experiments on Linguistic Profiling of Three American Dialects," unpublished PhD qualifying research paper, University of Michigan, 2019.

3. AAL is also referred to as African American English and African American Vernacular Language, among similar titles. For this essay, we use "AAL" to refer to the several language varieties spoken by African American communities in the United States, descendant from African and enslaved people's language traditions, and the distinct language features that identify these varieties. See also Sonja L. Lanehart, Jennifer Bloomquist, and Ayesha M. Malik, "Language Use in African American Communities: An Introduction," in *The Oxford Handbook of African American Language*, July 2015.

4. Wright, "Experiments on Linguistic Profiling."

5. Justin T. Craft, Kelly E. Wright, Rachel Elizabeth Weissler, and Robin M. Queen, "Language and Discrimination: Generating Meaning, Perceiving Identities, and Discriminating Outcomes," *Annual Review of Linguistics* 6.1 (2020): 389–407, https://doi .org/10.1146/annurev-linguistics-011718-011659

6. John R. Rickford, and Sharese King, "Language and Linguistics on Trial: Hearing Rachel Jeantel (and Other Vernacular Speakers) in the Courtroom and Beyond," *Language* 92.4 (2016): 950, https://doi.org/10.1353/lan.2016.0078

7. Rickford and King, "Language and Linguistics."

8. Craft et al., "Language and Discrimination."

9. Taylor Jones et al., "Testifying While Black: An Experimental Study of Court Reporter Accuracy in Transcription of African American English," *Language* 95.2 (2019), https://doi.org/10.1353/lan.2019.0042.

10. Emily A. Vogels et al., "53% of Americans Say the Internet Has Been Essential during the COVID-19 Outbreak," Pew Research Center, May 31, 2020, https://www.pew research.org/internet/2020/04/30/53-of-americans-say-the-internet-has-been-essen tial-during-the-covid-19-outbreak/

11. Valerie Strauss, "Perspective: A Novel Proposal to Help Millions of Kids Struggling with Online School," *Washington Post*, September 23, 2020, https://www.washi ngtonpost.com/education/2020/09/23/novel-proposal-help-millions-kids-struggling -with-online-school/. See also digitalequityforlearning.org for specific data on Internet access among low-income communities.

12. Kelly M Hoffman et al., "Racial Bias in Pain Assessment and Treatment Recommendations, and False Beliefs about Biological Differences between Blacks and Whites," *Proceedings of the National Academy of Sciences of the United States of America*, April 19, 2016, http://www.ncbi.nlm.nih.gov/pmc/articles/PMC4843483/

13. Borja Andrino Kiko Llaneras, "El mapa de la renta de padres e hijos: Cómo la riqueza de su familia influye en su futuro," *El País*, July 14, 2020, https://elpais.com/soc iedad/2020-07-14/el-mapa-de-la-renta-de-padres-e-hijos-como-la-riqueza-de-tu-fam ilia-influye-en-tu-futuro.html

14. Rusi Jaspal and Ioanna Sitaridou, "Coping with Stigmatized Linguistic Identities: Identity and Ethnolinguistic Vitality among Andalusians," *Identity* 13.2 (2013): 95–119, https://doi.org/10.1080/15283488.2012.747439

15. José Luis Venegas, *The Sublime South: Andalusia, Orientalism, and the Making of Modern Spain* (Evanston, IL: Northwestern University Press, 2018).

16. Inmaculada Gordillo-Álvarez, "La autorrepresentación del Andaluz en webseries," *Palabra Clave—Revista De Comunicación* 15.1 (January 2012): 54–81, https://doi.org/10.5294/pacla.2012.15.1.3

17. Alberto Grimaldi, "Andalucía será de las regiones con menor impacto por el Covid-19, según Funcas," *Diario de Sevilla*, June 16, 2020, https://www.diariodesevilla.es/economia/Andalucia-regiones-menor-impacto-Covid-19-Funcas_0_1474352972.html; Javier Martín-Arroyo, "En busca de explicaciones a la anomalía andaluza," *El País*, April 27, 2020, https://elpais.com/espana/2020-04-26/en-busca-de-explicaciones-a-la-anomalia-andaluza.html

18. Craft et al., "Language and Discrimination."

19. Zoe Phillips, Amber Galvano, and Ellie Maly, "Socially Distant Yet Intellectually Close," *Inside Higher Ed*, August 12, 2020, https://www.insidehighered.com/advice/2020/08/12/students-online-class-describe-four-elements-made-it-highly-positive-experience. In this article, students in an online class describe four elements that made it a highly positive experience.

20. Anne Curzan, "What Makes a Word 'Real?'" YouTube video, 17:13, June 17, 2014, https://www.youtube.com/watch?v=F6NU0DMjv0Y

21. Jonny Lupsha, "Merriam-Webster Says Word of the Year Is 'They'—But Why?," *Great Courses Daily*, December 20, 2019, https://www.thegreatcoursesdaily.com/merriam-webster-says-they-is-word-of-the-year-but-why/

# CHAPTER 28

# Quarantine Rebellions

## Performance Innovation in the Pandemic

*Anita Gonzalez*

## OVERVIEW

The pandemic of COVID-19, which began to impact the United States in March 2020, has drastically impacted the performing arts industry. Modes of theatrical production have shifted perceptibly, perhaps irretrievably, amid a global health crisis. Artists responded to the disrupted order in a multiplicity of necessary and inspiring ways. Quarantined at home, distant from familiar studios or theatres, artists are reassessing, recognizing the fragility of their profession and of their personal economies. This brief series of essays examines artistic responses to COVID-19 quarantine. By looking at specific artistic works, these essays will break down how isolation of individuals from their artistic communities has led to creative reflection and eventually direct, embodied political action.

January and February 2020 were scheduled to be eventful and dynamic months for the American theatre.[1] Ivan Van Hove's reimagination of *West Side Story* was set to open on Broadway with newly imagined choreography by Anna Teresa de Keersmaeker. The blockbuster hit *Hamilton* had tours running or planned for fourteen venues across the United States.[2] New, progressive leaders of color were appointed at regional theatres like the Oregon Shakespeare Festival (Nataki Garrett), Baltimore Center Stage (Stephanie Ybarra), and the Round House Theatre in Bethesda, Maryland (Nicole Watson). San Diego and Fort Worth opera companies were commissioning a new work about Frida Kahlo and Diego Rivera for a spring 2020 premiere. From my perspective as an African American theatre artist of Cuban descent, things were looking up. Then the coronavirus disease began to spread. First cases appeared in Washington State on January 21. By March 21 there were 17,935 cases.[3] As of this writing, the infection rate continues to grow, surpassing five million infections worldwide. American theatre—and theatre worldwide—came to a screeching halt.

People across the globe have experienced—and continue to experience—the impacts of this disease and the social transformations it has wrought. For the sake of clarity and sequencing as I describe each artists work, it will be important to distinguish between and define the terms COVID-19, the coronavirus, the quarantine, and the pandemic. The coronavirus is a type of virus that causes the disease properly called COVID-19.[4] A pandemic is the worldwide spread of a disease. On March 11, 2020, the World Health Organization categorized COVID-19 as a global pandemic.[5] The general public sometimes refers to this time of quarantine and the continuing circulation of the COVID-19 disease as the time of the pandemic. Quarantine is locally determined. Each state within the United States closed businesses at different times and asked residents to stay inside. Quarantines varied in restrictions and duration, but in almost all cases of quarantine, arts institutions, deemed "nonessential services," were shuttered.

For those with enough privilege, mandatory quarantines during the pandemic brought about extended periods of isolation. This isolation presents major challenges for art forms like performance, dependent upon the intimacy of touch and the presence of an audience. As the pandemic spread, and with it mandatory quarantine, performing artists and arts institutions moved from isolation to despair to innovation, and ultimately many mobilized into communities of protest. BIPOC artists (Black, Indigenous, and people of color), caught in the downward cycle of the social and economic distress, were especially impacted both by the virus and by its social effects as white fears, coupled with frustrations about confinement, led to visible incidents of racial violence. Performing artists are inherently innovative, but COVID-19 forced many artists to confront their mortality in a real way. As a result, artists became first fearful, and then politicized in their art-making.

When I departed the country for a theatre symposium in Addis Ababa, Ethiopia, US theatrical activities were flourishing, so my personal response to the impact of COVID-19 closures on the art community was disbelief. When I returned on March 17, artists were at home, theatres were closed, and quarantine had begun. Both artists and arts institutions were looking inward, and two things became clear: quarantine created a heightened awareness of the importance of community and connection, and artists realized how fragile the performing arts really are in the United States.

This essay series sprang from a fascination with artists' flourishing innovation in a time of immense fear and isolation in the United States. After the initial shock of the pandemic and its implications, performing arts companies and artists began to reimagine themselves and their place in American culture. They invented new modes of production even as they mobilized to address political and social inequalities. In the following sections I will examine three distinct themes that categorize the arts community's process of reimagining their role in the current cultural landscape: "Working in Isolation," "Creating Community," and "Mobilization and Restructuring."

## WORKING IN ISOLATION

Isolation: artists once in a community were left to deal with and explore their creativity alone. This section looks at the work of three young artists who developed and shared performance work during the quarantine. I selected these artists because all are relative newcomers to the performing arts profession, and were therefore most impacted by the dearth of opportunities to continue to work within their art forms. Each of these artists is part of a generation familiar with digital technologies, so they were able to easily and efficiently produce new digital works.

Julia Register is an actress and comedian who—five days after New York shut down on Friday, March 13—began posting videos to a YouTube channel to express her frustration and disbelief. Julia, in an online interview with me, explained that she was feeling such palpable fear that she was ranting with her roommates about all that seemed to be wrong. They suggested she film herself and post it. What evolved was a series called *Live! From Bed!*

The video segments are both comic and poignant. The actress uses a hairbrush as a microphone in a close-up image of her head on a pillow. The choices are deliberately tacky. The viewer can see that the hairbrush cost $3.99. Each segment begins with an audio overlay of the intro music to a news broadcast. Then the dialogue begins:

> Ladies and gentlemen, welcome to *Live from Bed*. I'm Julie "Freaking Out" Register here with your nightly news. Breaking news: I'm currently having one long panic attack.[6]

She then declares that her body is numb with "Jewish anxiety at its finest." Comedy emerges as she self-reflexively comments on her fake and very bad Australian accent. Julia's post captures the immediacy of the moment. She is suddenly at home, without work, and trying to cope with rapidly changing artistic circumstances through comedy. Over the course of the pandemic, Julia developed and refined her broadcast, eventually turning it into a full-length series of thirty-one episodes, each focusing on a different aspect of her miniature apartment world. She shows images of the dishes in her sink or herself washing her hands in the shower. One episode even includes a section of "Remembrances" from the days of holding hands and dining in restaurants.[7]

In an interview, I asked Julia how creating the series shifted her artistry. She says:

> It completely shifted everything. I am still trying to figure out what that means. It has been all about autonomy for me and how I can create this stuff with just me and my phone. I feel excited about this now. This pandemic has forced people to get rid of the things they have been meaning to get rid of and move towards the things they imagined.[8]

Julia's homemade television series is an excellent example of first responses to the pandemic. Her comedic take on how to cope with a feeling of disbelief was not to deny all that was happening around her, but rather to immerse herself in the irony of depending on the news to inform her about what, for her, was quite literally moving from bed to shower to kitchen within a cramped New York City apartment. While broadcast and cable stations marked the progression of the virus through body counts, charts, graphs, and politics, for Julia, and so many others, the virus was about losing her job, being confined to her apartment, and the effects that had on her daily reality.

Opera vocalist Jenny Cresswell adopts a very different approach to coping with the isolation than Register, choosing to bring the formal world of opera into her home rather than elevating the everyday into performance. Cresswell is a soprano singer and lyricist currently working toward her PhD at the University of Michigan. In her video entitled *What Good Would the Moon Be?*, she uses the upholstered chair in her living room as a backdrop for a fantasy immersion in the world of formal opera.

Wearing a red-and-black velvet evening dress, she enters the space with a glass of red wine and turns on her television set. Pianist Kathleen Kelly appears on the screen and plays accompaniment to the song "What Good Would the Moon Be," from Kurt Weill's American opera *Street Scene*. After her grand entrance, Jenny crosses her legs and begins to sing in her stunning soprano voice.[9] The lyrics of the song reference diamonds and dreams, a primrose path without a lover at your side.[10] When the singer finishes singing this solo as if it were a diva aria, she sips her wine and the video abruptly ends. Cresswell, in an interview,[11] says the idea for the performance came after she completed a performance residency with Kathleen Kelly on February 29.[12] Because both of them like to problem-solve, they embraced the idea of continuing their collaboration from afar.

They didn't know what kind of technology was available to them, so they improvised with what they had on hand. Technology has been an important and finicky friend to artists everywhere during quarantine. It allows for so much experimentation and collaboration, but at the same time is unreliable and is not a universal medium for the artistic mind. Kelly first lay down an audio track with video and then sent it on to Cresswell. The singer decided that, rather than merely playing the recording in the background, it would be much more fun for her stream the video through the television so she could sit with the pianist over her shoulder as if she were leaning over the keyboard. Because of her many previous live performances, she had an innate sense about where the pianist would sit. The resulting collaboration catches the imagination because it uniquely replicates spatial components of live solo operatic performance digitally.

One outcome of the collaboration was that after producing the video Kelly and Cresswell decided to collaborate on a chamber opera together. They also founded a new not-for-profit organization called GDQ Arts to increase opportunity and accessibility in opera. From her perspective, the COVID-19 health crisis was a great equalizer in terms of artistic accessibility. Even though there are financial losses, everyone was suddenly given the same platform with which to create. She and her collaborator have been able to do live readings and performances via Zoom. They have also found the time and space to write new material together.

Yet another example of innovative collaboration in isolation, *Nothin' Else 2 Do* describes a state of being and the title of a song released by University of Michigan senior Gian Perez as he watched the pandemic signal an end to his scheduled Broadway opening. While still a senior, Gian was tapped by Broadway director Rebecca Taichman to play a supporting role in the musical *Sing Street* based on the 2016 movie of the same name. During fall 2019, the production premiered at New York Theatre Workshop, the same theatre that spawned the hit musical *Rent*.[13] Although reviews were mixed,[14] a Broadway opening at the Lyceum Theatre was scheduled for April 19. By opening night, all Broadway theatres were closed. These closures and the isolation that followed sparked the virtual collaboration *Nothin' Else 2 Do*.[15]

The video begins with a close-up of a trap drum playing a syncopated rhythm. Gian's collaborator Jacob Ryan Smith counts, "Check one two three," then turns around in circles with his arms overhead. The video next cuts to Gian lying down on a bed next to girlfriend Nina White. He sings into a tube of deodorant, using it as microphone. Smith says: "OK, let's go!" and the listener is propelled into a funk beat featuring Gian on electric bass.

This artistic product is about isolation, yet it is produced with a tightly coordinated musical team. Gian writes:

> *Nothin' Else 2 Do* came out of a collaboration with Jake Smith, a Michigan MT [musical theatre] graduate, who has an Instagram account called The Songsmith where he writes a song a day. He asked me to write a piece with him, and what we created was this song about what life during quarantine looks like. We wrote the whole song together, and I contributed vocals, as well as bass parts. Apart from the song literally being about quarantine during the pandemic and everybody "getting funky," the remote way in which it was recorded was my first interaction with the "new normal" of music making. We wrote the whole song via FaceTime, recorded our parts separately, and pretty much produced it without even seeing each other face to face.[16]

What I appreciate about the song is how it keeps the listener in a walking groove of steady rhythm that maintains its pattern and develops into—well— nothing. Lyrics assert: "Let's just waste the day away . . . 'cause there's nothing else to do." One highlight is when Jake shrugs his shoulder while jabbing his arms away from the side of his body in perfect time with the funky rhythm. He looks silly like a duck because, after all, there's "nothing else to do" but feel the funk of your own body making its own rhythms. The song eloquently captures the sense of boredom and uselessness felt by many artists during the time of quarantine.

In a similar way to Julia Register, Gian viewed the quarantine as a moment to reassess his arts practice. When the pandemic began, he was a young artist excited about entering mainstream performance. By the time the coronavirus pandemic shuttered New York, he had reassessed what he wanted from his career.

> Once the pandemic hit, I had to leave New York because our Broadway transfer of *Sing Street* was postponed. In New York, life is so fast. You're always moving, going places, doing things, boogeying. But, since COVID-19, life has slowed down. I've taken up a much more dedicated spiritual practice and focused on my inner life. In doing this, I've realized that my art and creativity are much

more fluid than I'd always thought. I've been able to sit and write another album entitled *No Love for Cowboy*, which I'm still recording and producing. I've also decided to go back to my hometown in Puerto Rico and excavate the rich musical history there. Ultimately, this has led to a huge paradigm shift in my career. I'm no longer married to the path I thought I'd be taking and instead I'm excited to see where life takes me.[17]

The music video *Nothing Else 2 Do* alluded to a feeling of isolation during quarantine, but it was already signaling a shift to the next phase of the quarantine—collaborative performance. Register and Cresswell created their artistic works all alone by working with materials easily accessible to them in their living spaces. Perez's work was an early collaboration with musicians in multiple spaces that marked the start of a surge of online collaborative performances from artists seeking community. Amid immense seclusion and isolation across the world, these artists found ways to connect with each other through sharing relatable anxieties, and creating innovative virtual collaborations that brought people together in new and necessary ways.

CREATING COMMUNITY

Community: Artists coming together for mutual aid and exchange creating new communities. Amateur singers in communities throughout the world responded to quarantine isolation by singing together from balconies and street corners. In Italy, patriots sang from balconies to lift spirits and to pass the time.[18] New York City joined the international choir as the city shut down, first singing the Beatle's song "Yellow Submarine" in March.[19] Videos of community singing at a distance quickly became an internet sensation. These videos provided both hope and a feeling of togetherness as people everywhere were experiencing extreme loneliness. Then later, in April, as the health situation became more critical, apartment residents joined together in support of health care workers by singing Frank Sinatra's "New York, New York" from their windows.[20] The collective event, organized by the Peace of Heart Choir,[21] unified New Yorkers in a common chorus of "We'll come on through, New York, New York." At a time of great physical and financial stress for so many, these community performances brought hope and connection, but the performing arts world was not immune to the realities of the massive wave of unemployment. Few artists, if any, had ever experienced a universal shutdown of theatres, concert halls, and opera houses all at the same time.

Johanna Kepler, a senior at the University of Michigan in spring of 2020, was preparing to graduate and move to New York City to begin a professional career as a dancer and choreographer. When the quarantine began in March she felt she had lost control, and her plans to move to New York and perform with companies were dashed. Kepler channeled her creative energies into connecting with other artists through the development be of a website called The Power of the Performing Arts.

The website, a series of published interviews with two hundred artists, allowed her to be in community through dialogue about the impacts of the pandemic on a broad swathe of artists.

The website is impressive in its breadth and depth. Kepler asked each artist to submit a biography and photo, and then she interviewed them. They were asked to speak about how the COVID-19 pandemic affected their personal lives and their artistic practice. She selected artists and producers from a wide range of institutions, including artistic directors in Canada, performers from Broadway, and dancers from nationally recognized concert dance companies.

Johanna, deprived of the opportunity to physically connect with artistry of the dance profession, maintained connections with dance through the aspirations of hundreds of artists who participated in her interview process. The sheer labor of conducting two hundred interviews consumed much of her time and allowed her to investigate how others coped with changes brought about by the pandemic. When the labor of completing the project became overwhelming, Kepler created a managing production team of eight individuals: editors, webmasters, transcribers, and production managers who helped her to complete the massive project of transcribing and translating materials.[22]

Johanna considers her project to be social activism because she features primarily artists of color on the website. She writes:

I have brought voices together and stories from all walks of life to one page in the palm of the reader's hand. Diversity, equity, and inclusion is at the core of everything I do and how I look at the world around me. I used this platform to highlight artists of color, stand in solidarity with Black Lives Matter, and translate the entire website into Spanish to reach a larger demographic of people who are often left out of these conversations due to social and language barriers. I have also gotten every artist I have interviewed to think about diversity, equity, and inclusion within the arts. I ask each artist during the Zoom interview, "How can the performing arts be a platform for social

Figure 28.1. Screen capture from Johanna Kepler's project "The Power of the Performing Arts"

justice issues?" and "What do you think needs to change and shift in the performing arts community in terms of diversity, equity, and inclusion?"[23]

Even though many of the artists were already directly involved in issues of social activism, others had never thought about questions of social justice in relation to their work. Kepler states that creating the website allowed her to create community using technology in the most authentic way possible. Through the interview process, she has come to understand that returning to "normal" should not be the goal, because the normal of the past did not serve many people, such as minorities, artists of color, LGBTQ+ artists, or Indigenous artists.

Q: How has the COVID-19 pandemic affected you as a performing artist and business owner?

We are starting a mini grant for tap dancers. I am starting the fundraising this week. There will be mini grants 100-500 dollars for people who can't pay the rent for COVID19. All of my work has been cancelled or postponed. We produced the DC Tap Festival which is the biggest tap festival in the world. We moved it online. I'm pretty sure that we were the first dance event to go online during this pandemic. We did it as a buy 1 give 1 model. We work with kids all over the world in orphanages and low income so every package someone purchased we gave one for free for a child. All you had to do was ask for a package and we said yes.

Read full interview here

Figure 28.2. Screen capture from Johanna Kepler's project "The Power of the Performing Arts"

Themes of inequity emerged from discussions about art-making during the quarantine across all of the arts disciplines. Priorities have shifted as artists reassess the impact of their work within a landscape of death and unemployment. The Power of the Performing Arts project documents shifting attitudes across a broad cross section of artists during the time of initial disruption. Kepler continues to build the project and expand upon the initial interview set. In so doing, she documents a process of coping and acceptance as artists realized the pandemic would extend beyond a few weeks and continue to affect the performing arts industry.

Of course, building community happens in different ways. Serious discussions about arts and art practices were just one approach to coping with isolation. Performing artists also constructed social events to connect with one another. Some artists sought relief from the drudgery of isolation by just having fun. Zoom was the theatre platform of choice for social as well as theatrical gatherings.[24]

During normal times, the Players Club functions as a members-only space where select colleagues of the arts and entertainment community attend

Figure 28.3. Screen capture from Johanna Kepler's project "The Power of the Performing Arts"

play and poetry readings or music events. There is a dress code to enter the building, and the physical space of the club—a mansion on Gramercy Park—features a great hall, a pub, a dining space, and multiple meeting rooms. The club was founded by Edwin Booth in 1888 as a gathering place to bring together professional actors and business entrepreneurs.[25] After decades of scandal, the club was revitalized in 2014 with a new, forward-thinking board of directors.[26]

By April the club had initiated a series of social events to substitute for our inability to gather, meet, and greet. The first COVID events were happy hours designed to replicate the post-work gatherings most familiar to members of the club. Later the events became more structured activities. Drag Bingo, for example, allowed members to dress in drag while playing online Bingo. Two Truths and a Lie was a simple recorded guessing game. While these theatrical games were party games, other organizations directly addressed the challenge of developing theatrical games for Zoom.

James Woodhams, the Young People's Officer from the Barbican Theatre in London, developed an informative video available on YouTube.[27] It reimagines theatre games generally used in theatre improvisation classrooms as engaged Zoom activities. The video, posted on March 30, 2020, was an early entry into what would become a wave of educational videos about how to do theatrical "stuff" online. His video uses the hashtags #keep moving and #COVID19Exercises. Games like Grandma's Footsteps, One-Word Story, and Ball of Energy are familiar among theatre practitioners and were thoughtfully converted into Zoom activities to allow for connection and play when being in the same space was not possible.

The Barbican's video, as shared by Woodhams, is an example of the kinds of adaptations developed within the performing arts community to replicate and sometimes enhance what was usually performed live and in person in the performance studio. As the quarantine continued, Zoom innovations became more and more complex. The digital platform was reluctantly activated, then innovated, institutionalized, and mobilized for ongoing performing arts activities. One of my favorite products of Zoom instruction is the ninety-minute video created by Dominic D'Andrea for the Queens Theatre about how to create an effective Zoom production.[28] The video was widely circulated as artists struggled to deliver their storytelling through what was then a foreign medium.

The video is detailed. He begins with the philosophical question of whether Zoom is theatre or not. While performers on the screen are indeed simultaneous in virtual space, they are not live and in the room. Philip Auslander's groundbreaking book *Liveness: Performance in a Mediatized Culture* (first published in 1999 and revised in 2008) was one of the first to challenge the premise that performance must be live in order to effectively express energy and community.[29] He argues against an intrinsic opposition between live and mediatized forms of performance.[30] Thomas F. DeFrantz, on the other hand, argues: "Performance, as I imagine it, involves the excitement of breath to create subject or subjectivity."[31] The Barbican video demonstrates how performers might share a broadcast breath through the Zoom screen, but human embodiment of touch and feel was not in the room. Indeed, I would argue that human touch and kinesthetic sharing were what artists most missed during the quarantine. While digital images of human beings were widely available, in-person interactions for many performing artists were limited to excursions to the grocery store. Still, something—regardless of its shortcomings—was, and is, necessary to keep us all going. D'Andrea's video demonstrates how artists in separate spaces might collaborate on a storytelling event through a collective and collaborative Zoom meeting.

He begins with an assertion about his desire to ensure that artists can practice and communities can convene during the pandemic. After reminding listeners that Zoom is designed for meetings and not production, D'Andrea explains how principles of theatrical production can be applied to this technology. Approximating a theatrical production from top to bottom means holding a rehearsal process on Zoom, employing a stage manager, instructing the house manager about how to control audience entry into the digital platform, and managing entrances and exits of actors. D'Andrea explains how to reboot or relocate routers for optimal signal as well as how to stage actors within the frames, how to invite applause, and tips for holding post-show events. With this kind of detailed instruction on managing productions within the Zoom platform, many artists were able to optimize play readings and performances.

One professional producing company in Oxford, UK, called Creation Theatre[32] staged a production of *The Tempest* that modeled professional Zoom artistry. The production, which ran from April 11 to May 10, 2020, was coproduced with Big Telly Theatre Company, based in Northern Ireland. It was an early experiment in monetizing theatrical performances behind a paywall. The company set the ticket price at GBP20 per viewing device. Creation Theatre specializes in interactive performances of texts in unusual locations. The desire of producers Lucy Askew and Zoe Seaton was to entertain audiences and to find ways to pay freelance teams for making work. Lecturer Laura Wright from the University of Oxford maintains:

> *The Tempest* lends itself to such a production. It's a play about isolation and exile, about characters moving around a small island without ever meeting one another. Creation's performance did nothing to disguise its new medium. In fact, the most powerful part of the performance came as Prospero spoke the famous epilogue which begins: "Now my charms are all o'erthrown."[33]

Actors used green screens to create imaginative backdrops in their individual spaces that would support the production. The directors coached them on how to adjust sightlines for Zoom and how to make creative use of props. The experiment was successful, as the company sold 1,428 tickets to seventeen performances. The interactive ethos of the company was maintained in the production as audience members were able to participate in two different ways: they could ask questions of characters by using the Zoom chat function, and they could create sound effects at certain points in the play. For example, they created the storm by drumming through their fingers on their computer microphones. According to a follow-up survey conducted by researchers Pascale Aebischer and Rachael Nicholas from the University of Exeter, audience members felt a sense of community and connection through their engagement with the show.[34]

The Aebischer and Nicholas case study and digital toolkit published after the production is an informative document.[35] It explains, in detail, the process of developing a business and artistic model for the production. While a normal summer production would have generated almost GBP 30,000 in net income, the Zoom production, which netted GBP 15,400, generated less income.[36] Even though one impetus for the production was financial, the production also demonstrated that Zoom could build community and engage global audiences in performing arts viewership. Similar trends were occurring in other performing arts disciplines as well.

The dance community in particular adapted very quickly to Zoom performance, in part because of the necessity of maintaining daily practice to ensure continuing proficiency in the art form. Just as dance faculties within university settings were required to teach technique online, so too did individual studios adapt to delivering instruction from living rooms. Classes were easily made accessible through password-protected links where teachers could be paid for delivering lessons online. And there were some advantages to this forced digitization. Class size was no longer limited by studio space, so classes could be offered to hundreds of students simultaneously. Dancers were also able to experiment with new forms of dancing taught by experienced teachers from across the globe. Halen Hilton, on the Dance Spirit website, even offers a primer on virtual dance protocol titled "The Do's and Don'ts of Taking Zoom Dance Class."[37] This is an etiquette guide that elucidates rules about lateness, attire, advance charging of devices, and when to turn your camera on and off.[38]

More challenging than the delivery of dance instruction was the creation of collaborative dance works. Despite the challenges, some of the most exciting performance work of quarantine emerged from the dance community. Dance is visual as well as kinesthetic; as a result, dynamic movement within the mediated frame communicates well. Synchronizing and coordinating spatial patterns was not nearly as difficult for collaborative dance choreography as it would be for coordinated sound. The *New York Times* offered suggestions and commentary about twelve different online streaming platforms early on in quarantine (April 7, 2020).[39] Throughout the following months dance productions became even more sophisticated. One of my favorite high-concept dance works produced for Zoom is *Immediate Tragedy*, a collaboration of twenty-two artists from locations across the United States and Europe.[40] Christopher Rountree[41] composed a score to animate a Martha Graham solo from 1937. The original dance, created the same year that Picasso painted *Guernica*, was inspired by women's activism during the Spanish Civil War.[42] The work-in-motion was lost, but dancers working under the leadership of Janet Eilber brought photographic stills of the original choreography to life.[43] Fourteen dancers, working from within their living rooms, recreated gestures of sadness and melancholy following choreographic guidelines introduced by Eilber. The editing of the performance is particularly evocative as the camera shifts the framing of individual dancers to accelerate the velocity of each performer's contribution. The structure of the work is circular. Black-and-white frames of isolated poses transform frame by frame into full-movement compositions rendered in color. After eight minutes of active motion, the visual choreography resolves into black-and-white stillness reminiscent of the original images.

Vocal and instrumental music performers faced the greatest challenges in creating community through sound. The latency of most digital technologies does not allow for simultaneous playing and synchronization. Even though co-created videos circulated widely, they depended entirely on editing artistry to create a feeling of synchronicity. In the world of live performance, instrumentalists responded to scientists sharing information about the toxicity of COVID-19 aerosol dissemination by developing new protocols. Performing artists envisioned installing barriers between players and implementing social distancing on the stages of indoor auditoriums. As early as March 12, the Berlin Philharmonic performed an orchestral composition in a near-empty space. The performance was designed to be distributed digitally though the orchestra's Digital Concert Hall series.[44] The Berlin Philharmonic was also one of the first to distribute detailed information about how to best stage instrumental performances safely.[45] By May 14, instructions and suggestions for staging musical performances were circulating widely. Justin Davidson published an article in *Vulture* magazine titled "What Socially Distanced Live Performance Might Look Like."[46] He describes the potentiality for performances in outdoor public spaces and hangar-like halls, even for a one-on-one concert series where a single musician plays for a single audience member within a vast space. Yet how to perform live orchestral or choral music in real time while remaining socially distanced remained, and still remains, a challenge.

However, digital renditions of awe-inspiring music did emerge from music organizations. Artists at home contributed voices and instrumental melodies to opera companies as a marker of solidarity during trying times. African American composer Nkeiru Okoye was in upstate New York when the pandemic began. Her most recent engagement had been at the Detroit Symphony Orchestra, where she was commissioned to compose a work called *Black Bottom* about a historically Black neighborhood in Detroit.[47] Quarantine left her alone in a primarily white hamlet in lower New York State. She observed how artists living in New York City were able to join in celebrating essential workers with sirens and singing, and she thought about how she could join and support as a Black woman living in a white suburb.

The idea of being surrounded by white people advocating for Black Lives Matter with fists raised while shouting was unappealing to her. In an interview, she says she found this idea ironic, scary, even triggering.[48] A group of people gathering in the streets was not something she wanted to participate in. Fortunately, the American Opera Project based in Brooklyn contacted her and asked if she would be interested in having the aria "Keep on Going" from her 2014 opera *Harriet Tubman: When I Crossed That Line to Freedom* recorded as a tribute to health care workers.[49] The American Opera Project arranged to have singers from multiple casts of *Harriet Tubman* participate. Okoye was able to select voices she particularly liked. She says: "We got these casts together and I ended up rearranging some of the music." The resulting video brought multiple singers who performed within a Zoom frame that was later synchronized with the musical orchestration. Composer Okoye reflects upon what she learned from the project.

> It was healing and it contributed to Universal Good. If you just do something to contribute to the Universal Good, that is God's work and it makes everything better. As an artist, I use my art as an agent of change. Not in a grandiose sense, but I mean each person has their way of contributing. Essential health care workers are people who look like us. They are people of color who are forced to put their lives on the line. They are putting bread on the table.

By collaborating with New York City artists and reinvigorating one of her earlier works, this African American composer was able to feel a sense of community even while isolated and away from the concert hall.

A more expansive classical music recording was produced by the service organization Opera America. The *Light Shall Lift Us*[50] video was shared widely on the internet as part of a promotional effort to demonstrate the vitality and resiliency of opera. Because of the prestige of the producing organization, funds were funneled into a high-fidelity recording with a large number of artists. More than one hundred opera singers united in a song of hope and solidarity by participating in a virtual performance of this composition by the Pulitzer Prize–winning team of composer Paul Moravec and librettist/lyricist Mark Campbell. The project, disseminated on YouTube, credited every artist who participated in this celebration of choral sound.[51] Director/producer Cara Casilvio edited the project.[52] The first image on the screen is a single singer framed by his dining room. The sense of community accelerates as the solo becomes a duet, then a quartet. Casilvio's skillful editing amplifies each recorded sound track so that the voices linger; the sound of each operatic voice persists in the background. Eventually, the overlay voices include the sounds of one hundred singers with the conductor featured in a single frame, gesturing from the center of a multitude of faces. The swell of the final vibrato note raises emotions while confirming the impact of community. The message is clear. Opera singers unite in song, defying the constrictions of the quarantine. All of these acts of community building within isolation reminded artists simultaneously of their collective strengths and of the systemic problems that have been reflected in the performance world. With a pandemic raging and racial violence in the streets, performing artists were faced with how they could make a difference in their communities.

## MOBILIZATION AND RESTRUCTURING

Mobilization: disparate individuals coming together to elicit change in the performing arts industry. The character of the quarantine took a turn after the police killings of George Floyd, Breonna Taylor, Ahmaud Arbery, Tony McDade, Rayshard Brooks, and others. Visceral videos of violence against black men and women led to global demonstrations against police brutality. The demonstrations accelerated processes of social unrest already brewing from the confinement of the quarantine. Public protests against white supremacy and anti-Blackness began to proliferate, building upon earlier protests activated by the Black Lives Matter collective of activists. Artists and scholars responded quickly and vocally to the disrupted order. Clearly, the extreme visibility of the murders triggered a public recognition of the pervasive and systematic anti-Blackness that contains the lives of Black people in all aspects of public life, including the arts. Black people united in the streets and also within the arts community to demand recognition and, more importantly, change.

Tonya Pinkins, for example, a Tony Award–winning actress, published an online blog about her rage.

> 2020 gifted us the perfect storm to herald the winds of societal change. . . . The American theater has been dying a slow death from its racist, nostalgic, blacklisting and anglophilia on top of its soon to be extinct subscription audience. It has flat-lined, and debating whether there will be a Lazarus resurrection in 2022 seems so frivolous to me while young men and women are shot with rubber bullets, Black men are being lynched from trees and Americans are being brutalized by the Police who are sworn to serve and protect their constitutional right to free speech.[53]

Unacknowledged racism had long been an entrenched part of the professional theatrical infrastructure. Pinkins's rage builds upon her previous activism when, in 2015, she spoke out about demeaning practices in the theatre industry. She achieved notoriety for her refusal to play the title role in *Mother Courage* after white director Brian Kullick objected to the broadness of her character depiction. The actress's physical embodiment of the iconic figure irked him.[54] She preferred using a broad gesture—snatching a coat—to express the inner life of a dignified character the director viewed as "delusional."[55] This simple physical act of snatching reverberated within the rehearsal studio as a disruption of spatial orders, a challenge to structural hierarchies embedded within a performance ecosystem based upon upper-middle-class market preferences. Then her rebellion against preconceived expectations about her artistry emboldened Pinkins and several of her cast members to walk away from the production. Now, as a convergence of economic and health crises halts theatrical productions across the globe, Pinkins is somewhat vindicated.

While Pinkins's statement represented a personal response, a broader and powerfully visible movement erupted with the We See You, White American Theatre campaign,[56] initiated by a coalition of three thousand artists and cosigned by fifty thousand US artists. High-profile artists in the arts and entertainment industry published a statement the week of June 6, 2020, which decried racism on Broadway and beyond. "The signatories include the Pulitzer Prize winners Lynn Nottage, Suzan-Lori Parks, Quiara Alegría Hudes and Lin-Manuel Miranda; the film and television stars Viola Davis and Blair Underwood; and many Tony Award winners, including the actor and director Ruben Santiago-Hudson and the playwright David Henry Hwang, who is the chair of the American Theater Wing."[57] We See You, White American Theater included a website manifesto demanding overdue change and a sweeping new social contract for the American theatre. Equitable presence, codes of conduct, and transformative practices are central to these demands. The manifesto builds upon an earlier (2016) statement by playwright August Wilson called "The Ground on Which I Stand" about unequal funding for Black arts.[58] Both manifestos describe a need to destabilize underpinnings of hierarchical economies in order to shake loose new methodologies for imagining redistribution of resources.

As the summer progressed and protests continued to circulate, the coalition continued its work. By July they had developed principles for building antiracist theatre systems with recommendations for transformative practices. The online statement was only the beginning of a series of activities and policy protests that would continue across institutions. The trend was so pervasive that almost every arts institution—galleries, opera companies, producing organizations, unions and guilds, university training programs— began to issue statements about their support of BIPOC artists.[59] As pressures increased, organizations began to schedule summits and seminars to self-assess and come to terms with ongoing, entrenched, and systematic exclusions of BIPOC artists.

The Theatre Communication Group, an advocacy organization for professional American theatre, responded to the moment with a bold step. It canceled all of the scheduled opening events at its annual 2020 conference and replaced them with presentations by BIPOC artists. This was a significant, high-profile intervention because the organization represents seven hundred member-theatres and organizations and ten thousand individual members. This shift in programming was sudden. The day before the conference organizers issued the following statement:

> Part 2 of the 2020 TCG Virtual Conference, *Convening*, **will go Dark on Tuesday, June 2** in an expression of solidarity with our Black colleagues who are enduring the pain of continued acts of violence in their communities. **We will craft a new way forward for the remaining days of Convening**, in order to center the needs of our Black colleagues and colleagues of color. Just as we have done during the current pandemic, we are taking this emergency action for the safety and well-being of our community members.[60]

The keynote address was delivered by three BIPOC artists: artistic director Jamil Jude,[61] actor/dramatist/educator Nikkole Salter, and actress/poet/director Monique Holt. Its intensity shifted dialogues about diversity throughout the industry. Jude was the first speaker. After expressing his gratitude for being invited to speak, he talked about how he entered the field with bushy-tailed enthusiasm as an intern at the Arena Theatre. After his internship, he followed the trajectory of someone working his way up to a position of artistic leadership, eventually winning a TCG fellowship grant. When invited to speak, he was originally planning to talk about changes in the industry. However, his plans shifted after what he calls the public lynching of George Floyd. He connected to his own grief. He watched institutions put out antiracist statements, and he came to one conclusion: "It has all been a lie. The idea that anyone can become a successful artistic director is a lie because we have built our edifices on the pillars of white supremacy." He says that for years he accepted the lie and the belief that he could make a difference. He believed that change would happen. Jude maintains that the lie exists because under-qualified leaders have assumed positions when qualified people of color are not allowed access because of white privilege. "We have been bamboozled," he says. He ends with a prayer and a hope that his beliefs are untrue but culminates with the statement, "You fix it." Jude's speech directly confronts the industry by telling leaders and organizers they are facing a crisis in moral leadership.

The second speaker, Monique Holt, aka MoMo, communicated with sign language on behalf of the disability and deaf community, with a speaker interpreting her gestures. Holt grew up with a deaf family and never thought she would become a part of a hearing community.[62] Her career, including her work for the Oregon Shakespeare Festival, makes her a bridge between two worlds. In her speech, Holt questioned how BIPOC artists could feel safe within a racist community/state like Oregon. Even though more deaf actors are being hired on Broadway in productions like *Big River*[63] and *Spring Awakening*,[64] she wonders why more BIPOC people aren't involved. MoMo, at the end of her speech, advocates for intersectionality instead of the notion of inclusion, expressing the need for theatre communities to educate themselves with diversity, equity, and inclusion training programs.

Finally, Nikkole Salter began her talk with a broad rhetorical embrace: "What a time this is . . . an opportune time."[65] Salter acknowledged that the industry and society are crumbling around her, and she was excited because breaking down and falling apart are just natural cycles. The middle of a storm is a chance to stand still, take a wide view, see things whirling around and reassess. Destruction, she maintained, is an appropriate response when you are out of alignment with nature. Salter suggested that notions of hierarchy and scarcity are lies, belief systems that are out of alignment with a truth of abundance. Society perpetuates lies of divisions and difference that cause suffering in the world and in the field of the performing arts. "Our field is not excluded because it is well intentioned or because it has a 501(c)3." The world, she maintained, is a circle and a sphere. We made up the existing systems, and we can make up something else that does not cause suffering within the "best practices" of our institutions. Salter reminded us that we are artists telling stories in order to bring consciousness to story making, and everyone has a right to contribute to the human narrative. The actress and director ended by asking the industry to correct its lack of integrity by genuinely working in solidarity. "The theater-making of the past may just be of the past."

Collectively, the three speakers' critiques of the industry shifted dialogues from conversations about diversity, equity, and inclusion toward more potent discussions about antiracist institutional change. The BIPOC community was asking for accountability and effective actions instead of lip service to generalized and unrealizable concepts of inclusion. The challenge reverberated throughout the conference. The plenary presentations were followed by multiple "breakout" sessions where coalitions of white producers and Black artists met in separate Zoom rooms to debrief and strategize. As an African American artist, I participated in the BIPOC breakout, where we primarily expressed our feelings of relief at not being called upon to solve the problem for institutional leaders assessing their own relationship to systematic racism.

Organization and institutional reassessment were only one way in which artists responded to escalating racial violence during the quarantine. Artists also made art. Performers, very aware of the power of a performance image, responded viscerally to the murder of George Floyd. The video recording of a callous policeman using his knee to press down on the neck of a dying human being affected viewers globally. Public response implicated the observers who watched the murder as much as the callousness of the perpetrator. How many white people stand by, witnessing the suffering of Black people, without turning a head or only mumbling a muted call of protest? Black response to ongoing disregard of Black lives engendered outrage. Black performing artists realized how our advancement, our lives, and our livelihood were stymied by the inaction of the institutionalized white artistic managers and implementers.

The day after the George Floyd murder, on May 26, 2020, a seemingly tamer incident occurred. Amy Cooper, walking her dog in Central Park, called the police on a Harvard University–educated bird-watcher, a Black man named Christian Cooper. Public emotions were raw after the deluge of social media images of Floyd's death. New Yorkers and others, already sensitized to what could happen to a Black man when the police were involved, responded with horror to the callous way in which white Amy called for unnecessary police intervention because she wanted to break the law by walking with her dog unleashed. The press and social media began to refer to her as "Karen," an internet slang term for an annoying, middle-aged, white woman who wants to share her trivial complaints with someone in authority (often a manager). The term had been around for a few years, but it's became more common during the pandemic as a shorthand for ignorant and abrasive white women.[66] The incident became inspiration for poet and spoken-word artist Decora, who created and disseminated the musical composition "Dear Karen." I highlight his work because it was an immediate response to ongoing and systematic racism.

"Dear Karen" follows the format of a breakup letter to a girlfriend. Decora explains that he had to write this with his "fists in a tight grip" because he "felt mike-less and voice-less, and homeless in the land of the free."[67] The metaphor of his relationship with America continues throughout the four-minute song-poem, with its easy beat accompaniment. The speaker, who is trying to become whole, comes to the "table" with expectations of inclusion only to find there are no seats. He questions the emotional commitment of a symbolic Karen who holds no justice or caring for the speaker, presumably a Black man. After a narrative that recounts the circumstance of what happened in Central Park, the protagonist recognizes a betrayal. The lyrics indicate that he is not surprised "Karen" didn't respond to his letter, and notes that it's all right, because there are now pyro/peaceful protests. This is where he is finding protection because fighting the unjust system is like fighting a whale. He speaks about how this metaphorical "Karen" could help by joining protests and talking to other "Karens" about their advantage. This, Decora raps, is an opportunity to change the world.

Decora is an Afro-Latinx artist who says the following about his rationale for creating the work:

> I wrote "Dear Karen" because I had to. As an artist, I feel that I am the messenger and not the originator of my work. That being said, the work has to be produced for humanity, especially in the state we are in, where people are finally willing to listen to what's going on and take the time to reflect. COVID

has forced people into a corner where they can't help but to hear the reverberations of injustice bounce off the wall. As an artist, I've had to redefine myself, and it's been hard, but that's why we are made from clay and mud not skin and bones.[68]

Like many of the artists described in this essay, Decora viewed the COVID-19 quarantine as an ideal opportunity to make a change, first within himself, and ultimately within the world. His journey continues as shifting political waves inundate the United States during an ongoing health pandemic. Artists have created powerful movements of change within performance communities and beyond at a time when it is difficult not to be engulfed in isolation and despair.

## FINAL THOUGHTS

In some ways, the onset of the COVID-19 pandemic, coupled with a crisis of isolation, propelled artists in the performing arts industry through a grieving cycle matching the Kübler-Ross paradigm of denial, anger, bargaining, depression, and acceptance. The denial, which happened during the first month of quarantine, March 2020, was the belief that the viral circulation of illness would not change the nature or frequency of live performance. Most artists, unsure about the public health implications of the disease, believed things would return to normal within a relatively short period of a few weeks. Health expert Kimberly Holland equates this with the belief that "this will be over tomorrow."[69] The second stage, anger, also associated with bitterness or resentment, erupted as political and social distress: "How dare they let this happen to us." It's important to mention how perceptions of anger or resentment differed substantially across racial and social groups. For those who worked from positions of privilege, isolation felt restrictive, but paychecks still arrived. For temporary workers in the gig economy, there was limited cash flow.

A type of bargaining emerged within the industry as performance companies offered previously recorded streamed performances for free or at minimal costs, promising audiences that all would return to normal by the fall season. I view the bargaining as a belief among artists that "they will see how valuable we are." From a production standpoint, the intent was to retain theatre subscribers and eliminate as many refunds on ticket sales as possible. Finally, depression set in as industry professionals realized the inevitability of needing to close theatres and performance spaces through at least the end of 2020, leaving entire teams of performers, designers, technicians, and production staff without work. Artists and production companies reassessed their economic circumstances, with some concluding, "I don't know how to go forward from here," or asking, "Why go on at all?"

At this point, the trajectory of the performing arts community veered away from this imaginary Kübler-Ross paradigm. Instead of passive acceptance, artists mobilized two types of responses: innovation and protest. By July 2020, artists were quickly developing new technological expertise, new modes of interaction, and inventive modes of presentation. As of August 2020, performing artists were redefining modes of production that focused on new organizational structures to address a second pandemic of systematic racism within the profession. The process, as Nikkole Salter artfully describes, requires destruction and reimagination of long-standing practices and policies.

Technological and production innovations are developing quickly, and organizations collaborate to share models of innovation and best practices. One website, for example, called Innovations in Socially Distant Performances, is a worldwide, open-access list of productions and their innovations for anyone to consult.[70] The site includes models for creating innovative work through cutting-edge, frequently avant-garde, processes and collaborations. In the commercial world, companies like DLR Group have developed architectural plans for reopening theatrical buildings that accommodate socially distanced audiences and performers.[71] The company's "Pathways to (Re)opening Night" document visualizes how performance might happen in a post-pandemic world.

More difficult will be the challenge of expunging racism within the performing arts industry. Many BIPOC artists whose work I describe consider the COVID-19 health emergency to be a unique opportunity for removing infrastructures and hierarchies that have limited access by disenfranchised communities. In isolation, we have watched as norms of performance have broken down. In isolation, we have watched the previously privileged cohorts panic as they are forced to release control over modes of production previously normalized in their favor. The COVID-19 pandemic exposed systematic injustices within neoliberal global paradigm. Like a blinding light of merciless whiteness, the health crisis and its accompanying economic breakdown revealed cracks and crannies of deeply embedded inequities, making them clearly visible. The performing arts, like institutions throughout the United States, continue to reassess their willingness to reconstitute for the sake of inclusion.

## Notes

1. "Spring Preview 2020."

2. "Hamilton 2020 Tour Dates."

3. Gamio et al., "Watch How the Coronavirus Spread."

4. Sauer, "What Is Coronavirus?"

5. Centers for Disease Control and Prevention, "New ICD-10-CM Code."

6. Register, *Live from Bed!*

7. Register, *Julia Register YouTube.*

8. Register, interview by Anita Gonzalez.

9. Cresswell, *What Good Would the Moon Be?*

10. "Kurt Weill."

11. Cresswell, interview by Anita Gonzalez.

12. Kelly, "Calendar."

13. Gardner, "Meet the Kids."

14. Brantley, "'Sing Street' Review."

15. Smith et al., *Nothin' Else 2 Do.*

16. Perez, interview by Anita Gonzalez.

17. Perez, interview by Anita Gonzalez.

18. *New Yorker, Italians Making Music.*

19. ABC News, *New Yorkers Sing Together.*

20. CBS New York, *Coronavirus Update.*

21. "New York Sings Along."

22. Kepler et al., "TPOTPA."

23. Kepler, interview by Anita Gonzalez.

24. Zoom is "simplified video conferencing and messaging across any device" ("Video Conferencing").

25. The Players NYC, "Home."

26. Crain's New York Business, "Historic Comeback."

27. Barbican Theatre, *B-Hive Activity.*

28. Queens Theatre, *Zoom Theatre.*

29. Auslander, *Liveness.*

30. Auslander, *Liveness,* 11.

31. DeFrantz, in DeFrantz and Gonzalez, "Introduction," 6.

32. Creation Theatre Company, "The Tempest."

33. Wright, "Shakespeare on Zoom."

34. Aebischer and Nicholas, *Digital Theatre Transformation.*

35. Aebischer and Nicholas, *Digital Theatre Transformation.*

36. Aebischer and Nicholas, *Digital Theatre Transformation,* 21.

37. Hilton, "Zoom Dance Class Etiquette 101."

38. Turning your camera on and off is a primary consideration in all aspects of live Zoom performance interactions because the camera determines which and how many faces appear on the screen.

39. *New York Times*, "12 Places to Watch."

40. Martha Graham Dance Company, *Immediate Tragedy*.

41. Rountree, "Home."

42. Martha Graham Dance Company, *Making of "Immediate Tragedy"*.

43. Martha Graham Dance Company, *Making of "Immediate Tragedy"*.

44. "Berliner Philharmoniker's Digital Concert Hall."

45. "Berlin Study Issues Recommendations."

46. Davidson, "Socially Distanced Live Performance."

47. "Celebrating Detroit's Historical Black Bottom."

48. Okoye, interview by Anita Gonzalez.

49. Okoye, "Harriet Tubman—AOP."

50. Opera America, *Light Shall Lift Us*.

51. "Artists who lent their voices to this project come from all across America and represent a broad variety of backgrounds and experience. Their participation is an example of the vitality and resiliency of our field and a demonstration that even while we are apart, music brings us together. They are: Singers: Javier Abreu Danielle Beckvermit Daniel Belcher Andrew Bidlack Matt Boehler Amanda Lynn Bottoms Liz Bouk Marnie Breckenridge Erica Brookhyser Raehann Bryce-Davis William Burden Jennifer Johnson Cano Leonardo Capalbo Joyce Castle Lisa Chavez Hailey Clark Sarah Coit Troy Cook Sasha Cooke Olivia Cosío Tara Curtis Adrienne Danrich Joseph Dennis Mary Dunleavy Jason Ferrante Jessica Fishenfeld Emily Fons Daryl Freedman Blake Friedman Joseph Gaines Blythe Gaissert Priti Gandhi Sara Gartland Eve Gigliotti Nathan Granner Devon Guthrie Jasmine Habersham Sam Handley Roger Honeywell Soloman Howard Briana Elyse Hunter Craig Irvin Zachary James Keith Jameson Jessica E. Jones Michael Kelly Maya Kherani Michael Kuhn Claire Kuttler Tesia Kwarteng Sarah Larsen Anna Laurenzo Victoria Livengood Cecilia Violetta López Zulimar López-Hernández Alexandra Loutsion Daniela Mack Amanda Majeski Alex Mansoori Trevor Martin Robert Wesley Mason Aundi Marie Moore John Moore Dylan Morrongiello Brian James Myer Miles Mykkanen Luis Alejandro Orozco Edward Parks Ailyn Pérez Dimitri Pittas Matthew Polenzani David Portillo Stephen Powell Katherine Pracht Gabriel Preisser Emily Pulley Elise Quagliata Brenda Rae Zoie Reams Morris Robinson Lisa Marie Rogali Adrian Rosas Annie Rosen Jordan Rutter Christian Sanders Lucy Schaufer Laurel Semerdjian Alek Shrader Benjamin Sieverding Jake Stamatis Dane Suarez Jack Swanson Talise Trevigne Richard Troxell Maria Valdes Jamie Van Eyck Miguel Angel Vasquez Craig Verm Yunpeng Wang Andrew Wilkowske William Ferguson Karin Wolverton Caroline Worra Matthew Worth Wei Wu Adriana Zabala Jennifer Zetlan Conceived by Mark Campbell and Paul Moravec Music Direction: Andrew Whitfield Video Editor: Cara Consilvio Assistant Video Editor: Alex Charner Orchestral Simulation and Final Audio Mix: Peter Lurye Vocal Mix: Andrew Whitfield Special Thanks: Adelphi University David Charles Abell Jennifer Johnson Cano Elizabeth Dworkin Alison Moritz Opera Orlando Gabriel Preisser Kent Tritle, Oratorio Society of New York Subito Music Justin Werner, Stratagem Artists Light Shall Lift Us

was originally written for One Voice Orlando, a benefit organized by Opera Orlando in response to the shooting at the Pulse nightclub in 2016. Light Shall Lift Us—Music by Paul Moravec, Words by Mark Campbell Copyright ©2016 by Subito Music Publishing (ASCAP) All Rights Reserved."

52. "Cara Consilvio."
53. Pinkins, "Why I Am Fed Up."
54. Soloski, "Star of 'Mother Courage.'"
55. Gans and Viagas, "Exclusive."
56. We See You, White American Theater, "Demands."
57 Paulson, "Theater Artists Decry Racism."
58. Wilson, "Ground on Which I Stand."
59. E. G., "Message to Our Audience"; Cartagena, "Kennedy Center"; Goodman Theatre, "Commitment to Action"; Robb, "Actors' Equity."
60 Eyring and Budhu, "Home."
61. "Jamil Jude."
62. Holt, "Monique Holt."
63. Hernandez, "Deaf West's *Big River.*"
64. Isherwood, "Review."
65. Salter, "A Time Such as This."
66. Elliott, "Outrage Erupts."
67. Decora, *Dear Karen.*
68. Decora, interview by Anita Gonzalez.
69. Holland, "Stages of Grief."
70. "About Innovations."
71. "Pathways to (Re)opening Night."

## References

ABC News. *Body Camera Footage of George Floyd's Death Released.* Video. August 10, 2020. https://www.youtube.com/watch?v=Pzjln_SCxY8

ABC News. *New Yorkers Sing Together Out Windows during Coronavirus Pandemic.* Video. March 19, 2020. https://www.youtube.com/watch?v=hcjO_cETMUI

"About—Black Lives Matter." Black Lives Matter. 2020. https://blacklivesmatter.com/about/

"About Innovations in Socially Distant Performance." 2020. https://www.sociallydistantperformance.com/?fbclid=IwAR2QsymPUNdoMKNsyBRSmmzS3kKO8ObqzZWyD6X6rZcQZGM4eLP_Cn7NByg

Aebischer, Pascale, and Rachael Nicholas. *Digital Theatre Transformation: A Case Study and Digital Toolkit.* E-book. Exeter: University of Exeter, 2020. https://www.creationtheatre.co.uk/wp/wp-content/uploads/2020/08/Digital-Theatre-Transformation-A-Case-Study-Digital-Toolkit-Web2-1.pdf

Auslander, Philip. *Liveness: Performance in a Mediatized Culture.* London: Routledge, 1999.

Barbican Theatre. *B-Hive Activity: Zoom Games—Theatre / Drama Warm Up Games (Or Just For Fun!).* Video. 2020. https://www.youtube.com/watch?v=6ZHuCkekyrE

"The Berliner Philharmoniker's Digital Concert Hall." Digital Concert Hall. 2020. https://www.digitalconcerthall.com/en/home

"Berlin Study Issues Recommendations for Orchestral Distancing." The Strad. 2020. https://www.thestrad.com/news/berlin-study-issues-recommendations-for-orch estral-distancing/10641.article

Brantley, Ben. "'Sing Street' Review: New Wave Music As Sweet Deliverance." *New York Times,* December 16, 2019. https://www.nytimes.com/2019/12/16/theater/sing-str eet-review-off-broadway.html

"Cara Consilvio—Opera 'Light Shall Lift Us: Opera Singers Unite In Song.'" Cara Consilvio. 2020. http://caraconsilvio.com

Cartagena, Rosa. "The Kennedy Center Announces Anti-racism Initiatives with #Blackculturematters, the Cartography Project, and More," Washingtonian. 2020, https://www.washingtonian.com/2020/07/09/kennedy-center-announces-anti -racism-initiatives-blackculturematters-cartography-project/

CBS New York. *Coronavirus Update: NYC Residents Join "New York, New York" Sing-Along to Honor Essential Workers.* Video. 2020. https://www.youtube.com/watch?v=wt -u34qbwfs

"Celebrating Detroit's Historical Black Bottom Neighborhood through Music." FOX 2 Detroit, March 6, 2020. https://www.fox2detroit.com/news/celebrating-detroits -historical-black-bottom-neighborhood-through-music

Centers for Disease Control and Prevention. "New ICD-10-CM Code for the 2019 Novel Coronavirus (COVID-19)." Atlanta: Centers for Disease Control and Prevention, 2020.

Crain's New York Business. "A Historic Comeback for One Of NYC's Oldest Social Clubs." September 7, 2016. https://www.crainsnewyork.com/article/20160907/SM ALLBIZ/160909937/new-management-revives-the-128-year-old-players-club

Creation Theatre Company. "The Tempest | Live, Interactive & In Your Living Room | Creation Theatre Company." Creation Theatre Company. 2020. https://www.creati ontheatre.co.uk/shows/the-tempest-live-interactive-in-your-living-room/

Cresswell, Jenny. Interview by Anita Gonzalez. Zoom. 2020.

Cresswell, Jenny. *What Good Would the Moon Be?* Video. 2020. https://www.youtube .com/watch?v=Zx3Y6FdgSKQ&feature=youtu.be

Davidson, Justin. "What Socially Distanced Live Performance Might Look Like." Vulture. 2020. https://www.vulture.com/2020/05/what-socially-distanced-live-perfor mance-might-look-like.html

Decora. *Dear Karen Official Music Video.* Video. 2020. https://www.youtube.com/wat ch?v=sdBSn5Uw5z8&ct=t%28BREAKDOWN+%3D+BREAKTHROUGH_COPY_01 %29

Decora. Interview by Anita Gonzalez. Text message. 2020.

DeFrantz, Thomas F.. "Introduction: From 'Negro Expression' to 'Black Performance.'" In *Black Performance Theory*, edited by Thomas F. DeFrantz and Anita Gonzalez. Durham, NC: Duke University Press, 2014.

E. G. "A Message to Our Audience," Metopera.org. 2020. https://www.metopera.org/us er-information/a-message-to-our-audience/

Elliott, Josh K. "Outrage Erupts over 'Karen' Who Called Cops on Black Birdwatcher in Central Park." Global News. 2020. https://globalnews.ca/news/6986111/central-pa rk-karen-amy-cooper-dog/

Escoyne, Courtney. "6 of Our Favorite Digital Dance Projects to Come out of Quarantine." *Dance Magazine*, August 7, 2020. https://www.dancemagazine.com/best-onl ine-dance-videos-2646888257.html

Eyring, Teresa, and Adrian Budhu. "Home—2020 TCG Virtual Conference—Re:emerg ence." Circle.Tcg.org. 2020. https://circle.tcg.org/tcg20/home?ssopc=1

Gamio, Lazaro, Mitch Smith, Karen Yourish, and Sarah Almukhtar. "Watch How the Coronavirus Spread across the United States." *New York Times*, March 21, 2020. https://www.nytimes.com/interactive/2020/03/21/us/coronavirus-us-cases-spre ad.html

Gans, Andrew, and Robert Viagas. "Exclusive: Tonya Pinkins Issues Unedited, Full Statement Detailing Abrupt Departure From CSC's Mother Courage." Playbill, December 31, 2015. https://m.playbill.com/article/exclusive-tonya-pinkins-issues -unedited-full-statement-detailing-abrupt-departure-from-cscs-mother-courage -com-377196

Gardner, Elysa. "Meet the Kids Who'll Make 'Sing Street' Rock." *New York Times*, December 11, 2019. https://www.nytimes.com/2019/12/11/theater/sing-street-cast .html

Goodman Theatre. "Commitment To Action." Goodmantheatre.org. 2020, https://www.goodmantheatre.org/season/1920-Season/A-Statement-from-Goodman-Th eatre/

"Hamilton 2020 Tour Dates & Top Events." Blog.Ticketcity.com. 2020. https://blog.tic ketcity.com/theatre/hamilton-2020-tour-dates/

Hernandez, Ernio. "Deaf West's *Big River* Shines on Broadway as Roundabout Revival Opens, July 24." *Playbill*, July 24, 2003. https://www.playbill.com/article/deaf-wests -big-river-shines-on-broadway-as-roundabout-revival-opens-july-24-com-114432

Hilton, Haley. "Zoom Dance Class Etiquette 101." Dance Spirit. 2020. https://www.dan cespirit.com/zoom-dance-class-etiquette-2645744609.html

Holland, Kimberly. "Stages of Grief: General Patterns for Breakups, Divorce, Loss, More." Healthline. 2020. https://www.healthline.com/health/stages-of-grief

Holt, Monique. "Monique Holt." Oregon Shakespeare Festival. 2020. https://www.osfa shland.org/en/artist-biographies/guest-artists/monique-holt.aspx

Isherwood, Charles. "Review: 'Spring Awakening' by Deaf West Theater Brings a New Sensation to Broadway." *New York Times*, September 28, 2015. https://www.nytimes

.com/2015/09/28/theater/review-spring-awakening-by-deaf-west-theater-brings
-a-new-sensation-to-broadway.html

"Jamil Jude | Kenny Leon's True Colors Theatre Atlanta." Kenny Leon's True Colors The-
atre Company. 2020. https://truecolorstheatre.org/about/staff2/jamil-jude/

Kelly, Kathleen. "Calendar—Kathleen Kelly." Kathleenkellymusic.com. 2020. http://
www.kathleenkellymusic.com/calendar/

Kepler, Johanna. Interview by Anita Gonzalez. Zoom. 2020.

Kepler, Johanna, Shannon Nulf, Zion Jackson, Sammy Sussman, Casey Tin, Kristin
Hanson, Allie Taylor, and Shea Carponter-Broderick. "TPOTPA: About." Thepower-
oftheperformingarts.com. 2020. https://www.thepoweroftheperformingarts.com
/about

Kourlas, Gia. "'If I Was Martha, What Would I Do?' For One, Stay Upright." *New York
Times*, June 16, 2020. https://www.nytimes.com/2020/06/16/arts/dance/martha
-graham-immediate-tragedy-virus.html

"Kurt Weill—What Good Would the Moon Be Lyrics." Allthelyrics.com. 2020. https://
www.allthelyrics.com/lyrics/kurt_weill/what_good_would_the_moon_be-lyrics
-218812.html

Martha Graham Dance Company. *Immediate Tragedy—Martha Graham Dance Company and Wildup*. Video. 2020. https://www.youtube.com/watch?time_continue
=37&v=L_CxbzdXStI&feature=emb_logo

Martha Graham Dance Company. *The Making of "Immediate Tragedy"*. Video. 2020.
https://www.youtube.com/watch?v=dMj0LfmIWNE&feature=youtu.be

*New Yorker. The Italians Making Music on Balconies under Coronavirus Quarantine*.
Video. March 20, 2020. https://www.youtube.com/watch?v=EBByYjjvNzs

"New York Sings Along—Peace of Heart Choir." Peace of Heart Choir. 2020. http://
www.peaceofheartchoir.org/new-york-sings-along

*New York Times*. "12 Places to Watch Dance Online." April 7, 2020. https://www.nytimes
.com/2020/04/07/arts/dance/stream-dance-online-virus.html

Okoye, Nkeiru. "Harriet Tubman—AOP." AOP. 2020. https://www.aopopera.org/tu
bman

Okoye, Nkeiru. Interview by Anita Gonzalez. Zoom. 2020.

Opera America. *Light Shall Lift Us: Opera Singers Unite in Song*. Video. 2020. https://
www.youtube.com/watch?v=u8A8fIGbYyY

"Pathways to (Re)opening Night—DLR Group." View.Ceros.com. 2020. http://view.cer
os.com/dlr-group/pathways-to-reopening/p/1

Paulson, Michael. "Theater Artists Decry Racism in Their Industry." *New York Times*,
June 9, 2020. https://www.nytimes.com/2020/06/09/theater/theater-artists-decry
-racism.html

Perez, Gian. Interview by Anita Gonzalez. Zoom. 2020.

Pinkins, Tonya. "Why I Am Fed Up with Performative Activism from White and Black
Theater Makers." Medium. July 10, 2020. https://medium.com/@tonyapinkins/why
-i-am-fed-up-with-performative-activism-from-white-and-black-theater-makers
-d46564ec94fe

Queens Theatre. *Zoom Theatre: Best Practices.* Video. 2020. https://www.youtube.com
/watch?feature=youtu.be&v=AC_AS4zs9ZQ&fbclid=IwAR22OFT3F1lIAYl6gT1Ft
PY9zXxje3htJ56p9X-Lyo-AK1BWjoNWJVcmG5I&app=desktop

Register, Julia. Interview by Anita Gonzalez. Zoom. 2020.

Register, Julia. *Julia Register YouTube Channel.* Video. 2020. https://www.youtube.com
/channel/UCf1uSiMhmj0S3uy7vU1ahCg

Register, Julia. *Live from Bed! Coronavirus NYC Day 5: "Shelter At Home"? My Buttocks.*
Video. 2020. https://www.youtube.com/watch?v=ryGakKZzszk

Robb, David. "Actors' Equity Acknowledges Its 'Historic Culpability In Perpetuating
Inequity,' Vows Reforms." Deadline. June 18, 2020. https://deadline.com/2020/06
/actors-equity-acknowledges-its-historic-culpability-in-perpetuating-inequity-vo
ws-reforms-1202963420/

Ross, Alex. "Coronavirus Concerts: The Music World Contends with the Pandemic."
*New Yorker,* March 14, 2020. https://www.newyorker.com/culture/cultural-comm
ent/coronavirus-concerts-the-music-world-contends-with-the-pandemic

Rountree, Christopher. "Home." rountreemusic.com. 2020. https://rountreemusic
.com

Salter, Nikkole. "A Time Such as This." nikkosalter.com. June 3, 2020. https://www.nikk
olesalter.com/single-post/a-time-such-as-this

Sauer, Lauren. "What Is Coronavirus?" Johns Hopkins Medicine. 2020. https://www
.hopkinsmedicine.org/health/conditions-and-diseases/coronavirus

Smith, Jacob, Gian Perez, Alain Sullivan, Eliza Salem, Nina White, Zan Berube, and
Wilson Plonk. *"Nothin' Else 2 Do" (An SMTD Collaboration).* Video. 2020. https://
www.facebook.com/umichsmtd/videos/225711998793292/

Soloski, Alexis. "Star of 'Mother Courage' Quits in Creative Dispute." *New York Times,*
December 31, 2015. https://www.nytimes.com/2015/12/31/theater/star-of-mother
-courage-quits-in-creative-dispute.html

"Spring Preview 2020: Get the Lowdown on THE 18 Broadway Shows Opening in the
Next Three Months." Broadway.com. February 4, 2020. https://www.broadway.com
/buzz/198308/spring-preview-2020-get-the-lowdown-on-the-18-broadway-shows
-opening-in-the-next-three-months/

Theatre Communications Group. *TCG 2020 Virtual Conference—Opening Session.* Video. 2020. https://www.youtube.com/watch?fbclid=IwAR3QFd7gMJ29wha6iY0IM
Lov8KpJPxMG91fEd3nVQmg53uL1x4kcM6CS_cs&v=hgpB-XlMbwc&feature=you
tu.be&app=desktop

The Players NYC. "Home—The Players NYC." Theplayersnyc.org. 2020. http://theplay
ersnyc.org

"Video Conferencing, Web Conferencing, Webinars, Screen Sharing." Zoom video.
2020. https://zoom.us/meetings

We See You White American Theater. "Demands." 2020. https://www.weseeyouwat
.com

Wilson, August. "The Ground on Which I Stand." *American Theatre*, June 20, 2016. https://www.americantheatre.org/2016/06/20/the-ground-on-which-i-stand/. This is a reprint of a speech delivered by playwright August Wilson on June 26, 1996.

Wright, Laura Jayne. "Shakespeare on Zoom: How a Theatre Group in Isolation Conjured Up a Tempest." The Conversation. 2020. https://theconversation.com/shakespeare-on-zoom-how-a-theatre-group-in-isolation-conjured-up-a-tempest-136974

# Contributors

**Abiola Akiyode-Afolabi** was born in 1971 in Ilorin, Kwara State, Nigeria. Akiyode-Afolabi studied law at the Obafemi Awolowo University. She received her LLM from the Notre Dame School of Law in the United States and a PhD from the School of Oriental and African Studies, the University of London, where she specialized in women's peace and security studies. In 2002, she established the Women Advocates Research and Documentation Center, a not-for-profit focused on maternal and reproductive health advocacy, gender-based violence, and social justice. She also teaches international humanitarian law at the University of Lagos. Akiyode-Afolabi organized grassroots networks connecting women in Nigeria. Such networks have been established in colleges across Nigeria.

**Patrick Bates** is a researcher and community collaborator for the Carceral State Project, a workshop facilitator for the Prison Creative Arts Project, and a community activist. He is also the host and executive producer of the web series *Living on Loss of Privileges: What We Learned in Prison*.

**Sara Blair** is Patricia S. Yaeger Collegiate Professor of English and Faculty Associate of American Culture and Judaic Studies. Her publications include *How the Other Half Looks: The Lower East Side and the Afterlives of Images* (Princeton University Press), *Harlem Crossroads: Black Writers and the Photograph in the Twentieth Century* (Princeton University Press), *Remaking Reality: U.S. Documentary Culture after 1945*, coedited with Joseph Entin and Franny Nudelman (University of North Carolina Press), as well as numerous essays in such venues as *American Literary History, Images, PMLA, ELH, The Cambridge Companion to Alfred Hitchcock*, and *The Oxford Handbook of Global Modernisms*. Her current work focuses on the lives of the image as material object, aesthetic form, and resource for literary and cultural narratives from the advent of photography through the digital era.

**William A. Calvo-Quirós** is Assistant Professor of American Culture at the University of Michigan. He holds a PhD in Chicana/o studies from the University of California, Santa Barbara (2014) and a PhD from the Department of Architecture and Environmental Design at Arizona State University (2011). His current research investigates the relationship between state violence and religiosity, faith, and migrations along the US–Mexico border region during the twentieth century. He looks at this region not only as a sociopolitical space of conflict and struggle but simultaneously as a two-thousand-mile strip of "haunted" land, inhabited by many imaginary creatures, monsters, popular saints, and fantastic tales. His other areas of interest include Chicana/o aesthetics, Chicana feminist and queer decolonial methodologies, and the power of empathy and forgiveness in formulating new racial, gender, and sensual discourses. You can find more about his research, and teaching at www.barriology.com

**David Caron** is Professor of French and Women's and Gender Studies at the University of Michigan. He is the author of several books on the culture of HIV/AIDS and queer theories of community and is currently at work on a book on transnational queer cinema.

**Eimeel Castillo**, originally from Nicaragua, is a PhD candidate in the joint program in History and Women's and Gender Studies at the University of Michigan, Ann Arbor. Her research interests are Central America's encounter with the United States and gender histories of empire. She is interested in combining scholarly work with innovative pedagogical strategies.

**Sueann Caulfield** is Associate Professor of History and the Residential College and former Director of the Center for Latin American and Caribbean Studies at the University of Michigan. She specializes in the history of modern Brazil, with emphasis on gender and sexuality. She has won awards and fellowships from the Fulbright Commission, National Endowment for the Humanities, and American Council of Learned Societies. Her publications include *In Defense of Honor: Morality, Modernity, and Nation in Early Twentieth-Century Brazil*, the coedited volume *Honor, Status, and Law in Modern Latin American History*, and various articles on gender and historiography, family law, race, and sexuality in Brazil. Her current research focuses on family history with a focus on paternity and legitimacy in twentieth-century Brazil. She is particularly interested in questions of human rights in Latin America, and has participated in a number of workshops, cross-country teaching projects, and exchanges around topics of social justice and social action.

**James Cogswell** is a multimedia artist and Arthur F. Thurnau Professor at the Penny W. Stamps School of Art & Design. Attracted to interdisciplinary projects, he has collaborated in performance works and installations with poets, dancers, musicians, composers, cosmologists, astronomers, archaeologists, microbiologists, a biostatistician, and computer science and mechanical engineers. His latest project, *Vinyl Euripides*, will be installed in 2021 at the Michael Cacoyannis Foundation in Athens, Greece, based on Cacoyannis's film adaptations of three plays by Euripides.

**Suzanne L. Davis** is an archaeological conservator and Associate Curator and Head of Conservation at the Kelsey Museum of Archaeology at the University of Michigan, Ann Arbor. She believes in the power of historic places, objects, and artwork to delight, connect, and inspire us, and sees her work as an act of both remembrance and hope.

**Abigail A. Dumes** is a medical and cultural anthropologist and Assistant Professor in the Department of Women's and Gender Studies at the University of Michigan. Her first book, *Divided Bodies: Lyme Disease, Contested Illness, and Evidence-Based Medicine*, was published by Duke University Press in 2020.

**Amal Hassan Fadlalla** is Professor of Anthropology, Women's and Gender Studies, and Afroamerican and African Studies at the University of Michigan. She is the author of *Branding Humanity: Competing Narratives of Rights, Violence and Global Citizenship* (Stanford University Press, 2019) and *Embodying Honor: Fertility, Foreignness, and Regeneration in Eastern Sudan* (University of Wisconsin Press, 2007). She is also the coeditor of *Humanity* journal issue "Human Rights and Humanitarianism in Africa," 7.1 (Spring 2016) and the book, *Gendered Insecurities: Health and Development in Africa* (Routledge, 2012). Some of her other publications appear in *Identities: Global Studies in Culture and Power, Urban Anthropology, Signs*, and the School for Advanced Research seminar series coedited volume *New Landscapes of Inequality: Neoliberalism and the Erosion of Democracy in America*. As part of her commitment to engaged anthropology and public scholarship, Professor Fadlalla has also written short articles for various media blogs and has given interviews to various popular media outlets, including BBC, Al Jazeera, and NPR. She is the recipient of many fellowships and awards.

**Marisol Fila** is a PhD candidate in Romance languages and literatures, Spanish and Portuguese, at the University of Michigan. Her dissertation, "Content and Form: Twenty-First-Century Black Press and Articulations of Blackness in Buenos Aires, São Paulo, and Lisbon" explores how the twenty-first-century Black presses of these three cities reveal different articulations between diasporic and national Black identities. Fila places her analysis of the recent digital and print Black press in dialogue with a reading of the historical printed Black press published in each of these cities between the end of the nineteenth century and the first decades of the twentieth century.

**Sara Forsdyke** is Josiah Ober Collegiate Professor of Ancient History in the Departments of Classical Studies and History at the University of Michigan. Her research interests focus on democracy and on slavery and the law, both ancient and modern.

As a graduate student, **Alexandra Friedman** worked as an intern for the Prison Creative Arts Project as well as research assistant for the Carceral State Project at the University of Michigan. She graduated from UM in May 2020 and currently works as a program specialist for Big Brothers Big Sisters of Colorado.

**Anita Gonzalez**, PhD, is a Professor of African American Studies and Performing Arts at Georgetown University. At the time of writing, she was Associate Dean for Faculty Affairs and a Professor of Theatre in the School of Music, Theatre & Dance at the University of Michigan, where she promoted interdisciplinary and intercultural performance initiatives. Her edited and authored books are *Performance, Dance and Political Economy* (Bloomsbury), *Black Performance Theory* (Duke University Press), *Afro-Mexico: Dancing between Myth and Reality* (University of Texas Press), and *Jarocho's Soul* (Rowman & Littlefield).

**Kristin Ann Hass** is Associate Professor of American Culture at the University of Michigan. She has been the faculty coordinator of the Michigan Humanities Collaboratory since 2017. Her publications include *Carried to the Wall: American Memory and the Vietnam Veterans Memorial* (University of California Press) and *Sacrificing Soldiers on the National Mall* (University of California Press). Her current book project is *Blunt Instruments: A Field Guide to Racist Cultural Infrastructure*. Her interests include visual culture, material culture, museum studies, memory, and twentieth-century cultural history.

**Nicholas Henriksen** is Associate Professor of Spanish Linguistics at the University of Michigan. He uses methods in experimental phonetics to research language varieties of the Spanish-speaking world. Some research areas include intonational structure and prosody, bilingual phonology, and sound change in Andalusian, Argentinian, and Castilian Spanish. He is the principal investigator of Michigan's Humanities Collaboratory project "From Africa to Patagonia: Voices of Displacement."

**Daniel Herbert** is an associate professor in the Department of Film, Television, and Media at the University of Michigan. He is the author of *Videoland: Movie Culture at the American Video Store* (University of California Press, 2014) and *Film Remakes and Franchises* (Rutgers University Press, 2017) and the coauthor of *Media Industry Studies* (Polity, 2020).

**Roland Hwang** is an attorney and a lecturer in the Department of American Culture, Asian / Pacific Islander American Studies at the University of Michigan. He serves as President of American Citizens for Justice / Asian American Center for Justice, an Asian American civil rights organization. He also serves as Vice President for Public Affairs for OCA–Asian Pacific American Advocates, headquartered in Washington, DC. He serves as Co-Vice Chair of the Michigan Advisory Committee to the US Commission on Civil Rights. He chairs the advisory board to the Center for Health Disparities, Innovation and Solutions at Eastern Michigan University. Hwang received a BS in mechanical engineering and an MBA from the University of Michigan and a JD and master of laws from Wayne State University Law School.

**Verena Klein** is a Marie Skłodowska-Curie Postdoctoral Fellow at the Stigmatized Sexualities Lab at the University of Michigan, Department of Psychology. Her major research interests focus on gender inequalities, women´s sexuality, sexual desire and entitlement to pleasure, and gender differences in sexual behavior.

**Adam Kouraimi** is a formerly incarcerated college student driven by the desire to change the world through film. He has worked with the Prison Creative Arts Project, the Carceral State Project, the Undergraduate Research Opportunity Program, the Youth Justice Fund, and A Brighter Way.

**Jayati Lal** is a Visiting Associate Professor in the Department of Women's, Gender, and Sexuality Studies at Wake Forest University. Her scholarly interests include transnational feminism, postcolonial studies, neoliberalism and capitalism in the Global South, and feminist labor studies. Her research has been published in *Signs, Feminist Studies, Critical Sociology, Sociological Review*, and various edited anthologies. She was a founding codirector and co-principal investigator of the feminist digital archival project on global feminisms at the University of Michigan, as well as site co-coordinator for the India interviews (https://sites.lsa.umich.edu/globalfeminisms/about/).

**Donald Lopez** is the Arthur E. Link Distinguished University Professor of Buddhist and Tibetan Studies in the Department of Asian Languages and Cultures at the University of Michigan.

**Ashley Lucas** is Associate Professor of Theatre and Drama, the Residential College, English, and the Penny Stamps School of Art and Design at the University of Michigan, Ann Arbor. She is the co-principal investigator of the Carceral State Project, the former director of the Prison Creative Arts Project, and the author of the book *Prison Theatre and the Global Crisis of Incarceration* (Bloomsbury, 2020).

**Christopher Matthews** teaches in the creative writing and literature faculty in the University of Michigan's Residential College, where his courses often focus on monstrosity, ghost stories, and apocalyptic tropes rooted in Romantic, Victorian, and contemporary literature and culture.

**Michelle McClellan**, PhD, is the Johanna Meijer Magoon Principal Archivist at the Bentley Historical Library, University of Michigan, where she collects materials that document the history of the state of Michigan. Michelle has worked in academia, museums, and historic preservation over the course of her career and is especially interested in intersections of place and story.

**Aprille McKay** is the Lead Archivist for University Archives at the Bentley Historical Library at the University of Michigan. Before she became an archivist, she practiced law and maintains a strong interest in copyright, privacy, and ethical issues in archives.

**Matthew Neubacher** is currently in the Master of Public Affairs program at Brown University. At the time of writing, he was an undergraduate at the University of Michigan, majoring in political science with a minor in Latin American and Caribbean studies. At the Speech Production Lab with Professor

Nicholas Henriksen, he researched hesitation phenomena in the Humanities Collaboratory project "From Africa to Patagonia: Voices of Displacement."

**Ronke Olawale** is a PhD candidate in social work and anthropology at the University of Michigan. Broadly speaking, she is interested in culture, care, and infectious disease; death and dying, care at the end of life, and meaning-making; kinship and child welfare/well-being; and intergenerational care. Olawale is also very interested in clinical pastoral care. Her dissertation explores the social and cultural context in which the 2013–16 Ebola virus disease epidemic occurred in Liberia.

**Sriram Papolu** is a Chicago-based filmmaker whose work consists of internationally acclaimed narrative and documentary films as well as music videos. If you are interested in his work or would like to get in touch, please visit www.srirampapolu.com

**David Patterson** is a PhD candidate in history at the University of Michigan. His research explores early medieval conceptions of weather and climate, and reactions to meteorological adversity.

**Özge Savaş** is a faculty member in psychology at Bennington College. She received her PhD in psychology and women's and gender studies from University of Michigan. Her research on activism, political behavior. and migration examines people's sense of belonging in groups, institutions, and nations.

**Abigail J. Stewart** is Sandra Schwartz Tangri Distinguished University Professor of Psychology and Gender and Women's Studies at the University of Michigan. She has a PhD in psychology and social relations from Harvard University, an MSc. in social psychology from London School of Economics, and a BA from Wesleyan University. Her research interests include political activism, personality development and change in the context of experience and social history, and institutional change in higher education. She is coauthor with Virginia Valian of *An Inclusive Academy* (MIT Press, 2018) and with Sarah Fenstermaker of *Gender, Considered: Feminist Reflections across the US Social Sciences* (Palgrave Macmillan, 2020).

**Melanie Tanielian**, PhD, is Associate Professor in the Department of History at the University of Michigan and an anxiety-driven amateur photographer. Her research concerns the history of war and society in the Middle East, Ottoman Lebanon in particular, at the beginning of the twentieth century. She is the author of *The Charity of War: Famine, Humanitarian Aid, and World War I in the Middle East.*

**Nick Tobier** studied sculpture and landscape architecture and has worked at Storefront for Art & Architecture in NYC and as a designer with the NYC Department of Parks and Recreation, Bronx Division, and LandWorks Studio, Boston. His focus as artist-designer is in the social lives of public places, both in built structures and events, from bus stops to kitchens and boulevards in Detroit, Tokyo, Toronto, and San Francisco. His work has been seen at the Smithsonian; the Queens Museum, New York; the Mattress Factory, Pittsburgh; and as part of the 2019 Prague Quadrennial. Nick is cofounder of the Brightmoor Maker Space in Detroit, a Libra, a midfielder for the Penguins (a 4th Division soccer team), and Professor at the Stamps School and the Center for Entrepreneurship and Senior Counsel to the Provost on Civic Engagement at the University of Michigan.

**Frances Kai-Hwa Wang** is a journalist, essayist, poet, and lecturer at the University of Michigan Department of American Culture Program in Asian / Pacific Islander American Studies. She is a Knight Arts Challenge Detroit artist and is working on a book and digital arts archive about the Vincent Chin case (Franceskaihwawang.com).

**Cozine Welch**, formerly incarcerated, is Executive Director of the Washtenaw County nonprofit A Brighter Way and co-instructor of both the Atonement Project and Theatre and Incarceration courses at the University of Michigan. He is also an accomplished poet who has been published in the *Michigan Quarterly Review*, *Plough Quarterly*, and eleven volumes of the *Michigan Review of Prisoner Creative Writing*. His first poetry collection is forthcoming from Dakota West Publishing.

# Index

Page numbers in italics refer to illustrations

abortion rights, 251, 252, 254n17, 272
Abu Ghraib prison, 98, 114n3
accountability, 83, 85–86
activism, Black feminist, 246, 256–61
activism, digital, 247, 252
activism, social, 364–66. *See also* Black
  Lives Matter movement
activism, women's, 272, 300, 314–15,
  319–20
ACT UP, 109, 111
Adam, Barbara, 99
Adaptive COVID-19 Treatment Trial, 267
Aebischer, Pascale, 370
African American Language (AAL), 345–
  46, 347–48, 355n3
African American Policy Forum, 112
Afro-Argentines, 273–74, 275n28
Afro Women's Day, 273
AIDS pandemic. *See* HIV/AIDS
  pandemic
AKP (Justice and Development Party),
  313, 314, 315
Alliance of Motion Picture and Televi-
  sion Producers, 223
All Souls College, 40–41
Alternative für Deutschland, 283
Altom, Akram, 134
Amazon region (Brazil), 257, 258
AMC theater chain, 228
American Citizens for Justice (ACJ), 332
*The American Four Seasons* (Glass), 30
American Opera Project, 372
"ancestrality," 256, 260–61
Andalusia, 349–53, *350*
Andalusian Spanish, 350–53

Anganwadi workers, 291–92
antechambers, 97
anti-Asian American hate, 82, 132, 219–
  20, 329, 332–33, 337
anti-Black racism: and arts community,
  373–79; and Catholic Church, 183–85;
  and deaths from COVID-19, 165, 266;
  as genocide, 111; and linguistic prejudice, 345–48, 353; and portraiture,
  50–52; and public statuary, 56–57. *See
  also* Black Lives Matter movement
anti-Chinese riot (1871), 330
Anti-Defamation League Michigan, 332
anti-Japanese sentiments, 330
anti-Semitism, 332, 337
anti-trans violence, 271
Apple+ TV, 226, 227
*Approaching Storm*, 122
Arbery, Ahmaud, 52, 329, 373
archives, historic, 73–74, 86. *See also*
  Bentley Historical Library
archivists, 73–74, 76, 83
Argentina, 247, 271–74
Arruzza, Cinzia, 298, 299
artists: and anti-Blackness, 373–79;
  and Black Lives Matter, 373–74; and
  community, 363–73; and George Floyd
  murder, 377–78; innovation of, 358–
  59, 380; and isolation, 359–63; and
  technology, 361, 380. *See also* artists of
  color; performing arts industry
artists of color: impact of COVID-19 on,
  358; inclusion of, 377, 380; and social
  activism, 364–66; unequal funding
  for, 375

art-making, politicization of, 358
ASHAs (accredited social health activists), 291–92
Asian Americans, 329, 333–34. *See also* anti-Asian American hate
Asian Americans Advancing Justice, 332
Asian Pacific American Advocates. *See* OCA-Asian Pacific American Advocates
Asian Pacific Policy and Planning Council, 332
Askew, Lucy, 369
Association of Chinese Americans in Detroit, 331
Athens, 176–78, 179
*The Atlantic*, 283, 296
attention, redirection of, 47
audiences and sense of community, 370
*Auschwitz and After* (Delbo), 98
Auslander, Philip, 368

Badiou, Alain, 104
Baltimore Center Stage, 357
"bamboo ceiling," 333
Barbican Theatre, 368
Barthes, Roland, 97, 106
al-Bashir, Omar, 133–34, 136, 142
Bates, Patrick, 64
Batista, Luíza, 259–60
Bay, Michael, 223
BBC, 28
Beck, Glenn, 28
Beckett, Samuel, 99
"being human," 40
belonging, 162. *See also* community
Bentley Historical Library, 72, 73–75, 83, 86–87. *See also* "Documenting COVID-19 at the University of Michigan"
Berlin Philharmonic, 371
Bersani, Leo, 111
Bhattacharya, Tithi, 298, 299
bias, implicit, and auditory cues, 345–47, 353
Bidaseca, Karina, 271, 272
*Big River* (Broadway musical), 376

Big Telly Theatre Company, 369
biomedical research, sex and gender differences in, 266–68
BIPOC artists. *See* artists of color
*Black Bottom* (Okoye), 372
Black Lives Matter movement: and artists, 373–74; in Brazil, 260; and Catholic Church, 183; and collective grief, 9; and "distant justice," 142, 144; founding of, 347; and streaming platforms, 227; use of images, 52, 55–57; and waiting, 105–6; and yards as resistance spaces, 147
*Black Voices Matter* (DeVito), 51
*Black Widow* (2021 film), 225
blame, 336–41
*The Bloody Chamber* (Carter), 36
Bolsonaro, Jair, 256, 257, 258, 260, 261, 339
Booth, Edwin, 367
"born digital," 74–75
Bould, Mark, 287, 292
Boys and Men of Color, 332
Brazil, 256–61, 339
Bridges, Leon, 93
Brooks, Rayshard, 373
Brown, Michael Christopher, 10, 59, *60*
Browne-Springer, Chad, 50
Bruni, Matteo, 191
bubonic plague, 336, 337
the Buddha, 119
Buddhism and suffering, 117–21
Bull Moose (retail store), 225
*The Bus, The Environment, The Human,* *143*
businesses, small, federal aid for, 298
bus systems, 142

Cacoyannis, Michael, 127
Campaña Nacional por el Derecho a un Aborto Legal, Seguro y Gratuito (National Campaign for the Right to Legal, Safe, and Free Abortion), 272
Campbell, Mark, 373
Canada, blame of COVID-19 on outsiders in, 338
cancel culture movement, 190

capitalism, coronavirus, 298, 302
capitalism, patriarchal, 245, 288, 297
Carceral State Project, 64
care work, unpaid: gender inequality in, 295–97; in Nigeria, 320, 321; as social reproduction, 296–99, 302; visibility of, 287–88, 313–14
caring, bond between waiting and, 113–14
car ownership, 141
Carter, Angela, 36
Casilvio, Cara, 373
Castilian Spanish, 351
Catholic Church, 181–85, 251
Católicas por el Derecho a Decidir (Catholics for the Right to Decide), 251, 252
Centers for Disease Control (CDC), 43, 331
Central Bank of Nigeria, 323
certainty, 31–33
#ChallengeAccepted movement, 312, 314
Change.org, 56
Chapek, Bob, 227
Charro Azteca apparel retailer, 187
Chauvin, Derek, 52, 183
childcare, burden of, 320. *See also* care work, unpaid
Chin, Vincent, 219–20, 330, 331–32
China, ineffective COVID-19 leadership in, 339
"China virus," 29, 337. *See also* xenophobia and COVID-19
Chinese Exclusion Act (1882), 330
Christ, Mystical Body of, 183–84
Christian Democratic Union, 283
Citizen University, 179
civic responsibility, and portraiture of health care workers, 44–45
"Civic Saturdays," 179
civil rights, Asian American quest for, 333–34
class assignments and documenting COVID-19, 78–79
clinical research, exclusion of women from, 244–45

CNN, 44
code switching, 346
coincidental communities, 239
Coleridge, Samuel Taylor, 25
Collective Action and Dissent under COVID, 233
comedy, 359–60
commemoration, public, 9
Commission for November 8, 273, 275n28, 276n30
communication technologies: and Afro-Argentine women, 273–74; as bridges of physical distance, 144–45; and linguistic profiling, 344, 349; and sensationalism, 146
communities, coincidental, 239
communities of color, 185, 258–60
community: and artists, 363–73; and music performers, 371–73; portraiture as form of, 49; sense of, 158, 160, 370; and technology, 365; virtual rosaries as, 191–95
commuter trains, 141
Comprehensive Law Against Violence against Women (Law 779), 251, 253
concentration camps, Japanese-American, 172, 330
conditioning, suffering of, 119, 121
connections: with neighbors, 233; with objects, 154, 171. *See also* community
"contemporaneous collecting," 72
Cooper, Amy, 378
Cooper, Christian, 378
Cooper, Larry Ray, 162–64, *163*, 166, 168
Cooper, Susan, 166, *167*
coronavirus: derogatory naming of, 29, 329, 331, 337; genome mapping of, 15; image of, 43. *See also* COVID-19
"coronavirus capitalism," 298, 302
"Coronavirus: How a Misleading Map Went Global" (*The Sun*), 28
"The Coronavirus Is a Disaster for Feminism" (Lewis), 296
corruption in essential services, 321
cosmic kingship, 338, 339–40

Council of Europe Convention on Preventing and Combating Violence against Women and Domestic Violence, 312–13

"Courage is Beautiful" ad campaign, 46–48, *47*, *48*

COVID Memorial Project, 8

COVID-19: economic relief packages, 271–72, 298, 313, 320–21, 323; gendered nature of, 283, 287, 290; as kind of war, 164; and lack of empathy, 165, 168; and leadership, 245, 281–84, 298, 338–39; naming of, 3–4, 337; as patriarchal, 297; tracking apps, 43, 135; and xenophobia, 3–4, 29, 132, 329, 331, 332–33, 337

COVID-19 Government Response Tracker, 289

"COVID-19 Response and Recovery: The Roles of Women Politicians" (webinar), 322

@cozboylenz, 51

Craft, Justin, 348–49, 352

Creation Theatre, 369

Cresswell, Jenny, 360–61, 363

criminal justice system and racial inequality, 65, 173, 178

Criola, 260, 261

Cristero War, 187

cultural centers and monster stories, 34–35

culture, fragmented, and film industry, 222

Curzan, Anne, 353


D'Alessandro, Mercedes, 272

Dalits, 290, 293

dance community, 370–71

dance lessons, online, 370

Dance Spirit (website), 370

dance works, collaborative, 370–71

D'Andrea, Dominic, 368, 369

da Silva, Lula, 257

Davidson, Justin, 371–72

Davis, Mike, 288

A Day without Women Strike, 288

deaf actors, 376

"Dear Karen" (Decora), 378–79

deaths, COVID-19: grief of those left behind, 168; and mass graves, 9, 55, *55*; obituary project, 54, 165; photography of, 52–53, *53*, *54*, 54–55, *55*

Decora, 378–79

DeFrantz, Thomas F., 368

de Keersmaeker, Anna Teresa, 357

Delbo, Charlotte, 98

del Valle, María Remedios, 273, 275n28

democracy, 177–78

depression during COVID-19, 321

"Designated COVID-19 Compliance Officer" position, 223

Detroit Association of Black Organizations, 332

Devault, Derek, 44–45

DeVito, Peter, 50–51

Día Internacional de la Mujer Afrolatina, Afrocaribeña y de la Diáspora (International Day of Afro-Latin, Afro-Caribbean, and African Diasporic Women), 272–73

dialects, marginalized, and code switching, 346

digital activism, 247, 252

Digital Collecting Toolkit (University of Virginia), 77

Digital Concert Hall series, 371

digital divide, 344, 348

digital information creation, 74–75

digital media: distribution of, 226–28; production of, 359–63. *See also* streaming media

digital platforms, 368. *See also* Zoom platform

Dirección de Economía, Igualdad y Género (Office of Economy, Equality, and Gender), 272

disasters and coincidental communities, 239

Disney+, 226, 227, 228

Disney, Walt, 96

"distant justice," 144

distribution: of digital media, 226–28; of films, 224–26

diversity: in archival collections, 86–87; in performing arts industry, 375–77

Dixon, Troy, 80–81, *81*, 87

DLR Group, 380

"Documenting COVID-19 at the University of Michigan," 76–88; and class assignments, 78–79; diversity in, 86–87; evaluation of initiative, 87–88; publicity for, 79; submission of materials to, 80–85

"Documenting in Times of Crisis: A Resource Kit" (Society of American Archivists), 77

domestic violence. *See* violence, domestic

domestic workers: economic vulnerability of, 294; hiring of by women, 295–96; impact of COVID-19 on, 258–60, 294; Indian women as, 293–97; return to work of, 294–95; rights for, 259–60

"doortraits," 49–50

"The Do's and Don'ts of Taking Zoom Dance Class" (Hilton), 370

Douglass, Frederick, 43

Dove brand, 46–48, *47*, *48*

"Do You Speak Andalusian?" survey, 352–53

*Dracula* (Stoker), 25, 27, 29, 31

Dreamers, 185, 196n11

Dumes, Abigail, 244

"The Dungeon" (Coleridge), 25

Dunham, Nancy Cross, 212

*Echoes of Revolution*, *145*

ecological crises, blame for, 340

economic relief packages: in Argentina, 271–72; in India, 298; in Nigeria, 320–21, 323; in Turkey, 313

education, importance of, 179, 291, 333

educational videos, 368

Eichmeyer, Adam, 78–79

1882 Project, 333

Eilber, Janet, 371

elderly, impact of COVID-19 on, 165

*Electra* (1962 film), 127

Emergency Family Income (EMI), 271–72

empathy, lack of, 165, 168

"enhanced social distancing," 134–35

En Nuestra Lengua, 353–54

entertainment industry. *See* film industry; streaming media

Epstein, Steven, 267

Erdoğan, Recep Tayyip, 313

escapism and streaming media, 227–28

essential services, corruption in, 321

essential workers: domestic workers as, 259; as expendable, 164, 289; photographs of, 80–81; and social inequality, 185; support for, 299; women overrepresented as, 287. *See also* health care workers

Etsy, 188

Euripides, 127

European Court of Human Rights, 313

Evelle, Monique, 260

exercise, *238*

face masks, 51, 164–65, 186–90, *188*

Family Video, 225

fatalities, military, 163–64, 165–57

Fauci, Anthony, 103, 108

fear: as just, 32–33; and monster stories, 30–31

Federation of Muslim Women Associations, Nigeria, 322

femicide, 251, 254n10, 271, 313, 314, 315

feminism: in Argentina, 272; in Brazil, 246, 256–61; in India, 298–99, 300

*Feminism for the 99%: A Manifesto* (Arruzza et al.), 298, 299

Fernandez, Alberto, 271

Fernandez de Kirchner, Cristina, 271

Filipino American National Historical Society, 331

film industry: distribution sector, 224–26; production sector, 221, 222–23; streaming media, 222, 226, 227–28, 229

flight path map as misleading, 27–28, 29, 31

Flores, Martha, 251

Floyd, George: and artists, 377–78; and collective grief, 9–10; images of, 52, 56–57, *57*; and Mystical Body of Christ, 183–84; and police reform, 113; and second wave of Black Lives Matter movement, 105, 107, 142, 323, 329
*Forbes*, 281
forgetting, 132–33, 146
Foucault, Michel, 102, 106
Four Noble Truths, 117
Fox News, 44
*Fracture* (Neuman), 37
Francis (pope), 181, 191
Franco, Francisco, 350
*Frankenstein* (M. Shelley), 25
Frankenstein's creature, 34–35
Fraser, Nancy, 298, 299
Freud, Sigmund, 95
frontline workers. *See* essential workers; health care workers
*Frozen II* (2019 film), 227
funerals, political, 111
future, envisioning of, and waiting, 106–7
future tense, 120–21

gardening, 133, 147–48
Garner, Eric, 10, 52
GDQ Arts, 361
Geledes, 260
Gender and Constitution Reform Network, 319
Gender and COVID-19 Working Group, 267
gender differences: in biomedical research, 266–68; and leadership, 245, 281–84
"gendered familialism," 297, 299
gender inequality. *See* inequality, gender
GenderSci Lab (Harvard), 268
"gender/sex," 268
gender stereotypes and leadership, 245, 282
@Genithecrankynurse, 46
genocide, AIDS as, 110–11, 112
Gen Verde, 193
George, Kennedy, 56–57, *58*

George Floyd Hologram Memorial Project, 56, *57*
German National Academy of Sciences Leopoldina, 283
Germany and COVID-19, 282–83
Giuliani, Alberto, 46
Glass, Philip, 30
Global Feminisms Project (GFP), 13, 243, 248
Global Health 5050, 267–68
Gonçalves, Cleonice, 259
Google forms, 78, 79, 86
"governmentality," 102, 106
governments: blamed for natural disasters, 339–40; and waiting, 102–3
Governor's Forum, 323
Graduate Employees Organization (GEO), 85
Graham, Martha, 371
grassroots organizing of Indigenous peoples, 257–58
graves, mass, 9, 55, *55*
Greenblatt, Jonathan, 332
Gregory the Great, 336
Greyson, John, 112
grief, collective, 8–10, 168, 172–73, 211
grief, personal, 211–13
grieving cycle and performing arts industry, 379–80
Griffith, D. M., 267
Grinberg, Keila, 260
"The Ground on Which I Stand" (Wilson), 375
Gültekin, Pınar, 312, 314

Hadendowa-Beja groups, 140
Hage, Ghassan, 104
*halafa*, 140–41
*Hamilton* (Broadway musical), 357
*Handheld Device* (Cogswell), *130*
hands, symbolism of, 123
*Hands 1* (Cogswell), *124*
*Hands 2* (Cogswell), *125*
*Hands 3* (Cogswell), *126*
Hanks, Tom, 221
Hans Böckler Foundation, 283

*Harriet Tubman: When I Crossed That Line to Freedom* (Okoye), 372
Harris, Kamala, 1, 2, 10, 23
Hart, Eric, Jr., 50
Hart Island, mass burials on, 55, *55*
*A Hat Full of Sky* (Pratchett), 23–24
HBO Max, 226, 228
health care, racial inequality in, 108–9, 171
health care workers: celebration of, 45; and communication technologies, 146; effect of COVID-19 on, 136, 291–92; increased risk of COVID-19 among, 320; photographic portraiture of, 44–48; tributes to, 372
*Heavy Headed* (Yeh video), 81, *82*
"herd immunity," 165
Hilton, Halen, 370
historians, 211
historical records, shaping of by archivists, 76
HIV/AIDS pandemic: as genocide, 110–11, 112; and introspection, 101; as ongoing, 108, 109; and othering, 103; racial inequity of, 108–9; and waiting, 94
Hochschild, Arlie, 296
Holland, Kimberly, 379
Holloway, Ava, 56–57, *58*
*Hollywood Reporter*, 221
Holt, Monique, 376
home video businesses, 225
hope and blame, 340–41
househusbands, 296
Howell, Katie, 77
Hulu, 226
*The Human Face of COVID-19—New York City* (Turnley), 57, *59*
humanitarianism, 146–47
the humanities, importance of, 179, 180
hydroxychloroquine, 339

IANS news agency, 291
*Immediate Tragedy* (dance work), 371
Immigration Act (1965), 330
*Inclusion: The Politics of Differences in*

*Medical Research* (Epstein), 267
India: COVID-19 relief package, 298; lockdown in, 289–92, 291; second surge in COVID-19, 301; Spanish flu (1918 influenza) in, 288; unpaid care work in, 295; women as domestic workers in, 293–97
*The India Forum*, 289
Indian Protection Service, 257
Indigenous peoples, 257–58
inequality, economic, 171, 275n4
inequality, gender: in Argentina, 247, 271, 272–73; and COVID-19, 248, 287, 290; and Nigerian women, 319; and stereotypes, 282; of unpaid care work, 295–97
inequality, racial: and COVID-19, 35, 107–8; and criminal justice system, 65, 173, 178; in health care, 108–9, 171; and language perceptions, 345–46
inequality, social: of Andalusians, 351; and essential workers, 185; and streaming platforms, 227
influence, 25–26, 47
informal employment, 272. *See also* care work, unpaid; domestic workers
innovation and artists, 358–59, 380
Innovations in Socially Distant Performances (website), 380
Instagram, 214
Institute of Medicine (IOM), 266
Institute of Social Studies Trust, 294
International Committee on Taxonomy of Viruses (ICTV), 337
International Day of Afro-Latin, Afro-Caribbean, and African Diasporic Women (Día Internacional de la Mujer Afrolatina, Afrocaribeña y de la Diáspora), 272–73
International Labour Organization, 290, 294
International Society of Gender Medicine, 266
internet access, 344, 348
introspection and global crises, 101–2
invention and waiting, 106

invisibility: and loss of words, 214; of migrant workers, 290; of unpaid care labor, 314

*Iphigenia* (1977 film), 127

isolation and artists, 359–63

*Isolation Mood* (Tanielian), 200–210

Istanbul Convention, 312–13

"Is the Rectum a Grave?" (Bersani), 111

Italy: balcony singing in, 363; blame of migrant workers for COVID-19 in, 337–38

Jalisco region (Mexico), 187

Japanese Americans, concentration camps for, 172, 330

Jeantel, Rachel, 346

*Jekyll and Hyde* (Stevenson), 26

John Hopkins University, 43

journaling, 82–83, *84*

journalists *vs.* archivists, 83

Jude, Jamil, 376

*Jurassic World: Dominion* (2022 film), 223

Justice and Development Party (AKP), 313, 314, 315

"Keep on Going" (Okoye), 372

Kelly, Kathleen, 360–61

Kelsey Museum of Archaeology, 153–54, 155

Kepler, Johanna, 364–66, *365, 366, 367*

King, Martin Luther, Jr., 94, 184

Klein, Naomi, 298

Köhler, Andrea, 94–95, 97–98, 99, 102, 106, 109

Kracauer, Siegfried, 97

Kramer, Larry, 109

Kullick, Brian, 374

"Kung Flu," 29, 329, 331, 337. *See also* xenophobia and COVID-19

Kurdish women, 247, 312, 314–15

Kurdistan Worker's Party (PKK), 314

*The Lancet*, 267

language and power structures, 346

Law 779 (Comprehensive Law Against Violence against Women), 251, 253

leaders: downplay of COVID-19 by, 298, 338–39; and gender stereotypes, 245, 281–84; Indigenous women as, 258

Lee, Robert E., statue, 56–57, *57, 58*

*Legenda aurea* (Jacobus), 336

Legislative Advocacy Coalition on Violence against Women, 319

Lepore, Jill, 213

Leroy, Vanessa, 59, *60*

Lewis, Helen, 282, 283, 296

Lewis, Sarah, 52–53

*Light Shall Lift Us* (Opera America video), 373

Lilla, Mark, 102, 109

linguistic profiling: and implicit bias, 345–48, 353; and online communication, 344, 349

linguistics and policy change, 348–49

*Live from Bed* (video series), 359–60

*Liveness: Performance in a Mediatized Culture* (Auslander), 368

*Living on LOP: What We Learned in Prison* video series, 64–71

lockdown. *See* stay-at-home orders

Lockhart, Jeff, 85, *85*

Lorraine American Cemetery, 162

Los Angeles, anti-Chinese riot in, 330

"loss of privileges," 64–65

Lourenço, Maria Izabel Monteiro, 260

Lovekin, Stephen, 49–50

*A Lover's Discourse* (Barthes), 97

Lui, Eric, 179

Macri, Mauricio, 271

making as way of thinking, 122–23

Mallisham, Artaysia, 65–67, *66*

marginalized populations: and capitalism, 288; impact of COVID-19 on, 271, 320, 351; and internet access, 344, 348

Marielle Franco Institute, 261

marriages, arranged, 291

Martin, Trayvon, 10, 346, 347

masculinity and face masks, 186, 189–90

"Mass Observation Project," 75–76

Massumi, Brian, 212, 213

maturity, collective, and waiting, 102–6
McDade, Tony, 373
McMichael, Gregory, 52
Merkel, Angela, 281–83
Michael, Saint, 190
Michigan United, 332
Middle Ages, blame during, 338, 339–40
migrant workers: blame for COVID-19 in Italy, 337–38; invisibility of, 290; and lockdown in India, 289–90, 301; as undocumented, 185
Miller, Virginia M., 266
Ministry for Women and Family, 313–14
Ministry of Family, Labor and Social Services, 313, 314
Ministry of Family and Social Policies, 313–14
Ministry of Labor and Social Services, 314
Ministry of Women, Gender, and Diversity, 274
"Mirando la realidad desde la intersección: Afrofeminismos en Argentina" (Looking at Reality from the Intersection: Afro-Feminisms in Argentina), 273–74
misinformation: images as, 27–28, 29, 31; spread of, by leaders, 338–39
mobilization of change and performing arts, 373–79
Modi, Narendra, 289, 298, 301
monster stories, 23–41; attacks on centers of power, 35–37; and cruelty of humans when afraid, 30–31; pandemic as, 26; transformation in, 37–40; as warnings, 34
monstrosity, concept of, 26–27
monuments. *See* statuary, public
Moravec, Paul, 373
morgues, mobile, 9
*Mother Courage* (play), 374
Mount Sinai Hospital, 54, *54*
movie theaters. *See* theaters, movie
*Mulan* (2020 film), 228
Murillo, Rosario, 250
music making, 361–63

music performers and community, 371–73

National Assembly (NASS), 323
National Campaign for the Right to Legal, Safe, and Free Abortion (Campaña Nacional por el Derecho a un Aborto Legal, Seguro y Gratuito), 272
National Centre for Disease Control, 294
National Coalition on Affirmative Action, 319
National Council of Asian Pacific Americans, 334
National Council of Women's Societies, 319
National Day of Afro-Argentines and Afro Culture, 273
National Domestic Workers Movement, 293
National Social Register, 323
National Women's Encounters, 273
National Women's Marches, 273
Native American Graves Protection and Repatriation Act (1990), 171
natural disasters, blame of governments for, 339–40
Neetha, N., 297
*Neighborhood Window*, 233, *234*
neighbors, connections with, 233
Netflix, 226
Neuman, Andres, 37
"New York, New York" (Sinatra), 363
New York City, balcony singing in, 363
*New York Native*, 109
*New York Post*, 44
*New York Times*: obituary project, 8, 54, 165; and streaming platforms, 371
Ng, Tiffany, 82–83, *84*
Nicaragua, 246–47, 250–53, 253n9, 254n17
Nicholas, Rachael, 370
Nigeria, 318–24
Nigerian Women Trust Fund, 322
*Night of the Living Dead* (1968 film), 31–33, *32*, *34*, 35
NIH Revitalization Act (1993), 266
nirvana, 121

Ni Una Menos movement, 272
*No Love for Cowboy* (Perez), 363
Northam, Ralph, 56
*Nothin' Else 2 Do* (music video), 361–63
"Nude Selfies are Now High Art" (*New York Times*), 214

Obata, Chiura, 172
objects: as artifacts of remembrance, 168–69; and connections, 154, 171; inability to retain, 171–72; power of, 153
Observatory for Women's Lives, 251
OCA-Asian Pacific American Advocates, 332, 333
Office of Economy, Equality, and Gender (Dirección de Economía, Igualdad y Género), 272
Office of Research on Women's Health (NIH), 266
Ogilvy (ad agency), 46
Okoye, Nkeiru, 372
*Old News* (Cogswell), *131*
"one percent feminism," 288
"1,112 and Counting" (Kramer), 109
*On Waiting* (Schweizer), 95
opera, 360–61, 373
Opera America, 373
opioid crisis, 108
oral history projects, 76
Oregon Shakespeare Festival, 357
Ortega, Daniel, 250, 251, 252, 253n4, 254n17
othering: and AIDS pandemic, 103; of Asian Americans, 329–30; and blame, 337–38; of slum-dwellers, 292–93

Palriwala, Rajni, 297
pandemics as monster stories, 26
*A Paradise Built in Hell* (Solnit), 239
*Passing Time: An Essay on Waiting* (Köhler), 94–95
"Pathways to (Re)opening Night" (DLR Group), 380
patience and waiting, 94
patriarchy in capitalism, 245, 288, 297
Patterson, Megan, 45–46

peace activists, women, 314–15
Peace and Social Change Fellowship, 322
Peace of Heart Choir, 363
Pence, Mike, 108
Perez, Gian, 361–63
performance, collaborative, 363
performing arts industry: and diversity, 375–77; grieving cycle of, 379–80; mobilization of change in, 373–79; systemic racism in, 374–79, 380. *See also* artists; artists of color; theatre; theatres, performing arts
Pericles, 176, 177–78, 179
"perpetual foreigners," Asian Americans as, 329, 333
personal protective equipment (PPE), 45–46, 136, 164–65, 291–92. *See also* face masks
personhood and photography, 53–59, 114n3
Pew Research Center, 344, 348
Philippine Association of Medical Technologists – Michigan, 331
photographers, impact of COVID-19 on, 48–53
photographs: of Covid-19 deaths, 52–53, *53, 54*, 54–55; of essential workers, 80–81; and personhood, 53–59, 114n3. *See also* portraiture, photographic
*The Picture of Dorian Gray* (Wilde), 26
Pinkins, Tonya, 374
PKK (Kurdistan Worker's Party), 314
plague, Athenian, 176–78
plague, bubonic, 336, 337
Players Club, 366–68
"PM Cares" fund, 298
police: abolishment of, 113; brutality by, 239, 373. *See also* Black Lives Matter movement
policy change: and linguistics, 348–49; in Nigeria, 324
politicization: of art-making, 358; of portraits of health care workers, 46–48; of waiting, 95; of women, 299–300
Poo, Ai-jen, 299

portraiture, photographic: and anti-Black racism, 50–52; in Black Lives Matter movement, 53, 55–57; as form of community, 49; of health care workers, 44–48; social function of, 43–44
poverty in Nigeria, 318
power, centers of, attacks on, 35–37
power, distribution of, and waiting, 96–99
*The Power of the Performing Arts* (website), 364–66, *365, 366, 367*
power structures and language, 346
Pratchett, Terry, 23–24
pregnant women and COVID-19, 140
"Preparing Your Mind for Uncertain Times" (Weiner), 38
Prime Video, 226, 227
prison, lessons from, to adjust to life during pandemic, 64–71
prison releases in Turkey, 247
production, film, 221, 222–23
*Protest Platform, 236*
protests: criminalization of, 250; use of portraiture in, 53; of white nationalists, 105–6. *See also* Black Lives Matter movement
public office, minorities for, 261
Puff, Helmut, 97, 100
Punit, Ikita, 295–96

Queens Theatre, 368
*quilombo* communities, 258

race: COVID-19, 2; and grief, 9; and linguistic profiling, 347–48; and wealth gaps, 171
racialization as social distancing, 134–35
racial purity, 29
racism, anti-Asian, 82, 132, 219–20, 329, 332–33, 337
racism, anti-Black: and arts community, 373–79; and Catholic Church, 183–85; and deaths from COVID-19, 165, 266; as genocide, 111; and linguistic prejudice, 345–48, 353; and portraiture, 50–52; and public statuary, 56–57

racism, systemic, 329, 333, 347, 374–79, 380
radio programs and Nigerian women's groups, 322, 323
"rapid-response collecting," 72
Ray, Nikolas, 51
Real Academia Española, 351
Reclaim the Streets, *236*
Redbox, 225
Register, Julia, 359–60, 363
religious freedom: and face masks, 186; and stay-at-home orders, 181
religious images and face masks, 186–90, *188*
religious practices, resurgence of during COVID-19, 181–82
religious studies, 120
remdesivir, 267
remembrance, objects as artifacts of, 168–69
Rendleman, Julia, 56–57, *58*
reproductive rights, 251, 252, 254n17, 272, 320
residents welfare associations (RWAs), 294, 295
Rhode, Jeff, 53
Rice, Tamir, 10
"The Rich Love India's Lockdown" (Sharma), 292
Robins, Rosemary, 99
Rodriguez, Robertino, 44
rosaries, virtual, 191–95
Rosenzweig, Roy, 73
Rothrock, Theodore, 183
Round House Theatre, 357
Rountree, Christopher, 371
Rousseff, Dilma, 257
Roy, Arundhati, 290, 292, 300
Rundell, John, 110

SAG-AFTRA, 223
Salter, Nikkole, 376–77, 380
Sanctuary Movement, 185
Sanders, Bernie, 46
SARS-CoV-2. *See* coronavirus; COVID-19
Sartre, Jean-Paul, 104

Saterfield, Teresa, 353–54
Saudi Arabia, 136
Scheherazade, 112
school closures, 295, 296
schools, online, 348
Schweizer, Harold, 95
scolding, 337
Seaton, Zoe, 369
self-blame and COVID-19, 336–37
self-documentation, 72–73
self-quarantine. *See* stay-at-home orders
"sex- and gender-based medicine"
   (SGBM), 266
Sex and Gender Women's Health Collaborative, 266
sex differences in biomedical research,
   266–68
sexual offenders, release of, 252
*Shadows: Living in Between*, 137
Sharma, Ruchir, 292
"shecession," 287
Shelley, Mary, 39
Shelley, Percy, 30, 41
*Sing Street* (Broadway musical), 361,
   362
Skrdla, Larry, 80–81, *81*, 87
slavery, legacy of in Brazil, 260
slum-dwellers and stay-at-home orders
   in India, 292–93
Smith, Jacob Ryan, 362
social distancing: and global citizenship,
   133; and *halafa*, 140–41; and music
   performances, 371–72; racialization as,
   134–35; and streaming media, 226, 229;
   and theatrical buildings, 380
social distrust and COVID-19, 176
social identity and linguistic profiling,
   345–47
socialist feminism, 300
social justice: and Black Lives Matter
   movement, 144; and waiting, 94
social media, use of, 144, 214, 322, 323
social norms, breakdown of, 177
social relations and waiting, 95–99
social reproduction, 296–99, 300
social threats and portraiture, 50–52

Society of Women's Health Research
   (SWHR), 266
Solnit, Rebecca, 239
*Songbird* (2020 film), 223
*Song of Myself* (Whitman), 49
*Sorry to Bother You* (2018 film), 346
Soth, Alec, 50
"Sound Change in Western Andalusian
   Spanish: An Acoustic Analysis of Phonemic Voiceless Stops" (Galvano), 353
Southern American English (SAE), 345
Spanish flu (1918 influenza), 74, *75*, 288
spiritual rituals, modification of during
   COVID-19, 182
*Spring Awakening* (Broadway musical),
   376
#StateOfEmergencyGBV, 323
statuary, public: and anti-Black racism,
   56–57, *57*, *58*, 173; removal of, 112
stay-at-home orders: impact on slum-
   dwellers, 292–93; increase in family-
   based violence in Nigeria, 318; lessons
   from prison to adjust to, 64–71; and
   migrants in India, 289; and religious
   freedom, 181; rise in femicides in Turkey, 313, 315; and women in India, 291
St. Columba Catholic Church, 183, *184*,
   185
stelae, funerary, 155–58, *156*, *159*, *161*
Stelter, Brian, 53
stereotypes: of Andalusian Spanish, 351–
   53; of gender in leadership, 245, 282; of
   "perpetual foreigner," 329
Stislow, John and Stephanie, 49–50
Stop AAPI Hate Center, 331, 332, 337
storytelling, 112–13
streaming arts performances, 379
streaming media: and escapism, 227–28;
   increased reliance on, 222; social
   distancing and rise in consumption
   of, 226, 229
streaming platforms, 226–28
*Street Scene* (opera), 360
strikes of health care workers, 292
subscription video-on-demand (SVOD),
   226. *See also* streaming media

Sudan, 133–34, 136, 142, 144, 146, 149n10
suffering and Buddhism, 117–21
*The Sun* (Ireland), *28*
"Sweeter" (Bridges), 93
Sweetman, David, 78

Taichman, Rebecca, 361
Taylor, Breonna, 53, 329, 373
tear gas, *237*
technology: and artists, 361, 380; and
    community, 365
telemedicine and minority communi-
    ties, 348
*The Tempest* (Shakespeare), 369
"Temporal Horizons of Modernity and
    Modalities of Waiting" (Rundell), 110
Terenouthis, Egypt, 155, 158, *159*, 160, *161*
testing, Covid-19, 38
Thao, Tou, 52
*That's What They Say* (podcast), 353
theaters, movie, 221, 223–25, 227, 228,
    229
theatre: monetizing of, 369; and racism,
    374–79, 380; and Zoom platform,
    368–70
Theatre Communication Group, 375–77
theatre games, 368
theatres, performing arts: closing of, 358,
    379–80; social distancing in, 380
theatrical windows, 225, 228
"This World Is Full of Monsters" (Van-
    derMeer), 39–40
Thucydides, 176–77, 178–80
*Tiger King* (Netflix miniseries), 12, 221–22,
    229
TikTok videos, 82
time as linear, 99
The Time Is Now project, 261
Tocqueville, Alexis de, 179
Topaz War Relocation Center, 172
*To Protect*, *237*
tourism, 351
Tragedy Response Initiative Task Force,
    77
transformation in monster stories,
    37–40

transgender persons: in Argentina,
    275n5; and COVID-19, 271, 290
*The Trojan Women* (1971 film), 127
*The Trojan Women: Hecuba's Grief* (Cog-
    swell), *130*
*The Trojan Women: Pyre* (Cogswell), *129*
*Trolls World Tour* (2020 film), 227
Trump, Donald: downplay of COVID-19,
    1, 9, 239, 298, 338–39; and face masks,
    186; as irresponsible, 103, 178; xeno-
    phobic naming of virus, 3–4, 29, 329,
    331, 337
trust, importance of building, 178–79
Turkey, 247, 312–16
Turnley, Peter, 57, *59*

uncertainty as good, 38–40
unemployment of women, 271, 287,
    291
*Unhinged* (2020 film), 224
Universal Pictures, 227, 228
University of Michigan. *See also* Bentley
    Historical Library; Kelsey Museum
    of Archaeology: accountability of, 83,
    85–86; documenting COVID-19 at, 76;
    multiethnic education at, 333
"U.S. Deaths Near 100,000, an Incalcula-
    ble Loss" (*New York Times*), 8

vaccine manufacturing in India, 301
Valeroso, Romando, 67–68, *68*
vampires *vs.* zombies, 40–42
van Anders, Sari, 268
VanderMeer, Jeff, 39–40
Van Hove, Ivan, 357
Vaswani, Neela, 211
Vietnam War, public commemoration
    of, 9
*Vinyl Euripides* (Cogswell), 127–28
violence, domestic: in Brazil, 258, 261; in
    Nicaragua, 252, 253n9; in Nigeria, 318,
    321; in Turkey, 315
violence, gender-based: in Brazil, 246; in
    Nicaragua, 246–47, 250–53; in Nigeria,
    319, 323; in Turkey, 247, 312
violence, state, 314–15

Violence against Persons Prohibition Act, 319

Virgen de Los Angeles, 181

virtue: and fear, 32–33; and monstrosity, 26–27

"The Virus Has Seized the Means of Production" (Bould), 287, 292

"Visitation Fridays" series, 193–94, 195

*Visitors' Platform*, 235

*Vulture*, 371

Wages for Housework Campaign, 288

waiting, 6, 93–106; bond between caring and, 113–14; change in meaning of, 99–100; and collective maturity, 102–6; dimensions of, 95; and distribution of power, 96–99; and envisioning the future, 106–7; as gendered activity, 97; and governments, 102–3; and invention, 106; as member of a group, 110–12; and patience, 94; as political act, 95; and protests, 105–6; refusal of, 104–6; shared spaces of, 96; and social justice, 94; and social relations, 95–99

*Waiting for Godot* (Beckett), 99

"Waiting for Rain in the Goulburn Valley" (Robins), 99

"Waiting in the Antechamber" (Puff), 97

"Waiting Out the Crisis" (Hage), 104

walking, 133, 138–41, 160

*Walking as an Act of Remembering*, 139

Walmart, DVD sales through, 225

WARDC (Women Advocates Research and Documentation Center), 319, 320, 321, 322, 323

Warner Bros., 228

*Washington Post*, 299

Weill, Kurt, 360

Weiner, Eric, 38

Welch, Cozine, 64

"The Werewolf" (Carter), 36–37

We See You, White American Theatre campaign, 374–75

*West Side Story* (Broadway musical), 357

We the People of Detroit, 331

"wet markets," 292

"What do countries with the best Coronavirus responses have in common? Women Leaders" (*Forbes*), 281

*What Good Would the Moon Be?* (performance video), 360–61

"What Good Would the Moon Be" (Weill), 360

WhatsApp, 144

"What Socially Distanced Live Performances Might Look Like" (Davidson), 371–72

"What's Really behind the Gender Gap in COVID-19 Deaths?" *(New York Times)*, 268

White, Nina, 362

white fear, 32

white nationalist protests and waiting, 105–6

Whitman, Walt, 49

Whitmer, Gretchen, 15, 147, 186

Willis, Juan Juan, 68–71, *69*

Wilson, Alfred Wilkinson, *75*

Wilson, August, 375

Wilson, Rita, 221

*Winter Light + Power*, 238

Womanifesto group, 323

women: and care economy, 313–14; exclusion from clinical research, 244–45; as health care workers, 291; hiring of domestic workers by, 295–96; increased risk of COVID-19 among, 318, 320; politicization of, 299–300; and stay-at-home orders, 271, 287, 291; use of social media to organize, 322, 323; wage discrepancy, 275n4. *See also* care work, unpaid; domestic workers; health care workers; violence, domestic; violence, gender-based

Women, Peace, and Security, 322

Women Advocates Research and Documentation Center (WARDC), 319, 320, 321, 322, 323

Women in Nigeria, 319

Women International League for Peace and Freedom, 322

Women's Aid Collective, 322, 323

Women's Autonomous Movement, 250–51, 252
Women's Freedom Assembly, 315
Women's Network against Violence, 251
Women's Peace Initiative, 315
Women's Rights Advancements and Protection Alternative (WRAPA), 322
women's shelters, closure of, 313, 315
Womersley, Kate, 267
Woodhams, James, 368
*Words at the Window: Self Isolation and the Coronavirus* (Lovekin), 49–50
World Bank, 291
World Health Organization, 331
World Population Project, 28
World War II, military fatalities during, 163–64, 165–67
Wright, Kelly, 345, 353
Wright, Laura, 369
"Wuhan flu," 331. *See also* xenophobia and COVID-19

xenophobia and COVID-19, 3–4, 29, 132, 329, 331, 332–33, 337

Yang, Andrew, 332
yards as spaces of resistance, 147
Yeh, Tiger Russell, 81, *82*
"Yellow Submarine" (The Beatles), 363

Zeno, 212
*Zero Patience* (1993 film), 112
Zia, Helen, 333
Ziibiwing Center, 171–72
zombies *vs.* vampires, 40–42
Zoom platform: and dance community, 370–71; musical performances through, 372; socializing through, 144; and theatre, 368–70
zoonotic diseases, 115n7, 340